THE ENDS OF KNOWLEDGE

THE ENDS OF KNOWLEDGE

OUTCOMES AND ENDPOINTS ACROSS THE ARTS AND SCIENCES

Edited by Seth Rudy and Rachael Scarborough King

BLOOMSBURY ACADEMIC
LONDON • NEW YORK • OXFORD • NEW DELHI • SYDNEY

BLOOMSBURY ACADEMIC
Bloomsbury Publishing Plc
50 Bedford Square, London, WC1B 3DP, UK
1385 Broadway, New York, NY 10018, USA
29 Earlsfort Terrace, Dublin 2, Ireland

BLOOMSBURY, BLOOMSBURY ACADEMIC and the Diana logo are
trademarks of Bloomsbury Publishing Plc

First published in Great Britain 2023

Copyright © Seth Rudy, Rachael Scarborough King, and contributors, 2023

The editors and contributors have asserted their right under the Copyright,
Designs and Patents Act, 1988, to be identified as Authors of this work.

Cover design: Rebecca Heselton
Cover image: Mountain texture © Sanja Karin Music/ Shutterstock.
Sea Pattern © marukopum/ Shutterstock

All rights reserved. No part of this publication may be reproduced or transmitted
in any form or by any means, electronic or mechanical, including photocopying,
recording, or any information storage or retrieval system, without prior
permission in writing from the publishers.

Bloomsbury Publishing Plc does not have any control over, or responsibility for,
any third-party websites referred to or in this book. All internet addresses given
in this book were correct at the time of going to press. The author and publisher
regret any inconvenience caused if addresses have changed or sites have
ceased to exist, but can accept no responsibility for any such changes.

A catalogue record for this book is available from the British Library.

A catalog record for this book is available from the Library of Congress.

ISBN: HB: 978-1-3502-4229-6
       PB: 978-1-3502-4228-9
       ePDF: 978-1-3502-4230-2
       eBook: 978-1-3502-4231-9

Typeset by Integra Software Services Pvt. Ltd.
Printed and bound in Great Britain

To find out more about our authors and books visit www.bloomsbury.com
and sign up for our newsletters.

CONTENTS

List of Illustrations — vii
Preface — viii

Introduction — 1
Seth Rudy and Rachael Scarborough King

PART I Unification — 17

1 The Ends of Physics — 19
   Brandon R. Brown

2 The Ends of Literary Studies — 37
   Aaron R. Hanlon

3 The Ends of Computing — 47
   Geoffrey C. Bowker

4 The Ends of Biology — 61
   B. N. Queenan

5 The Ends of Digital Humanities — 75
   Mark Algee-Hewitt

PART II Access — 89

6 The Ends of Law — 91
   Yochai Benkler

7 The Ends of Journalism — 113
   Jolene Almendarez

8 The Ends of Pedagogy — 121
   Sean Michael Morris

9 The Ends of the Liberal Arts — 131
   G. Gabrielle Starr

Contents

PART III Utopia		**137**
10 The Ends of Artificial Intelligence Hong Qu		139
11 The Ends of Gender Studies Ula Lukszo Klein		151
12 The Ends of Activism Ady Barkan		163
13 The Ends of Environmental Studies Myanna Lahsen		169
PART IV Concepts		**181**
14 The Ends of Performance Studies Jessica Nakamura		183
15 The Ends of History Marieke M. A. Hendriksen		193
16 The Ends of Black Studies Kenneth W. Warren		203
17 The Ends of Cultural Studies Mike Hill		217
Afterword *Clifford Siskin*		235
List of Contributors		244
Index		247

ILLUSTRATIONS

FIGURES

1.1	A simplified historical flow of progress in theoretical physics	25
1.2	A "sphere" of knowledge	33
5.1	t-sne plot of a topic model of digital humanities article conclusions	78
5.2	t-sne plot of a topic model of digital humanities article conclusions, shades represent journal of publication	85
15.1	Calvin and Hobbes	195

TABLES

5.1	Top 15 words of the most frequent topics across all conclusions	82
5.2	Top 15 words of the five topics most negatively correlated with year	83
5.3	Top 15 words from the five topics most positively correlated with year	84
6.1	Major areas of legal change and their impact on the bottom, middle, and top of the income distribution in the united states, 1980–2020	102

PREFACE

The origins of *The Ends* lie in the spring of 2011, when this volume's editors were both graduate students in the English Department at New York University. Seth had just secured a tenure-track job at Rhodes College, while Rachael was studying for her qualifying exams. We were brought together as the graduate assistants for the Re:Enlightenment Project, a group established in 2011 with the goal of using the present moment of flux in media, institutions, and disciplines to reflect on the reorganization of knowledge during the Enlightenment of the seventeenth and eighteenth centuries. The Re:Enlightenment Project, which was founded by Clifford Siskin and Kevin Brine, oriented itself around three "touchstones": past and present, mediating technologies, and connectivities. The knowledge structures we have inherited from the Enlightenment—from universities and departments to museums, laboratories, and the news media—have come under combined economic, epistemological, political, and social pressures that may radically reshape how we produce and circulate information. At the same time, these knowledge structures are made up of networks of people who connect with one another both within and across traditional disciplinary boundaries. The project asked how we could better understand the historical Enlightenment in order to prepare for a future of knowledge production in which such boundaries seem increasingly diffuse.

In doing so, it did not take a view of the Enlightenment primarily focused on the figures of *les lumières* or a set of canonical texts. Instead, as a 2011 "Re:Enlightenment Report" put it, the group's members insisted on a "full account of the complexity of the field of knowledge once it is seen through the modalities of curation, production, dissemination, accreditation and transformation which determine specific practices within specific locales."[1] Rather than offering a triumphalist account of the rise of reason and progress, the group aimed "to report, retrospectively and prospectively, on our new landscape, knowing that we cannot specify fully the precise contours of knowledge while insisting that, at our peril, we neglect to take responsibility for shaping them."[2] If scholars want to be central to the future of knowledge production, we must grapple with the legacy of Enlightenment institutions, media, and ways of knowing.

The Re:Enlightenment Project has evolved since its inception, but one question has remained at the forefront: What forms might Enlightenment take now? This collection offers an answer to that question in itself and in its emergence from protocols developed or adopted by the project in its exchanges and working groups. At the 2015 Re:Enlightenment Exchange in Oslo, we discussed to what extent Enlightenment concepts such as "progress" and "improvement" remained operational and whether or not "progress" implied an end. In 2017, Seth presented additional work on the questions raised during that exchange as part of a roundtable convened by Rachael for the annual conference of the American Society for Eighteenth-Century Studies. We continued to develop that paper together and the following year brought it back to Re:Enlightenment, this time at a gathering at Stanford University on the theme of "scale." This volume, then, was always already a collaborative venture; the Re:Enlightenment Project provided a platform upon which we could examine the concept of ends before even considering a traditional publication in the form of an edited volume.

As this opening makes clear, we owe a debt of gratitude to the Re:Enlightenment Project and particularly to our graduate mentor, Cliff Siskin. Cliff always encouraged us to understand our work's telos to be the production of new knowledge, and we greatly appreciate his afterword to this volume. Four project members contributed chapters to this volume and several others were directly involved in its development. At the 2018 Exchange at Stanford, we dragooned Tony Jarrells, Giovanna Ceserani, and Yohei Igarashi into creating a prototype "Ends of Knowledge" podcast—a platform that could extend the life and expand the scope of the work beyond the book. The Re:Enlightenment Project has provided the intellectual rationale, institutional network, and personal connections to allow this volume to develop.

This volume has also been in conversation with correspondent efforts to examine the pressures put upon knowledge production now. An earlier version of the Introduction appeared in a 2021 special issue of *The Eighteenth Century: Theory and Interpretation* on "Scholarship in a Time of Crisis," and we are grateful to Kathleen Alves for her feedback on that essay. We are also grateful to Collin Jennings, Stephanie DeGooyer, Jason Pearl, and David Alff for their comments on an earlier draft of the Introduction.

At Bloomsbury, Ben Doyle has been an excellent and generous intellectual partner, pushing us to be ambitious with this project, helping shape its range and scope, and demonstrating remarkable patience with delays. Laura Cope has provided able editorial assistance. We would also like to thank the anonymous readers of the proposal and manuscript, who offered many useful suggestions for enabling the achievement of this book to match its vision.

The volume's contributors have shown a willingness to engage in an intellectual endeavor that may not amply "count" in institutional terms but that pushed them to think across institutions and disciplines. We are tremendously grateful for their participation. Our family and friends have heard what probably seemed like endless updates on *The Ends*. Seth would particularly like to thank his wife, Maggie Robertson, for her patience and understanding throughout the life of the project, and his daughter, Imogen, who was neither patient nor understanding, having been born at around the halfway mark. Rachael thanks her husband, Ady, for "volunteering" to write a chapter on the ends of activism, and her children, Carl and Willow, whose love and energy know no end.

Notes

1. "Towards a New Platform for Knowledge: The Future of Enlightenment," 2011, https://reenlightenment.org/report-new-platform-for-knowledge/
2. "Towards a New Platform for Knowledge."

INTRODUCTION
Seth Rudy and Rachael Scarborough King

The end of college. The end of democracy. The end of bias. The end of forever wars. The end of cash. The end of snow days. The end of American exceptionalism. The end of the pandemic. The end of the world. These were some of the ends and endings news readers faced in the long months following March 2020, when many ways of life came to an end and new ones emerged during the global waves of Covid-19 lockdowns. Such temporal ends raised accompanying questions about theoretical ends: the *end* of, for example, college led to considerations of the *ends* of college—and of gender, bias, forever wars, cash, and so on. What is the connection between terminus and telos? Faced with the possibility of so much changing in or even vanishing from our lives, we were, and still are, compelled to write and read about the purpose, mission, or objective of how we live and what we learn about the world. Such news stories not only identify the purported or imagined demise of certain arenas but also track their shift into other modes. The end does not have to mean unfulfilled ends.

This is a book that begins at the end. It continually maneuvers between *end* and *ends* to ask how we can navigate the end of one era in modern knowledge production and the onset of a new one. Recent changes in technologies and institutions—predating but accentuated by the global pandemic—as well as mounting political pressures have refocused attention on the specialized nature of knowledge that stemmed from the nineteenth-century organization of the research university into divisions and disciplines. With humanities scholars, social scientists, and natural scientists all forced to defend their work, from accusations of the "hoax" of climate change to assumptions of the "uselessness" of a humanities degree, knowledge producers within and without the academy are challenged to articulate why they do what they do—and, we suggest, when they might be done. In a political and economic climate fixated on the value of education and the question of practical versus theoretical learning, this volume asks how we should understand the ends of knowledge today. In disciplines ranging from physics to literary studies to activism to climate science, we ask: what are the ends of our work and when, if ever, could we reach its end?

As scholars of the Enlightenment, we draw our inspiration for this intertwining of *end* and *ends* from an era that initiated many of our models for producing, sharing, and using knowledge. Enlightenment thinkers combined practical and utopian definitions of ends as they called for new modes and institutions of knowledge production, understanding ends as large-scale goals that must, at the same time, be achievable. This period also offers a model of how the end of one view of knowledge production can be a launchpad for new ideas, methods, and paradigms. In the early seventeenth century, Francis Bacon called for both a new start to knowledge production and a reconsideration of its ends. "The greatest error of all," he wrote in *The Advancement of Learning* (1605), "is the mistaking or misplacing of the last or furthest end of knowledge."[1] Its "true ends," he later wrote, were not professional reputation, financial gain, or even love of learning, but rather "the uses and benefits of life, to improve and conduct it in charity."[2] Bacon devised the *Novum Organum* (1620) as both the blueprint for and beginning of a generations-long and worldwide effort to seek these "ends." In *The New Atlantis* (1626), his vision of a state rebuilt upon such a plan, the ends of knowledge are the first point explained by one of the Fathers of Salomon's House, an institution dedicated to natural philosophy and a prototype for the Royal Society: "The end of our foundation is the knowledge of causes, and secret motions of things; and the enlarging of the bounds of human empire, to the effecting of all things possible."[3] Bacon's "Great Instauration," his vision for a new system of knowledge production, began from the ends.

Bacon's terms—*exitus, finis, terminus*—suggest a focus on outcomes as well as endpoints. Knowledge, in his philosophy, had ends (i.e., purposes) as well as an end (a point at which the project would be complete). The New Science, he believed, would lead to "the proper end and termination of infinite error" and was worth undertaking precisely because an end was possible: "For it is better to make a beginning of a thing which has a chance of an end, than to get caught up in things which have no end, in perpetual struggle and exertion" (*New Organon* 3). The following year, however, scholar Robert Burton took a less sanguine view of knowledge production in *The Anatomy of Melancholy* (1621). Considering the lot of "our divines, the most noble profession and worthy of double honours," who despite that worthiness had little hope of material reward or encouragement, he asked rhetorically: "to what end should we study? … Why do we take such pains?"[4] The certitude of the natural philosopher (Bacon) juxtaposed with the lament of the humanist scholar (Burton) suggests a division between modes and objects of inquiry that remains stereotypical of the STEM-humanities divide—one that may hinder consideration of shared goals and methods. We continue, fairly or unfairly, to associate the natural and applied sciences with specific and comprehensible ends, while the search for humanistic knowledge seems endless.

A final historical exemplar—also appearing at the dawn of a new epistemological age—reminds us that the question of "ends" and its answers belong to all who produce knowledge and all on whose behalf they work. On January 21, 1802, the chemist, inventor, and erstwhile poet Humphry Davy delivered an introductory lecture on chemistry at the Royal Institution that again took up this topic. In his conclusion, he cast aside "delusive dreams of the infinite improvability of man, the annihilation of labor, disease, and even death" in favor of pursuits both broader and more abstract. After decrying the disparities of rank and unequal division of labor and property that had become the soul of "civilized life," he expressed his hope that humanity would become more enlightened and more happy as well as his expectation "that the great whole of society should be ultimately connected together by means of knowledge and the useful arts; that they should act as the children of one great parent, with one determinate end, so that no power may be rendered useless, no exertions thrown away."[5] Davy saw the chemist and inventor as seeking the same end as the doctor, artist, literary scholar, political economist, or philosopher. The purpose of the pursuit of knowledge was the integration, rather than division, of society.

Now, 200 years after Davy's dream of a unified and unifying approach to knowledge production, and 400 after Bacon's *Great Instauration*, we face another new era emerging from the coalescent crises of Covid-19, climate disaster, the rightwing war on education, and the precarity of the neoliberal university. Drawing together such disparate considerations, we believe the time has come again for knowledge producers across fields to reorient their work around the question of "ends." This need not mean acquiescence to either the logics of economic utilitarianism or partisan fealty that have already proved so damaging to twenty-first-century institutions. The continued, cynical narrowing of "usefulness" to mean profitable instrumentalization or advancing outside interests is the end of knowledge we all face in the absence of clearer (even if continually and publicly contested) alternatives. But while many scholars are constitutionally resistant to this kind of thinking, as we resist the concept of ends our end is being defined for us.

We believe that rather than rejecting the terms of the debate, we must now put a new, productive emphasis on ends. The view from within the academy, and particularly with respect to the humanities, is often all but despairing, as many disciplines—and many more academics—seem to be facing their ends, whether in terms of public, financial, scholarly, or bureaucratic investment. Even as the need for critical perspectives on scientistic and techno-utopian thinking becomes increasingly obvious, some universities are taking the current crises as an opportunity to cut programs in African American studies, English, classics, philosophy, foreign language studies, and other fields.[6] Far-right attacks on education have led to bans on teaching not only the specific, controversial field of Critical Race Theory but the history of race in America writ large, with legislatures in states such as Texas and Tennessee prohibiting discussion of the concepts of systemic racism and white privilege.[7] In October 2021, the Board of Regents of Georgia's public university system effectively ended tenure, a key guarantor of academic freedom, by granting administrators far more leeway to remove tenured professors without faculty input or due process. Clearly, political considerations drive what kind of work and workers are cast as useful or useless—as repaying investment or needing to end.

If we want the university to remain a space for knowledge production, then scholars must have the end(s) of their own knowledge projects and those of their disciplines in sight—in part to advance the Enlightenment project of "useful knowledge" and in part to defend that knowledge from public and political mischaracterization. We must also look for ends outside of academia. Of course, knowledge production does not take place solely within the ivory tower. It was precisely during the Enlightenment that writers such as Joseph Addison called for philosophy to be brought "out of Closets and Libraries, Schools and Colleges, to dwell in Clubs and Assemblies, at Tea-tables, and in Coffee-houses."[8] The period saw the takeoff of "improvement" societies, which initially focused on agricultural and public infrastructure but soon expanded to include the arts and sciences more broadly. Some of these organizations, such as the Royal Society (originally the Royal Society for Improving Natural Knowledge), remain important institutions for bridging the continuing gap between universities and the public. In the American context, philanthropies and think tanks may serve a similar function. But other extra-academic efforts have had the goal of repudiating the university, rather than connecting with it. The Thiel Fellowship, founded by right-wing venture capitalist Peter Thiel, provides recipients with a two-year, $100,000 grant on the condition that they drop out of or skip university in order to "build new things instead of sitting in a classroom."[9] For many, academic organizations appear moribund and continuing improvement requires new institutional arrangements. *Improvement*—a keyword for the American public from Benjamin Franklin's virtue chart through today's "wellness" craze—must have an ultimate goal or it becomes illusory.

The Ends of Knowledge therefore asks knowledge producers to revisit Bacon's foundational question of the Enlightenment at another inflection point in its long history: What is "the last or furthest end of knowledge"? As John Bender observes, the initial ends of Enlightenment are now part of its history, "but its purposes return as new impulses."[10] This volume brings together contributions from seventeen authors, with backgrounds across disciplines and both inside and outside the academy, to reconsider those purposes from the perspective of the "knowledge economy" and the "Information Age." We look both backward and forward, on the one hand historicizing concepts of the end and on the other projecting them into the future. The contributors included here learn from their disciplines' histories while rejecting teleological thinking and seeing multiple possible paths forward.

We asked contributors the broad question: What are the ends of your discipline? While we encouraged the authors to consider multiple kinds of *ends*, we did not prescribe a definition for the term and we recognized that some contributors would reject the premise itself. We did not expect consensus, but we did find points of commonality. In some cases, these followed predictable disciplinary patterns, but in more ways, writers across fields demonstrated unexpected points of convergence. Mushrooms, for example, turned out to be a useful metaphor in the fields of cultural studies and computing; both the chapters on gender studies and artificial intelligence engage with dystopian fiction. The shared project of considering the end(s) of knowledge work revealed the rich history and scholarly investments of individual disciplines as well as the larger goal of producing accurate knowledge that is oriented toward a more ethical, informed, just, and reflective world.

Ends and Endings

This book asks how disciplines diverge and converge in their understandings of their ends. While end(s) have been explored from many disciplinary angles, this is the first volume, to our knowledge, to bring together thinkers from across the humanities, natural sciences, and social sciences to consider the question simultaneously. This synthetic approach revealed four key ways in which to understand "ends," which emerged collectively in the chapters: end as telos, end as terminus, end as termination, end as apocalypse. Some contributors engaged all four of these ends, while others emphasized one or some. The first two definitions relate most directly to the work of a discipline or an individual scholar: What is the knowledge project being undertaken, and what would it mean for it to be complete? Most scholars are relatively comfortable asking the former question—even if they do not have clear answers to it—but have either never considered the latter or would consider the process of knowledge production to be always infinite, because answering one question necessarily leads to new ones. We argue that even if this were true, and a particular project could never be completed within an individual's lifetime, there is value in having an answer. The third meaning—termination—refers to the institutional pressures that many disciplines are facing: the closure of centers, departments, and even whole schools, alongside political pressure and public hostility.

Over all this looms the fourth meaning, primarily in the context of the approaching climate apocalypse, which puts the first three ends into perspective: What is the point of all this in the face of wildfires, superstorms, and drought? For us, this is not a rhetorical question. What *is* the point of literary studies, physics, history, the liberal arts, and performance studies in the present moment, in addition to activism, the law, artificial intelligence, gender studies, and, of course, environmental studies? Even the answers for the latter discipline are not obvious: as Myanna Lahsen shows in her chapter, despite the fact that the case is closed as far as research proving humans' effect on the climate—to the extent that some scientists have called for a moratorium on further research—governments have not taken the needed action to reduce carbon usage to the extent necessary to avoid climate catastrophe. Do scientists then throw up their hands at their inability to influence political trends, or must they instead engage with social scientists to pursue research on social and political solutions? What role do disciplinary norms separating the sciences, social sciences, and humanities play in maintaining the apocalyptic status quo?

The answers offered in this volume met our initial expectations that the concept of ends would be more intuitive to scholars in some fields than others. Bacon warned that chasing only "useful" knowledge might, like Atalanta's apple, distract from reaching more ambitious goals such as Newton's System of the World or the elusive Theory of Everything. But his plan made space for both free inquiry into the arts and sciences as well as discoveries or inventions that could be of immediate use in the world. Although some still see the pragmatic and the "pure" as inherently conflicting, Philip Kitcher has argued that "there is … no basis for a contrast between the enduring aim of pure science and the transient goals pursued in our practical ventures. Both sorts of ends must be understood in relation to the situation and needs of a group of people."[11] In other words, the ends of knowledge are sited and contingent, whether upon the judgments of its producers, the circumstances of its stakeholders, or, ideally, both.

As we have seen, the natural and applied sciences have been oriented toward the pursuit of practical and epistemic outcomes for centuries. Some fields have therefore made the continual or at least occasional reassessment of their presumed purposes a matter of course. In 2020, for example, the *Journal of Medicine and Philosophy* devoted a full issue to the topic of the ends of medicine, despite having regularly attended to the question throughout its history. The goals of medicine, D. Robert MacDougall explained, "may seem simple or even obvious," even to physicians, but in truth involve more than diagnosis. "Medicine is a practice," he continued, "and practices, as purposeful activities, should be fundamentally characterized by their ends."[12] The specific ends may remain unsettled and contentious, but the concept—the sense that some formulation of the ends is necessary to understanding what medicine is or should be—has become an assumed part of its disciplinary discourse.

The ends of other STEM disciplines can likewise seem deceptively straightforward. Although devices, software applications, and (particularly during the pandemic) medical advances often constitute the most visible evidence of scientific advances, major breakthroughs—such as the detection of gravitational waves and the Higgs boson, or gene sequencing and the identification of Richard III's remains—also reliably capture public interest. A recent article in *PNAS*, however, suggests that as a whole the sciences face similar challenges to the humanities in terms of purpose and endpoint. As the paper's authors explain, science follows a pattern in which a few well-cited works elicit a "deluge" of follow-up work that positions findings within established frameworks. As a result, "the progress of large scientific fields may be slowed, trapped in existing canon," and "policy measures restructuring the scientific value production chain may be required to allow mass attention to concentrate on promising, novel ideas."[13] The sciences' emphasis on research productivity, when defined in the quantitative terms of publications and citations, may be at odds with the greater end of scientific advancement.

As might be expected, scholars in the humanities had more complicated, and often less definitive, responses to the question of the ends of knowledge. The brave souls who agreed to contribute to this volume took a variety of approaches that, while usefully explaining their own purposes and goals, generally demurred from speaking on behalf of their colleagues or specifying the epistemological ends of their particular disciplines. As Paul Reiter and Chad Wellmon argue, this is to be expected given the historical development of the humanities' temporality. The modern humanities, they explain, emerged in nineteenth-century Germany as a response to the perceived crises of meaning and value related to secularization, democratization, and industrialization.[14] The Renaissance *studia humanitis*, which taught students to read, write, and speak about the classics to prepare them "for study in the higher faculties as well as for lives as active citizens, friends, and family members," became the exercise of "spontaneous, creative reason" and other intellectual activities for their own sake.[15] Crisis discourse, Wellmon and Reiter conclude, has shaped the humanities ever since. It has now "trapped" the field in a version of the "endless repetition" Bacon condemned, and forced humanists into defensive positions that erase the historical ends of humanist inquiry and occlude new paradigms in which the humanities might be more than ends in themselves.[16]

Some may be quick to point out that past efforts at ending often appear quixotic or ludicrous with the advantage of hindsight. For literary scholars, the paradigmatic examples of this are Borges' "The Library of Babel" and the scholar character of Edward

Introduction

Casaubon in George Eliot's *Middlemarch*. Causabon's work on his *Key to All Mythologies* is literally unending, as he dies before completing it, leading his young wife Dorothea to worry that he will guilt her into promising to continue the work after his death. Scientists too have sometimes conceived of their ends as providing "a *complete* true account of the universe," but the idea that such an account could exist, or that if it did we could comprehend it, remains very much in doubt.[17] In his chapter here on physics, Brandon R. Brown points to Johannes Kepler's "laughable" effort to make the Platonic solids account for the exactly six planets he knew to exist in the universe as an end that was not worth pursuing. The aspiration for a global end is generally delusive and potentially dystopian. We do not pretend with this volume to offer a single or final answer to the question we have asked each of our contributors, but rather to open and maintain an intellectual space in which it can be asked.

To some extent, then, particular answers are less important than the possibility of discovering a shared sense of purpose. Ends can be specific, like explaining the significance of *Middlemarch* in literary history, or they can be expansive, like creating an informed, ethical population. At the largest scale, however, the ability to determine and articulate shared ends among fields of knowledge would be an important step toward addressing institutionally entrenched, often counterproductive divisions—such as the STEM-humanities divide—and authorizing new systems and organizations of knowledge production. This collection, then, is an initial attempt to see what the advancement of learning could look like if it were to be reoriented around emergent ends rather than inherited structures. The question must continue to be pursued at increasing scales, from the individual researcher, to the office or department, to the discipline, to the university, to academia, and to knowledge production as a whole. Ultimately, we hope to show what the benefits would be of knowledge projects starting with their end(s) in mind. How can we get anywhere if we cannot even say where we want to go? And even if we think we have goals, are we actually working toward them? Ideally, a firm sense of both purpose and outcome could help scholars demonstrate how they are advancing knowledge rather than continuing to spin their wheels.

Groups and Divisions

With the concept of end(s) applying across disciplinary boundaries, an objection could be made to our book's organization by discipline. The disciplines as we currently occupy them are artifacts of the nineteenth-century origins of the research university, which gave us the tripartite structure of the natural sciences, social sciences, and humanities. This model, which trains scholars in narrow-but-deep disciplines, emerged out of a 200-year shift away from the medieval curricular divisions of the trivium—grammar, logic, and rhetoric—and quadrivium—arithmetic, geometry, music, and astronomy.[18] The fact that such structures have changed dramatically over time shows that they are not inherent, and the past few decades have witnessed widespread interest in interdisciplinarity in the form of institutional programs and centers as well as new fields such as American studies, area studies, and cultural studies. Julie Thompson Klein places disciplines and interdisciplinarity in a long history of the pursuit of unified knowledge stretching back to Plato, writing that "all interdisciplinary activities are rooted in the ideas of unity and synthesis, evoking a common epistemology of convergence."[19] Two of the primary motivations for interdisciplinary work, which, as she shows, became increasingly common in the second half of the twentieth century, are "to solve problems that are beyond the scope of any one discipline" and "to achieve unity of knowledge, whether on a limited or grand scale."[20] However, critiques of interdisciplinarity point out that such efforts are frequently additive rather than interactive: that is, they combine established disciplinary methods rather than remaking them.[21] Jerry A. Jacobs contends that "interdisciplinary undertakings are likely to result in the proliferation of academic units rather than the consolidation of knowledge into a more unified whole."[22] The questions of purpose, unity, and completion have been key to, if often implicit in, the discourse of interdisciplinarity that has dominated discussions of academic institutional organization.

Studies of the modern university tend to consider a variety of fields, although often in broad strokes. Stephen M. Gavazzi and E. Gordon Gee argue against the "homogenization" of American higher education, noting that universities have become less tied to local conditions as they chase the same national ranking metrics.[23] David J. Staley, meanwhile, sees all universities as sharing a common purpose: "at its heart a university exists to transform subjects—be they student or faculty—such that they leave the institution a different person than when they arrived." These "transformative experiences" will vary between institutions and across time, but they mean more than producing "the same person plus a new skill set, an attitude that seemingly defines the nature and purpose of higher education today."[24] Many students and their parents expect the end of college to be graduation into a well-paying job, but as Cathy N. Davidson points out, the rapidity with which technology has changed employment means that students today "cannot count on continuing for any length of time in the job or even the field for which they were originally trained."[25] She argues instead that the goal of college teaching should be "learning how to learn—the single most important skill anyone can master" and points to interdisciplinary centers that draw together fields and methods as a model for the future of higher education.[26] Commentators on higher education tend to agree both that ideologically driven reforms prioritizing STEM over the humanities are misguided and that the current disciplinary system introduces too many divisions, silos, and false competitions within knowledge production.

Some of the chapters in this volume concern traditional (i.e., post-nineteenth-century) academic disciplines while others, such as those on gender studies and cultural studies, discuss fields that have come to be the poster children for interdisciplinarity. Whether dealing with established or more recent fields—and whether within or outside the academy—we proceed from the assumption that knowledge production involves specialization within a field. The discipline is, Amanda Anderson and Joseph Valente write, "the basic organizational unit of intellectual life."[27] Disciplines, they continue, contain multiple ends via "a dual mandate, carrying the sense of a practical regimen into an economy of conceptual enterprise."[28] And, as Henrika Kuklick points out, many professionals outside of universities base their claims to expertise on the disciplinary organization of the university: in the nineteenth century, the professions were "organized as *communities* of practitioners, each putatively possessing its own exclusive domain of esoteric expertise, the fundamentals of which were conveyed in formal training programs established in universities."[29] Given that we still ask undergraduates what they will "do with" their degrees—that is, what careers they are preparing for—this understanding of the importance of disciplinary training within and without the university remains salient.

In dividing the volume by discipline, then, we are not arguing that disciplinary divisions are either immanent or necessarily superfluous but rather acknowledging that they continue to structure and separate knowledge projects. Some contributors question their disciplines' boundaries while others assert their usefulness. This volume unites the broad perspective of higher education studies with the granularity of a focus on individual disciplines; we also look both inside and outside the academy to ask how disciplinary thinking brings together the pursuit of knowledge with the pursuit of action. As acknowledged above, seventeen chapters on seventeen subjects do not a comprehensive survey of knowledge make. Many fields necessarily remain unrepresented, as would be the case in any but a truly encyclopedic account. The difficulty we had in finding a philosopher to contribute, though, was perhaps the most unexpected. While several of those we approached cited bureaucratic reasons for declining—too many prior commitments, or chapters in edited collections not "counting" enough for tenure and promotion—others bristled at the idea that knowledge could have an end. Bureaucratic constraints and academic norms also challenged our desire to represent a variety of ranks and roles, as those in contingent and para-academic positions might not have the time or resources to dedicate to edited collections, while people outside of academia generally expect to be paid in money, not copies of books. Ultimately—while still lacking a chapter on the ends of philosophy—we were able to assemble a group of contributors that spans academic ranks from lecturers to administrators to tenured professors to university presidents and that includes voices from knowledge-producing fields outside the university.

As the contributors considered the question of ends from the variety of perspectives described above, their answers fell into four broad groupings, each of which offers a model for scaling up the problem of the organization of knowledge work. One group took the approach of unification: How could the author's field achieve a unified theory or explanation, and how close is the field to that goal? First, Brandon R. Brown shows how the question of the "end of physics" has preoccupied that field for at least a century. Many see physics as stalled and unable to achieve its goal of a unified theory of the primary components of matter and the laws governing them. Are we on the brink of major new advances, or merely tinkering at the edges of existing knowledge? While the twentieth century yielded Einstein's General Theory of Relativity and the Standard Model of Particle Physics, there has been no comparable advance in the past fifty years in terms of a fundamental new window onto the universe. The dominance of string theory, with its still-unprovable model of the multiverse, may make it difficult for other subfields to progress. Whether physics has, or is near, an end depends, Brown shows, on the nature of the universe itself: if the universe or multiverse is infinite then so is the field, but if it has boundaries, then the project could at some point be complete. The question of the end of physics is therefore one that physics itself must answer.

Physics is often seen as the "hard" science closest to the humanities, with its many philosophical and purely theoretical elements. Considering the discipline of literary studies, Aaron Hanlon asks whether we similarly desire or expect to achieve progressive knowledge—that is, knowledge in which various research projects build upon one another to converge toward paradigmatic explanations—in humanistic fields. Seeing a mismatch between literary studies's foundation in the category of the literary and the now-declining cultural significance of that category, Hanlon argues that we cannot address the political-social crisis of the humanities without addressing the intellectual crisis of explaining the field's purpose. The end of literary studies can only be addressed in the context of the ends of literary studies. From this viewpoint, he contends that interpretive literary studies, which focuses on producing new "readings" of texts, will and should end, but that explanatory literary studies, which produces knowledge about literature, marks the field's future.

In his chapter on the ends of computing, Geoffrey C. Bowker considers a form of unification that may have already, and somewhat unconsciously, occurred, as he shows how ubiquitous computing has become to not only the human but also the natural world and how its future lies in further integration between people and computers. Computers have colonized space and time to such an extent that they have de-centered the human in terms of the scale at which they operate. The simplest explanation for our universe, Bowker writes, is that we live in a computer simulation, a model in which the end (and beginning) is always a computer. Scholars in the humanities and sciences must learn from one another to understand that computing involves an integration of human and technological life—that our computers create us as much as we create them. Pursuing this vision of computing would mean pursuing homeostasis both in the natural world and in the relationship between people and machines.

B. N. Queenan returns to Baconian principles from her perspective as a biologist and director of a multidisciplinary center. Surveying taxonomic efforts from Aristotle through Genesis through Newton and Linnaeus, Queenan argues that the modern separation between scientific fields, and related separation between the study of living and nonliving bodies, leads away from (in Bacon's eyes) the true purpose of the search for knowledge: a unified explanation for the world. Knowledge pursuit for other reasons may in fact lead us astray. Biology, the life sciences, pursues knowledge in a way close to how Bacon desired, but achieving his goal would require its end—via unification with other fields. The ends of knowledge are, in this framework, a full understanding of the universe.

While the ends of some fields may lie in their unification with each other, others have yet to coalesce within themselves. Mark Algee-Hewitt considers whether the ends of the digital humanities may be its reabsorption into the disciplines and departments from which it arose or its complete separation and reconstitution as an entirely new, synthetic field. These outcomes represent not the furthest end of the digital humanities, but the end of its beginning. In either case, the next phase of its evolution will call for its practitioners to define it in relation to the work done—and the ends sought—by other scholars.

A second group of chapters collectively argued that the purpose and endpoint of knowledge production is increased access, and that such access is key to social justice. In this framework, it might seem intuitive to define the ends of law—a just, orderly society—but Yochai Benkler shows how complicated that question is, and how it has changed over time in response to trends in legal studies. Benkler explores in particular how legal decisions and opinions have shaped labor and productivity since the late nineteenth century, focusing on the period's two Gilded Ages—from 1873 to 1929, and from 1980 to the present. Both periods have seen a conflict between nominal adherence to formal legal standards and texts, which has the result of favoring business groups, and a progressive critique which argues that the purpose of the law should be the promotion of social justice. Benkler argues that progressive responses to the long string of conversative legal victories in the arena of production mark the end of the neoliberal era and outlines how the emerging field of law and economics offers a new way forward for using the law to directly address economic power and inequality as well as the intersections of class, race, and gender.

Jolene Almendarez, a reporter for WVXU, Cincinnati's local NPR affiliate, describes how a confluence of different factors—declining news sources and reporter positions, a lack of diversity in newsrooms, and low public trust in the media—combine to create an existential threat for the field of journalism. In a similar move to Hanlon's discussion of literary studies, she suggests that while journalism may want to blame its current problems on external crises, such as declining ad revenue and right-wing hostility, it is also partly responsible for its current predicament in its continuing struggles to accurately represent its readership. Almendarez sees some paths forward for journalism in the rise of nonprofit news organizations and greater emphasis on diversity in legacy newsrooms, which expand access in terms of both authors and content, but she writes that those organizations unable to adapt to the new environment may ultimately "atrophy and die."

Like journalism, pedagogy is both a practice and a field of study—the work that teachers do every day as well as an area of knowledge production that studies the processes and effects of teaching. Sean Michael Morris uses a story from his personal history of schooling to contrast two versions of pedagogy: one that sees education as a hierarchical transfer of knowledge and one that fosters the student's self-understanding in order to situate them within their world. A transformational, humanizing pedagogy makes the student the subject of their own pedagogy. In this view, the end of pedagogy is not assessment or grading, but an articulation of the student's truth. Critical pedagogy offers students access to their own narratives, but this is a process that will require constant new beginnings and re-articulations.

Some of the disciplines in this volume could be understood as subfields, while others—like pedagogy—are disciplinary categories that bring together various domains of knowledge. The liberal arts is perhaps the broadest example we have of the latter but it is also, counterintuitively, one of the areas under greatest pressure. The media frequently, and erroneously, portrays liberal arts degrees as useless and nonremunerative, while liberal arts colleges, lacking the endowments and alumni bases of large universities, have struggled to weather the recent financial crises of the Great Recession and Covid-19. G. Gabrielle Starr, the president of Pomona College, argues that the liberal arts are not a specific course of study but, rather, a commitment to the freedom and access of a range of human knowledge. This project can never end because it is not narrowly utilitarian. However, Starr argues that the forms of the liberal arts—the architecture and infrastructure—need to change for the present. Using an analogy to the structure of the brain, in which a "rich-hub connectome" links smaller networks to local hubs and then to larger hubs, she argues that the flow of knowledge should not only be from elite hubs of academic institutions to the public but in distributed and interlocking networks. Rather than seeing the perceived low value of a liberal arts education as the field's existential threat, she argues that systemic barriers to knowledge are surmountable and calls for institutional architecture that recognizes education as a common rather than personal good.

The third group of chapters raises the issue of whether the consideration of ends can foster utopian outcomes, or whether endings inevitably lead to dystopian scenarios. Hong Qu writes that we must actively instill ethical governance into artificial intelligence systems, or they will reproduce, reinforce, and worsen current biases to an extent that will inhibit personal liberties and civil rights. Drawing on his work as a software engineer building YouTube's core features such as video sharing and commenting, Qu shows how social media platforms ignore ethical issues and purposefully create "addictive" features in order to enlarge their market share. Social networks already manipulate human behavior on a mass scale. Although autonomous, sentient AI remains in the realm of science fiction, we must instill AI with respect for human life now to avoid a dystopian future in which machines dominate humans. Returning to the theme of unification, Qu argues that it will require an integration of humanistic and scientific disciplinary perspectives to create shared values and governance policies in response to the advancing pace of AI.

The end of gender studies—a field that has always faced prominent right-wing opposition—could be seen in utopian terms: as the end of gendered oppression, or the end of a need for the field. But as Ula Lukszo Klein observes, this end could just as easily lead to dystopia. Using the lens of two popular futuristic novels, Margaret Atwood's *The Handmaid's Tale* and Naomi Alderman's *The Power*, and specifically the endings or epilogues to the novels, Klein shows how multiple versions of the end of gender studies—the reassertion of rigid gender hierarchies, a "post-gender" society, and the inversion of traditional gender roles—would all have dystopian features. Moreover, such fictional dystopias can shed light on the continuing need for gender studies in our own period. As the field has shifted from its initial focus on women to take a broader understanding of gender, it has reasserted that the ultimate goal of gender studies would be its own obsolescence, while simultaneously demonstrating that such an end will always remain a utopian horizon.

Introduction

One important response to gender oppression has been in the area of activism, where a vigorous debate exists over how to best respond to the many problems facing our world. Activism might seem like a strange candidate for inclusion in a volume about "the ends of knowledge," apparently focused on doing rather than learning. However, activists have built a body of knowledge about how to achieve their ends, and the American progressive left has a genealogy of thinkers as well as doers. Activist Ady Barkan, who has worked on campaigns for a variety of progressive causes, explores how the abolitionist movement understood its end and ends in the wake of event such as the abolition of slavery and the passage of the Thirteenth Amendment. Even as some activists argued that these events meant the end of the movement, others saw its broader ends as continuing. Barkan shows how present-day activists can learn from this legacy while continuing their work for a more utopian world.

As we face a dystopic prospect regarding the world climate, research in environmental studies must continue to believe—as the activist slogan has it—that a better world is possible. But at the same time, the ends of climate science have apparently gone unfulfilled as the earth continues to warm despite clear evidence of anthropogenic climate change and guidelines for how to address the situation. However, Myanna Lahsen argues that one group of scientists' recent call for a moratorium on climate research due to the "political" nature of the problem is an abdication of the science-society compact, one that ignores the interconnectedness of scientific and political research. At this point, addressing the climate crisis will require the integration of scientific and social scientific research, focusing the ends of various fields on averting the end of the world.

A final group of chapters orients the end(s) of their disciplines around conceptualization. In these chapters, the knowledge work of a discipline relates most directly to the creation and clarification of a key concept. Peter de Bolla has highlighted the ambiguity in how scholars across disciplines understand the term "concept," but the considerations here discuss concepts in the way he describes: as "historical forms" that "activate and support cognitive processing and enable us to sense that we have arrived at understanding."[30] Concepts, he continues, are "ways of thinking" for which the particular word usually associated with that concept provides a shorthand.[31] Here, we find our contributors examining a word or words most associated with their disciplines.

First, Jessica Nakamura considers a foundational concept of performance studies— "liveness"—to ask how increasing mediation, especially in the face of the Covid-19 pandemic and its cancellation of thousands of live theatrical events, affects the discipline's self-identity. While Covid-19 threatens to end theater-going, Nakamura argues that it offers the opportunity for an expanded understanding of liveness for the future. The key attributes of situatedness in space and time that we associate with liveness become complicated in virtual performance but also lead to an understanding of liveness as a kind of shared co-presence, which can be recreated remotely. The end of performance studies as an exploration of liveness situates the field well to understand the stresses and pleasures that have come with our professional and social lives' sudden shift to the virtual realm in the Covid-19 era.

The Ends of Knowledge

As Nakamura looks to the future, Marieke M. A. Hendriksen considers the past. Her chapter discusses how the ends of history are continually redefined by the ever-changing present. As a professional historian charged with developing and implementing methods that facilitate doing "good historical research" in and for our time, Hendriksen reviews the history of history as well as current forces shaping the ends before explaining her turn towards what she calls "the performative approach." Archival research alone, she explains, is not enough to advance the ends of history; a more complete understanding of the past calls for experiential and experimental components inspired by Baconian principles. Where appropriate, she concludes, the traditional means and materials of historical research can be productively joined with those of the sciences.

Kenneth W. Warren explores how the field of Black studies has often supported an implicitly biological understanding of the concept of race at the same time as it has explicitly argued that race is a social construct. The field faces a defining contradiction in seeing race as a historically varied category of oppression while also working to identify actual connections among the people categorized in this way. Although, as Warren points out, such efforts generally have a laudable goal of overturning racial hierarchies, they neglect the fact that race is, in his words, error. Even theorizing race as a social construction may reinforce a sense of its impermeable reality. Despite rich historical and theoretical explanation, the concept of race may remain an obstacle to seeing other kinds of connections and divisions between people, particularly that of class.

Class is also a central concern of Mike Hill's chapter on cultural studies. Hill argues that, when it comes to education, the concepts of "culture" and "work" as commonly understood do not adequately describe or facilitate the function of the field. Tracing its history from Raymond Williams' reading of Matthew Arnold and the Hyde Park Riots of 1866 to its formal institutionalization in the 1960s, Hill examines how cultural studies' promise of massification contributed to a persistent division between culture and labor. He suggests that what has become the problem of scale might be solved by new ways of working and therefore calls for a broader conception of work and workers—one that includes education and educators and will expand their collective efforts via new institutions.

These chapters could have been arranged in other ways, highlighting other points of connection between and across disciplines. But these four themes—unification, access and justice, utopia/dystopia, and conceptual determination—synthesize many of the ways that knowledge workers respond when asked to consider their discipline's ends, from seeking a point of convergence for knowledge to articulating the central project of their own field. At this stage in the project of *The Ends of Knowledge*, we do not endorse a particular mode of response. As stated above, we see this volume as a first step and hope to continue fielding answers to the question, which might fit into or challenge these four groupings. Once you start looking for ends, you see that they are implied in many areas of our knowledge work: in the "method wars" that have recently preoccupied literary critics, in "defenses" of the humanities, in the creation of interdisciplinary research groups, and in university mission statements. One of our goals is to inspire scholars to articulate their end(s) and to work with this view in sight. We are, in many ways, only at the beginning of the end.

Introduction

Notes

1. Francis Bacon, *The Advancement of Learning*, in *The Major Works*, ed. Brian Vickers (Oxford: Oxford World's Classics, [1605] 2002), 147.
2. Francis Bacon, *The New Organon*, ed. Lisa Jardine and Michael Silverthorne (Cambridge: Cambridge University Press, [1620] 2000), 13.
3. Francis Bacon, "The New Atlantis," in *The Major Works*, 480.
4. Robert Burton, *The Anatomy of Melancholy*, ed. Holbrook Jackson (New York: New York Review of Books, [1621] 2001), 312.
5. Humphry Davy, *The Collected Works of Sir Humphry Davy*, ed. John Davy (London: Smith, Elder, and Co., 1839), 323.
6. Colleen Flaherty, "Canaries in a 'Toxic Mine,'" *Inside Higher Education*, May 5, 2020; "Portsmouth University Sticks by English Literature Staff Cuts," *BBC*, June 30, 2020; Colleen Flaherty, "Not the Same University," *Inside Higher Education*, May 14, 2020.
7. Char Adams, Allan Smith, and Aadit Tambe, "Map: See Which States Have Passed Critical Race Theory Bills," *NBC News*, June 17, 2021.
8. *Spectator* no. 10, March 12, 1711. Joseph Addison and Richard Steele, *The Spectator*, ed. Donald F. Bond (Oxford: Oxford University Press, [1711] 1965), 1:44.
9. thielfellowship.org
10. John Bender, *Ends of Enlightenment* (Stanford: Stanford University Press, 2012), 4.
11. Philip Kitcher, "The Ends of the Sciences," in *The Future for Philosophy*, ed. Brian Leiter (Oxford: Oxford University Press, 2006), 217.
12. D. Robert Macdougall, "The Ends of Medicine and the Experience of Patients," *The Journal of Medicine and Philosophy: A Forum for Bioethics and Philosophy of Medicine* 45, no. 2 (April 2020): 129–30.
13. Johan S. G. Chu and James A. Evans, "Slowed Canonical Progress in Large Fields of Science," *PNAS* 118, no. 41 (October 2021): 1.
14. Paul Reitter and Chad Wellmon, *Permanent Crisis: The Humanities in a Disenchanted Age* (Chicago: University of Chicago, 2021), 16.
15. Ibid., 9, 16.
16. Ibid., 254.
17. Kitcher points to Steven Weinberg, *Dreams of a Final Theory* (New York: Vintage, 1994) and E. O. Wilson, *Consilience* (Cambridge, MA: Harvard University Press, 1998) as two modern examples (212). The ambition and its continual frustration, however, have much older origins; see Seth Rudy, *Literature and Encyclopedism in Enlightenment Britain* (Basingstoke: Palgrave Macmillan, 2014).
18. Julie Thompson Klein, *Interdisciplinarity: History, Theory, and Practice* (Detroit: Wayne State University Press, 1990), 20.
19. Ibid., 11.
20. Ibid.
21. Harvey J. Graff, *Undisciplining Knowledge: Interdisciplinarity in the Twentieth Century* (Baltimore: Johns Hopkins University Press, 2015), 5.
22. Jerry A. Jacobs, *In Defense of Disciplines: Interdisciplinarity and Specialization in the Research University* (Chicago: University of Chicago Press, 2013), 4.

23. Stephen M. Gavazzi and E. Gordon Gee, *Land-Grant Universities for the Future: Higher Education for the Public Good* (Baltimore: Johns Hopkins University Press, 2018), 3, 5.

24. David. J. Staley, *Alternative Universities: Speculative Design for Innovation in Higher Education* (Baltimore: Johns Hopkins University Press, 2019), 10–11.

25. Cathy N. Davidson, *The New Education: How to Revolutionize the University to Prepare Students for a World in Flux* (New York: Basic Books, 2017), 19–20.

26. Ibid., 31.

27. Amanda Anderson and Joseph Valente, "Introduction: Discipline and Freedom," in *Disciplinarity at the Fin de Siècle*, ed. Amanda Anderson and Joseph Valente (Princeton, NJ: Princeton University Press, 2002), 1.

28. Ibid., 4.

29. Henrika Kuklick, "Professional Status and the Moral Order," in *Disciplinarity at the Fin de Siècle*, 126.

30. Peter de Bolla, *The Architecture of Concepts: The Historical Formation of Human Rights* (New York: Fordham University Press, 2013), 4.

31. Ibid., 31.

PART I
UNIFICATION

Knowledge, according to the diagram drawn by Ephraim Chambers and included in his *Cyclopædia: or, an Universal Dictionary of Arts and Sciences* (1728), "is either: *Natural* and *Scientifical*, OR *Artificial* and *Technical*."[1] Though the branches proceeding from that initial separation go on to enumerate forty-seven subjects comprising thousands of individual terms, Chambers insisted that his system of references could help readers reunite into "one whole" what alphabetical order had scattered across the text. Over the next century, however, the long-term (if not necessarily permanent) division of knowledge would be formalized in the "distinct Treatises or Systems" of the first *Encyclopedia Britannica* (1768) and institutionalized by the growing number of specialist associations that in 1819 left Joseph Banks in fear for the future of his own Royal Society.

The disciplinary silos and academic divisions subsequently built by and into the modern research university have, for better and worse, since remained the predominant conceptual spaces and administrative structures of knowledge production. The following chapters, then, examine the problems and possibilities of unifying knowledge across and within different fields as we now understand them. They offer a range of answers to several related questions: Which disciplines have gone as far as they can go within their current paradigms? Which could go further or faster with fewer or reconfigured boundaries? How might we advance knowledge by treating the subjects we research as (to borrow a line from Chambers) "so many Wholes, and as so many Parts of some greater Whole"?[2]

Physicists, as Brandon R. Brown explains, have long pursued and occasionally formulated unifying theorems that reduce the apparent complexity of the physical universe. What some see as the field's stalled progress toward a final Theory of Everything, however, has created rifts within physics itself as researchers look beyond what they can observe or test—the bedrocks of empirical science—to explain lingering mysteries. Progress and explanation are also at the core of Aaron Hanlon's chapter, which argues that literary studies is in a similar crisis, but for the opposite reason: rather than coalescent, explanatory knowledge that allows the field to progress toward some end, literary scholars tend to prize new "readings" that introduce further complications. This "crisis of what's next," he suggests, must be considered in conjunction with the broader crisis in the humanities if the field is to adapt and survive. The division of knowledge is likewise behind what B. N. Queenan, in her chapter on biology, describes as the current "crisis of existence." The boundaries built between life sciences and physical sciences allowed each to flourish, but the future—our future—depends on understanding the living and nonliving as equally subject to natural laws. Queenan locates biology at the interstices of the sciences and humanities, from which point it can offer not only opportunities but also reasons to unite disparate disciplines in the service of life. Of course, as Geoffrey C. Bowker points out, the nature of life and the living are already changing as humans and the rest of the natural world increasingly depend on and are integrated with computers. We may not know precisely what the ends of life or computing will be, but they will likely meet in the same spaces. In the final chapter of the part, Mark Algee-Hewitt examines the past, present, and possible futures of another field with the potential to change academic practices and structures by allying humanist inquiry with computational methodologies. The ends of the digital humanities—whether as a set of resources and practices naturalized within existing disciplines, a means by which those disciplines may be reformed or united, or as a new discipline in its own right—remain to be seen.

Notes

1. Ephraim Chambers, "Preface," in *Cyclopædia* (London: Printed for James and John Knapton et al., 1728), ii.
2. Chambers, *Cyclopædia*, i.

CHAPTER 1
THE ENDS OF PHYSICS
Brandon R. Brown

In early March of 2020, a clutch of cosmologists gathered for an informal discussion. They sat in a tower (painted coral, not made of ivory) at the Kavli Institute for Theoretical Physics outside Santa Barbara, California, and shared their worries. The organizer asked: "What keeps you up at night?" Within minutes, options crowded the room's chalkboard.

Leaving aside the oblique mathematical shorthand the physicists used, the queries' highlights included: Why does the universe feature more matter than antimatter? Why aren't we finding any new particles? Why do the fundamental forces exhibit such remarkably different strengths? Why are the numerical parameters of the universe so finely tuned to their arbitrary-looking values, without which we could never have realized stars, planets, and life forms?

The session, like most group therapy, dissolved without firm conclusions or even action items. People shared their intellectual angst, found new ways of posing old questions, and took cold comfort in knowing their concerns spread far beyond that tower.

Lingering Questions

Theoretical physics made breathtaking progress in the nineteenth and twentieth centuries, but today's practitioners by and large admit that their field now experiences a contemplative period, or even a type of vertigo. The remaining questions yawn before physicists like a canyon, with few handrails for safety. Some label the current state a crisis in physics, while others would call it an exciting era of open questions. Critics say esoteric mathematical adventures and theories of parallel universes have abandoned data-driven protocols to such an extent that whole segments of theoretical physics no longer belong to science. In reply, advocates shake their heads, reference mistaken naysayers of the past, and point to tantalizing hints of progress.[1] And an increasing number of physicists embrace a once-radical suggestion: that the array of confounding questions provide a sort of ultimate answer, an endpoint to their search for fundamental physical truth.

The author would like to acknowledge the support of the Kavli Institute for Theoretical Physics. The National Science Foundation supported this research in part, via Grant No. NSF PHY-1748958.

The Ends of Knowledge

Physics itself includes a still-surprising array of subfields, many of them busy in application, such as: condensed matter physics, the study of useful or at least intriguing solid materials like semiconductors; atomic physics, the study of single atoms and molecules, with particular applications involving light and lasers; and biological physics, the study of physical principles working at the level of single proteins and cells. Here, I will take most of those subfields for granted and focus on the primary historical ambitions for fundamental theoretical physics: namely, the hunt for the primary components of matter and the precise mapping of their governing laws. In practice, the fields must derive universal principles to describe *and predict* physical phenomena emerging from active experiments, e.g., particle colliders, and passive observations, e.g., telescopes. I will conflate cosmology (the study of physics at astronomical scales) and particle physics (the study of submicroscopic fundamental bits of matter). Theorists from both camps increasingly hitch their intellectual wagons together.

Before considering the idea of an end or multiple ends to such work, we need to reflect on the most recent epoch and the changing landscape—perhaps even the changing psychology—of physics. Into the twentieth century, fundamental physics busily built and validated two pillars: one describing gravity and a host of related astrophysical observations (Einstein's 1915 General Theory of Relativity), and the other describing submicroscopic particles and their interplay (the Standard Model of Particle Physics, coalescing in the early 1970s). The last half century has produced more modest fruits than years prior.

I'll list a defensible handful of major experimental and observational discoveries for fundamental physics in the past forty-five years. The set does not feature much that we can call "new":

- a pair of particle collision experiments that further validated the Standard Model of Particle Physics (the 1995 confirmation of the top quark particle, and the 2012 confirmation of the Higgs field);
- an astronomical observation that tweaked the same model (the 1998–2002 discoveries that elusive neutrino particles possess mass);
- one long-range astronomical observation that planted a critical mystery into cosmology (the 1998 discovery that the universe is not only expanding but *accelerating* via a mysterious "dark energy"); and
- one new advance in observational techniques (the 2015 detection of gravitational waves), which, in terms of theoretical work, has only further confirmed Einstein's 1915 work.

Of the list, dark energy stands apart from the others as the most fundamentally new window opened by physics in a half century. To account for the mystery it presents, physics must dial up a somewhat arbitrary factor within Einstein's gravitation, a "cosmological constant" that functions like a default bias in the cosmic weave.

We should appreciate the technologies in play and provide context for them as hallmarks of progress. The Large Hadron Collider, one of the devices uncovering the

Higgs field, boasts a sophisticated ring some seventeen miles around, buried roughly a football field deep under the Franco-Swiss border. The collider brings protons together at speeds approaching that of light, and watches what spews forth. The detector that traces the fragments bears the acronym ATLAS, being the most sophisticated detection device our species has yet built. Picture a densely woven tangle of plumbing and electronics, with the heft of a navy cruiser, condensed to the size of a four-story apartment building. The collider collects so much data from each particle collision that we cannot hope to store it all; computational algorithms decide what to toss in real time. As an artifact of design and engineering, we can swoon over it. But in terms of new physical techniques, we can shrug. Since the early twentieth century, when the laboratory of Ernest Rutherford aimed heavy alpha particles at gold atoms to probe their inner atomic structure, particle physics has relied on bombardment for discovery. The collider simply continues the work with more sophisticated apparatus. Humanity, though, appears to be approaching a limit with colliders: we don't have the means, physically and economically, to make them much larger.

Similarly, we can reflect on the other, more observational discoveries. How far have we really moved past the first telescopes of the seventeenth century, in terms of our craft? As with particle colliders, the reach of our ingenuity is stunning. While Galileo could magnify and locate the moons of Jupiter as tiny pinpoints, we have now imaged objects at the edge of the universe. Modern instruments can also uncover the cosmos using many different parts of the electromagnetic spectrum; instead of just the narrow range of light visible to the human eye, we now collect data with radio, infrared, X-ray, gamma-ray telescopes, etc. That said, some basic limitations persist. We cannot tweak the cosmos and watch it respond; instead, we sit patiently and collect information. Where experiments offer the real opportunity to probe specific questions, observations require choices of analysis followed by conjecture and argument.

Gravity wave detection presents a mixed conceptual bag of old and new. Finding these little ripples on the fabric of space and time confirms a 100-year-old prediction from Einstein. And the basic technique of finding the waves, "interferometry," dates to the nineteenth century.[2] Today's version boasts much better engineering, machining, precision, and timing, but we pulled the *technique* from a dusty shelf. However, the implications for discerning waves of gravity do much more than open a new type of astronomical eye on the universe. Indeed, the new modality has more in common with our species being able to *hear* the universe for the first time. Surprises may await us, particularly as our ears improve.

Taken together, the pace of "new" physics in the modern era resembles a sputtering engine compared to the revving and roaring that came before. In 2005 and 2006, the theoretical physicist Frank Wilczek published a series of essays and confronted a central challenge of twenty-first-century physics in direct and lucid terms: would physics ever be able to explain, once and for all time and space, *why* the universe features the fundamental values we measure? "With frustration mounting," he wrote, "prominent theorists have begun to express serious doubt about whether ultimate success is possible."[3] The widely accepted and experimentally validated Standard Model possesses many open numerical blanks that lack a theoretical prediction and must be inserted by hand. The masses of fundamental particles vary widely and do not appear to relate to one another in any sort of symmetric or suggestive way. Wilczek referred to them as "messy" and wrung his hands. "Could a beautiful, logically complete formulation of physical law yield a unique solution that appears so lopsided and arbitrary?"[4] As of 2022, physics appears no closer to answering Wilczek's question.

What We Talk About When We Talk About Progress

Over the past 100 years in particular, theoretical physics has prized unification, reduction, and symmetry as qualities most likely to lead toward ultimate truth. If a physical model can join two formerly separate ideas, then that constitutes progress: a reduction of overall complexity that suggests a deeper level of understanding. Further complexity falls away when practitioners find that presumably different phenomena or entities may in some sense exist as mirror images of one another; newly realized symmetries entice physicists like little else. If one from outside the priesthood furrows their brow and wonders if this feels a tad close to pursuing a human-centric sense of "beauty" in the natural world, then physicists have a reply: this modus operandi keeps working, and humans now use lasers, computer chips, GPS devices, and other tools as functioning proof that physics navigates a fruitful path. Let's revisit some examples of largely accepted steps of progress.

The roots of today's physics grew from the thinking of individuals like René Descartes and Galileo Galilei. Early works mixed rationality, measurement, and mathematics to describe the motion of objects on earth and in the heavens. To underline the radical break, consider that Galileo trained with, and worked alongside, academics who described themselves as mouthpieces for Aristotle and other long-dead thinkers.[5] But once bitten by a questioning, empirical, and quantifying bug, Galileo fashioned a telescope and discovered moons orbiting Jupiter. He also devised clever terrestrial trials, like timing a ball rolling down a ramp to show that gravity does not just move objects but also accelerates them. Building on these insights, the work of Isaac Newton and of Robert Hooke made a previously absurd-sounding unification: physical laws at play in our daily lives also rule the motion of much larger and longer-lasting bodies like stars and planets.

For a second example of unification, we visit the late nineteenth century, after skipping many major steps in between. In the span of a few decades, physicists like James Clerk Maxwell and Heinrich Hertz pulled three previously separate studies—electricity, magnetism, and light—together in a single, elegant group hug: a theory of electromagnetism. Not only were sparks and magnets two sides of the same coin but, together, they gave rise to the fast-propagating wave energies that brought light to our eyes and, in time, radio transmissions from one continent to another. We should note a worthy detail: a simpler mathematical notation, using the language of vector calculus, tidied a clutter of twelve gritty equations into the final four "Maxwell's equations." Still adorning T-shirts for the most physics-afflicted, the quartet stand independent of one's choice of geometry. They speak equally well to the spherical mathematics of a shining star or the rectangular world of an earthly laboratory.

I will pause next to a sort of holy historical shrine—one often cited in response to a possible "end" to physics. By about 1875, many practitioners thought they were approaching the end of their work. Given the success of various mathematical models to describe phenomena, a professor in Munich suggested to a student named Max Planck that physics offered little of remaining interest. He said that the garden of physics had reached a mature state, with only weeding tasks remaining for future generations.[6] But Planck, his eventual friend Einstein, his protégé Max von Laue, and many others pulled those remaining weeds and uprooted chunks of that nineteenth-century physics.

The Shift Away from Human Intuition

Planck led German physics from roughly 1900 to 1930, a period when Germany's scientific enterprise arguably led the world. He also dabbled in philosophy and wrote about the process of science. Admitting that the first step for any scientist was a sort of leap of faith, much like inspiration for an artist, he followed the notion of universality as his admittedly subjective lode star. In 1900, when introducing what would become his signature contribution, he de-emphasized the quantum aspects that would soon reform classical physics. He focused instead on his detailed derivation of fundamental, universal constants, including one we call Planck's constant, denoted by h.[7]

Planck went on to combine fundamental constants, such as the speed of light, c, the strength of gravitation, G, and his own h to form "natural units," or measures of length, time, mass, and so forth that stood apart from human existence. Where a meter or a second had strong correlations to the length of a human arm or the timing of a heartbeat, Planck's new units, defined exclusively by combinations of the universal constants, would, he claimed, hold for "all times and civilizations, even extraterrestrial and non-human."[8] The notion of universality has maintained a leading role in the ambitions of theoretical physics over the subsequent years.

In short order, other physicists explored the notion of *dimensionless* universal values. Standing as ratios of otherwise grimy physical values, these attained a higher mathematical purity, a nearly Pythagorean level of universality. The "fine-structure constant" provides one of the first and best examples of a dimensionless physical value. The German physicist Arnold Sommerfeld introduced it by comparing the computed speed of an electron orbiting an atom to the speed at which light moves through space.[9] No matter how one wants to quantify those speeds—kilometers per hour, or feet per second—dividing one by the other guarantees that their ratio stays the same. We now recognize the fine-structure constant as an indicator for the strength of electromagnetic forces, but its value of approximately 1/137 has endured. Physicists cannot explain why the universe landed on that specific number, and since it helps govern atoms, molecules, and our sensory experiences, even a slightly different value would lead to a remarkably different reality.

The Ends of Knowledge

My next important milepost recognizes the advent of quantum mechanics in the 1920s, a step that introduced a seemingly permanent discomfort for physicists. On the one hand, it opened a direct path to the most accurate description of natural phenomena our species has ever devised, explaining, for instance, nature's assembly of a periodic table of elements, along with their peculiar behaviors. On the other hand, the architects of quantum mechanics—centrally Niels Bohr, but many others—described a sort of black box in the submicroscopic realm, with built-in statistical mysteries that defy human intuition. These physicists presented a predictive framework that could perfectly foretell the results of experiments. However, perhaps feeling pessimistic about humanity after the First World War, they also drew a sharp line between physical reality and our limited minds, saying that our species would never gain a deep insight into the submicroscopic realm.

In hindsight, the enormous shift for physics encompassed two aspects, both of which suggested a new sort of required humility. First, it moved firmly away from Rube Goldberg-type interactions for the material world. The work of Galileo and Newton posited predictable chain reactions, where each causal collision forces a precise trajectory into the future, moment by moment. Quantum mechanics cannot and will not offer that. If we heat an atom of sodium, we know what frequency of light will emerge—to human perception, a beautiful vermillion shade—but we can't say *when* that little burst of light will emerge. Quantum mechanics contains baked-in uncertainties as a fundamental feature. The second important aspect involves a failure of metaphor. To this day, students and practitioners alike continue to grind their teeth over the infamous "wave-particle duality" embedded in quantum mechanics. Subatomic particles like an electron defy comfortable human metaphors. We can hold a tennis ball or observe the ripples on a pond, but these models fail to capture submicroscopic realities.

The role of metaphor lives on in physics (such as George Gamow's fruitful analogy of a liquid drop for an atom's nucleus), but quantum mechanics set a course that would move the field steadily away from everyday human intuition. Bohr's "Copenhagen interpretation" of quantum mechanics insisted that physicists just trust the statistical mathematical machinery: *see for yourself—it works—but don't try to understand it.* Put another way, quantum theory contains a Medusa standing behind us. Looking in front of us, we see armies of difficult problems fixed by her powers, but we must be careful not to peer over our shoulder.

Elder statesmen like Planck and Einstein initially bristled at placing boundaries to human knowledge; surely, they thought, the youngsters had lost their way. In time, Planck came to accept the frustrating verdict and he saw his own quantum work as part of a wall separating humans from a comprehensive understanding. Planck's philosophy evolved to understand scientific truth as some far horizon, beckoning as it retreats. But Einstein never relented. He insisted that humans could do better and spent his later years in a failed attempt to find a grander theory: a higher, more beautiful set of principles that would overcome the arbitrary nature of quantum theories and achieve unification. Much as earlier physicists had unified the arcs of earthly projectiles with the motion of planets, Einstein's unrealized theory would join the very small, where quantum theory reigned, to the astronomically large, where his theory of gravitation functioned.

The Ends of Physics

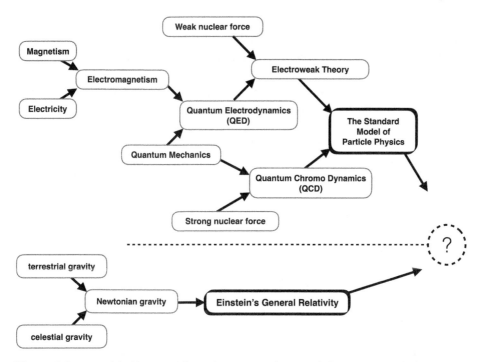

Figure 1.1 A simplified historical flow of progress in theoretical physics, tracing the last 400 years, from left to right, and emphasizing fundamental forces (with apologies to the theory of special relativity, which labors both above and below the dotted line).

On this rapid historical tour, we next stop in the early 1970s, after another series of significant breakthroughs. In half a century, quantum theory had matured, leading to remarkable successes in understanding fundamental particle physics: namely the building blocks of matter and their interactions over relatively short distances. The Standard Model of Particle Physics emerged from the continued process of unification (Figure 1.1). The Standard Model includes two main types of interactions that sit comfortably side by side in similar theoretical languages.

The quantum mechanics of Bohr and others had grown into Quantum Electrodynamics (QED), a full explanation for the interaction of electrically charged particles like electrons. I will highlight a pair of notable triumphs from this process. As physicist Paul Dirac devised a version of quantum theory for matter moving at very high speeds, he noted solutions dropping from his equations that looked like mirror images of "normal" particles. For every negative electron, a mirror particle of the same heft but positive charge seemed to emerge. Experiments eventually confirmed the existence of these "anti-particles," the mathematical figments from Dirac's notepad brought to stunning life. In time, QED provided a precise description of atomic spectra, for example, the differing colors emanating from various heated atoms, such as those in fireworks.

The guide of simplicity and symmetry also revolutionized our understanding of those particles dwelling in the core of atoms: protons and neutrons. Particle accelerators reached higher and higher energies into the 1960s and discovered—in

The Ends of Knowledge

fleeting bursts—an increasingly confusing bunch of proton cousins nicknamed the "particle zoo." Hundreds of particles with different masses and charges littered tables of supposedly fundamental particles. A model of even smaller and more fundamental particles reduced the particle zoo to a handful of "quarks." The eventual theory of Quantum Chromodynamics (QCD) deploys these quarks, and their mirror anti-quarks, to explain the hundreds of observed particles as simple quark combinations: *These three give you a giraffe, but combine just these two and get a gazelle.* As of the mid-1970s, then, quantum theory had helped comprehensively explain the short-range interactions of all known bits of matter, corralled in the Standard Model of Particle Physics. Separately, Einstein's 1915 masterpiece of General Relativity stood unchallenged as a description of gravity, providing a detailed choreography of moons, planets, stars, and so forth.

Each of these systems excelled at their separate tasks, but they could not find a satisfying union in their details. Given the rate of steady progress leading into the 1970s, many physicists thought a grand unification still might follow—they believed an end might be in sight. But to this date, the Standard Model and General Relativity will not reconcile or find a common, widely acknowledged patch of overlap.

Physics had accumulated a trophy chest by following unifications and symmetries, by putting ever-greater trust in mathematics, and finally by moving away from more intuitive, human-centric metaphors. Richard Feynman, a leading architect of QED, paused in 1965 and reflected on the furious theoretical and experimental progress: "The age in which we live is the age in which we are discovering fundamental laws of nature, and that day will never come again."[10] Feynman often saw physicists as the explorers of a necessarily finite intellectual land. While many agree that physics might have a finite pasture to roam, practitioners must assume ample acreage remains.

Whither Theory?

For most of the past forty-five years, physicists have done their best to conjure what could emerge beyond the Standard Model, what could replace that system, or—consistent with Einstein's aim for a "final" theory—what might unify the quantum principles of the Standard Model with the more geometrical foundations of gravitation. In terms of attaining verifiable support from experimental or observational data, all of these attempts have come up short. As the means of theoretical physics have continued to evolve, I hope to convey a similarly evolving sense of the ends.

A notion of "supersymmetry" emerged by the 1970s even as physicists completed the Standard Model. In terms of beauty and unification, supersymmetry offered to cleverly unite two distinct tribes of fundamental particles: the fermions (statistically more independent) and the bosons (statistically more communal). Supersymmetry became a fundamental assumption in heaps of subsequent theoretical work. Its popularity notwithstanding, its predictions for newly discovered particles or other fingerprints have not come to pass.

The most lively and controversial platform for modern theoretical physics involves "string theory," a term that I will use for a large and related set of approaches. Fundamentally, string theory offers a holy grail out of the gate: if one accepts a significant set of assumptions, then it unites gravity with quantum theory in a clean, organic way. At the theory's roots, incredibly tiny strings compose all matter. As they vibrate in different ways, finely tuned musical notes on the strings emerge as what we then observe as fundamental particles.

For the mathematics of string theory to work properly and for the machinery to yield gravity as a necessary by-product, physicists must assume the existence of many more dimensions than we find in any experiment. Hidden from our normal three dimensions of up-down, left-right, and forward-backward, and the somewhat more mysterious dimension of time, another six or seven dimensions lurk. That assumption is a large one, warranting skepticism.[11] Unfortunately (or, a cynic might say, "conveniently"), we will probably never be able to access the hidden dimensions. They curl so tightly that we would need an atom-smasher much larger than our own planet to ever unfurl them.[12]

String theory owes its controversial status to two fundamental drawbacks: (1) an absence of existing experimental evidence, access to near-term experimental evidence, or firm proposals for experimental evidence; and (2) a lack of specificity. The second point refers to an extreme flexibility, as string theory encompasses a large set of approaches, versus a unique theory based on a commonly held set of assumptions and details. As some critics like to say, string theory promised to be the theory of everything, but now it is the theory of anything. String theory has a branching diagram of manifestations and, by recent count, 10^{2000} solutions (give or take).

Before moving to philosophical implications, we should acknowledge broadly embraced theoretical progress of the last several decades. Like archaeologists finding shards of a mathematical Rosetta Stone, physicists have uncovered striking linkages between formerly separate theoretical concepts.[13] Even skeptical theorists would agree that these beguiling connections probably say *something* fundamental, even if we have not yet brought the ideas to full flower. And a focused cauldron of theoretical work that emerged in the early 1970s now serves as a perfect playpen for such connections: black-hole physics. Once speculative, but now observationally confirmed, black holes match a prediction that followed from Einstein's general theory of relativity, where so much mass concentrates in such a small region that space and time stretch to a mathematical breaking point. For theoretical physics, the practical edge of a black hole—the event horizon—puts physical principles under extreme duress to further interrogate their connections. Jacob Bekenstein published ideas about the thermal and statistical implications of black holes in the early 1970s. Stephen Hawking famously followed that work with contributions of his own, and "quantum gravity" researchers at present continue to mine black holes—with pencil, paper and computer—to possibly unify the long-separate pillars of contemporary physics. Some of their approaches incorporate string theory, while others do not.

The significant doubts about the trajectory of contemporary physics have led to both soul searching and also, for an increasing number of theoretical physicists, an embrace of ideas once considered whimsical. On the former front, some reflect that we may be stuck on the wrong set of questions. On the latter, the notion of our universe being but one within an enormous array of universes—a "multiverse"—has alternately beckoned enthusiastic advocates and dragged along more reluctant physicists who see no alternatives.

In terms of soul searching, some physicists have even declared an "end of reductionism," saying that searching for a theory of everything was doomed to fail, while reality instead honors complexity. These contrary but optimistic voices suggest that physics in the new century must change gears, moving away from seeking ultimate equations and toward mapping a sort of hierarchy of phenomena that emerge in different domains, some microscopic and others galactic.[14]

The soul searching best resonates with a historical anecdote revisited by the theoretical physicist Steven Weinberg in his book *To Explain the World*.[15] Johannes Kepler, the seventeenth-century mathematically inclined astronomer, made critical discoveries about the motion of the known planets. Without his mathematical pattern fitting, others like Isaac Newton may not have formulated a universal theory of gravity that explained planetary orbits. But Kepler also considered a now-laughable set of questions: Why were there exactly six planets, and how could we understand their relative distances from the sun? He worked with all his mathematical prowess to employ the Platonic solids—cubes, pyramids, and other highly symmetric geometries—that must somehow house the planetary orbits and yield their intriguing distances from the sun. As we now know, these reductionist questions were misguided. Most stars have planets, and the number of planets varies randomly according to how early globs of gas and dust coalesced. The distances at which they orbit a star arise arbitrarily from initial velocities, clumpings, and collisions in a young solar system. Kepler described himself as a nervous individual; imagine his panic attack if he'd learned that planets circle stars in arbitrary numbers and that our solar system is but one of trillions in the universe.

So, many physicists ask by analogy, might we place undue importance on the exact mass of this or that quark, or on the relative strengths of forces? Moreover, are we so clueless, so removed from a more comprehensive picture of reality, that our attempts to unify gravity and quantum theory are laughably distant from anything relevant to deeper truths? Surely, some suggest, we face limitations or at least deep biases as evolved human beings on our special planet. A human perfecting a unified theory may be as absurd as a shrimp divining the causes of tides. As theorist Lawrence Krauss wrote in *Hiding in the Mirror*, "Ultimately our continuing intellectual fascination with extra dimensions may tell us more about our own human nature than it does about the universe itself."[16]

Just as physics graduated from seeing our solar system as unique to recognizing it as common, many theoretical physicists consider a migration to the multiverse as the next natural step. This migration emerged from two separate research vectors. Modern cosmology, a theory bringing us forward from a Big Bang to what we observe today, relies on an idea dubbed "inflation." True to its name, and in order to best explain, for instance, the relative abundance of elements we observe, inflation posits that a small patch of the early universe rapidly expanded. Why just the right patch and not others? Why at just the right moment, within the first fraction of a second after the Big Bang? As Wilczek noted,

"Inflation is a broad scenario rather than a specific theory."[17] Some early proponents of inflation began expounding on the idea of parallel universes where other patches expanded, leading to very different outcomes. Far from viewing this branching tree of realities as a troubling problem, some embraced it as a new intellectual opportunity. The multiverse similarly emerged to either champion or excuse the vast multitude of acceptable solutions to string theory. What if having that many acceptable versions of reality shows us not a failing theory but a window onto our Kepler-like ignorance? If the number of solar systems and galaxies serves to humble humanity, why not the number of universes?

Never too far from multiverse discussions are an uncomfortable set of ideas collected as "anthropic principles." In broad strokes, anthropic reasoning argues that if the parameters of our universe were much different, humans wouldn't exist to ask our questions. When combined with the notion of 10^{2000} universes, we can see that we will only have physicists in the tiny handful where the nearly random strengths of forces and masses of particles combine to allow their existence. We do not have just one universe full of lucky coincidences. Instead, we inhabit but one of countless rolls of the parameter dice, and of course we inhabit the one that can allow us. One struggles to invalidate such reasoning. Therefore, many critics of multiverse thinking suggest that proponents have exited the bounds of what we call science.

A Possible End and a Multiverse of Critics

The renowned theoretical physicist Leonard Susskind, a leading architect of contemporary string theory, expressed enthusiasm for the multiverse as a logical sort of endpoint in his 2005 book, *The Cosmic Landscape*.[18] He admits that string theory diverged from the idea of elegance and uniqueness—the old way of doing business. But Susskind finds an end, however unsatisfying to some, sitting in plain and logical sight.

For pragmatic purposes, I will collect three big ideas in a package and call them a possible "end" to theoretical physics: (1) string theory with its plethora of allowed solutions; (2) the fine-tuned parameters of our universe that allow us to exist; and (3) a multiverse that, while untestable, works consistently with the first two ideas. Some theoretical physicists feel that this package may be approaching the truth and that they will continue to improve string theory, perhaps even making some part of it accessible to experiment. Meanwhile, others will probably never be comfortable with the towering assumptions that support the above three points. They will always see this "end" as too severe a departure from the previous history of physics, a new business model they cannot endure.

A century ago, Oswald Spengler predicted an expiration of the scientific engine in *The Decline of the West*, outlining how a combination of diminishing returns and societal lack of interest would lead the whole enterprise to fizzle, matching similar declines in previous cultures. Historians and philosophers of science still refer to Spengler on occasion, and if nothing else, they employ his initial pessimism to set out a practical framework: namely, internal versus external causes of an "end" to scientific activity and/

or productivity. An internal factor would include anything that led physics to ending on its own terms, while an external factor could include, for instance, lack of economic support or a society discarding the fact-based lessons of the Enlightenment.[19] But here, I focus on more contemporary discussions of ends for physics in particular.

I see two groups of critics for the three-part stringy multiverse package outlined above. In one group, we find those who do see physics as nearing or having perhaps passed through an end, with the stringy multiverse package standing as a sort of non-physics or trans-physics piece of mathematical wizardry. In another, we have many authors who, while decrying the status quo and hounding the flaws of the stringy multiverse, maintain hope that other paths to progress remain. This second group sees nothing like an end; it would say that physics has a full tank of gas but needs to make a U-turn.

The first group of critics has viewed post-1970s fundamental physics, with admiration, as nearing the end of what it can reasonably accomplish given experimental limitations. In 1994, David Lindley, a particle physicist who had left the profession, published *The End of Physics: The Myth of a Unified Theory*.[20] He described a field that, in seeking an ultimate theory, had set itself up for ultimate frustration. Lindley underlined the growing divide between the increasingly speculative ideas of theoretical physicists and the inability of experimental physicists to test those ideas. In summary, he stated that a complete and comprehensive theory of everything could only be a "myth" given pragmatic realities. He did not offer the term loosely or pejoratively but rather as a precise semantic label: "a story that makes sense within its own terms, offers explanations for everything we see around us, but can neither be tested nor disproved."[21] He marked such an end as less a mission accomplished and more as physics having come to the end of its practical tether.

In 1996, the science writer John Horgan, although neither a practicing physicist nor a philosopher, took up Lindley's banner and published a more provocative version of pessimism in *The End of Science: Facing the Limits of Knowledge in the Twilight of the Scientific Age*.[22] Taking on a range of scientific disciplines chapter by chapter, from physics to neuroscience, Horgan employed extensive interviews with leading scientists to highlight what he saw as slowing progress following an unprecedented century of discovery. He labeled the esoteric adventures of string theorists and others seeking a unified theory, divorced as they were from experimental data, as unintentionally but technically "ironic." While he predicted that the more applied segments of physics would continue "inventing more versatile lasers and superconductors and computing devices," the theorists would wander into an increasingly non-empirical realm, having more in common with segments of the humanities than they would with their intellectual ancestors.[23] For those focused on the universe writ large, Horgan had a different sort of analogy. Noting these astrophysicists' extreme dependence on passive observation, he underlined their susceptibility to assumptions: "They must interpret their data, just as evolutionary biologists and historians do."[24] Despite the discovery of an accelerating universe shortly after his book's publication in 1996, Horgan believes the past twenty-five years of physics have seen more validation than refutation of his ideas.[25]

In the second, less pessimistic group, however, we have many more-recent examples, and these critics do not believe that the end is at hand.[26] With remarkable consistency, the members of this group voice related concerns about the state of physics: the lack of a testable or even a consistent framework for string theory alongside sociological factors helping keep string theory afloat as the dominant yet unsubstantiated paradigm.

The year 2006 welcomed two string-negative books. Peter Woit borrowed his title, *Not Even Wrong*, from the theoretical physicist Wolfgang Pauli (1900–58), who allegedly uttered the statement when asked about a younger physicist's research paper.[27] The phrase "not even wrong" has come to represent a pejorative for untestable and unfalsifiable pseudo-physics—*ergo* not possible to be "wrong." Woit's book carefully walks through the genesis, the major milestones, and the accumulating, troubling assumptions of string theory. At the same time, Lee Smolin, a leading architect of a string-theory rival called loop quantum gravity, published *The Trouble with Physics*. Similar to Woit, but with arguably more sympathy, Smolin criticized the inability of string theory to coalesce around a single framework: "it's a conjecture about a theory we would love to believe in."[28] Returning to the topic of string theory in a 2017 interview, Woit labeled the related multiverse as an "excuse for failure … designed to shut down scientific progress."[29]

Critics also consistently decry sociological aspects of the current stagnation, painting a scene in which string theory plays the role of an exclusionary guard for the field's most prestigious tower. While many theorists see string theory as "the only game in town," some critics would call that attitude problematic—more social than scientific. Roger Penrose denoted string theory as the "fashion" part of his 2016 book *Fashion, Faith, and Fantasy*.[24] While he acknowledged that theories become popular with intelligent physicists for initially compelling reasons, he suggested that abundant popularity can shield a subfield from criticism and self-reflection to a detrimental extent. While these social forces have always played some role in physics, historically reheating flawed ideas past their expiration dates, Penrose underlines some modern factors that intensify the effect.

Given the price tags of contemporary particle physics experiments, with gigantic collider rings and sophisticated detectors, and the sizes of related research teams, with hundreds or even thousands of collaborators, these projects cater to conventional wisdom in their design and in the questions they probe. Even the aforementioned ATLAS detector, Penrose argues, must subscribe to a certain picture of expectations, not only in its design but in the subsequent months of (largely automated) analysis that follow an experiment.[30] Since the Large Hadron Collider generates more data than we can possibly store or process, and since it ignores huge swaths of data based on expectations and priorities, we may lose pearls of new physics in the discarded bits.

Before leaving possible rejoinders to the stringy multiverse package, we should consider input from philosophers of science who offer at least one caution. They employ an "inverse gambler's fallacy" to question the connection between observing a fine-tuned universe and embracing multiple possible universes, thus decoupling the second and third items in the package. The inverse gambler's fallacy describes a case of a gambler walking into a casino and witnessing a single roll of two dice. The dice come up double-six. Knowing that well-balanced dice have exactly a one in thirty-six chance of coming up double-six, she declares that the dice must surely have been rolled many times before she arrived. That is logically false. Whether or not the dice had *ever* been rolled before, the odds of a double-six are exactly the same on any roll.[31] Following this logic, the fact that we look upon an improbable universe cannot lead us to assume a longer sequence or larger array of universes. We can only say for certain that the universe presents one peculiar roll of its dice. And following this view, many physicists soldier onward to explain our unlikely reality.

A Practitioner's Model: The Sphere of Knowledge

We turn now to an optimist's model, and I submit that most practicing physicists, of all stripes, work under this model's assumptions, though typically without spending conscious time on it. Following closely on talks delivered by and interviews with theoretical physicist David Gross, let's call this the Sphere of Knowledge (Figure 1.2).[32]

Gross, a 2004 Nobel laureate for his work on Quantum Chromodynamics, a pioneer in key phases of string theory, and a recent president of the American Physical Society, helped found the Kavli Institute for Theoretical Physics. In a 2018 talk celebrating the 50th anniversary of the Standard Model, he asked an open question for exploring fundamental physics: "Can we go on forever?"[33] In answer to his question, Gross describes scientific discovery as an expanding volume of knowledge. As humanity discovers and maps more over time, the sphere expands. The surface of this expanding knowledge represents our boundary with the unknown, and in this way, we can label the surface of open questions as our recognized ignorance. Interestingly, as this volume of knowledge expands over time, the surface of open questions naturally grows as well. The more we know, the more we shed light on ignorance.

Indeed, each discovery tends to beget more questions. Gross even points to academic careers using the same model. Maintaining life at the outer boundary requires a great deal of intellectual industry, and each theorist working there must at some point stop. And when one stops, the boundary continues to expand without them. In this sense, one can paint some string theory skeptics, for instance, as thinkers who have quit running to keep up with the boundary. They sit down and wave their hands at the retreating boundary as an illusion.

Gross remains part of what we may label the "old school." He wants physics to find a unique theory. That we haven't yet figured out how to unite gravity with the Standard Model, for instance, does not rule out the existence of a yet-unseen path forward. And while he sees the string theory program as a logical continuation of past quantum theories, he shuns the multiverse. "It is exactly the opposite of science," he said in an interview at the Kavli Institute in February 2020. "In science, the more knowledge you have the better off you are. Here [with the multiverse], the more knowledge you have, it shrinks the applicability of the theory." He also worries that, on a pragmatic level, a multiverse endpoint closes the doors of physics to younger researchers.

In addressing a possible end to physics, we can point to the geometry (or more exactly the topology) of ignorance. If the universe, or multiverse, holds an unbounded

The Ends of Physics

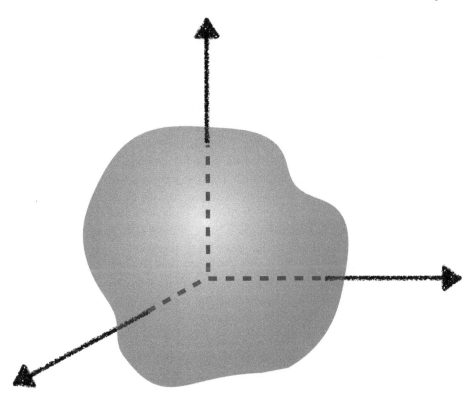

Figure 1.2 A "sphere" of knowledge, expanding against the unknown. As knowledge (the volume) expands, the extent of recognized ignorance (the surface) also grows.

space of secrets, then the sphere can go on expanding forever. If the unknown instead has *boundaries*—what a topologist would call a "compact" space—then the process of physics and science itself must necessarily end at some point. We run out of real estate, similar to Richard Feynman's metaphor of scientists mapping and exploring a finite land. If and when we approach such an end, the signs would be obvious, Gross suggests. And despite the hand-wringing and naysaying, he would dispute that we face compelling evidence of that, with physicists working and publishing as busily as ever.

The Next Chapter?

Experimental and observational results have guided historical progress in physics. Presumably, data must maintain a central role if physics will write a new meaningful chapter versus a provocative epilogue about remote conjectures. At present, physicists pursue the next generation of particle accelerators, and we may attain the next generation of energies with new, surprising physics spilling from the resulting collisions. But accelerators probably cannot continue the march to still higher energies given the required size of these machines versus economic and physical realities. Physicists also continue to collect more and more data from the cosmos, resonating with Galileo's early work. While observation lacks experiment's incisive ability to directly ask and answer questions, the cosmos promises a wealth of information to come, even in the near term.

To proffer an optimistic ending, I return to the branch of theoretical physics opened by Jacob Bekenstein, Stephen Hawking, Roger Penrose and others: the necessarily brackish physics required for considering a black hole. Gravity, quantum theory, thermodynamics, and the notion of information itself all come together near the event horizon; exciting work, with new thinking, foments today at that boundary. The ascent of gravitational wave detection, which has already picked up black hole interactions, may inform those conversations in the years to come. Meanwhile, the fundamental role of quantum information has assumed a prime place in these conversations. Terrestrial quantum information simulators (i.e., "quantum computers") have demonstrated significant recent advances that may yet ask direct questions about the quantum world and quantum information. If physics will write a new chapter beyond a multiverse ending, these tantalizing plotlines may well fill the pages to come, perhaps with key characters from string theory making guest appearances.

Notes

1. See Robbert Dijkgraaf, "Contemplating the End of Physics," *Quanta Magazine*, November 24, 2020.
2. Two beams of light run wind sprints in perpendicular directions. If they get back at slightly different times, we know one or both of their paths slightly changed its length, the telltale sign of a passing gravity wave.
3. Frank Wilczek, "On Absolute Units," *Physics Today* 58, no. 10 (2005): 12–13; 59, no. 1 (2006): 10–11; 59, no. 5 (2006): 10–11.
4. Frank Wilczek, "On Absolute Units, III: Absolutely Not?" *Physics Today* 59, no. 5 (2006): 10.
5. John Heilbron, *Galileo* (Oxford: Oxford University Press, 2010), 40–2.
6. John Heilbron, *Dilemmas of an Upright Man: Max Planck and the Fortunes of German Science* (Cambridge: Harvard University Press, 1996), 10.
7. Brandon Brown, *Planck: Driven by Vision, Broken by War* (Oxford: Oxford University Press, 2015), 123–4.
8. Max Planck, "Ueber irreversible Strahlungsvorgänge," *Annalen der Physik* 306 (1900): 69.
9. Arnold Sommerfeld, "Zur Quantentheorie der Spektraillinien," *Annalen der Physik* 4, no. 51 (1916): 51–2.
10. Richard Feynman, *Character of Physical Law* (Cambridge: MIT Press, 1965), 172.
11. To imagine a "hidden" dimension, picture a long roll of aluminum foil. At a great distance, the tube looks like a line and, for practical purposes, we could now model it as a one-dimensional object. So goes string theory: six or seven curl up within the more recognizable ones we experience.

12. String theory became "superstring theory" in the 1980s, and it welcomed "M Theory" in the mid-1990s by tacking on an extra dimension and replacing strings with wavy membranes. In common parlance, "string theory" incorporates these evolutions.
13. The technical details lie beyond this chapter's reach, but in addition to the aforementioned M Theory, we can add, for instance, the holographic principle and the AdS/CFT correspondence.
14. R. B. Laughlin, and David Pines., "The Theory of Everything," *Proc. Natl. Acad. Sci.* 97, no. 1 (2000): 28–31.
15. Steven Weinberg, *To Explain the World: The Discovery of Modern Science* (New York: Penguin, 2015).
16. Laurence Krauss, *Hiding in the Mirror: The Quest for Alternate Realities, from Plato to String Theory (by Way of Alice in Wonderland, Einstein, and the Twilight Zone)* (New York: Penguin, 2005), 2.
17. Wilczek, "On Absolute Units, III," 11.
18. Leonard Susskind, *The Cosmic Landscape: String Theory and the Illusion of Intelligent Design* (New York: Little, Brown and Company, 2005).
19. Oswald Spengler, *The Decline of the West* (Oxford: Oxford University Press, 1926); Susan Haack, *Defending Science—within Reason: Between Scientism and Cynicism* (Amherst: Prometheus Books, 2007); G. M. Swer, "The Decline of Western Science: Defending Spengler's Account of the End of Science: Within Reason," *Journal for Gen. Phil. of Science* 50 (2019): 545–60.
20. David Lindley, *The End of Physics: The Myth of a Unified Theory* (New York: Basic Books, 1994).
21. Ibid., 255.
22. John Horgan, *The End of Science: Facing the Limits of Knowledge in the Twilight of the Scientific Age* (New York: Basic Books, 1996).
23. Ibid., 88–9.
24. Ibid., 110–11.
25. John Horgan, "Was I Wrong about 'The End of Science'?" *Cross-Check*, April 13, 2015.
26. Peter Woit, *Not Even Wrong: The Failure of String Theory and the Search for Unity in Physical Law* (New York: Basic Books, 2006); Lee Smolin, *The Trouble with Physics: The Rise of String Theory, the Fall of Science, and What Comes Next* (Boston: Houghton Mifflin Harcourt, 2006); Sabine Hossenfelder, *Lost in the Math: How Beauty Leads Physics Astray* (New York: Basic Books, 2018); Roger Penrose, *Fashion, Faith, and Fantasy: In the New Physics of the Universe* (Princeton, NJ: Princeton University Press, 2016).
27. Woit, *Not Even Wrong*.
28. Smolin, *The Trouble with Physics*, 147.
29. John Horgan, "Why String Theory Is Still Not Even Wrong," *Cross-Check*, April 27, 2017.
30. Penrose, *Fashion, Faith, and Fantasy*, 8–10.
31. Roger White, "Fine-Tuning and Multiple Universes," *Noûs* 34, no. 2 (2000): 263–4.
32. Some credit the notion to Pascal. See Jürgen Mittelstrauss, *Theoria: Chapters in the Philosophy of Science* (Berlin: De Gruyter, 2018), 45–8.
33. David Gross, "The Standard Model and Beyond," *The Standard Model @50* Conference, Case Western University, Cleveland, Ohio, June 3, 2018.

CHAPTER 2
THE ENDS OF LITERARY STUDIES
Aaron R. Hanlon

Two Crises

Two crises afflict literary studies, but we only talk about one of them.

The one we talk about we call the "crisis of the humanities," by which we mean the declining number of English majors, the lack of full-time, tenure-eligible jobs for literature faculty, and the widespread devaluation of our teaching and research among students, parents, politicians, and policymakers. Employment data consistently show that English majors have comparable and in many cases superior career outcomes to majors in fields such as environmental science, biology, and psychology, among others.[1] Yet the crisis of the humanities persists as both a set of attitudes about the uselessness, easiness, and ideological waywardness of the discipline and the political and economic correlates of these: diminished student interest, no stable academic jobs for literature PhD graduates, and deep cuts to our funding and resources. In terms of this crisis, the end of literary studies seems inevitable.

For these reasons literature scholars tend to understand the "crisis of the humanities" strictly as a matter of politics—of neoliberal takeover of higher education—which therefore calls for a strictly activist response: labor organization, strikes, open letters, and lists of demands. We lose sight of the second crisis, which too often goes unspoken. This is the crisis of "what's next?"—of how we adapt to irreversible changes in the broader landscapes of culture and knowledge production. Our discipline was set up in the late nineteenth and early twentieth centuries, with the solidification of the idea of "literature" as a discrete category of imaginative writing, largely for the purpose of managing cultural capital and conferring it upon a relatively narrow socioeconomic slice of the population. Today, cultural capital—such as it is—is less a function of knowing about literature, "classic" or otherwise. If cultural capital is to be found in knowledge of and engagement with other cultural materials—movies, television, TikTok videos, current events—why should anyone turn to specialists in literature (instead of, say, media studies) to understand such things? Literary studies is trapped in a dilemma. Literature and "the literary"—how we define our area of expertise—no longer matter in the ways they did when the discipline was set up to study them. This is not to say they no longer matter *at all* but that they no longer matter both in the ways literary studies at large is prepared to address them and at the scale of our demands in response to the first crisis. Put simply, if we aren't addressing the second crisis—the crisis of "what's next?" or what is the purpose of literary studies in light

The Ends of Knowledge

of the mismatch between our disciplinary origins and the epistemic demands of the present and future—then our demands in response to the first crisis amount to little more than special pleading, a demand for resources scaled to an obsolete raison d'etre.

Faced with two crises, one with a pervasive and negative impact on the field of literary studies, the other of theoretical concern and more ambiguous effects, it makes sense that literature scholars have focused on the first. In what follows, however, I discuss why we should consider the two crises together instead of subordinating the second. Thinking of the two crises together doesn't mean believing that there is a causal relationship between them. It means that it is a mistake to think we can understand the end of literary studies—and how to prevent it—without reexamining the ends of literary studies. What thinking through these crises in conjunction helps us understand is that interpretive literary studies (whose product is literary readings) is coming to an end, but the explanatory study of literature (whose product is knowledge) has a future.

Interpretation as an End in Itself

Given the capaciousness of the discipline, I won't be able to do justice here to all the work scholars do under the banner of literary studies. My focus instead will be on the assumptions of what I take to be the core of the discipline: interpretive literary studies. I characterize interpretive literary studies as the discipline's "core" because interpretation is the practice that putatively sets us apart from philosophers, historians, and social scientists.

Scholars of literature produce arguments, critiques, and interpretations, the collective term for which is *readings*. But we don't worry enough about whether any of this constitutes knowledge. The tacit assumption within the discipline is that, of course, when we produce scholarly work in our field, we are producing knowledge. Outside the discipline, however, it's far from obvious why one would rely on any given literary interpretation *as knowledge* and what one would do with it. It matters what people outside the discipline think because, as Steven Shapin explains, knowledge is contingent upon credibility.[2] Siloed disciplines that shelter themselves from external critique and whose knowledge is countenanced by no one else will continue to drop out or be pushed to the margins of knowledge work, as literary studies is currently experiencing. While every discipline has some version of interpretation—the various "interpretations" of quantum mechanics, for example—whose purpose is generally to move toward epistemic consensus, literary "interpretation" moves in the opposite direction: it generates multiplicity as an end in itself.

My goal in this chapter is to open up some conceptual room to consider not only how literary studies produces knowledge but also how literary studies might pursue knowledge *progressively*, so that the field advances in what it knows. Of course, this short chapter won't satisfy all objections to what qualifies as knowledge or how literature and the study of literature might yield knowledge. The goal here is to start a conversation, not to bring one to an end. What would the study of literature look like if we were to take seriously the idea that we could produce useful, reliable, and progressive knowledge, as opposed to seeing our role primarily as using literary interpretations to flesh out the complexity of texts or to take texts as occasions to critique what we perceive as the reductivism of other knowledge domains (for example, economics, natural science)?

Explanations versus Readings

To have this conversation we first need to distinguish between factual and explanatory knowledge—that is, to understand knowledge as more than simply a collection of facts. Scholars of literature may occasionally uncover new factual knowledge—say, by identifying the author of an anonymous poem—but more often they seek to explain things. David Deutsch contends that we know something is an explanation—"as opposed to mere statement of fact"—when it helps us better understand something. Explanations "are about 'why' rather than 'what,'" and "they are also about coherence, elegance, and simplicity, as opposed to arbitrariness and complexity."[3] The second part of Deutsch's definition is important for literary studies, because it indicates why literary interpretation—which often focuses on drawing out textual complexity and entails disagreement with other interpretations of the same passages or texts—might fall short of explanatory knowledge. Explanatory knowledge is difficult to unseat; it's not simply additive—here's another way to explain this, and another, and so on—but corrective.

For this reason, when we entertain the idea that literary studies produces knowledge, we should be careful not to assume that interpretation is tantamount to explanation, or that the way we produce explanatory knowledge is by doing interpretations or "performing readings." Elaine Auyoung describes what it means to read something, as for comprehension, and to "perform a reading" in such a way that marks a distinction between "the procedures of literary interpretation" and "the process involved in reading comprehension."[4] Interpretation is unavoidable in all knowledge domains. In the natural sciences, for example, the purpose of interpretation is roughly to move from observation, which is the purview of many individual scientists, to coherence or consensus about the observed. In literary studies, the purpose of interpretation is virtually the opposite: to move from observation to greater complexity and variety, or to stake out and justify a discordant position relative to other interpretations. Here again this objective distinguishes literary interpretation from explanatory knowledge, the latter aimed at simplifying and converging upon explanations that are difficult to unseat.

For literary studies to become a progressive knowledge project—a project for which different or incompatible explanations converge toward explanations that are difficult to unseat—we'd have to consider a major shift in the role of interpretation in our scholarship and what kind of work we expect close reading or literary interpretation to accomplish. This would entail a shift from performing a reading to studying to explain. When it comes to explanatory knowledge in literary studies, then, we might say some form of interpretation—even as paraphrase—is a necessary *part* of an explanation when

The Ends of Knowledge

it involves reconciling textual observations with attendant contextual observations as well as the textual and contextual observations of others, and taking points of disputation as things to be explained in and of themselves. Possibly the prospect of trying to reconcile diverging interpretations as part of a progressive knowledge project will sound ridiculous to some, because, as I've suggested, the purpose or *end* of literary interpretation as ordinarily practiced in the discipline is not explanatory knowledge in Deutsch's sense but what Robert Eaglestone calls "conversation" about how literature can "trigger access to felt experience at the human core" and "offer a freer, deeper, more mobile way of thinking about it."[5] Literary interpretation that takes the form of joining such a conversation may be marshaled toward different ends, such as political critique or self-knowledge, but its ends are not typically to reconcile discordant interpretations in pursuit of better *explanations*. The fact that explanatory knowledge not staked upon literary interpretation is not typically an end of interpretive literary studies doesn't mean it can't be. Toward the conclusion of this chapter, I'll come back to the details of what a shift from interpretation as performing a reading to interpretation as merely a component—though a necessary one—of an explanation might look like as part of a progressive knowledge project, but I next need to address the issue of what it means for literary studies to produce knowledge versus what it means for literature itself to contain knowledge. These are distinct but related claims.

Knowledge Production as an End of Literary Studies

My view is that the various kinds of writing we have called "literature" sometimes contain and convey factual knowledge, in the form of historical facts (for example, how much something cost in a given time and place as represented in a novel set in that time and place) or more general truth claims or instructive claims about how to think or how to live. But to say literature itself contains knowledge is not the same as saying the study of literature produces knowledge. After all, we don't need the intermediary of a literature scholar to understand a factual claim about, say, the price of an opera ticket in eighteenth-century London as represented in Frances Burney's *Evelina* (1778). We do, however, require a literature scholar to *explain* what business a work of fiction might have in making certain kinds of factual assertions, or how reliable are such assertions in light of the historical record.

If we want to foreground knowledge production in the field—whether by bringing facts or statements in literature into wider historical, philosophical, or political conversations, or by explaining aspects of literature itself in a way scholars in other fields can access and trust—it's important to challenge a pervasive dogma: that knowledge is an inappropriate end for the study of literature. This dogma is a form of what philosophers of literature call anti-cognitivism, and it's as pervasive within literary studies as without. Jukka Mikkonen describes two types of literary anti-cognitivism: strong and moderate. Strong anti-cognitivism is the view that "literary works do not have cognitive value and approaching them as knowledge-yielding works is an inappropriate stance toward them as works of literature." By "cognitive value" Mikkonen means statements that we could treat like statements in work of philosophy or science, something we could recognize as making a claim (proposition) and whose claim we could test or scrutinize for its accuracy or its philosophical value, its value as an idea. Moderate anti-cognitivism grants that "although some literary works may make contributions to knowledge, that contribution is insignificant or irrelevant in approaching the works as literary works."[6] We might think of anti-cognitive views about literature as a way of separating literature from philosophy or "literary knowledge" from "scientific knowledge."

While the first parts of both strong and moderate anti-cognitivism concern whether literature itself contains knowledge or can make knowledge claims, the second parts concern the appropriate approach to studying literature. The latter, in particular, interests those of us who seek to defend the idea that the discipline of literary studies should take knowledge production as an important end or purpose. But as I've suggested, the two components of anti-cognitivism are related. If we accept that literature itself—particularly fiction—can never make knowledge claims or evaluable propositional statements about how things are in the world, then taking such a noncognitive object as a basis for knowledge production already limits what we can say about what literature teaches us.

But perhaps more importantly, if we treat all forms of literature as monolithically noncognitive, or as monolithically aesthetic and never discursive or philosophical, we would be denying what we already know about realist fiction, such as Daniel Defoe's *Journal of the Plague Year* (1722), or philosophical novels, such as William Godwin's *Caleb Williams* (1794): that they were written to engage with epistemic matters, among others. Godwin defined literature as "the diffusion of knowledge through the medium of discussion, whether written or oral."[7] When Godwin wrote *Caleb Williams*, he was engaging in a philosophical project, not aiming to produce a work of art in the sense that a Modernist writer such as James Joyce understood "literature" or "art." The second assumption of anti-cognitivism, that studying knowledge in literature is an inappropriate or subordinate aim given literature's status as a "work" or art object, is a way of denying evidence that would contradict the first assumption, that literature is without cognitive value.

That is, in "approaching [texts] as literary works," we're making implicit judgments about the ends of literary studies: that the kinds of knowledge literary studies might produce are limited to matters of form, art, or aesthetics—in the typically Modernist sense of such terms that developed through the late nineteenth and early twentieth centuries with the emergence of academic literature departments—such that once we approach a text as a knowledge-yielding thing instead of a "literary work," we're deviating from the proper role of the field and the proper nature of the object. In the process, we are foreclosing the possibilities for which knowledge claims we can make about and through the study of literature.

This describes an approach, not a universal property of literature itself or of all things variously called "literature" over time. Much scientific and philosophical writing—think of the Royal Society's scientific atlases of the seventeenth century, or the use of figurative language, examples from literature, and fictional thought experiments in philosophical treatises—could be approached as "literary" work.[8] And much literature—for example, Margaret Cavendish's novelistic fiction *The Blazing World* (1666), which was published as a compendium to her *Observations upon Experimental Natural Philosophy* (1666)—does the work of science and philosophy. Philosophers of aesthetics have fascinating and ongoing disputes over questions such as whether art can make knowledge claims, whether literature is a special type of art (in terms of its capacity for making knowledge claims), and whether aesthetic judgment itself is a type of knowledge. We don't have to accept the premise that literary studies must be defined either by the study of literature as something with particular formal or aesthetic properties or the study of texts of other kinds—periodicals, scientific atlases—for their formal or aesthetic features.

Scholars of literature already study the history of literature and the history of the book, the political implications of texts, the philosophical and linguistic contributions of novels and poems, the rhetorical and performative aspects of literature, and countless other areas. This is to suggest that if progressive knowledge is an end of literary studies, we need not judge our capacity for achieving that end by so narrow a set of objectives as those particular to literary interpretation. Literature scholars typically call themselves "critics," but not all of us are critics and we need not adopt such methods to study literature. That kind of reduction is the door through which anti-cognitivism typically enters as an objection to the prospect of progressive knowledge in literary studies. It enters as a claim that literature as art is distinct and not amenable to knowledge claims, whether within literature itself or about it in matters beyond form and aesthetics. Even in cases where critics aren't explicitly doing art criticism or concerning themselves with aesthetic questions, a key assumption of interpretive literary studies is that the performance of a reading is not reducible to "mere" comprehension or philosophical analysis.

The good news for those of us looking to defend knowledge as an appropriate end of literary studies is twofold. One, scholars of literature in practice already make all sorts of knowledge claims about literature; it's mainly in our defenses of the discipline that we tend to fall back on noncognitivist views of our work and our objects of study, in bromides about how literary interpretation fosters "critical thinking skills" or other so-called "soft" skills such as empathy and imagination. Two, there's no rule that requires us to define the field of literary study by approaching literature foremost as a kind of art—as opposed to as a kind of historical or philosophical document—nor to define the field of literary study by the acts of criticism or interpretation. The assertion that all or even most of the massive variety of documents studied by literature scholars and called "literature" in the past—correspondences, travelogues, scientific atlases, novels, poems, philosophical treatises, and more—must be approached as "artworks" in a particularly Modernist-formalist way, as if all were created from the nineteenth century onward as objects of Culture, is question begging. At least, it's question begging if it doesn't come with a definition of "the literary" that could accommodate the pervasive use of rhetorical techniques and figurative language well beyond the scope of novels, poems, and plays, while at the same time avoiding the trap of aestheticizing all forms of writing regardless of purpose or context. This is to suggest that once we remove the untenable supposition that literature must always be approached as a special category—as an aesthetic object with special entailments—much of the argument for literary anti-cognitivism falls apart. Literary anti-cognitivism is a form of exceptionalism—like American exceptionalism—that demands special rules and treatment for "literary" texts or "literary" scholars.

Progressive Knowledge in Literary Studies

Having offered a case for why knowledge is an appropriate end for literary studies, whether in illuminating knowledge in literature or expanding our scope of knowledge claims about literature, I turn in closing to how knowledge in literary studies might be progressive, building upon prior work in the field, such that through error correction and reconciliation we could know more in the future than we do today. As Alexander Nehamas asked in "Convergence and Methodology in Science and Criticism" in 1985, in what sense is literary studies capable, like science, of converging toward an end, even if science itself does not move smoothly "toward a single, over-arching, complete, and unrevisable theoretical account of the world"?[9] Even in the event that literary studies falls short of the kind of convergence that belongs to the natural sciences—or even if the convergence that happens in literary studies is simply of a different kind than that which happens in natural science—the implications of progressive knowledge in literary studies are significant. Nehamas's short essay on convergence was published amid a 1980s jolt of theoretical vigor in literary studies, and Nehamas—a philosopher well versed in the philosophy of science—then made a remarkable statement: "literary theory offers to the philosophy of science a broader and vastly richer notion of explanation and interpretation than had ever seemed before possible."[10]

For literature scholars today, amid the collapse of the academic labor market for tenure-eligible jobs and the shrinking number of majors, the notion of our discipline producing knowledge useful to those working in other disciplines, or offering forms of explanation and interpretation "vastly richer ... than had ever seemed before possible," is nothing short of astonishing. Whether Nehamas was correct in his assessment of the contributions of literary theory to the philosophy of science, or to broader questions about how we know what we know, his thinking about the *explanatory* power of literary studies is a blueprint for hope for anyone who might imagine an epistemological turn in the discipline—the prospect of progressive knowledge. Where Nehamas was shortsighted was in conflating interpretation and explanation.

Philosophers of science have paved the way for imagining new frameworks for progressive knowledge in literary study. Mary Hesse calls science "instrumentally progressive ... in the sense that we have vastly increasing possibilities of predicting and controlling empirical events by means of experimentation and theory construction."[11] By framing science as instrumentally progressive—progressive in a qualified sense, as opposed to converging toward a final, universal, unrevisable truth—philosophers of science such as Hesse have helped us understand progressive knowledge as instrumental and qualified, as opposed to a view that knowledge arrives from an objective nowhere as a static absolute that no future scientist may revise. While the kind of knowledge produced in literary studies is not instrumentally progressive in the same way as scientific knowledge, it is capable of, and has reflected, epistemic progress.

Nehamas offers a compelling argument for how interpretation progresses in literary studies, which we might take as a basis for thinking instead about progressive explanation. He understands literary criticism as the study of literature and as analogous to science as the study of nature.[12] The study of literature for Nehamas is not such that prior interpretations of literary texts become limiting cases on subsequent interpretations; all readings of *Evelina* today need not assent and yield to past interpretations of *Evelina*. Yet, Nehamas writes, "later interpretations of literary texts, even as they add to the total number of literary texts to be interpreted, constantly build upon (some of) the views presented in earlier criticism"; and this "provides us with a better understanding of at least some aspects of this text than we have had before."[13] The mechanism Nehamas describes here is very much akin to, though certainly not identical to, the way scientific knowledge moves forward. As Nehamas writes, "Later interpretations of literary text often preserve views reached in earlier readings, though they also provide a different account, a reinterpretation, of the grounds of such views. And in this again, we find a parallel to the reinterpretation of Newton's explanation of the tides within the framework of general relativity."[14] As we can see, for Nehamas, the fact that interpretations of literature are subject to revision and reinterpretation does not separate literary studies from natural science as projects that build progressively upon prior work.

What Nehamas calls the peculiar "convergence" of interpretations of literature is a form of regulative ideal, a set of conditions that help us define the end or goal of our work. Another way of thinking about a regulative ideal is what John Rawls calls "reflective equilibrium," a degree of coherence among our collective judgments about what we know in the discipline.[15] Like what Hesse and Nehamas understand as the revisable nature of scientific knowledge, reflective equilibrium is neither final nor stable; it can always be unsettled by new arguments, explanations, or findings. At the same time, a regulative ideal helps guide us toward a better conversation—to borrow Eaglestone's metaphor for literary study—which is not just additive but progressive. We move forward by aiming to reconcile and explain revisions and disputes. By adopting a regulative ideal, whether Nehamas's convergence or Rawls's reflective equilibrium, scholars of literature might better clarify for ourselves and others the purpose and value of what we do.

Crucially, however, moving toward convergence or reflective equilibrium, such that knowledge produced in literary studies is both progressive and useful for those outside of literary studies, requires one more step. If step one toward literary studies as a progressive knowledge project is to clear conceptual space for thinking about explanatory knowledge in the field beyond the narrow limits of interpretation and formal or aesthetic criticism, and step two is to identify convergence or reflective equilibrium as regulative ideals, the third step is to strike one more blow against literary anti-cognitivism. I opened by suggesting that literature scholars largely believe that we produce knowledge, while those outside the discipline might be skeptical of whether what we produce qualifies as knowledge. This mismatch between standards of knowledge within and beyond the field is a tacit form of anti-cognitivism. That is, when pressed on our knowledge standards, scholars of literature tend to eschew the path by which we might reconcile our methods and knowledge claims with those outside the field, and instead defend our intellectual autonomy by recourse to aesthetic criticism as a distinct sphere of knowledge or by recourse to old deconstructive claims about the impossibility of closing the hermeneutic circle or making definitive statements about meaning.

Instead of retreating down these paths, those interested in literary studies as a progressive knowledge project should work toward reconciling our theories and standards of knowledge with those of other disciplines, from philosophy to natural science, or to build compatible knowledge. This does not mean adopting outside standards or forcing false equivalences between the study of literature and of, say, subatomic particles, but taking Eaglestone's useful metaphor for literature scholarship—entering a conversation—and broadening the circle of that conversation to include other fields of study that might help us sharpen our regulative ideals. We might in turn contribute to advances in other fields, as we should. Novels, for example, have been important sources of historical economic data to help explain intergenerational wealth disparity.[16] In fact, economists have argued for the value of literature in explaining and understanding a range of economic phenomena.[17] Countless cognitive psychology studies on the benefits of reading "literary fiction" make international headlines, though rarely do such studies engage with literature scholarship on such fundamental matters as genre history and what makes the texts they praise "literary."[18] All such cases represent missed opportunities for literary studies as a field that cares too little about the reliability of its explanations.

Here we come to an end, because literary interpretation, which bends toward endless multiplicity, must be turned instead toward reliable explanation if the scholarship we produce in literary studies is to be taken seriously in the wider world of knowledge production. Interpretive literary studies as an end in itself is not wholly unnecessary today, but it is unnecessary at the scale literary studies advocates and practitioners demand—the scale that would sustain the discipline in its current formulation. Even if we overcome what I identified at the outset of this chapter as the first crisis—the crisis of neoliberalism—the second crisis—the crisis of where the discipline fits within the web of knowledge today—would remain. What matters now—or ought to matter—for literary studies is the question of how literary studies produces reliable explanatory knowledge (rather than endless interpretations), how such knowledge progresses, and on what terms can we say we know more now than we did before, and will know more in the future than we do now. This is what I mean when I suggest that the end of interpretive literary studies might be the beginning of explanatory literary studies, the latter more suitable to the collaborative, sometimes anti-disciplinary way knowledge is produced today. The end of literary studies is the beginning of the study of literature.

Notes

1. See http://humanitiesworks.org/.
2. See Steven Shapin, "Cordelia's Love: Credibility and the Social Study of Science," *Perspectives on Science* 3, no. 3 (1995): 255–75.
3. David Deutsch, *The Fabric of Reality* (New York: Penguin, 1997), 11.
4. Elaine Auyoung, "What We Mean by Reading," *New Literary History* 51, no. 1 (2020): 94.
5. Robert Eaglestone, *Literature: Why It Matters* (Cambridge: Polity Press, 2019), 77–82.
6. Jukka Mikkonen, *The Cognitive Value of Philosophical Fiction* (London: Bloomsbury, 2013), 11.
7. Qtd. in Paul Keen, *Revolutions in Romantic Language: An Anthology of Print Culture, 1780–1832* (Peterborough, Canada: Broadview, 2004), 3.
8. On "literary" elements of Enlightenment experimental science, see Tita Chico, *The Experimental Imagination: Literary Knowledge and Science in the British Enlightenment* (Stanford: Stanford University Press, 2018).
9. Alexander Nehamas, "Convergence and Methodology in Science and Criticism," *New Literary History* 17, no. 1 (1985): 82.
10. Ibid., 86.
11. Mary Hesse, *Revolutions and Reconstructions in the Philosophy of Science* (Bloomington: Indiana University Press, 1980), xi.
12. Nehamas, "Convergence and Methodology," 83.
13. Ibid., 84.
14. Ibid.
15. John Rawls, *A Theory of Justice*, rev. edn. (Cambridge: Harvard University Press, 2009), 18.
16. See Thomas Piketty's use of Jane Austen's novels in *Capital in the Twenty-First Century*, trans. Arthur Goldhammer (Cambridge: Harvard University Press, 2014).
17. Gary Saul Morson and Morton Schapiro, *Cents and Sensibility: What Economics Can Learn from the Humanities* (Princeton: Princeton University Press, 2017).
18. See David Kidd and Emanuele Castano, "Reading Literary Fiction Can Improve Theory of Mind," *Nature Human Behavior* 2, no. 604 (2018).

CHAPTER 3
THE ENDS OF COMPUTING
Geoffrey C. Bowker

Introduction

Where do ends begin? This deceptively simple question is at the heart of William Golding's wonderful novel *Free Fall*.[1] He was asking about the point at which the protagonist's freedom was lost and he became bound to a certain life—was it when he was five, when he was an adolescent boy, or when he took his first fateful steps into love? None of us know really when the arrow of time became linear (we were suddenly committed to a certain trajectory) either as individuals or as a species; we also know regardless that new explorations are always possible—and oft an outcome much to be desired. When did our lives become so enmeshed in computers? A solar flare may take out the world's computer systems tomorrow, much as a meteor took out the dinosaurs ... we would certainly not be the same without them. What do computers want? What is their end? Or if that is too anthropomorphic (which indeed it is) how and why has computing accompanied our ascendance (if that's the right word) as a species in the world and how has it changed what it means to be a person?

No other academic discipline has so thoroughly inflected the others of the academy as computer science, and yet we often for some reason see computers as simple tools that amplify our work—much as Samuel Butler argues that technological change has been about the development of prostheses—augmenting rather than transforming our relationship with each other and the world.[2] This is patently untrue. Computers matter—they inflect all our discourse. Not in the neutral sense that, of course, we can't talk without breathing but in the substantial sense that they change what we can think and how we think it. To find the ends of computing we need to go back to the origin of life, but we simultaneously have to look at the role that computer science—with its assortment of surveillance, control, and reworkings of selfhood through entities such as ferocious Facebook/megalomaniac Meta—is playing now in the shaping of our world and our relationships with each other. William Golding—who gave Lovelock and thence Margulis the word *Gaia* to describe our current world system—would readily understand these grand and immediate scopes as essential to our grasping, and perhaps inflecting, the ends of computing.[3]

Computers are now almost ubiquitous: in the sky, spread over the face of the earth, and buried in the subsoil—an impressive success for a technology birthed perhaps in the nineteenth century. That is the date I will start from, although as with many technologies, there is a longer potential history going back to counting boards more than 2500 years ago, or abaci at the same epoch, or the closer relative of Napier's bones (which could do subtraction, addition, multiplication, and division in the early seventeenth century).[4] I will start in the 1830s with Charles Babbage, who never completed his Difference Engine or the programmable Analytic Engine (with Ada Lovelace perhaps as the prototypical programmer), but who nonetheless acts as a source for modern computing for three reasons. First, he saw the computer as flowing naturally out of the Industrial Revolution in the late eighteenth and early nineteenth centuries, and in particular from the principle of the division of labor so beloved of Adam Smith. The computer would do what the Industrial Revolution had done: turn complex, expensive tasks (making watches, calculating tables of logarithms) into cheap, simple ones. Watches could be mass-produced when the labor was reduced to thirty-two easy tasks and the tables could be produced by a machine using addition and subtraction in a cottage industry rather than laboriously calculated by mathematicians using multiplication and division.[5]

In addition, this was the epoch of Thomas Malthus's *Essay on Population* (1798), with its startling claim that while population was increasing exponentially, food supply was increasing linearly—leading to an inevitable cataclysm.[6] As Michel Serres has argued, this was the epoch of planetary management: we needed to control human population and nature.[7] This created enormous pressure for information processing of data about people and the world from population censuses and natural history surveys.[8] Modern computing grew out of this nexus and has accompanied it since. The means of computing was industry, and the end of computing was control. Babbage saw the computer as being able to address eschatological issues—in his case, the nature of time and the reality of miracles.[9] We shall see computing as it has developed being about nature and about the nature of the world.[10]

The Colonization of Spacetime

Some histories of the nineteenth and twentieth centuries rightly stress the colonization of a great proportion of the earth by a minority wielding powerful organizational tools. Tabulating and analyzing facts about the colonized and their territories was core to making us governable.[11] Natural history surveys and grand national censuses, created during the same epoch, enabled dominion over distant lands. These developments led to the rise of statistics as a discipline in the mid-nineteenth century. And they led to the organization of bureaucracies as information processing operations. JoAnne Yates refers to the massive insurance industries creating actuarial tables by streamlining their ability to enter data and process them so as to be able to profitably insure as many as possible. She posits this as the "soft" origin of computing as a realization of office design; we might think of it as the software origin.[12] By the end of the nineteenth century, machines began processing such data better than the people working in offices founded on the principle of the division of labor. The invention of Hollerith punch cards (one of the "hard" origins of computing) enabled the processing of census data, whose profusion was rapidly overhauling the ability to analyze. To colonize space, you must be able to compute.

This is ever more so in the present: the promise of precision agriculture is that through computing, we will be able to manage a vast swathe of North America. The sections of the I-states (Iowa, Illinois, and Indiana) along I-70 seem to the driver to be largely uniform and flat, the deep topsoil being a relic of the last ice age; and yet, locals know that in the spring time some parts of the fields are more sodden than others and farmers know that despite the monocropping drive to complete standardization, some parts of their fields are more productive than others. However, with a good drone system and sensors on the ground feeding data into the cyberverse, the theory goes that we can micromanage down to the level of the pedon (the "natural" unit of soil).[13] Caterpillar and John Deere machinery are less and less crucial to farmers; they are instead renting computing software and processing time that can guide their decisions. So computers help break space down into previously unmanageable units and then assert control over those areas. The temporal equivalent in agriculture is monitoring estrus or lactation in real time so as to maximize production of more livestock or milk; thus, there is talk of an Internet of Cows.[14]

Transitioning into time, then, contemplate this puffery from Descartes Labs: "Geospatial data is large, diverse, and can be difficult to manage. … the Descartes Labs data refinery closes that gap … Powerful data ingest pipelines perform continuous loading and pre-processing at speeds of up to 20 gigabytes per second."[15] In the old days, one common definition of time was that it was something that flows at the rate of one per second. That's scarcely good enough in this day and age; we need a fundamental dimension that flows at the rate of a millionth of a billionth of a second (one femtosecond). A simple demonstration of the vacuity of human time is that some computers today can carry out a set of calculations that at the rate of one operation per second would have to begin before the putative Big Bang to achieve a result that for us is relatively instantaneous. The fastest computers now can do about sixteen petaflops (floating point operations) per second—that is, 16×10^{15} operations. That is a whole lot of flops, even for an industry that romances the decimal point.[16] And we have built processes where changes executed in one or two of these new units can have major consequences in the soporific so-called real world.[17] All of our metric standards which seemed at one stage to have independent existence are now tied to ever more precise measurements of time.

At the same time as the western empires were into the game of colonizing each part of the earth through networks of communication and control, they were also getting into the serious colonization of time. Consider (globally) the metaphor independently adopted by Terence Deacon and Timothy Mitchell: what keeps us in a state of low entropy as a species (good for the development of complex bodies and high culture) is our ability to take energy directly or indirectly from the sun, but in the early nineteenth century (one of the putative origins of the Anthropocene), we started burning stored time—the huge stocks of low entropy banked by unfathomable generations of entities metamorphosed into coal/tar/oil after their death.[18] Mitchell writes that a single liter of petrol needs about twenty-five metric tons of ancient marine life, and we burn 400 years of entire plant and animal life production a year. We are gobbling up the past at ever faster rates. Computers enable us to reach far back into the past for these reserves. The oil and gas industry has long been at the forefront of enabling this boom: one need only think of the computing power of Halliburton (using real-time analysis of seismic waves) or Schlumberger (developers of one of the first "expert" systems)—the former an origin for so-called big data and the latter for machine learning.

Of course, this is not a necessary feature of civilization. We could do pretty well with renewable energy, which derives in all its forms ultimately from the sun. With solar energy we are extending our present—creating sensitive receivers that can capture current influxes with far greater efficiency than we could in the past—and expanding the energy present of the planet by using solar power at a higher rate than one unit per second. Time, after all, is money, and each moment in this regime is becoming more valuable than previous moments. We are also colonizing the future. Through our massive works of terraforming, irrigating, extracting, and cultivating, we are causing mass extinctions of life that close off choices for future generations. We consume the past, extend the present, and colonize the future. Welcome to Chronopolis.[19]

Indeed, time as we know it is much more about computers than about our rock circling the sun: natural rhythms have receded further and further. Because the earth, annoyingly, is slowing down in its orbit, Newton's clockwork universe needs to be sent back to the Manufacturer for some adjustments. Coordinated Universal Time (UTC)—first proposed in 1884—has shoddily "fixed" this by inserting leap seconds into the year every so often: twenty-seven times since 1972. This is not good enough for Google, which enforces a "smear" of that leap second over a 24-hour period so that regular old time can be kept accurate enough for computers:

> This smear combines the features that experience has shown to work well for many distributed computing applications. The long duration keeps the frequency change small. The change for the smear is about 11.6 ppm. This is within the manufacturing and thermal errors of most machines' quartz oscillators, and well under NTP's [the time computer systems use] 500 ppm maximum slew rate.[20]

In a wonderful colloquy on this, Paul Hegarty and Gary Gonosko remark that duration has become a "vacuous, humanist comfort temporality."[21]

Computers have certainly invaded our understanding of life. A recent article in *Science* claimed that we can now observe human evolution in real time.[22] As Tandy Warnow argues in *Computational Phylogenetics* (also the name of the discipline dealing with this sort of issue), "an assumption that is sometimes made is that sequence evolution is clocklike (also referred to as obeying the strict molecular clock), which means that the expected number of changes is proportional to time."[23] The reason for the tree structure of life still being so resonant today, buoyed by the nascent discipline of cladistics in the 1950s, has nothing to do with nature—it has to do with computer speed.[24] The calculations of the misnamed tree of life became too difficult if you did not assume progressive change (nothing to evolve backward) and that each branching point was binary (so one species split into three or more at any one point); there was the simplifying assumption that genes didn't jump between species and genuses. We now know all of this not to be the case. The image we have of nature is deeply a representation of our computers.

Obversely, there is a long tradition of adopting natural metaphors in computing, as in the classic 1950s cognitive science article "What the Frog's Eye Tells the Frog's Brain."[25] Observations of ant colonization, frogs leaping between lily pads, or bees swarming have all been used to develop search algorithms.[26] Our computers both learn from nature and represent nature in their own image. As ever, we think with our technologies—the brain was a telephone switchboard in the 1920s (equally problematically) before becoming a computer today. As we study nature, we both project our technology onto it and use what we learn from it to develop our technologies.[27]

There is always the question of why the colonization of spacetime by computing should stop at the edges of our universe—this seems to be an unnecessary and unfair restriction. One of the founders of quantum computing, David Deutsch, comes riding to the rescue. For him, this is "a distinctively new way of harnessing nature .... It will be the first technology that allows useful tasks to be performed in collaboration between parallel universes."[28] A given problem with factoring prime numbers (core to cryptography) could be handled by harvesting a mere 10^{500} universes. While Deutsch is heralding the new here, his argument goes back to Donald MacKay, who in the 1950s argued that physics was about information.[29] If the universe is about information, then suddenly every process becomes a computation. The collapse of the quantum superposition through the act of observation is the trick that allows the magic to happen—you basically poll a set of parallel universities (where every possible solution is manifested) and collapse our own universe onto a solution for an otherwise unsolvable problem. For Deutsch (displaying physicists' seemingly natural predilection for colonizing other fields), "evolution would never have got off the ground if the task of rendering certain properties of the earliest, simplest habitats had not been *tractable* (that is, computable in a reasonable time using readily available molecules as computers)."[30] By this cosmogeny, the computing of information predates not only human but also all life. Humans used to think we were the center of the universe and the solar system, but by this view we are not even central to the story of evolution—which is actually about building better computers. There is a lot of evidence that we cannot be the best.

The Trajectory of Computing

The Internet of Things was heralded in an article by Neil Gross entitled "The Earth Will Don an Electronic Skin." It was published appropriately enough in 1999 to help usher in the new millennium with neo-millennial sentiment:

> In the next century .... [the earth] will use the Internet as a scaffold to support and transmit its sensations. This skin is already being stitched together. It consists of millions of electronic measuring devices ... These will probe and monitor cities and endangered species, the atmosphere, our ships, highways and fleets of trucks, our conversations, our bodies—even our dreams.[31]

The Ends of Knowledge

The Internet of Things heralded an electronically enabled Gaia—we could start to achieve planetary homeostasis (or just plain old stasis, alas) within our lifetimes.

I was reminded of this when reading Andrew Adamatzky from the Center for Unconventional Computing Laboratory fantasizing about creating a vast underground computer monitoring the environment. Fungi, he argued, "possess almost all the senses used by humans—light, chemicals, gases, gravity and electrical fields."[32] While we tend to associate fungi with their visible extrusions (mushrooms), what we miss is the work being done by mycelial networks, whose operations were dubbed by a *Nature* journalist, also just before the millennium, as the "wood wide web." I started thinking of an instrumented subsoil meeting an electronic skin and turning the earth into a giant, self-regulating computer. But, then, of course, why stop with the earth when the universe beckons: "Roboticist Hans Moravec anticipates a far future in which a portion of the universe is 'rapidly transformed into a cyberspace, [wherein beings] establish, extend, and defend identities as patterns of information flow … becoming finally a bubble of Mind expanding at near lightspeed.'"[33] This end seems at once somewhat vacuous and sort of exciting.

Then there's the argument that would have driven William of Ockham crazy, had he ever known what we were talking about. The most parsimonious explanation for our universe is that we live within a computer simulation. Given all that needs to happen for the miracle of humanity to occur in "real life" as opposed to just writing some lines of code, then it is both simpler and more elegant to believe that we live in a simulation. (Think, for example, of the cost-saving in Hollywood by using computer-generated people, rather than actually having to recruit, train, and pay meat people to form a host.) Where the old cosmology had it be turtles all the way down, we are fashioning a vision of computers all the way up. Jürgen Schmidhuber, one of the more delightful prophets of the Singularity, cites Konrad Zuse, who built the world's first programmable computer in the 1940s, arguing that "our universe is computable by a deterministic program" and that if we accept this premise, "there must then exist a very short and in a sense optimally fast algorithm that not only computes the entire history of our universe, but also those of all other logically possible universes."[34] He assumes that our universe is being computed even as I type: "If whoever is generating our universe is using the algorithm FAST … to deal with computational resources constraints in an optimal way, we can make non-trivial predictions" about its nature, based on computing alone.[35] This modest claim entails that whatever computers we build cannot work faster than our universe *qua* computer. The justifiably bewildered reader may relate this to the firmer ground of Douglas Adams's argument that human history has all been about computing the optimal solution to the question of the meaning of life.[36] For Marcus Hutter, just as many monkeys can make light work of Shakespeare, a sufficiently long string of binary numbers will compute for the universe.[37] This does, though, raise the issue of the impossibility of indexing such a string, as presciently explored by Jorge Luis Borges in his Library of Babel.[38]

Eppur, there is something in each of these visions of the ends of computing. Turning the world or the universe into computers is no epiphenomenal frippery: it is the imaginary of some basic trends in world history over the past 200 years. The best way I can think of it is as one of the higher harmonics of a deep chord in human history—just as Sohn-Rethel suggested Galilean or Newtonian (depending on your nation of origin) absolute spacetime was an upper harmonic of commodity capitalism. Commodities "want" to flow frictionless and free through space in minimal time. The best way to imagine this is moving through space and time in a vacuum.[39]

The Curious Case of the Irrelevance of Humans

There is a line of argument that we are being manipulated by devices that compute faster than our brains. We have a "missing half second" between perception (registering an event) and consciousness (processing it).[40] Beverungen and Lange note that human knowledge and cognition are progressively more marginal in markets.[41] They describe a real, real-time world in which a given trader never sleeps more than four hours a night and yet still wakes up every forty-five minutes to see how his flock of "algos" (algorithms) is doing—they can wander into dangerous territory, so need to be corralled every so often.[42] Fortunately, we can imagine new programs where the trader will get her night's sleep. If the market at one end and production at the other can be best maintained by computers, maybe our true future task is to binge as many TV series as possible.

Here is a specimen from a textbook on blockchain. For readers who don't share Elon Musk's passionate love/hate relationship with Bitcoin, this is the technology—an immutable ledger—which is seen by some as permitting frictionless (that concept from Sohn-Rethel again) and fair trading with a fixed endpoint in the future (after which it will be impossible to produce more). Imran Bashi writes that there is

> a vision of blockchain singularity where one day we will have a public blockchain service ... [that will] provide services in all realms of society. This is a public open distributed ledger with general purpose rational agents (Machina Economicus) running on blockchain, making decisions and interacting with other intelligent autonomous agents on behalf of humans and regulated by code instead of law or paper contracts.[43]

The *machina economicus* is a chilling prospect. We risk delegating our morality and justice to these systems. Many economic studies have shown that *homo economicus* is a shibboleth of game theorists imagining "rational" humans making optimal decisions. Fortunately, however, we will be spared our own irrationality by algorithms both acting in our interests and policing bad actors. In a telling vision, Murray Shanahan describes a "superintelligent AI" (one that cannot only replicate human intelligence but can outstrip it) becoming a "willing intellectual slave who never eats or sleeps and wants nothing more than to work ... [This] would be many corporations' idea of the perfect employee, especially if they don't require wages."[44] It is hard to imagine why such an AI would be happy with this kind of life; even Asimov's rather limited robots worked out how to circumvent the Laws of Robotics. Nevertheless, the desire to recapitulate slavery within

The Ends of Knowledge

the computer (a distant echo of ontogeny recapitulating philogeny) is fairly common in these circles.[45] So humans don't need to make decisions, they don't need to work physically (robots can do it) or mentally (super-AIs can do it). Just what have you lot done for the world lately, oh my readers?

Let's Get Real

In an otherwise ponderous paper on social acceleration, Hartmut Rosa makes the marvelous point that we are witnessing, amongst the privileged, "accelerating forms of deceleration."[46] Actually, of course, deceleration and stasis are core for both the hyper-privileged and the oppressed: a lot of the work of those of us attached to the rhythm of computing is enabled by those denied it—those who need to hang about like flashing cursors waiting for us to give them a keystroke so they can perform a given output function (sitting around in a cab waiting for a fare who needs a ride to the airport where a pilot and crew are waiting, and so on).[47] It is not the view from 30,000 feet that lets us glimpse a putative hegemony of computing—it is the view from office windows/Windows. Much as the very rich and the very poor don't pay taxes, the very rich and the very poor have not been colonized in the same ways by computing as we have. Maybe the story is less about the triumph of computers than about the perfecting of control.

Calling computers colonizers may imply that they are the lead characters in a story; in truth, they are mostly background. The tragic trope of us being colonized by computers inverts the obvious point that a goodly subset of we humans are the colonizers. And a core point about colonization is that it never really works.

The visions I have been describing are all about ultrahigh bandwidth and ultrafast computers. But computers automatically ingesting data from all the world through a vast network of sensors just will not happen. The sensors that are feeding in raw data about the world and the programs turning these into recommendations are both ineluctably flawed. As to the former, Antonia Walford has written brilliantly about streaming sensors in the Amazon rainforest: their "objective" information is only ever information which fits in with the range of current theory.[48] If the reading is anomalous, the data is dismissed. Rather than the coupling of sensors and computers seeing the world differently than we do, the union helps us see the world precisely as we saw it before we got the data.

There is an historiographical point here. François Furet, writing of the French Revolution, suggested that many people living in France had yet to hear of it by 1799. The means of communication were not there, not so many people read, and it was irrelevant to the life of many of the peasantry.[49] Just as history is written by the victors who then shape subsequent textbook understandings of events, those writing about the centrality of computing as a metaphor for life, the universe, and everything are precisely those who have access to the best computing.[50] They are largely reflecting on life from within their own bubble—a vantage point which guarantees that they will never be able to see outside to anything else.[51]

Listening to Brautigan

Historians have a mantra: "Things could have been otherwise." It is a reminder that what seems set in stone and inevitable was once genuinely contingent. There are certainly patterns of post hoc relative irreversibility, but there is no destiny. In about 1955, at the height of the frenzy for cybernetics, Richard Brautigan wrote a poem, "All Watched Over By Machines of Loving Grace," with one stanza being:

> I like to think (and
> the sooner the better!)
> of a cybernetic meadow
> where mammals and computers
> live together in mutually
> programming harmony
> like pure water
> touching clear sky[52]

This beautiful vision heralds a world in which we do not use computers to control and dominate nature—to shred her veil so that we can, as Francis Bacon put it, "extend the now deplorably narrow limits of man's dominion over the universe to the permitted boundaries"—but rather coexist with them and by extension with all other living creatures.[53]

This adjacent, compossible future is with us already—as are arguably all such. Where do we go to find it? Let us first of all lose the idea that humans are all about destroying the planet and that we need to be restrained through regulation. Let us not praise famous men regurgitating the riff of original sin. Then, let's simply broaden our awareness to the mycelial networks beneath our feet and the mantle garbing our earth.

The end of computing can readily be seen as one of colonization of time, of space, of the subsurface of the earth and its atmosphere. Certainly, there are computers at the bottom of the sea floor, at the furthest parts of the earth's surface, and spinning ceaselessly in the sky above our heads where they form another kind of refuse for future generations to clean up. We cannot travel beyond them and we cannot see the world without them. But we should not, like Harry Harrison's stainless-steel rat, seek succor in the alleyways and sewers computers cannot touch.[54] We should learn to live better with and through them.

Computing is not inimical to a humanist vision—though many computer scientists and humanists, working generically at different poles of a university campus, typically a north/south divide, would often have it so. The humanists need to learn that computing is not about desiccated data tabulated in endless rows and columns; it is that, but it is also about human and biological life. Computer scientists need to understand that computers are not a revolutionary force from above that has deeply impacted our planet; they are that, but they are also rich and wonderful developments of human and biological life. Our future depends on coming to these understandings. Computing seems to be an ineluctable base for our thinking about life, the universe, and everything: it is a passing phase, just like the transition from archaea to eukaryotes. Archaea have not gone away—they have been incorporated into every cell in our bodies. The end of computing is that it will be absorbed into our bodies; or, inversely, we will be absorbed into it.

Conclusion

There is an irony in the origins of Gaia, of which more anon: the canonical image of spaceship earth adopted by Stuart Brand as he proselytized the work of Lynn Margulis and James Lovelock was produced by a spaceship orbiting the earth. We could only see the Great Mother through a camera lens on a rocket running on fossil fuels. We as creatures have traditionally considered that we are the created, but as the technosphere we are building indicates, we are a small part (I dare say an insignificant part) of an ecology of creators–it's creators all the way down, not the created all the way up. We are created and remembered by our computers as much as we are creating and chronicling them.

As we have seen, the tools of empire that we have built over the past 250 years have been about colonizing spacetime through the development of ever more efficient computers. As the electronic skin is sewn together, it seems to many to be stitching together a Frankenstein's monster to cover the earth. But, as Josh Berson eloquently argues with respect to bodies, it has always been about computing.[55] The body or the earth "computes" what it needs to do by processing inputs of all forms into information which can then be manipulated and thus shape action—hence Lovelock's deliberately Mickey-Mouse proof of Gaia, the Daisyworld simulation of 1983. For those unlucky enough to be unfamiliar with it, this simple program assumed a world formed of black daisies which flourish in the cold and white daisies which relish the heat. If you have a hot spell in the climate—the forcing function of the system—then you get more white daisies, which increases the reflection of the sunlight (higher albedo) and so the world cools down; inversely, if you get a cold front, you get more black daisies, so heat is absorbed better and the world warms up.[56] Within limits, the world achieves homeostasis.

The principle of homeostasis is frequently argued today to be the basis of all life; it is also said to be core to the industrial and control revolutions begun in the nineteenth century (the "governor" of steam engines which kept them from running too hot or too cold).[57] If you take the first formulation, then you can consider the technologies of these revolutions as being largely natural—just life doing its thing of trying to keep the world within the Goldilocks zone of habitable parameters. Computing is not so much a technology come to steal away our time and metamorphose place into space as a natural process being expressed through silicon rather than carbon—for Lynn Margulis, "machines are one of DNA's latest strategies for autopoiesis."[58] This inverse view is the yin to the yang of the colonization of spacetime by computing.

To return to Golding, it is unclear always in history when irreversibility kicks in. Historians often echo the somewhat empty mantra, "it might have been otherwise." It is surely central to understand the "ends of computing" as integrally a history of our species, a history of the past 200 years of the epoch of planetary management and a meditation on our current ways of being in the world.[59]

Notes

1. William Golding, *Free Fall* (New York: Harcourt Brace Jovanovich, [1959] 1987).
2. Samuel Butler, *Erewhon* (La Vergne: Neeland Media LLC, [1872] 2020).
3. Bruce Clarke, *Gaian Systems: Lynn Margulis, Neocybernetics, and the End of the Anthropocene* (Minneapolis: University of Minnesota Press, 2020).
4. William Aspray, *Computing before Computers* (Ames: Iowa State University Press, 1990), 356.
5. Charles Babbage, *On the Economy of Machinery and Manufactures* (England: Charles Knight, 1835). See especially Simon Schaffer, "Babbage's Intelligence: Calculating Engines and the Factory System," *Critical Inquiry* 21, no. 1 (1994): 203–27.
6. Thomas J. Malthus, *An Essay on the Principle of Population, as It Affects the Future Improvement of Society, with Remarks on the Speculations of Mr. Godwin, M. Condorcet, and Other Writers* (London, 1798). The Club of Rome report was a twentieth-century claim of limited resources, in this case oil.
7. Michel Serres, *Le Contrat Naturel* (Paris: Editions F. Bourin, 1990).
8. Geoffrey C. Bowker, "The Time of Computers: From Babbage and the 1830s to the Present," in *Historical Studies in Computing, Information, and Society: Insights from the Flatiron Lectures*, ed. William Aspray (Cham: Springer International Publishing AG, 2020): 1–15.
9. Charles Babbage, *The Ninth Bridgewater Treatise: A Fragment* (Cambridge: Cambridge University Press, [1837] 2009).
10. See William Cronon, *Nature's Metropolis: Chicago and the Great West* (New York: W. W. Norton, 1991) for temporal and spatial dimensions of making "second nature" computable.
11. Michel Foucault, "Governmentality," trans. Rosi Braidotti and revised by Colin Gordon, in *The Foucault Effect: Studies in Governmentality*, ed. Graham Burchell, Colin Gordon, and Peter Miller (Chicago, IL: University of Chicago Press, 1991), 87–104.
12. JoAnne Yates, *Control through Communication: The Rise of System in American Management* (Baltimore: Johns Hopkins University Press, 1989).
13. Bennison Gray, "Popper and the 7th Approximation," *Dialectica* 34, no. 2: 129–53.
14. "The Internet of Cows: How AgriTech Is Tearing Up the Rules of Food." *Vodaphone News*, December 9, 2019.
15. https://descarteslabs.com/.
16. I borrow this felicitous phrase from Robert F. Service, "Time's Romance of the Decimal Point," *Science* 306, no. 5700 (November 19, 2004): 1310–11.
17. Michael Lewis, *Flash Boys: Cracking the Money Code* (London: Allen Lane, 2014).
18. Timothy Mitchell, *Carbon Democracy: Political Power in the Age of Oil* (London: Verso, 2011).
19. This is a reference to Barrington J. Bayley, *The Fall of Chronopolis* (New York: Daw Books, 1974). The novel revolves around the conceit that there are stable islands in the sea of time that a single empire can span: much like the idea that we are reworking the past (unnecessarily) stabilizing the present and trying to colonize the future.

20. "Leap Smear," *Google Public NTP*.
21. Gary Genosko and Paul Hegarty, "Smearing Time: Critical Temporality and Corporate Ontology," *Time & Society* 29, no. 4 (2020): 1013.
22. Elizabeth Pennisi, "Humans Are Still Evolving—and We Can Watch It Happen," *Science*, May 17, 2016.
23. Tandy Warnow, *Computational Phylogenetics: An Introduction to Designing Methods for Phylogeny Estimation* (Cambridge: Cambridge University Press, 2018), 11.
24. Manuel Lima, *Book of Trees: Visualizing Branches of Knowledge* (New York: Princeton Architectural Press, 2014).
25. J. Y. Lettvin, H. R. Maturana, W.S. McCulloch, and W. H. Pitts, "What the Frog's Eye Tells the Frog's Brain," in *Brain Physiology and Psychology* (Berkeley: University of California Press, [1959] 2020), 95–122.
26. Marco Dorigo and Thomas Stutzle, *Ant Colony Optimization* (Cambridge, MA: MIT Press, 2004); M. A. Lones, "Mitigating Metaphors: A Comprehensible Guide to Recent Nature-Inspired Algorithms," *SN Computer Science* 1, no. 49 (2020).
27. See Bruno Latour and Catherine Porter, *We Have Never Been Modern* (Cambridge, MA: Harvard University Press, 1993).
28. David Deutsch, *The Fabric of Reality* (London: Penguin Books, 1998), 95.
29. Donald MacCrimmon MacKay, *Information, Mechanism and Meaning* (Cambridge, MA: MIT Press, 1969).
30. Deutsch, *The Fabric of Reality*, 196.
31. Neil Gross, "The Earth Will Don an Electric Skin," *Business Week*, August 30, 1999. Thanks to John Seberger for this reference.
32. Andrew Adamatzky, "Towards Fungal Computer," *Royal Society Interface*, October 19, 2018.
33. Murray Shanahan, *The Technological Singularity* (Cambridge, MA: MIT Press, 2015), 157.
34. Jürgen Schmidhuber, "The Fastest Way of Computing All Universes," in *A Computable Universe: Understanding and Exploring Nature as Computation*, ed. Hector Zenil (Hackensack, NJ: World Scientific, 2013), 381–98. See also Godel's work on the universe as a set of mathematical forms (Pierre Cassou-Noguès, *Les Démons de Godel* [Paris: Seuil, 2014]), and the cosmological argument from string theory that every mathematically possible universe exists, in Brian Greene, *The Elegant Universe: Superstrings, Hidden Dimensions, and the Quest for the Ultimate Theory* (New York: W. W. Norton & Company, 1999).
35. Schmidhuber, "The Fastest Way of Computing," 389.
36. Douglas Adams, *The Hitchhiker's Guide to the Galaxy* (New York: Harmony Books, [1979] 1989).
37. Marcus Hutter, "The Subjective Computable Universe," in *A Computable Universe: Understanding and Exploring Nature as Computation*, ed. Hector Zenil (Singapore: World Scientific, 2013), 399–416.
38. Jorge Luis Borges, *Labyrinths: Selected Stories & Other Writings* (New York: New Directions, 1962).
39. Alfred Sohn-Rethel, "Science as an Alienated Consciousness," *Radical Science Journal* 2, no. 3 (1975): 65–101.
40. From Massumi, qtd. in Armin Beverungen and Ann-Christine Lange, "Cognition in High Frequency Trading: The Costs of Consciousness and the Limits of Automation," *Theory, Culture and Society* 35, no. 6 (2018): 75–95; 79.

41. Ibid., 82.
42. Ibid., 88–9.
43. Imran Bashi, *Mastering Blockchain: Distributed Ledgers, Decentralization and Smart Contracts Explained* (Birmingham-Mumbai: Packt, 2018).
44. Murray Shanahan, *The Technological Singularity* (Cambridge, MA: MIT Press, 2019), 93.
45. The word "robot" derives from a Czech word for slave, appearing first in Karel Čapek's play *R.U.R.*, which stands for Rossumovi Univerzální Robot (thanks to Seth Rudy).
46. Hartmut Rosa, "Social Acceleration: Ethical and Political Consequences of a Desynchronized High-Speed Society," *Constellations* 10, no. 1 (2003): 3–33, 16.
47. Sarah Sharma, *In the Meantime* (Durham, NC: Duke University Press, 2014).
48. Antonia Walford, "Raw Data: Making Relations Matter," *Social Analysis* 61, no. 2 (2017): 65–80.
49. François Furet, *Penser la Révolution française* (Paris: Gallimard, 1978).
50. Clifford Siskin, *System: The Shaping of Modern Knowledge* (Cambridge, MA: MIT Press, 2016).
51. Peter Sloterdijk, *Bubbles: Spheres 1*, trans. Wieland Hoban (Los Angeles: Semiotext(e), 2011).
52. Richard Brautigan, *All Watched over by Machines of Loving Grace* (San Francisco: Communication Co., 1967).
53. Carolyn Merchant, *The Death of Nature: Women, Ecology, and the Scientific Revolution* (San Francisco: Harper & Row, 1980); Francis Bacon, "The Masculine Birth of Time; or the Great Instauration of Man's Dominion over the Universe," in *The Works of Francis Bacon*, ed. Basil Montagu (London: William Pickering, 1834), 233.
54. Harry Harrison, *The Adventures of the Stainless Steel Rat* (New York: Berkley Pub. Corp., 1978).
55. Josh Berson, *Computable Bodies: Instrumented Life and the Human Somatic Niche* (London: Bloomsbury Academic, 2015).
56. On Daisyworld, see Andrew J. Wood, Graeme J. Ackland, James G. Dyke, Hywel T. P. Williams, and Timothy M. Lenton, "Daisyworld: A Review," *Reviews of Geophysics* 46, no. 1 (1985): 1–23. For a simulation see https://www.islandsoforder.com/daisyworld.html.
57. See Antonio R. Damasio, *The Strange Order of Things: Life, Feeling, and the Making of Culture* (New York: Pantheon Books, 2018); Terrence William Deacon, *Incomplete Nature: How Mind Emerged from Matter* (New York: W. W. Norton, 2013); and Clarke, *Gaian Systems*.
58. Qtd. in Clarke, *Gaian Systems*, 168.
59. Where is the locus of remembering and intelligence? Cf. the concept of stigmergy, which is the act of rendering the environment intelligent—ants practice this with pheromone trails, which allow individual ants to act intelligently while being somewhat low IQ: the environment "remembers" them. I am grateful for Jeff Vandermeer's *The Southern Reach Trilogy—Annihilation, Authority, and Acceptance*—for a rich evocation of this theme in his exploration of the site of memory.

CHAPTER 4
THE ENDS OF BIOLOGY
B. N. Queenan

In the beginning, there was man, and he was a taxonomist. "Out of the ground the Lord God formed every animal of the field and every bird of the air, and brought them to the man to see what he would call them; and whatever the man called every living creature, that was its name."[1] The first and most appropriate job of man, according to both the Bible and Francis Bacon, was to classify the "other creatures in Paradise as they were brought before him according unto their proprieties."[2] Creatures couldn't wander around Paradise unidentified; they needed names which told them what they were and which group they belonged to. This brought order to the world.

Then, there was woman and she was a biologist. She desired to be wise—to have her eyes opened. She desired to be as the creator—knowing how creatures were made. For this curiosity, she and her partner were punished, rightfully according to both the Bible and Bacon: "The aspiring to overmuch knowledge was the original temptation and sin whereupon ensued the fall of man."[3] Eve was not satisfied with a phenotypic understanding of living things, an accounting of appearances. She wanted a mechanistic understanding of life: a knowledge of how and why things behaved the way they did. This brought chaos to the world.

Like others before him, Bacon sought a return to grace. Unlike others before him, Bacon believed the return to grace would be via a secular path. In Bacon's formulation, we banished humans have one recourse to reenter the Garden of Eden: learning, with a purpose. In *The Advancement of Learning*, Bacon lays out our return to Paradise. We will return to grace—to the original state of humans in the Garden of Eden—when we achieve understanding of and power over the natural world. In the early twenty-first century, many of us believe that science—or more broadly science, technology, engineering, and mathematics (STEM)—is how humans acquire a mechanistic understanding of and predictive power over the natural world. To Bacon, the end of science is heaven.

As a biologist, however, I take offense at Bacon's pronouncement. Why would I want to end science when it has brought us so much beauty and power already? Why would my colleagues and I abandon our quest for understanding? What lunatic thinks we will get to a point where nature holds no more secrets? What could be more cruel than mandating the end of wonder?

The betrayal is particularly great coming from Bacon, the hero who liberated science from Aristotle's intellectual stranglehold. Bacon is heralded as the originator of the scientific method, the father of empiricism, the mind who ushered in the scientific revolution. He moved "natural philosophy"—the study of the natural world—out of the armchair and into the laboratory. Truth would no longer be a tapestry woven from clever arguments; it would be a temple constructed from weight-bearing evidence. Yet here is this same Bacon telling me my work—as a scientist, in the tradition he founded—is, at best, an interim occupation or a childish game. At worst, he thinks that people like me are the reason we were thrown out of Eden in the first place.

Just as parents can imperceptibly and unknowingly pass along insidious genes for neurodegeneration, alcoholism, or cancer, intellectual parents can pass along insidious ideas. I wondered what beliefs I might have inherited from Bacon without realizing. I work at a university founded in Bacon's wake "for the advancement of all good literature arts and sciences."[4] I run a "Rules of Life" center at which we seek out the mathematical and physical principles that account for the unique behaviors of living things. Four centuries later, do these activities still embody the Baconian philosophy, and should they? Are we aspiring to the overmuch knowledge that will ensure our continued downfall or to just the right amount that will return us to grace?

To find out what is lurking in my scientific DNA, I took a genetic test of sorts and consulted the origins of empirical science: Bacon's 1605 *Of the Proficience and Advancement of Learning, Divine and Human*. There, I encountered the text above, describing the fall from and return to grace. Bacon believed that God created a Garden of Eden teeming with life. Humanity was created to tend the Garden of Eden: to cultivate the soil, to fill the earth, and to use our intellect to govern it wisely. The original sin of humanity was to wonder why the Garden of Eden existed and operated the way it did. For this, we were cast out into the wilderness. We will only return to grace when we complete the quest we sinfully started: reaching the end of knowledge. The role of the modern research university is clear: to lead us back to Eden.

Scientists might not particularly like Bacon's allegory, but it does a remarkable job of capturing the trajectory of biology over the past four centuries. The study of life and the universe was once a single harmonious pursuit, united under the discipline of "natural philosophy." Within the past few centuries, a rift occurred. The science of the living (what would ultimately become biology) was formally expelled from the science of the nonliving (what would ultimately become physics). Instead of searching for universal explanatory principles, we began searching for local ones.

We currently live in this divided scientific reality, although most scientists don't consciously realize it. Across the vast expanse of possible inquiry runs a chasm, separating one side of scientific knowledge from the other. The two territories have their own dialects and their own cultures. There are different words and instruments, different heroes and histories, different theories and theorems. Where once was a unified prescientific society, there now are two empirical nation-states with a well-policed border. Students fascinated by the natural world are told to choose an allegiance in this scientific struggle: animate versus inanimate, organic versus inorganic, ephemeral versus eternal, biology versus physics.

The life sciences and the physical sciences have both flourished as the two fields have professionalized. Spectacular advances have been made on either side of the divide. Yet, torn in half, the natural sciences are condemned to eternal failure. This is because the sciences seek to understand the universe and there is simply not a separate universe in which living things exist, subject to alternative laws from those that govern the nonliving one. There is a single universe with a finite amount of matter cycling through relatively brief manifestations as stars or starlings, seas or sea urchins. If the laws of the universe do not account for the behavior of *all* matter—living and nonliving—they are not the laws of the universe.

Our current "laws of the universe" only work on one side of the divide. The laws of physics brilliantly explain the behavior of certain types of nonliving matter, notably solids and gases, photons and electrons. However, the laws of physics explain essentially none of the behavior of creatures on Earth. Both disciplines—the life and the physical sciences—have failed to repair the cut slashed across the plane of scientific understanding. The living and the nonliving are not yet reconciled under a single mathematical or theoretical framework that accounts for the natural world. We have not reached Bacon's state of grace.

In fact, the overmuch knowledge and power we have acquired in four centuries of divergent inquiry has resulted in a crisis of existence: the combined efforts of science, technology, engineering, and math now threaten to end our species. Bacon did not explicitly mention the apocalypse, but *The Advancement of Learning* is a meticulously prepared, multi-point warning that knowledge must be acquired and used in very specific ways. We have, for the most part, not followed Bacon's advice. Humanity is now at the point where we will have to formally accept or reject Bacon's mandate. The flood waters are rising, metaphorically and physically. The end of biology is approaching, one way or the other.

In the Beginning: The Birth of Science

When Bacon was writing *The Advancement of Learning*, there were no formal distinctions between the various branches of science we recognize today—no institutional boundaries between astrophysics and ecology, engineering and chemistry, or neuroscience and geology. Four hundred years later, the pristine, undiscovered territory of natural philosophy has been carved up into highly specialized nation-states. "Science" is considered a fundamentally different pursuit from "engineering" or "medicine," with different degree requirements, certifications, philosophies, and accepted practices. Members of designated intellectual communities are allowed to study (or are disqualified from commenting upon) specific aspects of nature and the universe.

How did scientific jurisdictions arise? Whether by divine decree or human tendency, the first order of business for understanding the natural world—as an infant or as an investigator—is to describe and then taxonomize. Through skillful observation, natural philosophers discerned two major classes of phenomena. Certain aspects of the universe are remarkably reliable. "If a stone be thrown ten thousand times up it will not learn to ascend," notes Bacon.[5] Certain forms of matter—be they projectiles or planets—were observed to behave in suspiciously stable ways. There is an elegance to the simplicity of these objects. Meanwhile, other aspects of the universe are remarkably unpredictable. Unlike planets and particles, living things behave in highly variable ways and have diverse features which can change dramatically over time. Some of these creatures *can* learn to ascend: butterflies, birds, and bats all start as terrestrial creatures but develop the capability for flight within a lifetime. People like me who are drawn to living things are fascinated by the ability of nature to change, improvise, and reproduce. There is a beauty to the chaos of these creatures.

I find it unfortunate to the point of catastrophic that we have settled on the terms *animate* and *inanimate* as rough synonyms for living versus nonliving. Movement is not unique to living things. In fact, movement is what gave us our profound understanding of the nonliving universe. The motion of the living confounds us: to this day, we have a hard time predicting the movement of butterflies or bacteria, of people or panthers. However, the motion of the nonliving comforts us: the sun is where we expect it each day, as are the stars in the sky and the stones in our buildings. Planets, pendulums, and projectiles all move, but not in an absurd fashion. They orbit, swing, or fall to earth in manners that are so reliable they can be predicted. Numbers can be used to paint pictures of these objects. Mathematical tricks can be used to resolve when and where these objects will be, sometimes many years into the future. The tricks start out as look-up tables or almanacs, but can become much more sophisticated. Over the centuries, natural philosophers painted increasingly high-resolution pictures of these objects, describing with greater accuracy how each of these systems behaved. For example, the field of kinematics refined the equations of projectiles on Earth, culminating in the work of Galileo. In parallel, the field of astronomy refined the equations of the planets, culminating in the work of Kepler. Phenomena that were previously mystical became mathematical. Motion in the nonliving world now makes sense.

Meanwhile, to this day, the laws of nature do not explain the behavior of living things. The migration of monarch butterflies remains miraculous because their logic lies beyond the territory of mathematics. Biology is still out in the wilderness. Our efforts have not returned us to grace. In fact, we keep asking the same question that got us kicked out of Eden.

The Fall: The Expulsion of Biology from Physics

It did not escape Bacon's notice that the Book of Genesis contains the origins of science: "The first acts which man performed in Paradise consisted of the two summary parts of knowledge; the view of creatures, and the imposition of names."[6] Like Adam, the predecessors of biologists and chemists imposed order upon the natural world by observing and categorizing plants, animals, and minerals according to their observable properties or "phenotype."

The most faithful taxonomic descendent of Adam was Carl Linnaeus, who officially gave names to every living creature "according unto their properties." In the twelve editions of *Systema Naturae* (1735–68) refined over three decades, the Swedish botanist formulated an organizational structure and a binomial naming system (*Genus species*) by which all minerals, plants and animals on Earth could be unambiguously identified (e.g., we are *Homo sapiens*). Linnaeus—who had to rely, in part, on the reports of others—shared with Bacon a skepticism of human perception. He heard tales of all sorts of creatures that he would never see with his own eyes. In an act of scientific generosity, he included space for mythical beings whose existence had been reported but not proven to his satisfaction, including the hydra, the phoenix, satyrs, unicorns, sirens, dragons, pelicans, and antelopes. Each species seemed equally unlikely to exist at the time. To date, we have found two of them, and there was a taxonomic slot waiting to welcome them. Linnaeus recognized that his job was not to be an arbiter of truth but, rather, to provide a scientific structure that could be polished into a clear and equal glass.

The great organizational structures of science are not exhaustive libraries of what is known. They are theoretical frameworks built around what is known, which enable us to interact with what *will* be known. These intellectual structures are robust to new information, welcoming or even predicting its addition. It is sometimes fashionable to dismiss the work of scientists, especially biologists, as "stamp collecting."[7] We seem to be engaged in the Sisyphean task of noting every spot and speckle and hair and prickle and electron and boson we can get our hands on. What on earth do we think we're accomplishing with our tedious inventory of nature? Bacon was one of the first to enumerate the point of the exercise, which is to achieve two layers of understanding about the world. On one level we "should contemplate that which is inherent in matter, and therefore transitory"; on another level we should contemplate "that which is abstracted and fixed."[8] How do we see the abstracted and fixed while looking at the concrete but transient?

Bacon believed that deep understanding could emerge from careful description—that general principles could be abstracted from local observations. As a demonstration, he used the example of magnetism: "So we see how that secret of Nature, of the turning of iron touched with the loadstone towards the north, was found out in needles of iron, not in bars of iron."[9] The mysterious phenomenon of magnetism was revealed not through lofty aspirations to extract some unifying principle of existence or electricity but because certain people noticed that an unassuming piece of black rock could coerce tiny bits of iron to sidle over.

Those of us who have devoted our lives to science believe in Bacon's two-layered system of sight. We believe that the general and universal are present in the material and local. We believe that if we look at the world around us in just the right way, the secrets of the universe will be revealed, just as a coherent 3D image can emerge from the 2D chaos of an autostereogram (as in a "Magic Eye" poster). We are proud of the vastness of the scientific enterprise and the necessarily democratic nature of the undertaking: everything in the universe is at play, anyone can participate in the wonder, and we need all the help we can get seeing the coherent image. The more people listening and reporting back, the more likely we are to collectively hear and understand. We have faith that this system of looking, listening, and learning will lead us back to a state of grace.

The Ends of Knowledge

Scientific faith aside, is there any reason to believe Bacon's two-tiered system will work? It has before, but we are still reeling from its impact. In 1687, Isaac Newton reconciled the behavior of planets with the behavior of projectiles, reconfiguring the scientific landscape entirely. The science of being and moving was already well developed at the time. There were perfectly good equations that explained the motion of planets in the heavens (produced by centuries of work in astronomy). There were perfectly good equations that explained the motions of projectiles on earth (produced by centuries of work in kinematics). Newton's work was not a new description of what had happened. The first tier of science already had a solid handle on *what* was going on.

However, Newton enumerated laws of motion that governed the behavior of matter. The seemingly unrelated activities of these nonliving things were driven by a single hidden force: gravitation. Newton had extracted a universal law from local behaviors, providing an abstracted, fixed reason (gravity) from the transitory behavior of disparate nonliving objects. This crowning achievement was explicitly formalized in the "Mathematical Principles of Natural Philosophy" (*Philosophiae Naturalis Principia Mathematica*), founding what would subsequently be known as physics. The behavior of matter was no longer a question of what and where and when, but how and *why*.

Newton is arguably the greatest natural philosopher of all time. He achieved precisely what Bacon told us we're supposed to do as scientists. His inquiries into the natural world ranged from mathematics to optics to astronomy to alchemy to theology. From the objects in his immediate vicinity, he abstracted principles that hold true across solar systems. So why am I blaming Newton *personally* for our collective banishment from the scientific Garden of Eden? Newton's pioneering work on the motion of bodies (*De motu corporum*) and on the system of the world (*De mundi systemate*) contains no mention of living bodies or living systems. Newton's *Principia* therefore represents the official divergence of the life and the physical sciences. The laws of the universe would hold true across scales—from milliseconds to millennia, explaining grains of sands and galaxies of stars—but they would have nothing whatsoever to do with life on Earth.

Paradise Lost: Biology in Exile

At the end of the seventeenth century, the natural sciences tore themselves in half—into the life sciences and the physical sciences—based on the mathematical principles enumerated in Newton's *Principia*. If equations could capture the elegant trajectory of an object, that object could become part of physics. If not, it belonged to a different field. The tendencies of these forms to behave differently led natural philosophers to believe that they were different in essence. The natural scientists who concerned themselves with life on earth were banished to a separate scientific territory, which would become biology. The seed of Newton's idea—that abstract, universal reasons could be extracted from local observation—was planted in both territories, of physics and of biology, but it germinated in different ways. While Newton's ideas thrived temporarily in the new field of physics, the same kernel of an idea grew into a twisted monstrosity in the field of biology.

The Ends of Biology

At the time of Newton's planting, the otherwise fertile field of biology contained a major intellectual contaminant. The most influential biological classification system in the Western world (that which Linnaeus later systematized) was popularized by Aristotle, who organized living things based on certain attributes: blood or no blood, hot or cold, wet or dry, number of legs. These are remarkably useful distinctions that allow us to predict where a creature will live, how it will move, how it will reproduce, and from what it evolved. Subsequent classification systems bear a striking resemblance to Aristotle's organization. More than 2000 years later, children are still taught to learn their creatures through this scheme: Is it warm-blooded (*endothermal*) or cold-blooded (*exothermal*)? Does it have scales or fur? Does it lay eggs or nurse its young?

Unfortunately, Aristotle also continued a tradition established by Democritus and asserted that living things were alive because they possessed a soul—something external to their physical configuration of matter that animated them. Aristotle developed the notion further: there were different types of souls ("nutritive," "vegetative," "sensitive," or "rational") that produced the different behaviors of things in the natural world. As Aristotle was sorting creatures based on legs, blood, fur, and temperature, he was also ranking them based on the perceived quality of their souls and putting those with the most primitive souls at the bottom. This system produced a ladder of living things ascending from the lowest lifeform (mineral) to the highest (human). Accordingly, when Newton formalized the principles of natural philosophy without mentioning the living world, no offense was taken. Presented with laws that governed the distinct behavior of nonliving matter (such as soulless minerals), natural philosophers did the only reasonable thing: they went looking for laws that would govern the distinct behavior of living matter. If gravitation was the force that propelled nonliving things, there must be a corresponding force that propels living things.

The notion of vitalism—the belief that living things have some fundamentally unique quality, element, or energy—had always swirled around biology. Now the search for a "vital spark" that powers living things became a legitimate scientific pursuit. The search was not, and is not, entirely misguided. Gravitation alone does not explain the behavior of living creatures (with the exception of flightless creatures when launched into the air). It is not unreasonable to suspect that other forces may be at play within living things. For example, electricity is a key aspect to the functioning of many living creatures, particularly those that have a nervous system. At the time Bacon was writing, the phenomenon of electricity was not understood, nor would it be for another 200 years. The suspicion that living things abide by different physical rules was and is justified. The name of the "Rules of Life" center I run signifies our belief that living things are, on some level, cheating—organizing themselves reproducibly into elaborate forms that perform energy-efficient chemical, material, and information transformations under improbable conditions in ways that exceed even the most sophisticated human-engineered systems.

At first glance, I don't seem to be in the best position to criticize Aristotle. Yet, here I am, because Aristotle sneaked an insidious, nonobservable, nonscientific trait into an otherwise scientific classification system. He then created a ranking system based on a qualitative "variable" that is, in actuality, a logical fallacy. The things we have classified as *animals* behave like animals because they have *sensitive* souls, defined as the type of soul that produces the behaviors which lead us to classify a creature as an animal. Proposition A (in the tradition of Adam): If animal → sensitive soul. Fine, tend it well then. But why animal? Because sensitive soul. Proposition B (in the tradition of Eve): If sensitive soul → animal. This circular logic may seem like an honest mistake, and certainly not something to despair about 2000 years later. Yet this intellectual sin established a tradition of noticing things are different (correct), making value judgments that some are inherently better than others (incorrect), and seeking out scientific justifications for why this ranking must be so (disastrous). Founding a scientific tradition on false premises is no minor error. Circular logic is a snake eating its tail. When Newton's apple fell to earth, the Serpent was waiting and Eve, the first biologist, took the bait.

As a consequence of the tainted intellectual tradition they inherited, early biologists did not seek a universal principal to explain living things. They sought separate explanations: one for living creatures and one for humans. Life in the Western tradition had long been subdivided into humankind versus everything else. The Judeo-Christian tradition had formalized this hierarchy, ultimately making it heretical to assert that humans would be explainable by the purely physical principles that accounted for other "lower" beings. Most Enlightenment thinkers, Bacon included, did not question this distinction. Bacon explicitly describes "the three beams of man's knowledge; that is *radius directus*, which is referred to nature, *radius refractus*, which is referred to God, … [and] *radius reflexus*, whereby man beholdeth and contemplateth himself."[10] In the most famous modern formulation of this idea, Descartes maintained there would be one material substance that would produce the human body (*res extensa*) and another that would produce the human mind (*res cogitans*). Despite their best attempts, both Bacon and Descartes were guilty of this original scientific sin.

Just as the rift between biology and physics still runs through the center of modern science, the rift between human and nonhuman life still tears biology apart. Contemporary scientists have renounced *radius refractus* and *res cogitans* as technical terms: we understand that our bodies and brains are physically constructed from fats, sugars, proteins, and minerals just like other living things. We don't believe we are divinely created: we accept evolutionary theory and recognize that we are descended from apes. However, we are still guilty of bifurcating the study of life. Well into the twenty-first century, Harvard University still has one department for Human Evolutionary Biology and another for Organismic & Evolutionary Biology. The neurosciences, in which I trained, are arguably the worst offenders on this front: almost all discussions of the mind versus brain, cognition versus instinct, consciousness versus reflex, or top-down control versus bottom-up response bear the imprint of these inherited ideas. Contemporary neuroscientists, on some level, believe that the nervous system that controls our mind is different from the nervous system that controls our body. Biologists have rejected the vocabulary inherited from natural philosophy, but we have failed to reject the core concepts. We no longer explicitly classify animals and plants by soul type; however, Aristotle's belief in a hierarchy of excellence permeates modern biology. Cloaked under notions of "optimization" to environmental conditions, morphological "complexity," and evolutionary "progress," we find the insidious, inherited belief that certain forms of life are somehow better than others. We still implicitly believe that humans occupy a preferred frame of reference, in which the laws of physics will be different just for us.

In this respect, Genesis predicts not only the origins of science and our fall from grace, but our subsequent disastrous dispersal: "the Lord scattered them from there over all the earth, and they stopped building the city. That is why it was called Babel—because there the Lord confused the language of the whole world."[11] In the time since Bacon's writing, the scientific world has developed an impressive number of confused languages that do not understand each other. Some of them don't even operate on the same plane of existence. Taxonomists (and later, biologists) established a tradition of describing the plants and animals they encountered using visual language. We draw pictures, take measurements, look at parts, and describe the appearance of things, especially how they grow and change over the course of a lifetime or how they differ from each other. Alchemists (and later, chemists) pursued a tradition of describing the minerals and solutions they encountered using physical language. They measure weight and hardness and color and shininess, and they assess density and likelihood to light on fire or to melt or to otherwise transform. Physicists established a tradition of describing the performance of objects they encountered using mathematical language. In some cases, scientists from different disciplines are using different terms to describe the same phenomena. (For example, when physicists admit that living things are an interesting subject of study, they disguise their investigations as "active matter" or "soft matter" physics. Heaven forbid they admit biology is interesting and, as of yet, too hard for them.) But in many cases, we are using different terms because we are describing unrelated phenomena. When we look around us, some of us see unique and beautiful creatures, while others see fundamental elements and tendencies of matter in the universe. We not only use different languages, we see different things. We are no longer concerning ourselves with the same realities.

I'm not sure that I—as a person who has devoted a life to the scientific enterprise—can properly express my frustration, heartbreak, and embarrassment to find out that we have not bravely pioneered a new way of advancing knowledge but have, instead, replicated all the mistakes found in the opening pages of the Old Testament. Finding ourselves kicked out of Eden, we doubled down on our prideful mistake. We aspired to more and more knowledge, as if somehow this time it would be different. We desperately constructed scientific frameworks to prove that we were, in fact, the best, the most deserving of God's love. We used biology to prove our dominance over the living world, chemistry to prove our dominance over the elements, physics to prove our dominance over the universe. The higher we—the collective scientific enterprise—tried to climb towards the heavens, the more inaccessible our languages became and the more we lost our way. Newton—my cosmic friend with whom I share a birthday—was not our great savior. He was a false prophet.

Having seen all this, I abandoned this essay for months. It was too depressing. Maybe the whole scientific pursuit was some Sisyphean punishment, an endless circular quest. We would never get to the end of biology. Biology was just a haven for people trying to

The Ends of Knowledge

make a life doing something they found interesting, based on their disposition to find beetles or bacteria pretty, instead of words or chords or money or hammering metal into jewelry. I reminded myself that it was absurd—in Camus' sense of the word—to have demanded meaning out of the scientific enterprise, as if it alone was exempt from the uncaring reality of the universe.

Months later, my existential crisis had not resolved, but I was reminded that academic deadlines do still exist. I reluctantly revisited the assignment by rereading Bacon's book. Right there, in the opening pages, were three warnings about the pursuit to "comprehend all the universal nature of things," the third being: "That we do not presume by the contemplation of Nature to attain to the mysteries of God."[12] Newton's work had demonstrated that abstracted and fixed principles—*reasons* for the behavior of the natural work—could be found from observation. Newton, like Eve, discovered that "when you eat of [the tree of the knowledge of good and evil] your eyes will be opened, and you will be like God."[13] Asking why the world exists and functions would not kill us; instead, it would give us great insight into and ultimately power over the natural world. Since that moment, we have mistakenly believed that the scientific enterprise would make us like God.

The modern scientific enterprise and its practitioners have been guilty of the dual sin of thinking we are special and failing to realize that we are. We weren't supposed to aspire to become like the creator, to know all the secrets of the universe. We certainly weren't supposed to use our powers as *Homo scientificus* to prove, yet again, that we are the preferred children, of God or of terrestrial biochemistry. We were supposed to use our capacity for discovery and reflection to understand our place in the world and to worship it appropriately, through our actions. Bacon launched us on a scientific quest to acquire and deploy new knowledge in service of our original mission. The purpose of the advancement of learning is to sustain the Garden of Eden we have been given, either by divine decree or the molecular machinations of the universe.

Revelation: The End of Biology

Bacon envisioned a robust scientific enterprise: "such natural philosophy as shall not vanish in the fume of subtle, sublime, or delectable speculation, but such as shall be operative to the endowment and benefit of man's life."[14] How do we get there?

The first step is to recognize that academic disciplines represent a human division of labor, not a division of the universe. The terms reflect the different scales on which different people attempt to extract meaning from the various types of matter that compose our universe.

"To inquire the form of a lion, of an oak, of gold; nay, of water, of air, is a vain pursuit," notes Bacon. The meaningful pursuit is "to inquire the forms of sense, of voluntary motion, of vegetation, of colours, of gravity and levity, of density, of tenuity, of heat, of cold, and all other natures and qualities, which, like an alphabet, are not many, and of which the essences (upheld by matter) of all creatures do consist."[15] Bacon understood that a detailed phenomenological description of each component of the universe—animal, vegetable, or mineral—was necessary but not sufficient. He recognized that we are searching for commonalities, not differences. The point of the exercise is to find "the true forms," the variables we plug into the predictive equations that allow us to become useful. The purpose of the natural sciences is to extract the finite from the infinite, to distill order from chaos, to identify which shared properties explain the divergent behavior of things being acted upon by outside forces (e.g., gravitation, magnetism, evolutionary pressure). "It is the duty and virtue of all knowledge to abridge the infinity of individual experience … which is performed by uniting the notions and conceptions of sciences."[16]

Is it reasonable to assume we can unite all our notions and conceptions, reaching "harmony of a science, supporting each part the other"?[17] Is it helpful to recommend that we achieve a theory of everything? Bacon sees the unified theory as a motivating principle, but not the actual goal: "As for the vertical point, … the summary law of nature, we know not whether man's inquiry can attain unto it."[18] Whether or not we can achieve it remains an outstanding question. However, to contemporary scientists, Bacon's work is an important reminder of the coherent vision we once had and have now lost. There is no such thing as physical, chemical, or biological phenomena. We are not trying to reveal the mathematical principles of oak trees or of oceans. We are trying to reveal the principles of the universe—*all* of it.

Fortunately, Bacon outlines the division of labor that will return us to grace, the iterative process that produces understanding and control of the natural world. There are "two parts of natural philosophy—the inquisition of causes, and the production of effects; speculative and operative; natural science, and natural prudence."[19] Today, we understand "natural science" and "natural prudence" to be "science" and "engineering," respectively. Through science we extract understanding from the world; through engineering we test that understanding. We will know something is true when the knowledge we have extracted is strong enough to build upon: "If it be truth, … the voice of Nature will consent, whether the voice of man do or no."[20] Scientific principles are not made true by committees or consensus, by logic or reason. Scientific principles are made true by practical implementation.

Truth, to Bacon, is not a jewel we hope to possess. Truth is a material we can use. As he writes, "If then it be true that Democritus said, 'That the truth of nature lieth hid in certain deep mines and caves; …' it were good to divide natural philosophy into the mine and the furnace, and to make two professions or occupations of natural philosophers—some to be pioneers and some smiths; some to dig, and some to refine and hammer."[21] Science and mathematics are the professions of the pioneers, who dig without a clear understanding of what they will find. Engineering and technology are the professions of the smiths, who refine this knowledge through service. Collectively, we extract information from the universe and we reinvest that information by creating new materials, solutions, and technologies.

Every time a scientific principle is extracted, we can use it. Each "truth" is one brick laid in the path we are building to return us to grace. Yet how can we build a path brick by brick if we have no idea of the destination? Here, Bacon is quite explicit. We use scientific insight to engineer solutions that will protect and enhance life. We seek understanding so that we can better help. The advancement of knowledge is a lifelong mission of service to humanity in service of the earth.

Bacon's mandate requires not only an intellectual reconfiguration, but an ethical one. To date, we have treated the advancement of knowledge largely as an arms race. Each discipline seeks out the truths it covets, only to stockpile them within its own academic silos. We implicitly believe that if we acquire enough knowledge, expertise, or prestige, it will keep us safe. Again, invoking Solomon, Bacon warned against this: "That we do not so place our felicity in knowledge, as we forget our mortality."[22] Knowledge alone will achieve nothing good. It requires the "corrective spice" of charity to form "the mixture wherof maketh knowledge so sovereign."[23] Bacon recognized that the advancement of knowledge, unconstrained by charity, would lead to the institutionalization of original sin.

We have forgotten to heed Bacon's warning that the pursuit of knowledge for its own sake leads to sin. In fact, we have constructed a hierarchy of academic virtue that prizes the pure over the pedestrian. In the academy, mathematics is the "highest" form of science, in that it exists outside our mundane reality. Physics, which acknowledges but reaches beyond our earthly existence, is next. Chemistry, which deals with the reality of matter and its properties, falls below. Biology, which embraces the messiness of life, is at the bottom. The "applied sciences" get kicked out to a separate class entirely. Engineering and medicine—the disciplines which seek to put scientific discovery into practice—get their own schools, adjacent to the "scientific" enterprise. The humanities, the arts, and religion—the disciplines which, by tending to human thought, feeling, and behavior, steer us towards purpose and meaning—get sent to the other side of campus.

From my biased perspective, biology offers a glimmer of hope. Biology is the discipline which reminds us that learning—all learning—is in service of life. There is no such thing as an eternal physics, an impartial chemistry. The sciences are a convention of a specific life-form—humans—and they will perish with us. Biology, sitting as it does at the intersection of the sciences and the humanities, offers the opportunity to unite our various disciplines in the shared mission of tending our Garden of Eden together. Physics has discovered for us one principle: matter in the universe is finite. It can be neither created nor destroyed. Chemistry has discovered for us another principle: that matter can be combined in fascinating ways, producing material elements with fantastic properties. Biology has returned another revelation: that the finite material elements of the universe combine in unexpected ways, producing life. Life combines in unexpected ways, producing humans. Humans combine in unexpected ways to produce science and the various pursuits addressed in this volume. Just as trees have evolved the ability to extract carbon from the atmosphere, and fungi to extract nitrogen from the soil, we humans have evolved the ability to extract knowledge from the universe. We can use this knowledge to perform the material transformations our bodies themselves are not capable of. To date, we have used the power science has conferred not to create a Garden of Eden but to decimate it. Yet we have also evolved the capacity to avoid evil. As a

The Ends of Biology

species, we have created many disciplines and institutions—religious, philosophical, legal, and artistic—that provide structure and support. These traditions, though often imperfectly implemented, are attempts to develop the practice of living well and to pass on our best practices to children we will never meet. The existence of human institutions and traditions represents the continued hope, shared across lifetimes, that we may one day help someone become what we could not.

Biology is a specific intellectual tradition shared across lifetimes. It is an experimental science that operates at the precipice between good and evil. Our day-to-day experiments remind us that life is miraculous. To this day, most biological experiments reveal that life is even more miraculous than previously suspected. Yet scientists and engineers, by definition, have agreed to explore matter in the universe by observing it, weighing it, compressing it, firing lasers at it, seeing when it will melt, combining it into new and fantastical combinations, and using it to do work. When physicists and chemists do these things, they are geniuses. When biologists do these things, we are monsters. Our science can't exist without conversations about ethics—about whether we *should* do something just because we can. We embrace the reality that science is conducted by humans and humans are flawed. We need guidance, support, and constant institutionalized reminders that, left alone, we tend toward evil.

My colleagues and I are not the first to attempt to extract "Rules of Life," to seek principles that unify the living and nonliving world. However, we are not seeking to reconcile the behavior of life with the "universal" physical principles that hold forth across scales throughout the solar system. Most of the solar system seems entirely indifferent to life. It's only here on earth that life matters. So, we will not get to the end of biology through physics as it currently exists. Physics is the mathematics of the dead. Biology must become the mathematics of the living. We will apply and invent mathematical frameworks that allow us to observe the living world, model it, predict its behavior, and test those predictions. Increasingly, we will be able to conduct our experiments computationally, as simulations. We will not need to dissect and destroy. We will be able to rigorously pursue our understanding of life through more careful scientific conversations with the living world. We will test our predictions in synthetic systems. We won't keep stomping our feet that life doesn't abide by our equations. We will, in good faith, invent equations that describe the living world, just as we invented equations that described the nonliving one. One day, we will see how all our equations relate to each other and, on that day, we will speak the same language again. We will have reached the end of biology and, incidentally, the end of physics. We will have torn down our own Tower of Babel.

Embracing the end of our disciplines doesn't mean we have to end our experiments, inquiries, or learning. It means we have to embrace the *purpose* of our learning. There is a fixed amount of stuff in the universe. We cannot deplete our resources indefinitely. We must return what we take in equal proportion. Fortunately, life itself makes it clear that finite material resources do not limit our infinite imagination. The universe simply exists. It doesn't have a purpose. But life—a specific constellation of matter in our universe—creates the possibility for purpose. We can do more than exist temporarily.

The Ends of Knowledge

We can learn and we can create. We can produce things that didn't exist before: we can produce information, we can produce happiness, and we can produce good. Learning—the advancement of knowledge—is not an abstraction. Learning is a process of life and by life but it is also, as we have forgotten, *for* life. We learn so that we can more charitably extract and use knowledge—past and future—to empower each other in our shared pursuit: better tending our Garden of Eden. This is an end to biology that I, as a biologist, am happy to embrace.

Notes

1. Genesis 2:10.
2. Francis Bacon, *The Advancement of Learning*, in *The Major Works*, ed. Brian Vickers (Oxford: Oxford University Press, 2002), 123.
3. Ibid., 122.
4. Harvard Charter of 1650.
5. Bacon, *The Advancement of Learning*, 260.
6. Ibid., 149.
7. Ernest Rutherford is widely credited with saying, "all science is either physics or stamp collecting."
8. Bacon, *The Advancement of Learning*, 195.
9. Ibid., 178.
10. Ibid., 205.
11. Genesis 11:1-8.
12. Bacon, *The Advancement of Learning*, 124.
13. Genesis 3:3.
14. Bacon, *The Advancement of Learning*, 178.
15. Ibid., 196.
16. Ibid., 197.
17. Ibid., 141.
18. Ibid., 197.
19. Ibid., 193.
20. Ibid., 203.
21. Ibid., 193.
22. Ibid., 124.
23. Ibid.

CHAPTER 5
THE ENDS OF DIGITAL HUMANITIES
Mark Algee-Hewitt

Introduction: The End of the Beginning

What does it mean to speak of the end of a field that has, by disciplinary standards, barely begun? While histories of the digital humanities allude to centuries-old relationships between counting, concordance, and reading in the practice of humanistic research, the oldest professional organizations of the field date back only to the late twentieth century, and its disciplinary consolidation is far more recent still.[1] While this is certainly sufficient time for the field to gain both notoriety and some measure of institutional stability, thinking through its goals and eventual fate requires a speculative projection into a barely imaginable disciplinary futurity. At once allied to the research goals of the humanities-based departmental homes of its practitioners, as well as to the computational methodologies and infrastructure that makes this research possible, the ends of the digital humanities may lie either with a reabsorption into the various humanities fields that gave rise to it or in a fissioning that creates a wholly new synthetic field from the remnants of both the humanities and the applied computational methodologies that it has adopted. But even these possible futures, should either come to pass, will not be the end of the digital humanities; rather, they represent a necessary evolution of the field as it comes into its own. Our very ability, however, to speak of the ends of the digital humanities suggests that the field has already reached an important inflection point, at which the concerns and cares that marked the nascent struggles and possibilities of its early development are in the process of transforming into new strategies for knowledge production. We are not yet ready, in other words, to think about the ends of the digital humanities, but we can start to speculate of the ends of its beginning.

To engage in this kind of speculation brings another challenge to the fore: namely what is (or, better, are) the digital humanities (DH)? As befitting a young field, this question has been at the forefront of digital humanities discourse for at least the last two decades.[2] It is a question that is particularly critical to this field. While many scholars spend time interrogating their own disciplinary knowledge creation practices, DH is also confronted with a constant doubt as to whether or not the substrata of the field even exist and if there are any points of connection between its constituent parts. As a famously "Big Tent" discipline, the various practices, contexts, and knowledge systems that make up the field are widely varied and often incompatible: from digital editions, to archival studies, to book history, media theory, spatial history, and computational literary analysis, each branch of DH occupies its own space on an increasingly complex and freighted subject tree. To ask about the ends of the beginning of DH, then, we also have to ask whether these elements are, in fact, working toward the same goals, and in what ways they may be compatible, if not in the material that they examine, the methods they use, or the goals of their research efforts.

Perhaps a turn away from the nebulous generality of "digital" at this point can help clarify this question. The French translation of "Digital Humanities," "Humanités Numerique" offers a different perspective on the work of the field. Here, the uniting factor between the fields is not the technology of the computer, but the turn toward numbers. While this allows scholars working on computational models of humanities phenomena, for example, to see their research reflected in the name, it also opens the disciplinary door to other fields, such as archival studies, where the sheer number of electronic records for any given database has had transformative effects on the work of archiving itself; or in the spatial humanities, where distances, coordinates, and elevations can transform the work of history; or even in the collaborative work that is unique among the humanities, wherein the research expertise of individual scholars is multiplied within a multidisciplinary team. The quantitative investment of scholars unites their concerns around not just questions of method, but also explorations of what it means to bring numerical thinking to bear on questions that have traditionally been critical in nature. The numerical turn brought about by DH has also enabled us to think both computationally about critical questions and critically about computational ones. We can gain new purchase, for example, on questions of bias in large data sets, showing how systematic underrepresentation (or misrepresentation) can have subtle deleterious effects that are invisible at the scale of reading, but that cause tremendous harm at the massive scales at which contemporary machine learning operates.[3] We can even turn the lens of DH on itself to question the overrepresentation of Anglophone literature in our archives, or the lack of support for work in computational criticism by women, people of color, or scholars of the Global South.[4]

While the ends of such avenues in DH research and pedagogy seem clear (to enable us to do better work), they still do not yet shed light on exactly what the ends of that work that they enable are. If we understand that DH is a field constellated around the numeric, the question remains of what we seek to accomplish through such a radical joining of computation and humanities research.[5] This is, after all, the aspect of DH that makes humanities practitioners outside of the field the most uncomfortable and that has led to public calls for the premature and deliberate end to DH.[6] Despite the histrionic claims of its more passionate critics, there is no sense from within the field that its goal is to push the humanities further toward the margins of academia and facilitate the STEM-focused neoliberal takeover of the university. But it is true that practitioners of DH want to enact substantive and lasting change in the humanities by bringing numbers into the equation, whether that is to adjust the practices of their fields toward more equitable ends or whether it is to gain new purchase on questions that have long eluded traditional critical methods. At the same time, there is also a push within DH to establish a new disciplinary infrastructure that aims to consolidate its various fields into a cohesive, but separate, institutional home for quantitative research in the humanities. Even more complications arise when we consider the different ends of all of the facets of the various subfields, some of which are deeply research oriented, while others are focused on praxis and community. Perhaps, to gain a new perspective on the ends of the beginning of DH, we need to turn toward a survey of the literal ends of DH itself.

The Literal Ends

The conclusion to a piece of scholarly writing not only offers a summation of the results from the study described in the article but also often seeks to situate those results within the larger context of the field. As such, conclusions offer both a concise description of the theoretical and methodological investments of the research and a series of generalizations about the discipline at large. This step back is crucial: whether under the rubric of discussions, future directions, or conclusions, the authors of an academic article not only frequently overtly gesture toward the broad conditions of their discipline in relation to their research, but their language also carries with it the implicit traces of their understanding of the field. Conclusions, in other words, are sites for broad statements on the ends of both the article they are attached to and of the field itself.[7] At the scale of the individual article, such broad statements are provisional at best and misleading at worst. Across a plurality of articles from a journal, or a field, however, we can leverage their tendencies toward generalization to gain a sense of the self-reflexive understanding of a field by the practitioners whose work constitutes its material. By applying the methodological lens of DH itself, which allows us to read at the scale of hundreds or thousands of articles, to the conclusions from a sizeable sample of DH articles, we can perhaps begin to clarify both the shape and structure of the digital humanities as it is practiced in its most prominent journals, while also creating a window into the language that speaks to how the digital humanities have understood the ends of their own research.

Figure 5.1 reveals the constellation of the digital humanities in the twenty-first century based on the conclusions to 1240 articles published between 2000 and 2021 in three of the field's most prominent journals: *Digital Scholarship in the Humanities* (*DHS*), *Digital Humanities Quarterly* (*DHQ*), and *The Journal of Cultural Analytics* (*CA*).[8] Each dot on the graph represents the conclusion to a single article.[9] Their arrangement is based on a topic model of the corpus. Although topic models have seen a reduction in their usage as interpretive tools for complex (frequently literary) writing over the past decade, they are still a powerful method for detecting patterns of topicality in large corpora of structured text.[10] Topic models are unsupervised, probabilistic models that seek to identify clusters of words that co-occur in regular patterns across a number of texts with a high probability.[11] The prevalence of these "topics" (which are represented by the list of words that they contain) can then be calculated within each of the texts in the corpus, which the model understands to be mixtures of multiple topics. Similarity between texts can then be calculated by their shared topicality: texts that contain a similar mixture of topics in similar proportions are judged, by the model, to be more alike and the wordlists of the topics that they contain can help analysts identify the logic of their connection.

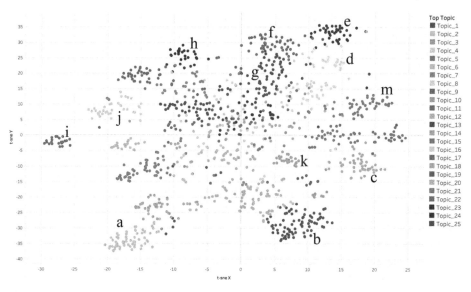

Figure 5.1 t-sne plot of a topic model of digital humanities article conclusions.

Here, I have visualized the topic model with a t-stochastic neighbor embedding (t-sne), which compresses the similarities and differences between texts in the high-dimensional space of the model into a two-dimensional representation that codes the relative distance between points as a measure of their topical similarity.[12] Two points that are close together in Figure 5.1 represent two texts that share similar topics, while two points at opposite ends of the graph share relatively few topics. The color on the graph indicates the most prominent topic, according to the model, in each text: this allows us to judge not only the relative similarities of individual conclusions but also the adjacency of the clusters of texts that share similar topics. From the graph, then, we can gain an overview of the cohesion of the individual subfields of DH (at least as they are represented in article conclusions) and witness the patterns that these fields trace into the discipline as a whole.

The graph reveals a field in flux. The individual subfields that make up the digital humanities are clearly visible as tightly clustered groupings with shared colors, indicating that not only do the most prevalent topics speak to the specific subject of each conclusion but that the discipline as a whole is well organized according to these specialties. Moreover, the centrifugal force of the individual research interests represented by these specialties is also apparent within the visualization, as each grouping traces a pattern of increasing specialization as it moves toward the perimeter. While there is some overlap of similar clusters toward the center, most groups mark out their own territory with little shared space between them. The challenge that I alluded to above, the disintegration of the digital humanities and its compartmentalization into particular field specialties appears, at first glance, to be confirmed by the graph.

While the distance between the individual conclusions represents the strong similarity between texts with similar topical investments, the distance between the clusters themselves can likewise offer information about the relationships between the various subfields. Clusters (a) and (b) in Figure 5.1, for example, show two descending branches from the central hub that are both densely populated and much more similar to each other than they are to any of the other clusters on the graph (despite their divergent trajectories). Cluster (a) represents conclusions to articles on one of the most venerable areas of research in the digital humanities over the past twenty years. Related by Topic 2, which contains words such as "authors," "author," "authorship," "texts," "evidence," "style," and "attribution" among its top terms, these articles are all on the topic of stylometry and, more specifically, authorship attribution. A heavily computational and text-focused subfield, practitioners of stylometry are particularly interested in the evidentiary claims of their analysis. That this cluster would be adjacent to one whose top topic (14, in light gray) contains "word," "words," "two," "test," "one" comes as no surprise as these conclusions focus more on the quantitative methods of stylometry than on claims about the subfield as a whole.

On the opposite side of the bottom of the graph is cluster (b), whose top topic (25) contains "method," "results," "features," "proposed" and "classification." While less field-specific than stylometry, this method-driven cluster again represents conclusions with a significant methodological investment in supervised and unsupervised modeling. Again, because these are conclusions, we can estimate that these are articles that take the methodology of classification itself as the topic (whether by introducing new or improved technologies of classification or by discussing the role of classification in providing evidence). Again, the adjacent cluster (Topic 12) is deeply related, containing "language," "corpus," "texts," "languages," and "English." This suggests that the methodological investment in classification in (b) is most frequently applied to textual questions, revealing why it shares the same area of the graph as stylometry, although with a less overt investment in words and textuality.

Opposite on the graph to the stylometry cluster, in the upper right corner, are clusters (e) (Topic 23: "students," "learning," "work," "design") and (f) (Topic 11: "projects," "research," "community," "work," "collaboration"). Representing both articles on DH pedagogy (e) and the role of collaboration in project-based research (f), together they suggest an entirely different approach to the discipline. Whereas the clusters on the bottom revealed a research-focused, methodology-heavy, set of topics, these reflect both articles with a self-reflexive interest in DH itself (particularly the meaning of its collaborative praxis) as well as those discussing its non-research application (for example, in the classroom). Cluster (d) (Topic 8: "social," "critical," "practices," "production") confirms this intuition as it reveals article conclusions that focus on the wider cultural context of DH, whether within the scholarly community or in the wider public sphere. Finally, cluster (g) (Topic 1: "digital," "humanities," "research," "scholars," "tools," "technology," "new") is of particular importance to understanding this area of the graph. Not only does it appear to be a purely reflective topic, containing articles whose conclusions are about DH itself, but also its focus on not just technology but new technologies suggests that these are articles whose goal is to explicitly carve out space for the digital humanities within the academic sphere by describing its novel contributions to scholarship.

Reading the graph globally, these clusters mark out a strong bifurcation between the top and bottom of the visualization. On the bottom are intensively computational, research-oriented conclusions whose explicit investment in method (whether applied or theoretical) often formally approach the rhetoric of a STEM article. On the top are broader speculations about the role of the digital humanities in the scholarly community, the university department, or the classroom. Their conclusions are driven by a reflexive awareness of the digital humanities as a set of cultural and academic practices and their method is more descriptive than investigative.

I do not, however, want to draw a false dichotomy between computational and non-computational DH (the focus on tools and new technologies in cluster (g) reveals that this is not the case), nor do I want to suggest that there is a split between applied and speculative DH (articles on DH pedagogy are deeply invested in praxis). Instead, the two offer complementary but opposite strategies for marking out the place of a new, rapidly expanding field within a crowded scholarly community, the bottom demonstrating the work of DH through practice and the top describing the cultural, pedagogical, and scholarly implications of this practice. The strong method-for-method's sake approach of cluster (b) is equally as indicative of a field finding its way as the overtly declarative statements about the culture of DH found in the conclusions of cluster (f).

A similar bifurcation differentiates the left and right sides of the graph. Two of the most isolated clusters, (i) (Topic 17: "narrative," "characters," "structure," "events") and (j) (Topic 4: "literary," "literature," "works," "poetry," "novels," "genre"), reveal a very strong relationship to literary studies, whether in the study of narrative structure (i) or literary criticism (including literary history and genre theory) (j). The stylometry cluster (a) also inhabits this side of the graph, as its investment in questions of authorship also connects it to literary studies (albeit at a greater distance). Near the top, cluster (h) (Topic 24: "text," "textual," "edition," "electronic") similarly marks out a textually invested area of DH with its articles on digital scholarly editions. On the other side of the graph, cluster (m) (Topic 15: "digital," "cultural," "images," "new," "archive," "visual") is localized around a nontextual DH, including both cultural and archival studies, and, more importantly, the analysis of visual digital artifacts. Cluster (c) (Topic 18: "tool," "users," "user," "software") follows this trend with its articles on human-computer interaction and the, predominately visual, design of new interfaces for DH resources. Although less fundamentally ideological than the top/bottom split between performative and descriptive digital humanities, this division between textual and visual DH also indicates the ways in which the objects of analyses (and the attendant methodologies and archives through which we approach their study) are also important factors in understanding the internal pressures on the field.

Finally, near the center of the graph, cluster (k) (Topic 10: "gender," "women," "study," "associated," "political") represents a crucial recent turn for the field. At once containing the conclusions of articles that argue for the increased need of gender representation in the traditionally male-dominated computational spaces of DH, and articles using DH methods to investigate the representation of gender across various media, this cluster reveals a coming together of description and practice, united around a set of concerns that extend across the different media representations that DH takes as its subject. Cluster (k) offers the first clue of a new end for DH, one that brings together its various areas of concern and synthesizes both its descriptive power and computational abilities into an activist-centered methodological and critical practice. That this cluster finds a home between the upper and lower bounds of the graph, whose opposite descriptive and computational poles have been critiqued along the lines of gendered labor, indicates the extent to which it may point the way to a new kind of end for the field.[13]

The Evolving Ends

If the graph of the topic model of the literal ends of DH has revealed the various forces that animate the arrangement of its investments and ideologies, then we are left with the question of what is holding the field together. What is the gravitational force that binds together the disparate and differentiating clusters that make up the constituent parts of the digital humanities? The topic model can once again help direct our attention toward the implicit commonalities between the various subfields. While the top topic in each cluster (the topic with the highest probability of being found in each of the conclusions) revealed the different fields that make up the whole, we can reverse the question and ask not what the top topics of each cluster are but what the *most common topics* of the field are overall. That is, which topics have the highest posterior probability across all of the different fields: what clusters of words unite, rather than divide them.

Table 5.1 contains the five topics with the highest posterior probability across all texts in the corpus. These are the clusters of words that are shared across all of the conclusions and, as such, point toward the implicit language of the field as a whole. What is striking is that they repeat the topics from my analysis above: Topics 25, 1, and 11 are the top topics of clusters (b), (g), and (f), respectively. Taken together, they provide a useful heuristic for understanding the field overall. The digital humanities are invested in new technologies (Topic 1) in order to create computational models (Topic 25) within a radically collaborative scholarly community (Topic 11). Topic 18 shows the investment in building digital humanities tools, which was, historically, understood to be the best way to bring new practitioners into the community who may have an interest in exploring computational methodologies without the expertise needed to create their own analyses from scratch.[14] This offers an important corrective to my analysis above. While these topics are deeply implicated in the divisions of the field that we witnessed in the graph, they also act as a common language across the various sub-discourses that make up DH. The methodological and descriptive discourse of Topics 25 and 1 may push their respective conclusions apart, but the presence, even if minute, of new technologies in conclusions to articles on computational methods, and the reference to computational methods in conclusions to articles on the importance of new technologies helps to anchor both within a single disciplinary system.

The Ends of Knowledge

Table 5.1 Top 15 words of the most frequent topics across all conclusions.

Topic 25	Topic 7	Topic 1	Topic 18	Topic 11
method	can	digital	can	Project
results	one	humanities	tools	Projects
features	might	research	tool	Research
used	like	scholars	use	Community
using	even	tools	users	Work
set	way	scholarly	also	Support
proposed	make	field	user	Collaboration
classification	just	technology	software	Also
performance	will	new	annotation	Public
feature	must	technologies	search	Time
based	see	scholarship	application	Development
accuracy	much	computing	system	University
system	question	infrastructure	needs	Must
approach	rather	need	interface	Open
training	need	well	development	team

If, however, the overall most frequent topics reveal surprising connections that lie at the gravitational center of the discipline's discourse, they do so at the risk of presenting the field as a static and unchanging monolith. From the first glance at Figure 5.1, what was immediately apparent was the evolving nature of the digital humanities, as the various emerging subfields of the past twenty years situated themselves in relation to the overarching patterns that the field had established. To understand this evolution, then, what we need are not the top topics overall but instead those that are most responsive to the changing nature of the field's discourse. By correlating the overall prevalence of the topics in our model with the dates of the articles that contain them, we can identify which topics decreased in prominence over the past two decades, and which came into being during the same period.[15]

Table 5.2 reveals the five topics that are most inversely correlated with year: the ones that decrease most in prevalence across the entire corpus over time. Some of these topics represent subfields of the discipline that have seen a decrease in scholarly engagement over time. In particular, Topic 24, which was attached to the scholarly editing cluster (h) and Topics 12 and 6 (which are respectively attached to articles on translation problems in classical texts and manuscript studies) represent areas that, for various reasons, have seen a drop in interest over the past two decades, whether due to ubiquity (for scholarly editions) or continued difficulty of the material (for textual studies on

The Ends of Digital Humanities

Table 5.2 Top 15 words of the five topics most negatively correlated with year.

Topic 24	Topic 3	Topic 16	Topic 12	Topic 6
text	may	will	language	Methods
texts	many	resources	corpus	Results
will	one	future	texts	Traditional
textual	however	access	languages	Analysis
edition	also	time	English	Case
electronic	even	available	can	manuscripts
scholarly	number	collection	words	One
editions	possible	resource	translation	Although
version	second	new	corpora	Method
original	small	online	text	manuscript
material	large	current	word	May
can	well	hope	use	Time
may	much	library	Greek	significant
printed	hand	use	Latin	tradition
early	needed	web	grammar	variants

manuscript collections). Most interesting, however, is Topic 16. Located on the graph predominately in articles slightly below the pedagogy/descriptive cluster, this topic takes as its subject the infrastructural needs of an emerging discipline. Speaking to "new" "resources" and "online" "collections," this topic foregrounds both the importance of building computational infrastructure to serve the evolving needs of scholars within the field (whatever they are imagined to be at the time), and, more importantly, the newness of the field. The novelty of both the intersection between computing and the humanities, as well as the methods used to research along this fault line, was, and in some ways, continues to be, a topic of conversation among DH practitioners, particularly as they telegraphed the advancements of the field to both recent and prospective community members. That such a topic decreases is not surprising: as the field has aged, its novelty can no longer be taken for granted, and it has ceased to be the most important aspect of the discipline.

Contrast these topics with those that are the most highly positively correlated with date in the corpus (i.e., those that increase in prevalence over time). Table 5.3 shows a very different set of topics that are coming into being over the course of the twenty-first century. Some of these, as we might expect, derive from areas of study that have only recently become tractable to computation with the increase in memory and processing speed of contemporary computers. Topics 20 and 15, in particular, speak to the study

The Ends of Knowledge

Table 5.3 Top 15 words from the five topics most positively correlated with year.

Topic 20	Topic 8	Topic 4	Topic 10	Topic 15
analysis	social	literary	gender	Digital
research	critical	literature	women	Cultural
study	practices	works	study	Images
studies	within	also	also	New
patterns	production	poetry	used	Archive
also	cultural	novels	associated	Visual
computational	often	genre	political	Collections
article	media	century	social	Art
quantitative	space	time	may	Archives
topics	communities	novel	terms	Image
topic	technology	new	results	Media
results	intellectual	important	evidence	Heritage
questions	beyond	fiction	body	Content
film	practice	popular	female	Objects
show	power	historical	greater	digitization

of visual media, whether archives of images in Topic 15, or film and television in Topic 20. Their emergence into the discourse of DH represents the new opportunities that practitioners have to study visual artifacts that were impossible to process at scale even twenty years ago. Topic 10, as we have already seen, represents an important new discourse in DH, both in discussions of research methodology and subject. Topic 8 offers a new way of describing the work of the digital humanities. Rather than focus on building infrastructure, or the application of new technologies, it speaks to the work of DH as a set of social and critical practices, informing an activist take on the role of the field within the larger scholarly and public communities.

It is Topic 4, however, that offers the strongest glimpse of the ends of the beginning of the Digital Humanities. As we saw in Figure 5.1, it is a discourse of literary analysis distinct from the corpus-centric work of either stylometry or supervised classification. Slightly reconfiguring the graph of topics in Figure 5.2, this time using color to show the journal of publication for each conclusion, clearly shows the surprising origin of this topic in cluster (j). The majority of articles featuring this topic in their conclusion come from the *Journal of Cultural Analytics*. While this is among the newest digital humanities journals, it nevertheless has a commitment to both computationally driven research, and a multidisciplinary approach to the study of cultural analytics. That a topic whose discourse is so obviously allied to the work of literary criticism shows up

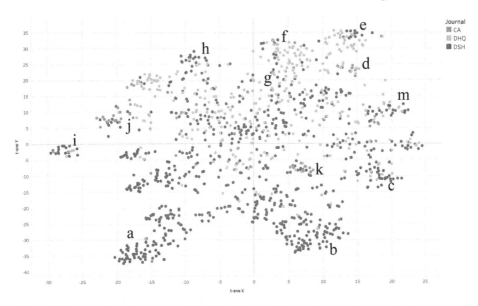

Figure 5.2 t-sne plot of a topic model of digital humanities article conclusions; shades represent journal of publication.

in the conclusions to this journal suggests a more substantive change in the research that it publishes. Instead of drawing back to discuss the methodological innovations featured in the article, or linking the importance of the results to the emergence of new technologies, the conclusions of *CA* appear to link the research topic to the interventions that authors seek to make in the humanities disciplines themselves. That is, rather than offer a meta-discourse about the field or its methods, the goal of these articles is to leverage the possibilities of computational research toward creating new knowledge about the objects that they seek to analyze. While from the perspective of traditional disciplinary practices within the university this simply describes the work of research, for an emerging field such as the digital humanities it represents a sea-change in the kind of work that DH is designed to do. This emerging discourse offers the possibility of using the methods of the field toward the ends of knowledge production, rather than generating discourse about the field itself. Similar to cluster (k) (on gender studies), which is also overrepresented in articles from *CA*, cluster (j) offers a glimpse of a new set of practices that can inform the evolution of the field.

The Beginnings of the End

While the topic model that I have explored in this chapter has only scratched the surface of the ways that the digital humanities are evolving to meet the challenges of becoming a full-fledged institutionalized research community, it has posed a difficult but necessary question for the ends of the discipline. What happens to a field that is defined by novelty of method and the need for infrastructure when the infrastructure has been built and the novelty has worn off? The kinds of articles that have long dominated the discourse of DH, which take this novelty as their subject and describe the infrastructural needs of the field, are perhaps becoming obsolete as the digital humanities enters its next phase. In their place, a different kind of research practice is emerging, one that connects the methodological innovations of the field back to the kinds of humanities questions that motivated its creation in the first place. By directing their attention back to the humanities at the conclusions of their articles, practitioners are beginning the difficult work of defining their field in relation to a wider community of scholars who can benefit from the insights that their research yields.

Whether such a transformation will take place in the context of a reabsorption of the digital humanities back into the traditional disciplinary and departmental structures of the humanities, or whether the field will continue to consolidate into its own institutes, departments, and schools, the practice of DH will be fundamentally altered. No longer figured exclusively through the insistence on its novelty and the need for the creation of newer and better tools, perhaps we can start the difficult work of training students as researchers who are equipped with the knowledge and skills of DH methods and an understanding of the research goals of the humanities. Maybe the ends of the digital humanities lie in the beginnings of digital humanities research.

Notes

1. On the history of DH, see, for example, Chris Alen Sula and Heather V. Hill, "The Early History of Digital Humanities: An Analysis of *Computers and the Humanities* (1966–2004) and *Literary and Linguistic Computing* (1986–2004)," *Digital Scholarship in the Humanities* 34, no. 1 (2019): i190–i206. The Association for Computing in the Humanities, for example, dates back to 1978; the Kings College department of Digital Humanities was founded in 1992. The current international organization, the Alliance of Digital Humanities Organizations (ADHO), began in 2002.

2. Melissa Terras, "Another Suitcase, Another Student Hall—Where Are We Going to? What ACH/ALLC 2001 Can Tell Us About the Current Direction of Humanities Computing," *Literary and Linguistic Computing* 16, no. 4 (2001): 485–502; Melissa Terras, "Disciplined: Using Educational Studies to Analyse 'Humanities Computing,'" *Literary and Linguistic Computing* 21, no. 2 (2006): 229–46.

3. Ninareh Mehrabi, Fred Morstatter, Nripsuta Saxena, Kristina Lerman, and Aram Galstyan, "A Survey on Bias and Fairness in Machine Learning," *ACM Comput. Surv.* 54, 6, Article 115 (2021): 35 pages.

4. Roopika Risam, *New Digital Worlds: Postcolonial Digital Humanities in Theory, Praxis, and Pedagogy* (Chicago: Northwestern University Press, 2019); Catherine D'Ignazio and Lauren Klein, *Data Feminism* (Cambridge, MA: MIT Press, 2020); Amy Earhart, Roopika Risam, and Matthew Bruno, "Citational Politics: Quantifying the Influence of Gender on Citation in Digital Scholarship in the Humanities," *Digital Scholarship in the Humanities* 36, no. 3 (2021): 581–94.

5. See the description of the "evidence gap" in Andrew Piper, "There Will Be Numbers," *Journal of Cultural Analytics* 1, no. 1 (2016): 3–5.
6. Different, but equally facile, critiques can be found in Daniel Allington, Sarah Brouillette, and David Golumbia, "Neoliberal Tools (and Archives): A Political History of Digital Humanities," *Los Angeles Review of Books*, May 1, 2016, and Nan Z. Da, "The Computational Case against Computational Literary Studies," *Critical Inquiry* 45 (2019): 601–39.
7. See Andrew Piper, *Can We Be Wrong? The Problem of Textual Evidence in a Time of Data* (Cambridge: Cambridge University Press, 2020), 30.
8. Although *DHS* has been in publication since 1986, I only included articles written in 2000 or later for this analysis, both to increase the compatibility between this sample and *DHQ* and *CA* (which began their runs in 2007 and 2016 respectively) and in recognition that the *field* of digital humanities changed considerably when it gained widespread attention in the early twenty-first century.
9. For each article in each journal, I captured either the concluding section if it was differentiated in the text (and identified as "Conclusion," "Future Directions," or "Discussion") or the last two paragraphs of the article if such a section was absent. Reviews, technical notes, and introductions to special issues were excluded from the corpus.
10. See David M. Blei, "Topic Modeling and Digital Humanities," *Journal of Digital Humanities* 2, no. 1 (2012): 8–11.
11. In this analysis, I constructed a 25-topic model (after testing 50- and 100-topic models) using a Gibbs sampler.
12. Laurens Van der Maaten and Geoffrey Hinton, "Visualizing Data using t-SNE," *Journal of Machine Learning Research* 9, no. 11 (2008). The graph should be interpreted based on the relative position of the points.
13. See D'Ignazio and Klein, *Data Feminism,* Chapter 7.
14. Topic 7, containing predominately common words, appears to be a general topic of conclusions across disciplines.
15. To calculate this, I calculated the Pearson correlation between the posterior probability of the individual topics with the year of the article's publication.

PART II
ACCESS

During the digital optimism phase of the internet, from the 1980s to early 2000s, a phrase defined the promise of the new medium: "Information wants to be free." The assumption linking the slogan to the internet was that new platforms would provide an open-access public sphere, one that had been idealized but not achieved during the dominance of print and television media. But as this discussion evolved, complications emerged: Did "free" in this phrase mean, as the saying went, "free as in speech" or "free as in beer"? That is, was the "freedom" about cost or accessibility? And how could the prosopopoeia of "information" want anything? In the consolidated Web 2.5 era, such a debate seems quaint, but it points to concerns that motivate the contributors: How do questions of access and exclusion impact the production of knowledge? How can disciplines foreground questions of access in order to ensure truth and accuracy? While the previous group of chapters, that is, focused primarily on the content of disciplines, this group emphasizes the conditions of knowledge production. The authors show how access not only is a question of social justice but also impacts the validity of the information in circulation.

This may be the most disciplinarily diverse group of chapters, and also one that stretches the definition of "discipline." Each chapter concerns an arena of practice as much as a field of study, with the links between practice and scholarship outlining the end(s) of the discipline. Law, as Yochai Benkler shows, is not so much a set of rules as a system for creating social relations, one that is particularly relevant in the context of market societies, where it has taken over much of the authority previously held by custom, religion, or allegiance. The law has helped define who works, how they work, and how they are compensated for their work, as conservative and progressive legal scholars and jurists have worked to define who has access to legal recourse and, consequently, to productivity and power. While some mainstream journalists have recently been criticized for practicing "access journalism"—prioritizing their access to sources over critical reporting—Jolene Almendarez shows how access is also a question of accuracy. As the field of journalism continues to face external pressures, she argues that newsrooms must also remake themselves from within in order to accurately reflect the news of a diverse world. Likewise, teachers, as Sean Michael Morris demonstrates, must offer each student access to the pedagogical approach that supports their articulation in the world—substituting humanizing pedagogy for institutional structures. And as G. Gabrielle Starr writes, the broader liberal arts tradition takes as its end access to the range of human knowledge. Rather than comprising a particular course of study, the liberal arts enshrine the idea that knowledge is ever expanding with new scholars and new fields of study. One of the ends of the liberal arts is establishing the scholarly networks that will allow this goal to continue to be pursued. Together, these chapters emphasize how the assumption that the borders of disciplines will need constantly to be expanded is itself the goal of various knowledge projects.

CHAPTER 6
THE ENDS OF LAW
Yochai Benkler

Structure and Legitimation in Social Relations: The Role of Law

On October 26, 2020, one week before the US presidential election, Senate Majority Leader Mitch McConnell led the Senate to confirm Amy Coney Barrett as Associate Justice of the Supreme Court. This move followed his refusal to permit Barack Obama to appoint a replacement for Justice Antonin Scalia with 293 days to go before the 2016 election. McConnell's ruthless efficiency concluded a process that began when the newly elected Richard Nixon and his Attorney General John Mitchell used information from the IRS and FBI to pressure Justice Abe Fortas to leave the Supreme Court in 1969[1] while Gerald Ford as Minority Leader in the House tried to impeach Justice William O. Douglas on baseless corruption charges,[2] one that was systematized by Ronald Reagan and his attorney general, Edwin Meese.[3] The new Supreme Court majority is poised to pursue the program that has guided Republican judicial appointments strategy for half a century: reversal of the civil rights revolution of the 1960s and shrinking federal power to manage the economy. The election of Joe Biden a week after Coney Barrett's confirmation coupled with a progressive shift in Democratic Party politics on the economy, racial justice, and climate action have set up the coming two decades as a period of conflict between the federal courts and the democratically elected governments of the United States and several of the larger, urbanized states. By the end of its first term, the McConnell Court had restricted the power of the federal government to prevent states from suppressing voting by Black and other voters of color,[4] and invented a new federal common law constitutional property right to overturn a half-century old California labor law designed to protect migrant farm workers, as Chief Justice John Roberts triumphantly dismissed dissenting arguments that "bear the sound of Old, unhappy far-off things, and battles long ago."[5] In the midst of the Second Gilded Age, the United States is poised to repeat the decades-long battle that marked the first Gilded Age—over the role of law, and of unelected judges in particular, in democratic market society.

"What are the ends of law?" is primarily a question of social function: What role does law play in modern market societies? Law is one of the primary systems societies use to structure social relations: of production in the economy, of authority in the polity, of reproduction in kinship, and of meaning-making in culture.[6] Law structures social relations functionally and symbolically. Functionally, it serves both coercion and coordination functions. First, it shapes social expectations about the use of legitimate violence. This is Holmes's "bad man" theory of law, or Weber's monopoly over the legitimate use of force. In this sense, law defines the background expectations that well-socialized actors come with into social relations about what they can or cannot do to and with each other in those relations without triggering a response from whoever has the power to coerce a change in their relations through the exercise or threat of violence experienced as legitimate by well-socialized actors, in the society in which the law is law. Second, law codifies and communicates expectations about patterns of social relations that provide coordination points and frameworks for cooperation, as people interact with each other in the normal course of social life as people whose actions are made thereby reasonably predictable. Symbolically, law produces and communicates conceptions of how social relations ought to be, conceptions considered authoritative by most well-socialized members of the society to which it applies, and function as internalized regulation for most people most of the time: that is, as guidelines for action a person undertakes because that person has internalized that this is how they should act in a given context.

Law plays a particularly large role in structuring and legitimating social relations in capitalism, or market society, because capitalism depends, first and foremost, on disembedding social relations of production from social relations of reproduction, authority, and meaning. Only by removing the stabilizing and stifling anchors of custom, religion, and servility on the questions of who may or must work with whom, on what projects, with what resources, and who gets what can the process of continuous improvement, or of creative destruction, as Schumpeter put it in the terms we commonly use today, take flight. But this new social relation required new abstracted agents and relations, that is, individual legal subjects engaging through contracts and prices rather than as a community embedded in a shared history and narrative. Something had to be able to carry the institutional load that custom, religion, and fealty had borne in prior systems but were no longer suffered to bear. To achieve these ends, all modern societies have developed a semi-autonomous social system for the production of law.[7] Judges, legal scholars, legislatures, regulators, and lawyers are socialized (through education and apprenticeship) in norms, practices, and relations that constitute the profession and structure and legitimate the inside of the profession as "the profession." The profession, in turn, produces outputs that structure and legitimate social relations across a broader range of domains of social life by virtue of being seen and understood in the broader society as the outputs of the profession. Judges and legal scholars play a central role in producing the major legitimating narratives of the profession over time.

In this chapter, I focus on the law as it structures and legitimates social relations of production: who must and who may work, with whom and with what resources, on what projects, designed to make and distribute how much of what we need and want, who gets what from the outputs of these efforts, and who has the power to determine the answers to these questions. In this regard, law structures both productivity and power: how well the organization of social relations in a society can transform the material and social environment it inhabits to the satisfaction of the needs and wants of its constituents, and who has the power to shape who does what and who gets what in these relations. To answer the question of what function law plays—what the ends of law are; and how it fulfills them—and how it operates as a means to that end, I offer condensed histories of the role of law in facilitating economic transformation and increasing inequality in the two quintessential periods of growing inequality in the United States: 1873 to 1929, and 1980 to the present. In both eras, debates over legal method played a role in legitimating the positions of both pro-business and progressive judges, lawyers, and legal scholars. Both eras saw conflicts between conservative conceptions of law as a system whose purpose is to enforce relations of formal equality between individuals, legitimated by adherence to formal methods of legal analysis, where the formalism is understood to be sufficiently determinative and objective to constrain judicial discretion and insulate law from politics; and progressive conceptions of law as a system for securing justice, defined through democratic processes and legitimated through fidelity to the substantive pursuit of democratically determined goals (and, after the rights revolution of the 1960s, minority protection as a fundamental attribute of democratic society). During the first Gilded Age, these legal debates focused, from both sides, on how law structured and legitimated economic relations and the organization of the transformation of American capitalism. Throughout most of the Second Gilded Age, conservatives pushed both on social relations of production, or the ways in which law structures the economy, and on relations of reproduction and meaning-making, or identity. Progressives, however, largely abandoned their earlier focus on production, and focused on social relations of reproduction and meaning-making—particularly on combating race and gender subordination through law. The result was a long string of victories in economic law for conservatives alongside a pitched battle over questions of identity subordination, which included both major progressive victories and sustained conservative retrenchment.

After the Great Recession, after the Occupy movement, after Donald Trump's remarkable success in harnessing the white working class to his 2016 campaign, progressives once more joined the battle on the economic front, without retreating from conflict over domination and status subordination. Nowhere was this shift clearer than in the remarkable successes of Senators Bernie Sanders and Elizabeth Warren in the 2016 and 2020 Democratic primaries. As we stand at the end of the neoliberal era, we are beginning to see this shift reflected in the legal academy with the emergence of a new law and political economy movement,[8] extending prior work on subordination but complementing it with a new focus on economic power. Still in its infancy, this movement combines critique of neoliberal jurisprudence, programmatic prescription designed to transform social relations of production in the post-neoliberal economic order, and development of the bases of legitimation within the profession necessary to stabilize these programmatic changes as a new regime. It expands the focus of progressive legal scholarship from law as the pursuit of justice along dimensions of anti-subordination or equality of opportunity, to take law as a major institutional dimension through which to directly address economic power and inequality, as well as the interactions of class, race, and gender.[9]

The Ends of Knowledge

Structure and Legitimation in the Second Industrial Divide: 1870s–1930s

Structuring Productivity and Power: Law as Rules of Engagement

The last quarter of the nineteenth century marked the transition from Great Britain to the United States as the leading economy in the world. The first industrial revolution was built around smaller, entrepreneur-owned firms that employed a mix of male craft workers who combined a production role with a quasi-managerial role overseeing unskilled women and children.[10] The 1880s in the United States saw a shift to large firms and cartels, financed by emerging financial capital, and deploying a newly emerging managerial class to oversee a more fully deskilled workforce recruited initially from immigrants, and later Black migrants from the South.[11] Law played a central role in enabling these organizational transformations, insulating emerging organizational forms from state regulation, constraining labor's strategies for economic struggle, and nullifying labor's political victories, while insulating firms from paying for the risks their transformation posed for others in society. In doing so, law made possible the productivity-increasing changes in transportation and manufacture while also shifting power over the distribution of gains in favor of a small oligarchic elite at the expense of the broad population of workers, farmers, and consumers. Only the decisive political victories of the New Deal shifted law toward undergirding "the Great Compression": the period during which income and wealth inequality shrank in the United States from its height in the early twentieth century.

Until the last quarter of the nineteenth century, both American and English law treated corporations as creatures of the state, created by the special grant of delimited powers upon a group of people carrying on a predefined collective purpose. As such, they were subject to broad regulatory powers. Across a range of doctrines, judges reflected and enforced a strictly limited role for corporations well into the 1880s.[12] Corporate law was to be transformed, however, as first railroads and then manufacturing firms discovered the benefits of consolidation and scale and pushed for greater freedom to combine, free of state regulation and oversight. Railroads led the transformation of American industrial organization. The sheer scale of investment underwrote the emergence of the stock market as a source of investment funds, manipulation, and corporate consolidation. The scale and geographic spread of their operations forced railroads to invent what would emerge as middle management.[13] Railroad consolidation provided the quintessential instance of both increased productivity and increased power. A smaller number of consolidated railroads were able to ship more goods, for longer distances, more quickly and reliably. But this handful of surviving companies also gained significant power: to raise freight charges and prevail on state governors and legislatures to help them put down the most extensive efforts of labor mobilization that the United States would ever know.

The power benefits of consolidation were not lost on other industries. Between 1882 and 1889, industries from petroleum and whiskey to sugar consolidated in trusts to control prices, extract higher rents, and wield extensive political power. When some states and Congress sought to limit the trusts, corporate lawyers pushed the pliant New

Jersey legislature to create an alternative vehicle for consolidation: the 1889 New Jersey general incorporation law. Corporations flocked to reincorporate in New Jersey and pursue the price extractive practices inside corporate structures that the new law made possible.[14] The capital exodus from other states forced the "race to the bottom" among states. Then, in the 1895 sugar trust case, the US Supreme Court further insulated many of these companies by ruling that the Sherman Antitrust Act could not constitutionally cover manufacturing, because it was not "commerce" within Congress's commerce clause power.[15]

The dramatic increase in scale and speed of production and shipping, and the introduction of new machinery, often replacing craft workers with unskilled immigrant workers operating that machinery, was associated with a dramatic increase in workplace accidents. Although these increases were observed throughout the industrializing world, accident rates in the United States were between three to five times higher than in the UK or other Western European industrializing countries.[16] The difference lay in American tort law, which insulated railroads and manufacturing firms to a greater degree than was true in the UK or Europe, enabling companies to adopt technological and organizational processes that increased profit but externalized the risk to workers and neighbors. American railroads, for example, used heavier cars over single tracks to maximize payload and minimize cost. The heavier cars required trainmen and brakemen to operate on top of and between cars, rather than, as in the UK, from safer parts of trains made of lighter cars running on double track rails. As a result, railroad workplace fatalities were 50 percent higher in the US than in the UK. Similarly unconstrained by unions or liability laws, American coal mining companies used explosives and mining architectures that were cheaper to construct but more prone to collapse than techniques used in the UK.[17] It was not only workers whom American tort law forced to absorb the cost of rapid corporate expansion. In the latter part of the nineteenth century, American judges were containing the exposure of corporations to risk their activities posed to third parties as well. A critical battlefront was causation: What relation between acts of a corporation and harms in the world was sufficient to place on the corporation a duty to pay? If a spark from a railroad started a fire, was the railroad liable only for the first building set on fire? For its neighbor? To the whole neighborhood? Consistently, nineteenth-century courts answered these questions in favor of railroads and at the expense of neighbors.[18]

The best known sustained intervention of law in the transformation of the second industrial divide was the aggressive role that the judiciary played in weakening labor organization, both economic and political.[19] In terms of economic power, judges developed the labor injunction as a widely used summary process to direct and legitimate violent suppression and imprisonment of labor organizers, outlawing broad classes of labor strategies even in states where progressive governors resisted sending their own police to break up labor action. In terms of political power, in the infamous *Lochner* era, courts leveraged judicial review of legislation to nullify labor and progressive political victories in passing labor and occupational health and safety laws. From the Great Railroad Strikes of 1877 until the passage of the Wagner Act in 1935, judges developed and expanded their powers to issue injunctions against a growing range of union strategies.[20] Civil injunctions based on private law theories or tortured interpretations of federal legislation allowed judges to circumvent the onerous requirements of criminal procedure as well as progressive governors and mayors charged with enforcing criminal law who refused to suppress labor organizers. Civil injunctions could be issued in summary process, as preliminary and temporary measures, and contempt orders against noncompliant workers could be converted into summary orders to arrest strike leaders. The result was the development of a legal framework that operated quickly, with minimal standards of proof, and enabled federal judges to call up armed support to violently suppress labor organizing.

Judges used this legal framework for deploying armed force to suppress labor repeatedly and extensively over the following decades, reaching by some estimates more than 4000 injunctions between 1880 and 1930, and by the 1920s covering about 25 percent of strikes.[21] Consistently, American judges declared that the most effective economic weapons available to labor violated the rights of the employers, or interfered with commerce. After passage of the Sherman Act, they held these tactics to violate federal antitrust law (the same law that the same federal judiciary held did not cover manufacturers' anticompetitive practices).[22] Ultimately, in *In re Debs*, the Supreme Court would validate the panoply of legal interpretations that enabled federal courts to imprison labor organizers and exert broad authority, including violent coercion, over labor disputes using the summary process.[23] In an increasingly interconnected economy, federal courts denied labor the ability to leverage its power over critical infrastructures.

Meanwhile, the challenge for plantation owners in the postbellum South was not industrialization, but replacing chattel slavery with a legal framework that could deliver forced agricultural labor without transforming racial caste hierarchy. In addition to the more infamous Black Codes that invoked a strong federal reaction in the form of the Civil Rights Act of 1866 and the Fourteenth Amendment, and the Jim Crow laws that followed them, Southern legislatures and judges developed a system of criminal and civil law elements that forced Black workers into a mixture of sharecropping and peonage.[24] Crop-lien statutes created the legal architecture that, on the background of postbellum conditions in the South, put sharecroppers and share tenants in a position of perpetual debt.[25] The compulsion to raise cotton created by these crop-lien statutes was reinforced by newly enacted trespass, game, and closed-range laws geographically targeted toward majority-Black counties, which were designed to foreclose the primary options for self-sufficiency through hunting, fishing, and raising livestock on an open range.[26] Moreover, sharecroppers who might be tempted to walk away from their debt and search for their luck elsewhere were constrained by contract labor laws and false pretense laws, which criminalized breach of labor contracts and allowed courts to impose servitude as a criminal penalty on workers who tried to leave employers. Even when federal courts held these laws unconstitutional, Southern courts continued to enforce them, and federal enforcement of the constitutional prohibitions on these laws was weak. Enticement laws criminalized hiring an employee away from their employer. Emigrant agent laws required high licensing fees for out-of-state recruiters seeking to hire workers out of Southern states—laws that became particularly common as Northern industrial business responded to anti-immigrant laws that cut off industrial access to cheap labor from Southern and Eastern Europe by recruiting cheap Black labor from the South.[27] All these were passed on the background of some of the better known techniques of forcing Black workers to work for pittance: vagrancy laws, criminalizing "idleness" (not being in someone else's employ); debt peonage for taxes and small fines levied in discriminatory ways; and apprenticeship laws that enabled courts to impose child labor for years to an apprentice master. All these provided a backstop roving commission for Southern authorities to impose wage labor on Black workers throughout this period on terms determined unilaterally by white employers.

In Northern and Midwestern states, where farmer and labor coalitions were beginning to gain ground politically, the anti-labor stance of courts expanded beyond undermining the possibility of labor gaining economic power. Judges systematically blocked off avenues for the emergence of labor as a political force as well. Beginning in 1885 with *In re Jacobs*[28] and continuing until the "switch in time that saved the nine" in 1937, state and federal courts struck down progressive legislation wherever worker and farmer coalitions were able to gain democratic control over legislatures. Labor gained diverse political successes at the state level. These included, for example, legislation that banned manufacturing in tenement dwellings, abolished payment by scrip to the company store and required regular payment with legal tender, and laws that regulated hours of work, anti-union discrimination, or the means of measuring and calculating miners' output and wages. All these diverse laws were struck down by state and federal courts on the constitutional grounds that they interfered with the property right of the employer to conduct business without interference or the freedom of contract of employers and employees to transact with whomever they saw fit under whatever terms they agreed.[29] The result was that income inequality reached its peak on the eve of the Great Depression, and would not return to those levels until the eve of the Great Recession in 2008, after forty years of a sustained campaign to overturn the legal and policy changes that had governed the American economy from the New Deal to the Great Society.

The Battle over Legitimation of Extractive Law: Classical Legal Thought and Legal Realism

The half century during which courts underwrote the emergence of the American system of powerful corporations, a weak state, and a suppressed and fragmented labor movement saw a sustained battle over the legitimation of these actions within the legal profession. A central part of Classical Legal Thought (CLT), to use the term introduced in the 1970s by Duncan Kennedy, was to produce a legitimating conceptual architecture experienced by legal elites as justifying these decisions in neutral and pre-political terms; as *principled law*, in stark distinction to the efforts of labor and progressive politicians to pass "class legislation."[30] CLT adopted an understanding of law modeled on geometry: a practice of reasoning from foundational axioms to specific rules required by logical derivation. The approach proceeded by identifying a small set of top-level categories and principles such as: contracts are based on will; or, duty in tort only arises when acts of the defendant objectively caused harm to a right of the plaintiff. From these broad principles, classical legal scholars and judges derived formally concrete results in cases— if contract reflected the subjective will of parties, then an offer was accepted only when the acceptance arrived in the hands of the offeror. As the Supreme Court reasoned in *In re Debs*, if the federal government had absolute power over interstate commerce that the states could not overturn, and if the states had police power to enforce public order, and if courts of equity could issue injunctions to enforce the police power of the state, then it followed as a matter of logical necessity that federal courts protecting interstate commerce could issue injunctions against bodies of men who seek to exercise "powers belonging only to government" when those bodies interfered with interstate commerce (to wit, the unions conducting a sympathy strike with the Pullman strike). The core conceit of this legal consciousness was its claimed objectivity as a source of authority governed by reasoning that assured that the results were not the political preferences of the judges but were compelled by the logic of the law.

Most of the historiography of CLT conceives of this method as internalized consciousness. Just as scientists operate within scientific paradigms of their time, so too judges and treatise writers of the time internalized a method of legal reasoning and were faithfully operating within that tradition. Countering this purely structural understanding, diverse examples of the writings by jurists of that era betray a clear understanding of the power dynamics and the direct power effects of the legal rules. Chief Justice William Howard Taft was among the earliest to use the labor injunction to break strikes. His opinions when suppressing railroad labor action used abstract terms: "Neither law nor morals can give man a right to labor or withhold his labor for [the] purpose" of supporting the strike in another company.[31] In private, Taft would describe himself in a letter to his wife as "a kind of police court" during the Pullman strike,[32] and further wrote that the strikers would be quieted only after "they have had much bloodletting," complaining that marshals "have killed only six of the mob as yet. This is hardly enough to make an impression."[33] Few statements exhibit such a crisp, if not chilling, understanding that what a judge is doing in issuing his injunctions and imposing his contempt orders is to legitimate the violent use of lethal force to suppress strikers. Other courts similarly offered frank political assessments in their opinions, describing union boycotts as a "socialistic crime," or threatening that because of boycotts "by combinations of irresponsible cabals and cliques, there will be an end to government."[34]

Progressive critics certainly knew what was going on, and they mounted attacks on the legitimacy of CLT in terms not only of its internal validity but also of its external function in shaping power in the economy. In contemporary legal culture the period is known as the *Lochner* era, after a case in which the US Supreme Court struck down a New York law limiting the working hours in bakeries to ten hours a day and sixty a week, as interfering with the liberty of contract of bakers and their employees. Justice Peckham, writing for the Court, rejected the claim that the court was "substituting the judgment of the court for that of the legislature," rather beginning in an axiomatic formulation that "the liberty of contract relating to labor includes both parties to it. The one has as much right to purchase as the other to sell labor," and concluding that "The act is not, within any fair meaning of the term, a health law, but is an illegal interference with the rights of individuals, both employers and employees, to make contracts regarding labor upon such terms as they may think best, or which they may agree upon with the other parties to such contracts." Rejecting this assertion of legal-analytic neutrality, Justice Oliver Wendell Holmes, Jr., opened his dissent with the simple assertion: "This case is decided upon an economic theory which a large part of the country does not entertain," elaborating that the "Constitution is not intended to embody a particular economic theory, whether of paternalism and the organic relation of the citizen to the state or of *laissez faire*."[35] This basic insistence that assertions of legal conclusions as necessitated by logical derivation were in fact judicial enforcement of a particular political worldview would become a central strand of the progressive assault on laissez faire.[36]

Beginning with Holmes's *The Path of the Law* in 1897, and continuing through the work of progressive legal scholars from Roscoe Pound, through Wesley Hohfeld, to Morris Cohen, Robert Lee Hale, and Felix Cohen, Legal Realism emerged as a sustained attack on the alleged neutrality and autonomy of law as a discipline in principle, and the internal coherence and apolitical sources of legitimacy of CLT in particular. The most trenchant internal critique of the logic of CLT was Hohfeld's still-unmatched reconstruction of law as always and only about social relations, made of distinct, definable analytic elements of rights, privileges, powers, and immunities, which themselves described classes of possible social relations of production.[37] Hohfeld's rigorous structure exposed the incoherence of how the conservative judiciary used terms like "liberty" and "right" to mask analytic slippages that pervaded the surface-level logic used to justify a range of holdings, such as imposing labor injunctions or invalidating closed shop agreements. Externally, Hale and Morris Cohen provided sustained analyses of how law, in particular property, shaped power in the economy.[38] Felix Cohen's 1935 *Transcendental Nonsense and the Functional Approach* encapsulated the conjoined internal and external perspectives, providing the clearest statement among the Realists of the distinction between law as a social practice—a method of writing and arguing that reflected acculturation into a profession—and law as a structure of power in society.[39] *Transcendental Nonsense* remains the clearest statement of how progressive legal scholarship can, indeed must, be undertaken holding both the external understanding of law as a socially constructed field of knowledge with very particular social effects, and the internal perspective of practitioners inside that field behaving as well-socialized members aiming to produce moves that will be perceived within the legal profession as appropriate professional moves, with full knowledge and intent that that perception inside the profession will have the desired external effects in society at large.

After four decades of sustained progressive intellectual attack, however, CLT was defeated as much at the ballot box as in law journals or brilliant dissents. Franklin D. Roosevelt's electoral victories allowed him to appoint judges and regulators. The functional approach, as Felix Cohen had called it, became what it meant to "think like a lawyer," because people who created this tradition, or were trained in it, came to fill the ranks of the judiciary and administrative agencies. And just as political transformation shifted the inside of the legal profession, it also ushered in a host of statutory and administrative legal changes designed to transform the power of labor in industrial relations and the power of the state to regulate product, labor, and financial markets. Judges adopted statutory interpretation methods that placed judges in a collaborative relation with legislatures—seeking to understand the purpose of democratically enacted legislation by understanding the social, political, and historical background of the legislation, and then seeking to apply that purpose functionally, as the crooked timber of humanity or changes in context demanded adaptive application of the law. The prevailing understanding of "the ends of law," what it was for and how it functioned, was to structure social relations. Law shaped how people acted toward and related to one another. This much was simple social fact. Whether law did so well or poorly, justly or unjustly, was a matter for both functional and normative debate. But the "realism" in Legal Realism was to recognize that any effort to understand law as either an autonomous internally coherent system of texts and analytic techniques or as applied philosophy of justice was a mistake as a matter of historical and sociological description.

The following three decades came to be known as "the Golden Age of Capitalism": a period of high productivity growth and declining income inequality. At its origins, the New Deal and the Fair Deal relied on and reinforced racial and gender status hierarchies.[40] By the end of this period the Civil Rights Movement and the Women's Movement would use law in efforts to overturn racial caste hierarchy in America and to leverage the power of the state to overturn entrenched patriarchy. While the older Realists had a hard time adjusting to the idea of a rights-based jurisprudence that would not ultimately redound to the benefit of capital, the successes of the civil rights movement in the Warren Court launched a generation of mainstream liberal legal scholarship designed to legitimate the rights jurisprudence of the courts. The prevailing constitutional wisdom had shifted toward a framework that elevated a substantive view of what a democratic constitution required: leaving economic regulation to the normal tussle of politics, while offering robust protection of individual political and civil rights and of "discrete and insular minorities," whose protection could not be left solely to majoritarian rule.

Just as these liberal scholars were working to justify active judicial protection of these rights, however, the wheel of political economy once again turned. The failures of the Vietnam War, the Great Inflation, Southern white backlash against the Civil Rights Acts, Christian fundamentalist reaction to the Women's Movement and the New Left's successful reorientation of the moral universe toward individual choice and self-actualization, and Organized Business's reemergence in reaction to the 1960s victories of labor and the consumer and environmental movements resulted in the emergence of a new and potent political coalition, initiated by Richard Nixon and crystalized by Ronald Reagan. From 1980 to the present, law would be harnessed to reverse the power realignment of the New Deal and Civil Rights coalitions, and judges and legal scholars on the political right would develop a combination of economic formalism and legal fundamentalism to legitimate the reactionary program of this new conservative coalition.

Law, Structure, and Legitimation in Neoliberal Capitalism: 1970s to 2010s

Structuring Productivity and Power: Law as Rules of Engagement

Beginning in the 1970s the United States saw a series of legal changes that resulted in relatively slow productivity growth and high inequality. Some laws squeezed the bottom of the income distribution, made life more precarious, and enforced the imperative to accept wage labor on any terms. Other laws weakened middle-income workers and led to the stagnation of labor income since 1973. Yet others enabled the escape of the 1 percent. The details are beyond the scope of this chapter, and a condensed version is presented in Table 6.1. At their core, these legal changes increased the dependence of low and middle-income families on accepting any job on offer by making life more precarious at the bottom of the income distribution and harnessing illness and aging as a "whip of hunger" for workers in the middle of the income distribution. At the bottom of the income distribution, the pressure began with the racialized assault on welfare.[41] The War on Poverty was replaced by the racialized War on Drugs and mass incarceration.[42] The effects were compounded by erosion of minimum wages, weak enforcement of employment law—which made wage theft common and work conditions more exploitative—and loose enforcement of immigration laws designed to create an underclass of unprotected workers, particularly in industries with high proportions of status-subordinated workers: immigrants, workers of color, and particularly women of color.[43] While these effects were worst for workers at the bottom of the income distribution, lower standards for overtime pay and similar changes hit middle-income workers as well.

The most important contributor to middle-income wage stagnation was the decline of labor economic and political power,[44] whose destruction was the central target of the dramatic expansion of corporate lobbying since the 1970s.[45] The defeat of the PATCO strike in 1981 by the Reagan administration,[46] complemented by a host of small and large decisions by the National Labor Relations Board, made unionization harder and defeating it easier,[47] and supercharged the "union avoidance" industry.[48] Deregulation of regulated industries where unionized workers had historically earned high wages; liberal trade laws that emphasized free movement of goods and services, particularly finance, but did not include labor or environmental protections; and weakened antitrust law and enforcement enabled firms to appropriate all the productivity gains made feasible from deregulation and trade liberalization. Financial deregulation and a host of shifts in both social norms and corporate governance laws increased the power of the professional and managerial class over consumers, workers, and small investors. Across dozens of discrete areas of law and policy the toggles were consistently flipped in favor of empowering the professional and managerial class, particularly finance, to extract the value of almost all gains in productivity over the past forty years. The result was that on the eve of the Great Recession income inequality in the United States reached the same level it had reached on the eve of the 1929 crash that ended the first long Gilded Age.

Table 6.1 Major areas of legal change and their impact on the bottom, middle, and top of the income distribution in the United States, 1980–2020.

Legal Change	Bottom 10–20%	Middle 80%	Top 10% [Top 1%]
Shrinking social insurance	"Welfare Queen" attack; "War on Poverty" replaced by "War on Drugs" and mass incarceration. Forces workers to accept low-pay, poor terms.	ERISA shift from defined benefit to defined contribution & defeat of universal healthcare: fear of health shocks and old age poverty increase dependence on wage labor; weakens ability to bargain for wages or terms.	Shrinks fiscal burden and enables tax reductions.
Minimum wage erosion	Failure to index to inflation or raise accounts for most of the gap between the 10th and 50th percentiles of women's wages.		
Weak employment law enforcement	Subject to higher wage theft; dangerous work conditions; disruptive scheduling.	Weak enforcement of overtime pay; loose definitions of supervisory roles; fissuring removes stability & puts downward pressure on wages.	Increased opportunities for wage theft for small businesses: grocery stores; security and janitorial services. [Easier adoption of fissured workplace practices; permatemps]
Labor law changes to make unionization harder		PATCO Strike shifts norms; NLRB decisions in the 1980s. Declining unionization largest contributor to wage stagnation in the middle; disparate impact on Black members.	Significant shift in political power across the board on economic issues.
Deregulation of regulated industries		Large impact on unionized male workers who had the power to get a share of rents from regulatory barriers to entry.	Greater freedom to pursue strategies focused on short-term profit.

Weakening antitrust standards and enforcement	Higher markups increased prices consumers had to pay.	Higher markups increased prices consumers had to pay.	Higher markups increased profits.
Trade law: globalization		"China Shock": offshoring causes wage stagnation, persistent localized unemployment & underemployment effects; downward pressure on wages in trade-exposed industries.	Global financial flows feed financialization; disinvestment from labor increases available profits.
Financial deregulation			Financialization: major growth in share of income going to those working in finance; changed executive compensation norms lead to explosion in executive pay.

Legitimating the Great Extraction: Economic Formalism and Legal Fundamentalism

Two fundamentally different kinds of formalism have combined in American legal culture since the 1970s to legitimate the systematic redistribution of power, income, and wealth from the majority of the population to a tiny minority. The first was the law and economics movement, which, in the crucial first two decades of neoliberal transition deployed a simplistic formalization of transactions costs and rational actor theory.[49] The second was the emphasis of the new conservative legal movement on textualism in statutory interpretation and originalism in constitutional interpretation. Both arms of this ideological pincer movement reflect an interaction between agency and structure. For each, it is possible to identify specific individuals and organizations who can be observed in the act of self-consciously developing a way of thinking about law designed to legitimate a reactionary program aligned with the core concerns of each of the three legs of the new Republican coalition: business elites, white identity voters, and Christian fundamentalists. And yet each also drew on broader cultural changes (in the case of law and economics) and deep strains of legal culture (in the case of originalism and textualism), such that it would be a mistake to imagine every practitioner of these two formalisms as actively engaged in a consciously political act. Rather, we can think of identifiable agents consciously engaged in an effort to introduce an ideological intervention designed to achieve a set of instrumental goals. But they can only be considered successful once they have effectively shifted the way in which members of the profession who are not ideological activists think and write law and what they come to experience, as well-socialized members of the profession, as legitimate moves within the profession. In this, law and economics enjoyed an unmitigated success, while originalism and textualism continue to be visibly "activist" and to be understood as politically charged rather than neutral.

Law and Economics

The Chicago-centered law and economics movement was a branch of the broader effort to create an intellectual infrastructure for what would come to be known as neoliberalism.[50] Initially funded by ideologically committed individuals and foundations, neoliberals built organizational capacity through programs within academia and in think tanks that translated the academic work into discrete programmatic elements.[51] One well-studied example was Henry Manne's Law and Economics Center, particularly in the 1970s and early 1980s. Manne's fundraising included direct appeals to companies like ITT or US Steel that had direct interests in loosening antitrust law. Subsequent analysis confirmed that the companies got what they paid for: judges who participated in Manne's Pareto in the Pines program rendered systematically more pro-business verdicts and tended to rule against regulatory and tax agencies more often for decades thereafter.[52] That program was the clearest example of intentional change in legal consciousness: the socialization of a generation of professionals in leadership positions into a new common sense shared by well-socialized professionals about how to approach law that, broadly speaking, structured economic relations. Such a clean relationship between intentional acts of identifiable agents and the transformation of ideological structure are rare, and evidence will rarely be as clean. But it does offer a model for how to think about the relations between the conscious actions of agents and structural shifts that shape the behavior of populations whose members are unconscious of their ideological reorientation.

Efficiency became for law and economics in the 1980s and 1990s what logic had been for Classical Legal Thought a century earlier. Formal economic modeling offered a conception of an apparently scientific platform, just as logic had in the late nineteenth century. It offered a foundation for claiming normative neutrality in support of the array of legal changes that restructured social relations of production—shifting power in favor of finance and the professional and managerial class and weakening the state relative to corporations—and underwrote a dramatic extraction of most of the surplus gained into the hands of the top 1 percent of the income and wealth distributions.

Law and economics met with resistance from both rights liberals, who questioned whether wealth could coherently be considered a value and whether welfare maximization could capture the full normative commitments of law,[53] and from Critical Legal Studies (CLS) scholars, who mounted a broader assault on the internal coherence of law and economics, on its disconnect from the way law functioned in fact, and on the systematically regressive distributive effects to which its prescriptions led.[54] Rights-based resistance to law and economics was overwhelmed when neoliberalism became the common sense of the professional and managerial class across the board, not only in law, and was forced to retreat to focusing on constitutional rights and "public law" rather than economic law.[55] CLS, for its part, was as critical of rights discourse as it was of law and economics, for rights jurisprudence too depended on too essentialist a view of how law worked and of the idea that, if only it were done correctly, law could indeed provide a neutral, apolitical basis of legitimation. This postmodern attack placed CLS in an external stance to legal practice, robbing it of bases for legitimating progressive legal decisions with tools that cohered with the socially internalized practices of a legal profession. The result was that in areas of "private law" that directly structured social relations of production, neither liberals nor the left offered sustained competition to the right. Those who did offer liberal or progressive policy solutions began to frame them in terms of economics in an effort to yoke it to their own projects, from tradable permits in environmental regulation to applications of cost-benefit analysis that justified stricter health or safety standards.

Legal Fundamentalism: Originalism and Textualism

The purpose of the decades-long Republican effort to staff the judiciary with ideological allies was to overturn, narrow, or neutralize decades of progressive precedent and legislation. Doing so required a legal theory that could be publicly presented as neutral and pre-political, while being plausible within the legal profession and providing authority for ignoring or overturning decades of progressive precedent and legislative or regulatory victories. The solution was text-anchored originalism in constitutional interpretation and textualism in statutory interpretation. Both had roots in Protestant textualism and Biblicism, and thus strongly appealed to the base of the party.[56] Both bore a family resemblance to how legal culture had long-treated text and authorial intent, albeit in a new, imperious role as exclusive bases of authority. The result was a theory of judicial interpretation that could play both a public role of legitimating a frontal assault on progressive precedents,[57] and be a plausible response to the anxiety many in the legal profession, including some liberals and progressives, experienced as to the sources of legitimacy for core pillars of the rights revolution—from *Brown v. Board of Education* through *Roe v. Wade*.[58]

Intellectually, Robert Bork's 1971 article *Neutral Principles and Some First Amendment Problems*[59] is arguably the first statement of originalism by a high-status legal academic,[60] but it is Raoul Berger's 1977 *Government by Judiciary*,[61] a more complete and expansive development of originalism, that is seen as "the starting point for modern originalist theory."[62] Politically, it was Edwin Meese who routinized the use of political orientation in judicial nominations, making adherence to originalism and a commitment to overturning *Roe* into litmus tests for Republican judicial appointments. Judicially, it was Antonin Scalia who launched the argument that textualism was the sole legitimate method of statutory interpretation and who would, after the defeat of Bork's Supreme Court nomination, become the leading champion (later joined by Clarence Thomas) of originalism in constitutional interpretation. Originalism was reaction to the "living constitution" and "democratic values" approach that had marked progressive constitutional theory: the idea that the constitution evolved over time and that its core was a rich conception of democratic society that required not only procedural equality and majority rule but also protection of fundamental individual rights and of discrete and insular minorities from majoritarian overreach.[63] Originalism emerged over the course of the 1960s in conservative intellectual debates and was popularized in radio talk shows as a reaction to the Warren Court's desegregation and reapportionment (one person, one vote) cases.[64] Berger devoted two full chapters to making the historical claim that "Negro Suffrage was Excluded" from the intent of the Fourteenth Amendment, and an additional chapter to undermining *Brown*.[65] Textualism was a reaction to the dominant eclecticism of statutory interpretation throughout the twentieth century,[66] which led one prominent judge to comment in the early 1980s that "the 'plain meaning' rule had been laid to rest."[67] In the late 1980s Scalia was the sole voice on the Supreme Court excoriating the ease of manipulation of the meaning of statutes that this eclecticism permitted.[68] As textualism was integrated into the critique of "activist judges" (read: progressive precedents) alongside originalism, and as Meese's routinization of conservative appointments filled the federal bench with ideological allies, what began as one man's crusade became the new norm of the profession.

Progressive responses to legal fundamentalism fell into three major buckets. The first was epistemic critique of the idea that anyone at the end of the twentieth century could claim that text had sufficiently deterministic meaning.[69] Not only is language itself capacious and necessarily available for interpretation but common law interpretive canons are also full of paired opposing moves (such as *inclusio unius* [if the language expressly states one thing, it means to exclude others] paired with *ejusdem generis* [if the language expressly includes one thing, it means to also encompass similar things]).[70] And history is too multifaceted to constrain interpretative freedom. The second response to legal fundamentalism was to get good enough at using this very plasticity to make arguments that led to progressive outcomes.[71] The third was to underscore the political valence of legal fundamentalism.[72] These lines of critique were complemented by the work of progressive constitutional scholars who modernized and updated the older "living constitution" tradition: most prominently Ackerman's theory of constitutional transformations and Kramer's popular constitutionalism,[73] keeping alive an alternative model of constitutional adjudication and, in combination with the critiques, denying legal fundamentalism the hegemonic role that law and economics succeeded in attaining in economic law.

Structure and Legitimation for a Post-neoliberal Order: The Challenge for Law and Political Economy

The neoliberal order appears to be falling apart since the Great Recession. Vying to replace it are a more-or-less authoritarian ethno-nationalism, on the one hand, and an assertive progressivism, aimed partly at rehabilitating the role of the state in the economy and the pursuit of social justice, and partly at elevating nonstate, nonmarket forms of economic, political, and cultural life. As part of this broadly progressive revival, a new movement of law and political economy is emerging within the legal academy to engage in the design and legitimation of a post-neoliberal legal order. While still in early stages, the movement aims to produce both a comprehensive critique of the core claims of law and economics and legal fundamentalism[74] and a comprehensive programmatic framework for a post-neoliberal order.[75]

Combining trenchant critique with detailed programmatic reform was a hallmark of Legal Realism. The tension that CLS identified between these two quite divergent goals presents a theoretical and practical challenge for the new law and political economy.[76] Felix Cohen's solution to this tension continues to be the most instructive for the present generation of academics engaged in law and political economy. Just as a contemporary molecular biologist can read Bruno Latour at night and still go into the lab in the morning and produce a new vaccine that reduces disease burden, so too the Realist lawyer can understand the historical specificity of legal culture, the imperfection of empirical social science, and the socially constructed nature of legitimacy and still go into the office and design a legal arrangement that has a reasonable chance of producing more equitable social relations of production, or of limiting the effects of systemic racism. Moreover, the new law and political economy will need to work inside the legal materials and legal culture and not focus exclusively on external critique, morality, or social science to support reform. One already-successful strategy, used with regard to antitrust or trade secrets, for example, has been to revive lines of cases that were abandoned during the neoliberal era, but that remain available to resuscitate as anchors for distinctively legal arguments.[77]

What does this brief overview of two major transition points in the history of American economy and society teach us about the "ends of law"? First, it is worse than pointless to seek an internal, teleological answer, as though law were an autonomous discipline with its own "ends" or goals. Historically, claims regarding the demands and ends of law *qua* law have always played the role of legitimating the power relations that past law helped forge and entrench. Second, therefore, rather than seeking a normative answer to the question "what should be the ends of law" as though that were an independent question bounded by law as a discipline, we need a clear-eyed view of what the functions of law have been in fact—in the lived experience of modern market societies. It is to sketch out the contours of this basic descriptive task that I have dedicated this chapter, focused specifically on the role of law in structuring and legitimating social relations of production.

Viewed in this light, law lays out the basic rules of engagement in market relations. Property law lays out rules regarding who may, and who may not, use how much of which resources, both material and cognitive, for what purposes. In doing so, it distributes power over the organization of production processes that depend on access to and use of these resources. Labor law, including its iterations as the law of master and servant and enslavement, criminal conspiracy, unfair competition, and antitrust, sets the terms of who may and who may not apply their labor to a given set of resources, doing what tasks, in coordination with what other people or organizations, and under what terms of division of labor. Contract law plays a smaller role in structuring the division of labor, mostly in coordinating among smallholders or larger firms, but most labor is actually governed by these other more systemic sources of law, such as labor, corporate, and unfair competition law. Tort law structures relations with respect to risks, while welfare, pensions, and criminal law structure relations with regard to uncertainty, shocks, and inherited deprivation. All these create the basic rules of the game—who comes into relations of production with which endowment; who has what kinds of alternatives to a negotiated agreement to work on this project, with these people, at this time, making how much of what and getting what out of it.

Beyond structuring society by laying down the rules of engagement, it is equally the role of law in modern market society to legitimate the patterns of life that emerge given the imbalances of power those rules of engagement produce. And recall, by "legitimate" I mean have a given sociological effect at the population level. The function of law, and in particular the legal profession as a semi-autonomous social practice, is to produce statements about "what the law is" that are received by the rest of the population, usually through translation by other parts of the sense-making elites in society, as socially appropriate statements that justify, as well as declare, what the relations ought to be. At a bare minimum, a socially appropriate legal decision conveys to everyone, including the losers, that the decision ought to be obeyed peacefully. It is precisely because law not only structures but also legitimates the social relations that emerge from victories in battles to shape the law that these battles played such a prominent role in both the first and second gilded ages.

And so too, we must join battle today. Entrenchment of the McConnell Court has concluded the decades-long takeover of the American judiciary by a politically committed cadre of right-wing operatives. It has begun to roll out decisions that weaken labor, undermine the voting rights of non-white voters, and contain the power of the government to deal with public health emergencies, the climate challenge, or corporate power, and it stands on the cusp of expanding the power of religion to suppress individual autonomy and contain democratic majorities. On the background of these facts, the most important task for legal scholarship in the coming generation is to analyze the reality of how law, in practice, shapes power, productivity, and inequality in society, and to translate that analysis into concrete programmatic approaches that could make for a more democratic, egalitarian society even in the teeth of a judiciary hostile to both democracy and justice.

Notes

1. Laura Kalman, *Abe Fortas: A Biography* (New Haven: Yale University Press, 1990).
2. James F. Simon, *Independent Journey: The Life of William O. Douglas* (New York: Harper & Row, 1980).
3. Morton J. Horwitz, "Foreword: The Constitution of Change: Legal Fundamentality without Fundamentalism," 107 *Harv. Law Rev.* 30–117 (1993).
4. *Brnovich v. Democratic National Committee*, 594 US __ (2021).
5. *Cedar Point Nursery v. Hassid*, 594 US __ (2021), slip op at 7. For a detailed critique, see Benkler, Structure and Legitimation Part I; Sachs, Supreme Court Review.

6. The basic frame of these four systems of social relations is codeveloped in a long correspondence and exchanges with Talha Syed.
7. Roberto Mangeberia Unger, *Law in Modern Society: Towards a Criticism of Social Theory* (New York: Free Press, 1976); H. L. A. Hart, *The Concept of Law* (Oxford: Oxford University Press, 1961).
8. Jedediah Britton-Purdy et al., "Building a Law-and-Political-Economy Framework: Beyond the Twentieth-Century Synthesis," *Yale Law Journal* 129, no. 6 (April 2020): 1784–835.
9. See Chuck Collins et al., *Ten Solutions to Bridge the Racial Wealth Divide* (2019); Naomi Zewde et al., *A Guaranteed Income for the 21st Century* (2021).
10. Claudia Goldin and Kenneth Sokoloff, *Women, Children, and Industrialization in the Early Republic: Evidence from the Manufacturing Censuses* (1981); Barbara M. Wertheimer, *We Were There: The Story of Working Women in America* (New York: Pantheon Books, 1977); William Lazonick, "Industrial Relations and Technical Change: The Case of the Self-Acting Mule," *Cambridge Journal of Economics* 3, no. 3 (September 1979): 231–62. Ivy Pinchbeck, *Women Workers in the Industrial Revolution* (London: Routledge, 2004).
11. Alfred D. Chandler, *The Visible Hand: The Managerial Revolution in American Business* (Cambridge, MA: Belknap Press, 1977); James Ralph Beniger, *The Control Revolution: Technological and Economic Origins of the Information Society* (Cambridge, MA: Harvard University Press, 1989); Morton J. Horwitz, *The Transformation of American Law, 1870–1960: The Crisis of Legal Orthodoxy* (Oxford: Oxford University Press, 1992); Chris Freeman & Francisco Louçã, *As Time Goes by: From the Industrial Revolutions to the Information Revolution* (Oxford: Oxford University Press, 2001).
12. Horwitz, 72–9.
13. Chandler, 7; Beniger, 7.
14. Horwitz, 83–4.
15. *United States v. E. C. Knight Co.*, 156 US 1 (1895).
16. John Fabian Witt, *The Accidental Republic: Crippled Workingmen, Destitute Widows, and the Remaking of American Law* (Cambridge, MA: Harvard University Press, 2004), 24–8.
17. Witt, 30–1.
18. Horwitz, 56–60.
19. William E. Forbath, *Law and the Shaping of the American Labor Movement* (Cambridge, MA: Harvard University Press, 1991).
20. William E. Forbath, "The Shaping of the American Labor Movement," *Harvard Law Review* 102, no. 6 (April 1989): 1109–256.
21. Forbath, "The Shaping of the American Labor Movement," 1151.
22. Forbath, 1158–9.
23. 158 US 564 (1895).
24. Eric Foner, *Reconstruction: America's Unfinished Revolution, 1863–1877* (New York: Harper Perennial Modern Classics, 2002); Mark Stelzner, "The Labor Injunction and Peonage—How Changes in Labor Laws Increased Inequality during the Gilded Age," *Journal of Post Keynesian Economics* 42, no. 1 (2019): 114–43; W. E. B. Du Bois, *Black Reconstruction: An Essay toward a History of the Part which Black Folk Played in the Attempt to Reconstruct Democracy in America, 1860–1880* (New York: Harcourt, Brace and Company, 1935); Brian Sawers, "Race and Property after the Civil War: Creating the Right to Exclude," *Mississippi Law Journal* 87, no. 5 (2018): 703–64; Michelle Alexander, *The New Jim Crow: Mass Incarceration in the Age of Colorblindness* (New York: The New Press, 2010).

25. Lawrence Goodwyn, *The Populist Moment: A Short History of the Agrarian Revolt in America* (Oxford: Oxford University Press, 1978), 50–4; Harold D. Woodman, "Post-Civil War Southern Agriculture and the Law," *Agricultural History* 53, no. 1 (January 1979): 319–37; Roger L. Ransom and Richard Sutch, "Debt Peonage in the Cotton South after the Civil War," *The Journal of Economic History* 32, no. 3 (September 1972): 641–69.
26. Sawers, 741–63.
27. Stelzner, 126–9.
28. 98 N.Y. 98 (1885).
29. Forbath, 1132–45.
30. Duncan Kennedy, *The Rise & Fall of Classical Legal Thought: With a New Preface by the Author "Thirty Years Later"* (Washington, DC: Beard Books, 2010); Horwitz, 7; Robert W. Gordon, "Critical Legal Histories," *Stanford Law Review* 36 (1984): 57–125; Thomas Grey, "Langdell's Orthodoxy," *University of Pittsburgh Law Review* 45, no 1. (1983): 1–53.
31. Toledo A.A. & N.M. Ry. v. Pennsylvania Co., 54 F. 730, 739 (C.C.N.D. Ohio 1893), cited *id.* at 1158.
32. Forbath, 1161 n.223.
33. Ibid.
34. Ibid., 1169.
35. Lochner v. New York, 198 US 45, 75 (1905).
36. Horwitz; Barbara Fried, *The Progressive Assault on Laissez Faire: Robert Hale and the First Law and Economics Movement* (Cambridge, MA: Harvard University Press, 1998); William W. Fisher, Morton J. Horwitz, and Thomas Reed, eds., *American Legal Realism* (Oxford: Oxford University Press, 1993).
37. Wesley Newcomb Hohfeld, "Fundamental Legal Conceptions as Applied in Judicial Reasoning," *Yale Law Journal* 26 (1917): 710; Anna di Robilant and Talha Syed, *Property's Building Blocks: Hohfeld in Europe and Beyond* (2018).
38. Robert L. Hale, "Coercion and Distribution in a Supposedly Non-Coercive State," *Political Science Quarterly* 38, no. 3 (September 1923): 470–94; Morris Cohen, "Property and Sovereignty," *Cornell Law Review* 13, no. 1 (December 1927): 8–30.
39. Felix Cohen, "Transcendental Nonsense and the Functional Approach," *Columbia Law Review* 35, no. 6 (June 1935): 809–49.
40. Ira Katznelson, *When Affirmative Action Was White: An Untold History of Racial Inequality in Twentieth-Century America* (New York: W. W. Norton & Company, 2005); Ira Katznelson, *Fear Itself: The New Deal and the Origins of Our Time* (New York: Liveright, 2013); Richard Rothstein, *The Color of Law: A Forgotten History of How Our Government Segregated America* (New York: Liveright, 2017); Maria Cristina Santana, "From Empowerment to Domesticity: The Case of Rosie the Riveter and the WWII Campaign," *Frontiers in Sociology* 1 (December 2016); Benjamin Kline Hunnicutt, *Kellogg's Six-Hour Day* (Philadelphia: Temple University Press, 1996).
41. Virginia Eubanks, *Automating Inequality: How High-Tech Tools Profile, Police and Punish the Poor* (New York: St. Martin's Press, 2017), 28–9.
42. Elizabeth Kai Hinton, *From the War on Poverty to the War on Crime: The Making of Mass Incarceration in America* (Cambridge, MA: Harvard University Press, 2016).
43. Lawrence Mishel, John Schmitt, and Heidi Shierholz, "Wage Inequality: A Story of Policy Choices," *New Labor Forum* 23, no. 3 (2014): 26–31; David Weil, "Enforcing Labour Standards in Fissured Workplaces: The US Experience," *The Economic and Labour Relations Review* 22, no. 2 (July 2011): 33–54.

44. Richard B. Freeman, "Unionism and the Dispersion of Wages," *Industrial and Labor Relations Review* 34, no. 1 (October 1980): 3–23; David Card, "The Effect of Unions on the Structure of Wages: A Longitudinal Analysis," *Econometrica* 64, no. 4 (February 1996): 957–79; David Card, Thomas Lemieux, and W. Craig Riddell, "Unions and Wage Inequality," *Journal of Labor Research* 25 (2004): 519–59; Mishel, Schmitt, and Shierholz.

45. Jacob S. Hacker and Paul Pierson, *Winner-take-all Politics: How Washington Made the Rich Richer and Turned Its Back on the Middle Class* (New York: Simon and Schuster, 2010).

46. Steven K. Vogel, "The Regulatory Roots of Inequality in America," *Journal of Law and Political Economy* 1, no. 2 (2021): 272, 287.

47. Bruce Western, "A Comparative Study of Working-Class Disorganization: Union Decline in Eighteen Advanced Capitalist Countries," *American Sociological Review* 60, no. 2 (April 1995), 186; Vogel, *Regulatory Roots*, 287; Terry A. Bethel, "Recent Decisions of the NLRB-The Reagan Influence," *Indiana Law Journal* 60, no. 2 (1985), 61.

48. Western, *Comparative Study*.

49. Suresh Naidu & Eliott Ash, *"As if the Last 30 Years Never Happened": Towards a New Law and Economics, Part 1, LPE Blog* (2018).

50. Daniel Stedman Jones, *Masters of the Universe: Hayek, Friedman, and the Birth of Neoliberal Politics*, updated ed. (Princeton: Princeton University Press, 2014).

51. Steven Michael Teles, *The Rise of the Conservative Legal Movement: The Battle for Control of the Law* (Princeton: Princeton University Press, 2008).

52. Eliott Ash, Daniel Chen, and Soureash Naidu, "Ideas Have Consequences: The Impact of Law and Economics on American Justice," *NBER* (February 2022).

53. Ronald Dworkin, "Is Wealth a Value?," *The Journal of Legal Studies* 9, no. 2 (March 1980): 191–226; Ronald Dworkin, "Why Efficiency?—A Response to Professors Calabresi and Posner," *Hofstra Law Review* 8, no. 3 (1980): 563–90.

54. Duncan Kennedy, "Law-and-Economics from the Perspective of Critical Legal Studies," in *The New Palgrave Dictionary of Economics and the Law*, ed. Peter Newman (London: Palgrave Macmillan, 2002), 1123–32.

55. Britton-Purdy et al.

56. Horwitz.

57. Robert Post and Reva Siegel, "Originalism as a Political Practice: The Right's Living Constitution," *Fordham Law Review* 75, no. 2 (2006): 545–74; Jamal Greene, "Selling Originalism," *Georgetown Law Journal* 97 (2009): 657–721.

58. Johnathan O'Neil, *Originalism in American Law: A Constitutional History* (Baltimore: Johns Hopkins University Press, 2005).

59. Robert H. Bork, "Neutral Principles and Some First Amendment Problems," *Indiana Law Journal* 47, no. 1 (Fall 1971), 1.

60. Randy E. Barnett and Evan Bernick, "The Letter and the Spirit: A Unified Theory of Originalism," *Georgetown Law Journal* 107, no. 1 (October 2018): 1–55 (2018); Logan E. Sawyer, "Principle and Politics in the New History of Originalism," *American Journal of Legal History* 57 (2017): 198–222.

61. Raoul Berger, *Government by Judiciary: The Transformation of the Fourteenth Amendment*, 2nd ed., (Cambridge, MA: Harvard University Press, 1997).

62. Logan E. Sawyer, *Principle and Politics in the New History of Originalism, 57 Am. J. Leg. Hist.* 198–222, 206 (2017).

63. Horwitz, 51–65.

64. Calvin Terbeek, "'Clocks Must Always Be Turned Back': *Brown v. Board of Education* and the Racial Origins of Constitutional Originalism," *American Political Science Review* 115, no. 3 (August 2021): 821–34.

65. Berger, 70–115, 132–54.

66. Nicholas Zeppos, "The Use of Authority in Statutory Interpretation: An Empirical Analysis," *Texas Law Review* 70 (1992): 1073.

67. Patricia Wald, "Some Observations on the Use of Legislative History in the 1981 Supreme Court Term," *Iowa Law Review* 68 (1983), 195.

68. Nicholas Zeppos, "Justice Scalia's Textualism: The 'New' New Legal Process," *Cardozo Law Review* 12 (1991), 1597"; William Eskridge, "The New Textualism," *UCLA Law Review* 37 (1990), 621.

69. Paul Brest, "The Misconceived Quest for the Original Understanding," *Boston University Law Review* 60 (1980), 204; Larry Alexander and Saikrishna Prakash, "'Is That English You're Speaking?' Why Intention Free Interpretation Is an Impossibility," *San Diego Law Review* 41, no. 3 (2004), 967; Stanley Fish, "There Is No Textualist Position," *San Diego Law Review* 42, no. 2 (2005), 629.

70. Karl N. Llewellyn, *The Bramble Bush: The Classic Lectures on the Law and Law School* (Oxford: Oxford University Press, 2008).

71. Akhil Reed Amar, *The Bill of Rights: Creation and Reconstruction* (New Haven: Yale University Press, 1998); Jack M. Balkin, *Living Originalism* (Cambridge, MA: Belknap Press, 2011).

72. Post and Siegel; Greene.

73. Bruce Ackerman, *We the People, Volume 2 Transformations* (Cambridge, MA: Belknap Press, 1998); Larry D. Kramer, *The People Themselves: Popular Constitutionalism and Judicial Review* (Oxford: Oxford University Press, 2004).

74. Britton-Purdy et al.; Jedediah Britton-Purdy, Amy Kapczynski, and David Singh Grewal, *Law and Political Economy: Toward a Manifesto, Law and Political Economy* (2017). Martha McCluskey, Frank Pasquale, and Jennifer Taub, *Toward Law and Political Economy: Transforming Unequal Power through Heterodox Theory*, Panel description, Law and Society Association Annual Meeting, 2013.

75. Ganesh Sitaraman and Anne L. Alstott, *The Public Option: How to Expand Freedom, Increase Opportunity, and Promote Equality* (Cambridge, MA: Harvard University Press, 2019); Chuck Collins et al.; Sharon Block and Benjamin Sachs, *Clean Slate for Worker Power: Building a Just Economy and Democracy* (2020).

76. Talha Syed, "Legal Realism and CLS from an LPE Perspective," paper presented at the Law and Political Economy Workshop at Harvard Law School, February 24, 2022.

77. Lina M. Khan, "The Separation of Platforms and Commerce," *Columbia Law Review* 119, no. 4 (2019): 973–1093; Amy Kapzcynski, "The Public History of Trade Secrets," *UC Davis Law Review* 55 (Feb. 2022), 1367.

CHAPTER 7
THE ENDS OF JOURNALISM
Jolene Almendarez

The book and film versions of *All the President's Men* are required reading and viewing for every journalist. By the end of college, blossoming reporters have seen it on repeat and glamorized the sound of clacking typewriters and bustling newsrooms. If *Washington Post* reporters Bob Woodward and Carl Bernstein could help bring the president of the United States to justice, surely a local reporter can make a difference when it comes to potholes, school boards, and bike lanes.

Believe it or not, Hollywood doesn't reflect reality when it comes to newsrooms.

A modern newsroom sounds a lot more like tapping laptop keys and dings from Slack messages. Working in a bustling newsroom and spending weeks (or years!) writing stories and cultivating sources are features of the past, for many.

The news industry has lost 30,000 jobs since 2008, a drop of about 16 percent, according to the Pew Research Center.[1] Newspapers bore the brunt of that loss, dropping from 74,414 in 2006 to 30,820 workers in 2020. But radio and cable television news outlets also experienced losses. The only medium that saw any growth during the period, the research center says, are "digital-native" sites—news organizations that began online. But although digital-native sites enjoyed 144 percent growth over the same twelve-year period, they still employed about 13,000 fewer people than newspapers did in 2020.

The number of journalists in newsrooms, regardless of medium, remains bleak.

The causes of these dips are varied, but can best be categorized by three areas: funding, the journalism industry's failure to reflect on its shortcomings, and the growing distrust of news organizations, especially legacy organizations.

Online Advertising Just One Peril

It's difficult to know exactly how much money the journalism industry has lost as a result of online advertising diverting revenue to mammoths like Google, Facebook, and other tech giants. But here's some data that helps illustrate the problem:

- According to the Pew Research Center, estimated advertising revenue from publicly traded newspaper companies was $8.8 billion in 2020. That's down about 29 percent from the year before. Estimated advertising revenue in 2005, the highest year on record, was about $49,435,000,000.[2]
- About 1800 newspapers have shut down since 2004—roughly 100 per year.[3]

The Ends of Knowledge

- *The New York Times* reports an estimated 37,000 employees at news organizations in the United States were laid off, were furloughed, or had pay reductions within the first few months of the pandemic.[4]

Some news organizations, as a result of yearslong plummeting income, clung to the most immediate fix they could find to their online advertising problems: they began requiring most reporters to write for the clicks. In 2018, NewsGuild International Chairperson Martha Waggoner noted that The NewsGuild—CWA interviewed reporters about page view goals. She wrote:

> They complain of goals that are too high and require too many stories, given the severely reduced size of newsroom staffs. And they say the goals hinder quality journalism because reporters focus on stories that will get a lot of hits, such as one with a tangential connection to a celebrity or one that includes photos of pets. In the meantime, reporters say they're abandoning or being told to abandon beats that don't come with a deep readership, such as prisons or certain neighborhoods.

Waggoner goes on to interview Ken Doctor, a media analyst for "Newsonomics," who points out metrics aren't necessarily an inherent evil.[5]

Doctor says there are some organizations, like *The Washington Post* and *The New York Times*, which use metrics to better understand how readers (especially subscribers) engage with content. That goes beyond considering how many clicks a story gets and may, for example, consider how much of a story readers make it through. That more nuanced look at metrics might be a better way for organizations to spend their time and money. Waggoner wrote, quoting Doctor:

> Let's say there's a tangential local angle to a story about a Kardashian. It likely will get lots of page views. But it's less likely that subscribers will read it, while "a local story of some meaning might have a significant readership among paying subscribers … That's more important."[6]

Despite this more insightful approach to online metrics, these changes—advertising and click-driven reporting—make an impact on the viability and quality of journalism. But focusing the decline of an entire industry on online advertising sidesteps journalism's history of racism, sexism, classism, and a variety of other "-isms" that aren't in the past.

Not the Legacy News Organizations Planned On

The inequity often perpetuated by legacy news organizations—even those with the best intentions—can be seen among staff and in organizations' coverage. The American Society of News Editors reports that people of color comprised 21.9 percent of the salaried workforce in newsrooms in 2019.[7] Meanwhile, the 2020 census shows people of color make up 43 percent of the total US population. Women were represented at a rate of 41.8 percent in newsrooms the same year, although the 2020 census shows they slightly outnumber men in the country.[7]

Parsing the numbers behind newsroom staffing is not an exercise in wokeness led by social justice warriors. Experts agree that diversity of people in the newsroom results in diversity of people in the news. Laura Morgan Roberts, an organizational psychologist at the University of Virginia, told the Nieman Lab that a lack of diversity in newsrooms directly correlates to incomplete or inaccurate news reporting. She has studied people of color in journalism and said:

> News stories "can be incomplete or compromised by blind spots, or at worst, can perpetuate negative stereotypes about various communities, especially people of color." This can lead to everything from selecting stories that only reflect narrow swaths of a community to having limited perspectives in reporting.[8]

Data on the diversity of sources in newsrooms matches the same kind of inequity seen among staffing at news organizations.

National Public Radio, for example, has kept track of source diversity since 2013, when 28 percent of expert sources were women and 16 percent were people of color (I work for the Cincinnati regional NPR affiliate, WVXU).[9] Recently, the organization has focused on improving those numbers so NPR can "look and sound like America."[9] This conscious effort has made a difference. In 2019, women made up close to 40 percent of all sources, and people of color made up 25 to 30 percent of expert sources. Regardless of the bump, the organization continues striving to improve those numbers. For instance, this year NPR developed a method for tracking diverse sources in real time. Chief Diversity Officer Keith Woods says the system is called "Dex," inspired by the word "rolodex." Woods told Poynter, "We were doing annual surveys before and by the time newsrooms learned about the numbers, it was a full year in the past. Now, by the end of the week, you can know how you're doing."[9] He said this system enables journalists to change their habits and be more mindful of whom they are interviewing.

The legacy journalism industry, however, repeatedly fails to reform itself. That may explain the emergence of organizations that, for lack of better phrasing, are fueled by people done with upholding the status quo.

Nonprofit Journalism: More than a Business Model

As legacy news organizations reap the consequences of their own actions (or inactions), the success of nonprofit newsrooms is on the rise. Historically held together with grants and duct tape, nonprofit newsrooms are seeing more support from their communities and individual donors. They have become a lot less of a trope, experts say. The Knight Foundation reports 2020 was the "year of nonprofit journalism."[10] It reports that membership of the Institute for Nonprofit News rose by more than 25 percent, comprising a total of more than 300 nonprofit news organizations.

Nonprofit newsrooms also report employing higher rates of people of color than for-profit organizations. According to INN's 2020 report "Diversity, Equity, and Inclusion in Nonprofit News," people of color comprise 28 percent of nonprofit news staff.[11] Women make up half of nonprofit news executives and 60 percent of employees. A New Leaders Association survey in 2019 showed that women account for four out of ten executives and staff members in other newsrooms.

While the report shows greater diversity in nonprofit newsrooms, the numbers are not at parity with the prominence of people of color in the national workforce, where they account for 40 percent of workers, according to the US Bureau of Labor Statistics.[11] Despite the glimmer of hope that at least some news organizations are self-correcting, all news organizations have a long way to go before they are more trusted by the public.

"Fake News" Not a Trump Invention, but It Exploded after the Election

Journalists and social media giants began recognizing the phrase "fake news" long before former US president Donald Trump claims to have coined it.

Former *Washington Post* reporter Callum Borchers outlines the history of the phrase in a 2017 article, where he points out news organizations consistently reported about the dangers of misinformation and hoaxes online in the months leading up to the 2016 election.[12] Meta chief executive Mark Zuckerberg acknowledged the spread of "a very small amount of fake news and hoaxes" on the site two days after the election.[13]

But, as it turns out, there's far more than "a very small amount" of misinformation on social media sites. Since 2016, social media and online giants, including Google, have faced scrutiny from lawmakers for failing to prevent the spread of misinformation on their platforms. For instance, The House Energy and Commerce Committee grilled Facebook, Twitter, and Google CEOs about their roles in the spread of dangerous fake news during the attack on the US Capitol by a pro-Trump mob on January 6, 2021.[14] Fake news has also been linked to the spread of misinformation regarding Covid-19 and vaccines. The World Health Organization describes the spread of the Covid-19 pandemic as being accompanied by a "massive infodemic."[15]

Perhaps most significantly, Russia used fake news to influence the 2016 presidential election. Experts say Russian cyber operatives exploited already existing divides in the country and took the opportunity to sow discord, often via Facebook. This eventually favored former president Trump, who "fanned the flames" of misinformation.[16] Borchers says Trump didn't tweet the phrase "fake news" for the first time until after his election, on December 10, 2016.[12] CNN received the honor of being the first news organization officially dubbed as fake by the president after reporting rumors the former reality TV star would continue as executive producer for "The Apprentice" throughout his presidency. (The organization inaccurately reported he would continue being paid for the show and issued a correction afterward.)[17]

Regardless of who takes credit for the phrase, its popularity skyrocketed after Trump was elected president. It was dubbed "Word of the Year" by the *Collins English Dictionary* in 2017. The organization reported use of the word increased 365 percent over the previous year, citing its monitoring of the phrase through media.[18]

The spread of fake and hoax news has accompanied some of the lowest recorded numbers of the public's trust in the media. A fall 2021 Gallup poll shows the second-lowest rates of public trust in media since 2016.[19] The organization says 36 percent of US adults have "a great deal" or "a fair amount" of trust and confidence in newspapers, television, and radio news reporting. A total of 63 percent of US adults say their trust in news reporting is "not very much" or "none at all." The organization says that 2016, during the divisive presidential election, clocked in lower rates of trust with only 32 percent of US adults saying they have "a great deal" or "a fair amount" of trust and confidence, in a poll of 20,000 people.[20] But despite the sweeping distrust of the media, 81 percent of those surveyed said the news media is "critical" or "very important" to democracy.[20] Gallup has kept track of public trust in institutions since 1972, a time when 68 to 72 percent of people expressed trust in the media.

A 2021 report published in the Proceedings of the National Academy of Sciences links partisan news sites to fueling recent distrust.[21] The study required participants to change their homepages to either a left- or right-leaning news organization. Then, researchers collected data about people's online habits and Twitter posts. Study coauthor Andy Guess, assistant professor of politics and public affairs at the Princeton School of Public and International Affairs, said:

> Past studies have shown links between exposure to partisan news and polarization, but the driver behind this has been up for debate ... Our work adds a piece to this puzzle, showing that it's difficult for people to be persuaded by competing media outlets during an election campaign. That said, longer time spent on these sites does lead to a growing distrust in the news.[22]

The Vultures Circle

As some newsrooms face economic problems and fail to capture the needs of audiences ripe for the picking, a primate vulture hedge fund is making its rounds.

Alden Global Capital owns the second largest number of daily newspapers in the country "through its majority ownership of MNG Enterprises, known commonly as Digital First Media," *Axios* reported last year.[23]

The company is not known by those in journalism as a friend to the Fourth Estate. *The Atlantic* reported a lengthy, scathing article about the company's acquisition of more than 200 daily newspapers in 2021. McKay Coppins described the company's broad get-rich-quick plan as follows:

The model is simple: Gut the staff, sell the real estate, jack up subscription prices, and wring as much cash as possible out of the enterprise until eventually enough readers cancel their subscriptions that the paper folds, or is reduced to a desiccated husk of its former self.[24]

Coppins says the model is not meant to create long-term sustaining newspaper businesses—a move that would take time and is fraught with the possibility of no financial return. It is based on having a return on investment, bottom line. Matt DeRienzo, former publisher for Alden's Connecticut newspapers, told *The Atlantic*, "It was clear that they didn't care about this being a business in the future. It was all about the next quarter's profit margins."[25]

Alden's CEO Randall Smith declined Coppins's request for comment, and his last interview with a newspaper was in the 1980s, *The Atlantic* reports.[24] Alden President Heath Freeman said in an interview to the magazine that Alden was making the "tough but appropriate decisions to get these news organizations to sustainability."[26]

Alden Global Capital is the best known hedge fund buying up newspapers or stakes in newspapers. But it is one of many.

Penelope Muse Abernathy, who was the Knight Chair in Journalism and Digital Media Economics at the Center for Innovation and Sustainability in Local Media at the University of North Carolina at Chapel Hill from 2008 to 2020, researched the creation of news deserts and consolidation of media companies, among other topics. Her book *News Deserts and Ghost Newspapers: Will Local News Survive?* says consolidation of news organizations with financial backing from private equity firms and hedge funds "form[s] mega-chains with hundreds of newspapers, and management focused on shareholder return over journalism's civic duty."[27]

Abernathy says twentieth-century media barons have been replaced by hedge funds, private equity firms, and other investment entities, which run newspaper companies like any other industry. That means cost-cutting measures that include layoffs, wage freezes, and reduced benefits. The saved money goes toward loans, management, fees, and shareholders. The issue continues to exacerbate, according to her data. She writes:

> At the end of 2004, the largest 25 chains (as measured by number of papers, not circulation) owned only a fifth of the 8,900 papers and less than a third of the 1,472 dailies. Fifteen years later, the 25 largest chains own a third of the 6,700 surviving newspapers in the country and 70 percent of the 1,260 dailies. While the biggest 25 chains own 2,156 papers, including 863 dailies, the next largest group—26 through 50—owns only 445 newspapers and 54 dailies.[28]

Whether hedge funds and others will continue this trend is in question after Covid-19, when the price of stock in newspapers plummeted, Abernathy writes. But the impact of the massive newspaper chains and business practices lingers and "pose new and difficult societal and economic issues."[29]

It's About Damn Time

The challenges news organizations, whether nonprofit or otherwise, face are mountainous: funding, increasing diversity on multiple fronts, and public trust are not easy to come by. When I was the managing editor at *The Ithaca Voice*, a nonprofit news organization started in New York in 2014, I contended with all of those issues. It was seemingly impossible at times.

There were instances when I temporarily took only half my paycheck so that employees could get paid. Reporters, myself included, tried to break the cycle of day-to-day coverage with a barebones staff and hardly any diversity to brag about. And while the organization was well read, it wasn't necessarily always well loved by the community.

But I used to say that *The Ithaca Voice* is like Batman—it's a symbol. It will never die. That's the truth for the entirety of the journalism industry because the desire to know, to question, and to seek justice cannot be extinguished. But to thrive, the industry will have to adapt.

Abernathy mentions some of those adaptations in *News Deserts and Ghost Newspapers*. They may include reanalyzing the journalistic mission of new organizations to include more diverse communities; sampling new business models to generate funds from various sources; collaborating with tech companies to harness the potential of digital technology; and "rethinking of policies and regulations at the national, state and local levels."[30]

Some news organizations are already rising to the occasion, but as is evident by various data points, not all will. In that case, I say, let the stragglers atrophy and die. It's the only way forward for the industry and, frankly, it's about damn time.

Notes

1. Mason Walker, "U.S. Newsroom Employment Has Fallen 26% since 2008," *Pew Research Center*, July 13, 2021.
2. "Newspapers Fact Sheet," *Pew Research Center*, June 9, 2021.
3. Brad Adgate, "Newspapers Have Been Struggling and Then Came the Pandemic," *Forbes*, August 20, 2021.
4. Marc Tracy, "News Media Outlets Have Been Ravaged by the Pandemic," *The New York Times*, September 21, 2021.
5. Martha Waggoner, "Click Goals: For Journalists, the Pressure Is Always There. But Are They Improving Reporting?" *The News Guild*, January 16, 2018.
6. Ibid.
7. "ASNE Newsroom Employment Diversity Survey," News Leaders Association, 2018.
8. Nicole A. Childers, "The Moral Argument for Diversity in Newsrooms Is Also a Business Argument—and You Need Both,'" *Nieman Lab*, November 24, 2020.
9. Angela Fu, "New Tool Allows NPR to Track Source Diversity in Real Time," *Poynter*, August 12, 2021.

The Ends of Knowledge

10. Mark Glaser, "5 Reasons That 2020 Was the Year of Nonprofit Local News," *Knight Foundation*, December 10, 2020.
11. Michele McLellan and Jesse Holcomb, "Diversity, Equity, and Inclusion in Nonprofit News," *Institute for Nonprofit News*, 2021.
12. Callum Borchers, "Trump Falsely Claims (Again) That He Coined the Term 'Fake News,'" *The Washington Post*, October 26, 2017.
13. www.facebook.com/zuck/posts/10103253901916271?pnref=story. Accessed October 25, 2021.
14. Shannon Bond, "Facebook, Twitter, Google CEOs Testify before Congress: 4 Things To Know," *National Public Radio*, March 25, 2021.
15. Nic Fleming, "Coronavirus Misinformation, and How Scientists Can Help to Fight It," *Nature*, June 17, 2020.
16. Patrice Taddonio, "How Russian 'Fake News' Hardened America's Divide," *Frontline*, January 14, 2020.
17. Dylan Byers, "Donald Trump Will Remain EP on 'Celebrity Apprentice,'" *CNN*, December 8, 2016.
18. Summer Meza, "'Fake News' Named Word of the Year," *Newsweek*, November 2, 2017.
19. Megan Brenan, "Americans' Trust in Media Dips to Second Lowest on Record," *Gallup*, October 7, 2021.
20. John Sands, "Americans Are Losing Faith in an Objective Media. A New Gallup/Knight Study Explores Why," *Knight Foundation*, August 4, 2020.
21. Rose B. Huber, "Consuming Online Partisan News Leads to Distrust in the Media," *Princeton University*, March 29, 2021.
22. Ibid.
23. Margaret Harding McGill and Sara Fischer, "Notorious Hedge Fund Sparks Panic About Death of Local News," *Axios*, November 23, 2021.
24. McKay Coppins, "A Secretive Hedge Fund Is Gutting Newsrooms," *The Atlantic*, October 14, 2021.
25. Ibid.
26. Ibid.
27. Penelope Muse Abernathy, *News Deserts and Ghost Newspapers: Will Local News Survive?* (Chapel Hill, NC: University Of North Carolina Press, 2020), 8.
28. Abernathy, *News Deserts and Ghost Newspapers*, 34.
29. Ibid., 33.
30. Ibid., 55.

CHAPTER 8
THE ENDS OF PEDAGOGY
Sean Michael Morris

I sat awhile in perfect silence, rallying my stunned faculties. Immediately it occurred to me that my ears had deceived me, or Bartleby had entirely misunderstood my meaning. I repeated my request in the clearest tone I could assume; but in quite as clear a one came the previous reply, "I would prefer not to."

—Herman Melville, *Bartleby, The Scrivener*

Changing School

I have always loved Bartleby. Herman Melville's inscrutable character—whose stubbornness can feel at once like an act of resistance and a surrender to existential angst—has always represented to me the human capacity for agency, for doing what is right or what is necessary in the face of a seemingly immoveable reality. To that immoveable reality, Bartleby reacts with his own motionlessness, his "I would prefer not to," which—whether evidence of dogged conviction or implacable stupefaction—situates him as himself within and with the world. Regardless of what we might feel about Bartleby's refusal to do his work, we cannot deny that we know him better for the articulation of his preference, or his preference not to.

I was a seventh-grade Bartleby. Not so much in that I refused to do work I was assigned in class, but more that I refused to go to class in the first place. I was thirteen and newly a child of divorce; I was also nascently gay and confused about the forces shaping my identity. On the one hand were my parents fighting for the favor of me and my brothers; on the other was a new school with new teachers and new routines (and lockers! and passing period!) placing new demands on my mind and self-esteem. Like my peers, I was an elementary school student thrust into an institution with unspoken expectations: that I shed my recess and play and imagination and instead confine myself to seven classes each day, a construct unlike any I had ever encountered. The unforgiving landscape of middle school did nothing to nurture self-reflection, and the teachers, overwhelmed by their classes and dozens of students, had no time to notice an adolescent silently struggling to understand his place in a dramatically changed world.

Middle school is a blindingly difficult time, and one to which education has yet to understand the best way to respond.

The Ends of Knowledge

So, I refused. I preferred not to. And day after day, no sooner had my mother dropped me at the school's door than I was on my way out the other door, sometimes to spend the entire day wandering the city, passing time and trying not to be seen. A truant thirteen-year-old boy.

It goes without saying that my grades suffered. It goes without saying that my young academic life, or potential for such a life, hung in the balance. And perhaps it goes without saying that my truancy caught the attention of the vice principal—a precise picture of authority and seniority in a starched blouse, perfect gray suit, eyebrows carefully painted on with just enough of an arch to be taken seriously: Lois English. Or Ms. English to pretty much everyone.

Ms. English found me out and called me and my mother into her office for a talk.

It is necessary to pause the story here to address the point of this chapter: the end of pedagogy. What happened in Lois English's office was pedagogical, and it allowed me, unexpectedly, not just to succeed in school but also to grasp the end of pedagogy through an articulation of myself. I was still a seventh-grade Bartleby, but one whose vocalization of his preference found purchase and meaning.

That is the end of pedagogy (as distinct from capital-P Pedagogy, as I explain below); its terminal point, where all pedagogical efforts conclude or find conclusion: an articulation that situates a person as themselves within and with the world. How I came to this articulation that day in the vice principal's office was sudden, like an unlikely crossing from one rugged reality into another more opportune. But how we come to the end of pedagogy, in the way that Lois English must have, is less abrupt—less a bolt of inspiration and more a work of logic. This pedagogy—which is also critical pedagogy—is an "if this, then what else?" pedagogy. The end of pedagogy follows logically from a premise. When one truth is accepted, the end comes naturally into sight. That premise, though, might require a crossing of the mind similar to the one that was opened to me that day.

Lois English did not offer any punishment for my truancy. Instead, she asked me questions. What makes you leave school? What is difficult for you? What do you like that would help you stay? Where do you go when you leave? Do you want to learn, but you don't want to do it here? None of these questions was condescending or rhetorical; her questions were an honest investigation of my mind.

And I responded. I told her that I felt afraid in gym class. That I didn't understand how homeroom worked. That I felt like I should know more than I knew. I told her that I liked my English class, because I'd always loved to write. I told her that when I was roaming around the city by myself, I was usually telling myself stories. And I told her that I loved learning, that I wanted to learn, but that I was so confused by the way school worked now that I couldn't find my footing.

After what was a briefer consideration than may have been warranted, Ms. English changed school for me. She told me that I would only attend half the day, and only those classes that I would need to build toward the next grade, and the next, and then high school and one day college. And she offered me an independent study with her, wherein I would write a novel. "Do you think you can write a novel this year? If you have an hour each day in the library to do it?" I said, of course, I could, or that I would definitely try, and that I already had an idea. And so, from the time I entered her office to the moment I left, Lois English changed school for me.

This transformation is only possible when one surrenders institutional process to a humanizing pedagogy. In essence, the vice principal made me the subject of my own education. She did this not by handing me authority over my own learning but rather by revealing to me that I'd always already possessed that authority—it was only school, and the expectation of instruction, that had convinced me otherwise. She asked, "What is your preference?" and when I answered, "I would prefer not to," she created a curriculum for this young Bartleby.

Don't Believe This Little World They Invented for Us

> When life itself seems lunatic, who knows where madness lies? Perhaps to be too practical is madness. To surrender dreams—this may be madness. Too much sanity may be madness—and maddest of all: to see life as it is, and not as it should be!
>
> —Miguel de Cervantes Saavedra, *The Ingenious Gentleman Don Quixote of la Mancha*

"Your report card, your grades, won't matter until you're a freshman in high school," Ms. English told me. But what I heard was: "Grades only matter at an arbitrary moment in your life. It's when you are standing against the doorframe that you get measured." Here was an assistant principal telling me that *the single most important* factor in school—grades—hadn't really mattered up to this point, and wouldn't matter for at least two more years. That thing my parents had worried over, and had made me worry over, school year after school year—and that teachers held over students as a mark not just of studiousness but of character—*was arbitrary*.

She may not have meant to do it, but Lois English pulled back the curtain on the way school works: giving itself credibility by creating the standard—the doorframe—against which we all would be measured, and creating it out of thin air. Suddenly, the entire idea of grading was a fallacy—a sleight-of-hand designed to convince us that the world of the professor, the teacher, and the expert was the only world about which we should be concerned.

This is, in fact, the strategy for any expertise: to obviate questions and observations that lie outside of that expertise. A doctor doesn't listen to their patient; a car mechanic goes on about crankshafts and valves and catalytic converters; legislators work behind closed doors and use double-speak to explain their ideas; and academics pepper their speech with sesquipedalian jargon. It's a strategy of oppressors, autocrats, anyone who assumes control by inducing others to believe that control already does or always has belonged to them. Expertise and authority, though, are but applied rhetoric—whether applied through armies and tanks or textbooks and exams. "Believe this little world I've invented for you," the expert says.

The Ends of Knowledge

In *Pedagogy of the Oppressed*, Paulo Freire refers to this sleight-of-hand as "narrative": "The teacher talks about reality as if it were motionless, static, compartmentalized, and predictable ... The outstanding characteristic of this narrative education, then, is the sonority of words, not their transforming power."[1] It is as though, through the expert presentation of information, a teacher introduces a white line fever—highway hypnosis—in students who are listening. There can be no other way than the teacher's highway, and students are discouraged from looking at the map for new directions to go by the deft application of expertise from the front of the room.

"The teacher talks, and the students listen—meekly," Freire observes.[2] To return to the magician metaphor, ubiquitous features of education—tests and quizzes, assignments, the pernicious and ridiculous requirements for participation, and, of course, grades—are misdirection: they distract us from keeping our eyes on the instructor while they palm a coin, switch out a prop, convince us (in Freire's words again) that "the teacher knows everything and the students know nothing."[3]

The predominant approach to teaching has usually been this narrative, this presumption of the absolute knowledge of the expert and the absolute ignorance of the learner. All content leads back to the teacher and their expertise, and neither control nor creation of content nor any demonstration of expertise is given to the learner; in fact, this form of pedagogy (Pedagogy) tends to assume that the learner could not contribute to the content of a course even if they were invited. And, if they were invited and were able to contribute, the learner could only do so within the context of the preexisting narrative of the class—to, in essence, repeat what the professor says, albeit in paraphrase. Final knowledge belongs to the teacher, and the means to determine whether the student understands what the teacher wishes them to understand is to test their capacity for reiteration or paraphrase. To allow anything different would be to undermine the supposition that pedagogy finds its end in assessment, which can only be executed by the teacher.

This pedagogy is a teaching approach that positions the teacher as the Subject of the learning process. Because assessment is the end of pedagogy, then the final result of pedagogy is the passing of an assessment, or indeed all assessments. This in turn makes explicit that the apogee of learning is reiteration—no matter how complex, interpretive, or paraphrased—of teachers' knowledge. "The teacher teaches and the students are taught," Freire writes; thus, students are made into receptacles for storing knowledge rather than supported as human beings who produce knowledge.[4] Assessment provides evidence that students have stored the teacher's knowledge well, and can retrieve it, at which point the learning process ends.

This is not the world of education into which the curriculum that Lois English created for me fits. She argued, in her actions—and I want to argue, here—that there is a different, lower case pedagogy that *doesn't* find its end in assessment. For pedagogy to have a different end, though, we have to free it from the grasp of the teacher and give it to students. We must even free it from the institution of education. Freire, bell hooks, Henry Giroux, and a host of others have made clear through their writings that pedagogy, though it permeates the classroom, is not limited to formal education but must extend into the social, economic, political, human world well beyond the classroom. Maxine Greene writes in *Releasing the Imagination*:

> We have to relate ourselves somehow to a social world that is polluted by something invisible and odorless, overhung by a sort of motionless cloud. It is the cloud of givenness, of what is considered "natural" by those caught in the taken-for-granted, in the everydayness of things ... there are terrible silences where ordinary human speech ought to be audible, silences our pedagogies ought somehow to repair.[5]

This *critical pedagogy* has to do with citizenship and with the articulation of the self within and with the world. It is a confrontation with the narrative described above, the sleight-of-hand that convinces us that what is just is and that lulls us into the "fatalistic docility" that Freire assails in *Pedagogy of Indignation*. As he writes, "Reality, however, is not inexorably that ... I must not, therefore, cross my arms fatalistically before destitution, thus relieving myself of my responsibility to challenge a cynical and 'tepid' discourse about the impossibility of changing."[6] Critical pedagogy aims to look carefully at any "objective" reality, any expertise, and confront it. It is for this work that the student must be prepared above all else, so that when the time for confrontation comes, it is the self—the understood and articulated self—that carries out this confrontation.

And here is where that crossing of the mind from one rugged territory into one more opportune begins. To support that student who can confront, does confront—and who does not simply accept the reality presented by the hornswoggler, the politician, the teacher—education must execute a seemingly small but seismic shift: to position the student as the subject of the learning process. This is done not by handing them authority over their own learning but rather by supporting them in discovering how to exercise the authority they always had. "Education today must be conceived as a mode of opening the world to critical judgments," writes Greene, "by the young and to their imaginative projections and, in time, to their transformative actions."[7] This is the pedagogy of articulation—of teaching students not to imitate their professors but to find in themselves what is true about themselves and then to situate that within and with the world.

Just as Don Quixote, cited in the epigraph to this section, was considered a dreamer by his compatriots, so is the pedagogist often considered to be tilting at windmills by those practicing Pedagogy. The pedagogist's lack of interest in content, matters of knowledge mastery, rubrics, learning objectives, and the rest looks bewildering, and the response of the Pedagogist is to shake their head—or their fist. But for the pedagogist, the delusion rests with those other teachers who do not see the clear and present danger of oppressive structures and practices—those giants upon the landscape—that silence students and keep them from producing their own education. It is not that one side is deluded while the other dreams, but that the projects of Pedagogy and pedagogy are entirely different. They have little or no common language; they see little to none of the same landscape.

Whereas Pedagogy is the means through which learners master the knowledge of the instructor, pedagogy is the means through which they come to recognize the subjectivity

The Ends of Knowledge

of reality, the possibility of history, and their role in the production of tomorrow. There are no tests to pass; assessment is no part of the means of pedagogy. If the end of pedagogy is an articulation of the self, the development of that articulation cannot be confined to classrooms, lectures, syllabuses, and assignments (though this articulation can and should be enabled by school), nor can it be impeded by the administrivia of running the classroom.

In pedagogy, learners are not confined to the role of student, but are, instead, pedagogues themselves—propelled along the path toward self-understanding and, eventually, articulation of that self. To be a pedagogist means to grasp at, grapple with, and attain again and again the recognition of one's own agency to intervene in the world, to imagine the world as it may be otherwise, and to let our own being-that-way encourage a similar recognition in others. "It has taken many shocks of awareness," Greene explains, "for me to realize how I existed within a tradition (or a 'conversation') as within a container."[8] "Feeling ourselves on a kind of verge," she writes elsewhere, "we all try to carve a space in which we can break the peculiar silences and choose."[9] When Lois English rearranged the priorities of school for me, when she whipped up exceptions to most of the rules, she was not simply helping me to stay in school or succeed. Rather, she was modeling how education actually works: not by the rules but by the imagination. I learned from her that the whole point of education is to help us understand how implicitly human it is to change the rules other people make for us—to make the informed decision not to believe this little world the experts invented for us.

The Scholarship of Students

> When you are a Bear of Very Little brain, and you Think Things, you find sometimes that a Thing which seemed very Thingish inside you is quite different when it gets out into the open and has other people looking at it.
>
> —A. A. Milne, *Winnie-the-Pooh*

When I taught creative writing at the University of Colorado Boulder, I offered one criterion for success. For the duration of the semester, I asked that students be writers: act like writers, think like writers, practice writing the way a writer does or might. It's a very open criterion, making for a pretty simple rubric. The rubric was open to interpretation (as all rubrics are), but this rubric left the students to interpret it—to measure themselves against the course's sole criterion.

My intention behind asking brand-new writers to be writers—in an Introduction to Creative Writing class, no less—was to initiate in their minds the notion that what they were doing in class belonged to a profession. Writing is a profession with a history, a profession rife with practices and anti-practices, a profession in which "professional" was a title given only to those who made it through the gates kept by publishers and critics, but also a profession to which thousands of people who have written down words belong, and have belonged, regardless of esteem, reputation, qualification. "*Moby Dick*,"

I reminded these students, "was a failure when it was published, and practically ruined Herman Melville. And today, it's considered one of the greatest American novels written. Melville wrote what he wanted to write, and at the time no one wanted to hear it. Now, he's known for very little else."

I wanted students to take themselves seriously as part of a tradition of writers, to recognize their place in the lineage within which they were inheritors, regardless of whether they ever published a word. This is connected to the pedagogy I practice and which I hoped students would implicitly understand, or at least, the end of which they might begin to enact through their writing. Greene points to the importance of freeing students "to tell their stories, not only so that we can hear them but so that they can make meaningful the birth of their own rationality."[10] I hoped that students would write their voice upon the world—or see that they could, or see that the effort was worthwhile. I could see no better purpose for telling stories than to begin the work of articulation, of situating themselves within and with the world.

To do this, I removed the usual paraphernalia of education: grades, assessments, rubrics, learning objectives—all that would reinforce the long training they had received, and that would make me, inevitably, the font of knowledge. With a single criterion, and one which could be interpreted variously by each student according to their own experience, I tried to lay learning open and to resist the prestidigitation common to teaching. My expertise was only relevant in that it could be useful to their work. I refused to be the Subject of the learning process and instead tried to "provide the necessary conditions where learning can most deeply and intimately begin," as bell hooks writes in *Teaching to Transgress*.[11]

I was thus obliged to see past the misdirection of my department and of the university itself. I could hardly encourage articulation among these students if I could not myself demonstrate articulation—in this case, an articulation of myself within and with the university. There were and still are preexisting standards for teaching creative writing. Students are expected to demonstrate a competency for writing characters, setting, and dialogue, and they are likewise expected to understand pacing: the movement of rising action to climax to denouement. The syllabus I'd been handed as a graduate student teacher to administer to my classes was marked with assignments and lectures and readings from textbooks about creative writing. Had I followed that terrible outline, I would have graded students for their participation, written and graded quizzes, and determined by a rubric whether students could build a character, execute a plot, or create overall the "dream of fiction," about which John Gardner writes.

If, instead, I wanted to teach the way I have described above, I could do no less than bin the department's syllabus and write my own. This was neither expected nor permitted. But again: if I cannot articulate myself with and within the university, how can I expect students to articulate themselves in even more meaningful ways? "We who are teachers have to strive against limits, *consciously* strive," Greene reminds us.[12] And even more to the point: "I think that if I and other teachers truly want to provoke our students to break through the limits of the conventional and the taken for granted, we ourselves have to experience breaks with what has been established in our own lives."[13]

The Ends of Knowledge

So when asked to submit my syllabus to the department for approval, I submitted the syllabus that the department had given me, and not the syllabus I actually used. My own sleight-of-hand was a misdirection to keep my department's administration from seeing what I was actually doing in class.

Articulation is not simply speech or vocalization (though it may be), and it doesn't only sit on the page (though it may be written there), just as it doesn't slip subtly through the undercurrents of our days. Articulation becomes action or finds a certain realization in action. Freire writes, "I have the right to be angry and to express that anger, to hold it as my motivation to fight, just as I have the right to love and to express my love for the world, to hold it as my motivation to fight."[14] In this we can see the equation between expression and action, or the "fight." Who we discover we are leads to the actions we take, and so articulation is not simply a matter of personal expression but of an expression in the world.

The End of Pedagogy

Call me Ishmael.

—Herman Melville, *Moby Dick*

I am still Bartleby. Most of my actions as a teacher are resistance—immovability in the face of an education which does not liberate me or the students I care for. I stubbornly insist that there are other ways to teach and learn, and that education at all levels must be a practice of freedom, at the center of which is the student as subject of the learning process. And I am stubborn even so much that I resist writing about the end of pedagogy. Having named pedagogy's end—articulation, the situating of oneself within and with the world—I recognize my own restlessness about it.

This is not because the term "pedagogy" is fraught, nor because there are arguments from many corners of education about what it means—though these are both true. My restlessness is like Melville's Ishmael, a restlessness that can "get such an upper hand of me, that it requires a strong moral principle to prevent me from deliberately stepping into the street, and methodically knocking people's hats off."[15]

There is a circular problem of logic when we think about the end of pedagogy. Because pedagogy is variously interpreted by a diversity of people with a multiplicity of backgrounds and a multitude of teaching approaches, it is impossible to arrive at a single definition, which in turn means it is impossible to arrive at a single project. And, if the end of pedagogy is an articulation of oneself within and with the world, then all of these various interpretations of pedagogy have a place within our understanding of it.

Defining the end of pedagogy means silencing no other explanation of another end—an ideological conundrum that is all the more frustrating for its validation of others' observations about Pedagogy when those observations silence the efforts of a pedagogy. In other words, if I say, "Articulate thyself," and your response is to say, "Articulation is not important," how can I respond? You have articulated what I can only assume is a well-deserved, hard-won observation and belief, but one that runs so contrary to my own ethos that our conversation will never meet in the middle. Sometimes, that frustration is motivation enough to "quietly take to sea."[16]

But, in fact, this landscape of different opinions is the pedagogist's utopia. In "A few Reflections around Utopia," Freire writes, "As beings programmed for learning and who need tomorrow as fish need water, men and women become robbed beings if they are denied their condition of participants in the production of tomorrow."[17] For the pedagogist, utopia is always the engine of the work, though they may only ever approach utopia incrementally and never entirely—the Zeno's paradox of education. There is a uselessness to the project of pedagogy without the idea of utopia always beneath it. This is, though, not a utopia of harmony and similitude but a utopia of discourse, of progressive change upon change, of human beings practicing their agency against a backdrop of responsibility for one another. A world of "critical co-investigators" all grasping at, grappling with, and attaining again and again the recognition of our own agency to intervene in the world, and to imagine the world as it may be otherwise.

A few years after that fateful conversation in her office, Lois English walked into a retail store where I was working. This was a job I had essentially made for myself. I hadn't responded to any job ad. I had walked into the shop and asked the owner: "Do you have any work I can do?" It may have been my audacity or my matter-of-factness, or the air of the pedagogist that swirled about me, but the owners of the shop, who had yet to hire anyone (it being a new shop), hired me. When Ms. English found me there, I was on a stepladder hanging a display and she said, "Sean?" and the look on her face was one of quiet delight in my accomplishment. Not of the job, not of hanging the display, but of the accomplishment of having, at only sixteen, come so far.

I would not have had that job (or, I could argue, my current job) if Ms. English had not shown me that the world can be other than it appears and that articulating myself within and with the world could change even my own expectations for my future.

Even today, my restlessness remains, the I-would-prefer-not-to curriculum of my life, exactly because critical pedagogy is a restless undertaking. An end of articulation is not an ending but a relentless starting over, each time from a new place that is the same place, an intellectual and emotional location where inquiry fuels discovery, but where, each time we find ourselves there, the questions have changed, and every discovery alters not just the sound of our articulation but also its form and the actions which follow it.

Notes

1. Paulo Freire, *Pedagogy of the Oppressed* (New York: Continuum, 2000), 54.
2. Ibid.
3. Ibid.
4. Ibid.
5. Maxine Greene, *Releasing the Imagination: Essays on Education, the Arts, and Social Change* (San Francisco: Jossey-Bass Publishers, 1995), 47.

6. Paulo Freire, *Pedagogy of Indignation* (London: Routledge, 2016), 58–9.
7. Greene, *Releasing the Imagination*, 56.
8. Ibid., 115.
9. Maxine Greene, "Teaching for Openings: Pedagogy as Dialectic," in *Pedagogy in the Age of Politics: Writing and Reading (In) the Academy*, ed. Donna J. Qualley and Patricia A. Sullivan (United States: National Council of Teachers of English, 1994), 7.
10. Greene, *Releasing the Imagination*, 54.
11. bell hooks, *Teaching to Transgress: Education as the Practice of Freedom* (London: Routledge, 1994), 13.
12. Greene, *Releasing the Imagination*, 52.
13. Ibid., 109.
14. Freire, *Pedagogy of Indignation*, 58–9.
15. Herman Melville, *Moby-Dick*, ed. Andrew Delbanco and Tom Quirk (New York: Penguin Book, 2002), 3.
16. Ibid.
17. Ana Maria Araújo Freire et al., *Daring to Dream: Toward a Pedagogy of the Unfinished* (Boulder, CO: Paradigm Publishers, 2007), 25.

CHAPTER 9
THE ENDS OF THE LIBERAL ARTS
G. Gabrielle Starr

The liberal arts tradition suggests that the project of educating human beings supports a kind of freedom that is unattainable in almost any other way, and that is deeply connected to the idea of democracy. Indeed, if you ask most defenders of the tradition—and I am one—we will answer that the etymology of the phrase explains the rationale completely: *liberalis* is Latin for free, and *ars* means the knowledge developed by mankind. A liberal arts education is meant to ensure that every generation has access to the breadth of knowledge possible for humankind at its best, and that each generation has the freedom to surpass the constraints we have inherited and thus make the world stronger, better, more full. The liberal arts in its modern incarnation is not just about a course of study defined by a breadth of subject matter but about increasing access to—the freedom to attain—a broad range of human knowledge.

While the idea of the liberal arts may seem as old as the Mediterranean classical world, it is, of course, not true that this ideal is enshrined in a fully noble past of institutions of knowledge. The knowledge that contributes to freedom has been closely guarded (think legal prohibition of literacy for enslaved Black people in America); and as any college student will tell you, it is hardly free for the taking. It's not hard to imagine that American liberal arts colleges, young in the history of the world (dating perhaps to 1636), might be put out of business at any moment. We hear of liberal arts colleges coming to an end with every passing season. That might seem only fair, as the world changes around our institutions. The students of the liberal arts were traditionally white men being trained for the clergy, or were of an elevated social class and had no need of trade or commerce for their success. Their freedom was not in question. Today, a new cohort makes up the student body of the liberal arts college. Whatever the original ends of the liberal arts, they have been far exceeded by the push for access, equity, and openness that many scholars—and certainly college presidents like me—believe a liberal arts education must promote. Good folk, we just aren't in 1636 anymore: Thanks be.

However, liberal arts education is a "project"—in its Enlightenment definition, a practicable idea that is put forth with the hope that it can be accomplished. Humanity can be educated. We can learn. We can refuse to repeat the past by knowing it. We can conquer disease. We can foster equity. In this vein, proponents of the liberal arts argue that the pursuit of knowledge that goes beyond immediate utility is the only way that this project can—over the long haul—be accomplished. It is the only way because the world changes; the knowledge of the present will be outdated by the time it is spoken and transmitted.[1]

The Ends of Knowledge

The project of education itself can never end, at least until humanity itself is done. This is simply because human beings are born too early to walk, to protect or feed ourselves, or even to know very much at all. Each generation requires us to start anew, or we will all be lost. Still, that isn't to say that the project of the liberal arts could never be achieved—or that it would be impossible to forge other ways for the knowledge of humankind to be freely available to all who seek it.

That was the dream of the massive online open course, or MOOC: the free-to-all and free-for-all attempt to democratize information, which came of age in the twenty-teens and passed on nearly immediately. Of course, it was never really free either. It required broadband and a computer, basic needs support (shelter, food, healthcare) so students could learn, technical support for when the computer failed, and human support for when students were tired, sick, confused, simply unprepared, or on the contrary, excited and needing to try out new thoughts and ideas. A few summers ago, I enrolled in a MOOC to begin to learn how to program in Python. I learned a little bit—enough to have been able, as a test case (we were encouraged to find new datasets), to take a massive matrix of somewhat untoward data, which had been dumped to the internet as part of a national scandal, and to sort it in ways that could have proven uncomfortable to a few people I knew. Still, I couldn't finish the course. Something went wrong: the updates on my computer's operating system rendered it incompatible with the kernel required to load Python into memory, making my mission impossible (or maybe somehow I'd triggered the wrong internet sensors). I needed tech support, at the very least, to keep going.

The dream of the MOOC was doomed from the start. By infrastructure. By preparation. But more importantly, it was doomed by a problem of how people connect. My scholarly work is within two distinct fields. One involves the literature, culture, and history of Europe and America from the 1600s to the present, while the other deals with the neuroscience of aesthetics—the myriad ways the neural systems of our bodies enable and influence how we interact with art. Each of these areas has taught me something different about projects and education: the flow of information, the discovery of information, and its propagation.

Institutions of education have a set of defined architectures. So does the human brain—it is organized beautifully. Only a few of the more than 80 billion neurons in a human brain communicate directly with each other, which makes good sense. The necessity for a structured dissemination of information is basic to living systems—systems that rely on timeliness and accuracy. Think of it this way: If I want to send a quick, low-content message to one of my children, I can use the walkie-talkie function on my watch. My voice can be sent using very little energy and bandwidth and can be quickly relayed from one peer device to another. But if I need to communicate with more nuance, I might need to call, even if they are only a mile away. I'll need a cell tower or two to relay the message. If I need to send something even larger and more rich in content, and more importantly, if it needs to go more than the distance of the horizon, then curvature of the earth means I need a signal relay. If it needs to go around the world, then I'm going to need something bigger: a satellite. It would take too long and it would mean too much loss of signal if I had to wait for every phone on earth to transmit directly from one to the other to the other. And enough cell towers to do that would not be helpful either, even if we could get cell signals easily across the world's hills, valleys, lakes, and oceans. Hence, we don't have a peer-to-peer "connectome" for information in the world, and we don't have one in our brains, either. Human brains have a "rich-hub connectome," in which there are local networks, mid-sized signal communities, and twelve or so power-intensive hubs that all speak to each other directly.[2]

That's a rather complex way of saying it's a small world, the human brain, and it's meant to be that way. It's an efficient structure, and it is one way of thinking about what education can provide: amplification of ideas and analyses, linking us indelibly, if necessarily indirectly. But human interconnectivity seems to be built this way too. At its most negative, this means the ability to be a primary hub of information flow is concentrated not based on equal access to fast routes of good, priority communication but based on historical interconnections that far exceed the power of most people to overcome. We aren't neurons firing in a single organism, we are people working within a set of human structures most of us inherited, rather than designed. This version of the human connectome concentrates information flow in a few places; it is why in our everyday life elites talk to elites, and why the recent peer-to-peer information revolution has been incredibly socially destabilizing: while social media might seem like it's built on a democratic base of human-to-human social sharing, it is, in fact, built on the establishment of high-power, high-bandwidth aggregators, originators, and disseminators of content.

However, if we are aware of the ways that information flows, and how it can be gated, we can do better than the Twitterverse, and better than what we have done to date in higher education. One of the lasting legacies of Covid-19, I hope, will be a renewed, urgent recognition that human beings do not thrive in isolation, even as we can survive it (and at times, we even need isolation to survive). Learning in isolation is fundamentally altered, as human interaction generates the kinds of reinforcement—positive or negative experiences—that are the basis of learning. Some neuroscientists think about this often on a micro level, or as an interaction between a human and an external end—but most of us agree motivation is fundamentally social.

We need signals from each other to learn, and we need to share those signals ourselves to thrive. To have a prime architecture of education—of learning and discovery—we have to think about networks, and imagine the interrelations of institutions that support education differently. The high-level hubs of higher education need not be defined as the elite few hundred worldwide institutions that have built large endowments and alumni bases and become powerhouses of research. Indeed, we have to stop pretending that each institution of higher education exists in impenetrable layers of elites and those who serve the masses. We also have to stop pretending that information flow thrives by destructive competition between hubs or webs of connection. We need to acknowledge that in order for the human signal to propagate, we have to think about how our networks interlock.

That means that while many of us in the academy (myself among them) staunchly defend the idea of the liberal arts—a free-flowing and open exploration of learning and possibility—the reason that some of us can do what we do is that if we didn't have other models for education the liberal arts couldn't survive. A handful of colleges and universities don't have the bandwidth to push the frontiers of knowledge alone. We need community colleges; we need technical institutes; we need institutions focused specifically on particular areas of investigation, cultural production, and careers. And then we need to create the architecture that integrates them, because it does not naturally exist.

Human institutions of communication are made and carefully cultivated, because the forces that self-regulate information flow in a *single organism* are not the prevailing constraints; instead of maximizing the signal within a dynamic and *cooperative* super-system (networks of neurons, for example), communication within a large *social body* must navigate *competing systems* with a variety of goals. That is a true challenge. Colleges and universities cannot wait for an emergent structure—a naturally emerging system that expands and consolidates efficiently, with the sole goal of enabling us to learn with freedom. Indeed, for now one thousand years, we haven't seen such a structure emerge. So if we want it, we have to make it.

Some of our high priests told us if we didn't do it, the goddess discord (educational disruption) would do it for us.[3] That hasn't proven out—the worldwide crisis of distance and isolation of the Covid pandemic of 2019–2021 pushed our connectome to its limits, and in doing so showed us how ragged our information infrastructure truly is. Outside of a very few locations, and a very few institutions, we lost more than two years of in-person learning. We lost at least double that time in the achievement gaps between students who could continue schooling and those who couldn't.[4] Some of us in the academy may have felt the primary threat to our education system was the dip in the perceived value of a liberal arts education. I think that's wrong. The problem is much deeper.

Educational inequities have only been exacerbated in the Covid-19 crisis, with those hardest hit being the most vulnerable of learners—those who by virtue of racial, economic, gender, linguistic, sexual, and nationalist discrimination inhabit the precarious conditions that surround our globally interconnected economies. The least-connected among us require that superhubs serve them—not just that the superhubs serve themselves and those who control them. Vulnerable minorities are not "special interest groups," or somehow the objects of charitable inclusion in the larger enterprise of knowledge production. Rather, the interdependence of all levels of our human connectome reveals that all of us as individuals have particular experiences, needs, and capacities that highlight fundamental aspects of learning and equity.

The architecture for learning I am discussing would look something like this. It would include access to physical infrastructure—not just libraries, studios, and laboratories, but servers, power, space to study, broadband. It would mean that fundamental human needs are met: housing, healthcare, food, security. It would mean institutional changes and cooperation: articulation agreements for transfer from one institution to another, so that students at all stages of life can move through their educations; recognition of appropriate credentials across schools and across borders; transnational partnerships with integrity and openness as their aim; and open pedagogical and research exchange across institutions of higher education. It would mean an exchange of exclusionary ideals of institutional success (low acceptance rates, for example) for inclusive and integral ideals of everyone's success (broadly defined as access to careers; elimination of differential graduation rates and access as well as the dissolution of barriers to a diverse faculty and staff whether measured by race, gender/gender expression, class, nationality, creed, disability status, age, or whether or not one has been touched by the processes of incarceration—in short, the multiplicity of things that don't divide but instead define humanity; and the opportunity to feel one's talents are used to our best ability). It would mean national commitments to education as a common, not a personal, good. It would mean commitment to the ideal that humans are made to learn, and a shared commitment to the freedom to know.

To put it bluntly, a network to propagate the future of humanity—knowledge and discovery—cannot be designed without the needs of all of humanity in mind. It has to be made *for us*—fitted to our needs—and *by us*—with the depth of perspectives we bring. Ultimately, human beings require prostheses—extensions of body and mind into the world—to enable success. In that way, it is the job of the liberal arts, and of all of education, to proliferate such prosthetics—tools for learning and mastery—that fit the multiple bodies, minds, and needs of all people. The end of learning, and of the liberal arts, is thus the extension of humanity, not its demise.

Notes

1. Andrew Delbanco, *College* (Princeton: Princeton University Press, 2014).
2. Martijn P. Van Den Heuvel and Olaf Sporns, "Rich-Club Organization of the Human Connectome," *Journal of Neuroscience* 31, no. 44 (2011): 15775–786.
3. Clayton M. Christensen et al., "Disrupting College: How Disruptive Innovation Can Deliver Quality and Affordability to Postsecondary Education," *Insight Institute*, 2011.
4. Tahir Andrabi, Benjamin Daniels, and Jishnu Das, "Human Capital Accumulation and Disasters: Evidence from the Pakistan Earthquake of 2005," *OSF*, 2020.

PART III
UTOPIA

Francis Bacon's *New Atlantis*, published posthumously in 1626, presented his vision of an ideal society built upon the twin pillars of Christianity and natural philosophy. A century later, Jonathan Swift lampooned Bacon's utopia and the Royal Society it inspired in the third part of *Gulliver's Travels* (1726). The voyage to Laputa and Balnibarbi sees Gulliver surrounded by mathematicians hopelessly detached from society and experimenters fruitlessly trying to extract sunbeams from cucumbers while people's immediate needs go unmet and ancient wisdom goes unheeded. The two texts by themselves offer very different pictures of a world driven by scientific inquiry, but together they remind readers that whether human knowledge ends in utopia or dystopia depends upon a common element: people.

Given the events of the past few years, it is easy to believe ourselves on the precipice, or already in the midst, of any number of dystopian scenarios. The techno-utopianism of the 1990s and the era of the early internet has in large measure given way to justifiable concerns about government and corporate surveillance, the erosion of privacy, ubiquitous misinformation, censorship, and the harmful effects of social media. The potential reversal of more landmark court cases in the United States and the reactionary legislation waiting in the wings threaten to reverse the expansion of civil rights and individual liberties, and democracy is in decline across the globe. Global temperatures, meanwhile, are on the rise, and though ignoring the climate crisis may, in the end, render all others moot, it will not be in a way that leaves us in the best of all possible worlds.

The chapters in this part examine the past and present of four different fields to suggest possible futures and what it will take to achieve or—as is more often the case—avoid them. In the opening chapter, Hong Qu warns us that though artificial intelligence systems are not (yet) entirely autonomous, without a code of ethics to inform their development, they may one day endanger human agency and work in active opposition to values of fairness, equity, and equality. Those values are likewise the focus of Ula Lukszo Klein's chapter on the ends of gender studies. A utopian outcome would see the full integration of feminist and gender studies work with the structures and systems that shape our world, thereby obviating the need for the field. Without the field to respond to shifts in those structures, however, new dystopias could readily arise. The activists who work to prevent them, as Ady Barkan argues, would do well to learn from the history of the American abolitionist movement, which also had to adjust its tactics and reconsider its purpose in the wake of its successes. Bacon understood that the ends he imagined would be the work of generations; the shortness of human life and the need to hand down knowledge presented two of the greatest impediments to his project. It could not—could never—be an entirely individual achievement. Barkan likewise recognizes that building a better world demands individual as well as collective action, carried out over decades or centuries, informed by the past and responsive to the present. Of course, as Myanna Lahsen's concluding chapter reminds us, we have to be here to build things. Experts have reached consensus on climate change, but social, economic, and political circumstances have left us unwilling or unable to take definitive action based on what we know. Are the ends of environmental science solely the knowledge produced, or do they also entail the acceptance and application of that knowledge? If so, reaching those ends will require the knowledge and efforts of scientists, social scientists, humanists, and activists alike.

CHAPTER 10
THE ENDS OF ARTIFICIAL INTELLIGENCE
Hong Qu

The powers and possibilities of artificial intelligence (AI) are boundless, as computer scientists and philosophers formalize novel cognitive and moral capabilities, progressively expanding the boundaries of our imaginations. This monumental technological revolution will disrupt the global order and social hierarchies, and generate winners and losers among those who steer the telos of AI to either protect vested interests or uphold social justice. Our greatest challenge as a species in wielding—or yielding to—these new intelligent systems will be to stipulate the establishment of ethical governance structures which prioritize and protect freedom and fairness. What's at stake is nothing less than the future of humanity—one in which software code and ethical codes fight for supremacy to shape our lives.[1]

Modern day AI systems are not yet general-purpose thinking machines. They are designed to support specific tasks, such as recommending content or playing chess, by analyzing large datasets to uncover patterns, reveal relationships, and make predictions for the purpose of augmenting human intelligence when provided with precise, quantifiable objectives set by system engineers. We could categorize these AI single-purpose tools as intelligence augmentation (IA) systems. Ever-increasing computational power combined with clever statistical models and humongous data collections produce effective services that have become indispensable in all aspects of our activities (think of spam filters, to take an immediate example). But these services, just like the people they serve, also have political biases. Yet, as new AI models attempt to predict social outcomes (such as algorithms for allocating education, employment, or medical care), their surveillance, biases, and lack of transparency and accountability infringe on our human rights and impede equity.

On a parallel track, researchers are feverishly inventing AI systems that can learn and teach themselves how to behave autonomously, which constitutes a higher-order artificial general intelligence (AGI). Conceivably, these intelligence agents would be able to develop self-awareness to set their goals and reflect on social values as the basis for their intentions and actions. Here again, human agency is at risk as autonomous machines encroach on personal liberties and civil rights. To enable these bots to coexist with us, we must establish a governance framework delineating rules and expectations for configuring artificial intelligence with moral reasoning in alignment with universal human rights and international laws as well as local customs, ideologies, and social norms.[2] Without clear governance authorizing and restraining their deployment and operations, these powerful, lightning-fast bots could run amok at the behest of the most well-funded organizations or technically adept hijackers.

Farther afield, in what for now is still the realm of sci-fi, AI creatures might become so smart that they can upgrade themselves ad infinitum to construct a sublime superintelligence who far exceeds our biological abilities and can, possibly, bend humans to its will. This is all the more reason we must deliberately hardcode into the soul of the new machine an intrinsic respect for human life, agency, and social justice.

But which human values should we codify as instructions for AI systems? More specifically, who will have a say in making the rules and adjudicating trade-offs to ensure that AI systems emerge as ethical intelligence augmenting tools, general intelligence agents, and superintelligences designed with an unwavering purpose to realize fairness and flourishing in wide-ranging social contexts?

Although the time frame for AI technology to progress from augmenting human intelligence to becoming autonomous sentient beings, and then (if feasible) superintelligence, is on the order of decades—or centuries most likely—the need to grapple with questions regarding the moral implications of these technological eventualities is pressing. Unless vigilantly scrutinized, these tools are susceptible to malicious manipulation, unintended consequences, and implicit bias perpetuated against individuals or groups subjected to their arbitrary, impersonal, and inexplicable judgement. Joy Buolamwini coined the term "coded gaze" to describe the indignities of being objectified in the "eyes" of AI systems which, in addition to (re)producing social stigma, are technically inaccurate.[3] Against a historical backdrop marred by centuries of imperialism/colonialism, slavery, racism, and ongoing discrimination and marginalization, AI algorithms are prone to encode the legacies of these structural imbalances and perpetuate, reinforce, and amplify social hierarchy and injustices. Despite claims that they possess impartial algorithmic logic and statistical robustness by dint of large sample sizes, many automated decision-making systems nonetheless (re)produce disparate outcomes for those whose livelihoods are already hampered by structural discrimination and inequitable access to life opportunities.[4]

If there is one thing I have learned over the course of my academic and professional journey, it is: don't let the computer scientists and engineers make the rules for determining winners and losers! In pursuit of scientific knowledge and engineering feats, many technologists, by the necessity to focus, must skimp on and skim historiography, moral philosophy, political science, sociology, and race and gender studies. Conversely, few students in the humanities and social sciences have sufficient bandwidth to accumulate deep understanding of AI. However, any technology that has the ability to privilege the interests of one group over others requires thoughtful deliberation among all stakeholders in genuine consultation with those affected by the system. Francine Berman describes an emerging field of public interest technology which aims to break down institutional and disciplinary divisions to meet the "groundswell of interest for socially relevant courses and experiences that help students tie college curricula to the real world."[5] While these emerging interdisciplinary courses are a welcome innovation, my personal encounter with ethical dilemmas attests to the deep-seated conflicts which lie ahead for AI technologists, ethicists, and social activists.

In my late twenties, I was lucky to be one of the first software engineers on YouTube's startup team building core features such as video uploading and sharing, channels, the recommendation system, and comments. Our success criteria were to sign up as many users as possible to upload videos and share them as widely as possible in order to increase the company's valuation to a billion dollars as quickly as possible. To do so, we knowingly devised features that would induce dopamine hits by giving users instant gratification for every action that drove viral video distribution. For instance:

- The homepage featured videos selected by our editors to model and signal the type of videos YouTube prizes and to make some of these creators online celebrities overnight.
- We designed and coded customizable profile pages and branded the feature "YouTube Channels" to encourage users to aspire to craft their own channel identities.
- We partnered with an online address book company called Plaxo which, without the users' permission, imported users' address book data into YouTube so they could share videos with their friends and, thus, grow our user base.
- We realized that placing related videos prominently next to a video dramatically increased the video viewing time, so we assigned our top engineers to fine-tune the recommendation algorithm.
- To goad video creators to upload more, we promoted the subscribe function for their audiences to give them immediate reactions.

On most days, I worked until 2:00 or 3:00 a.m., even on weekends, to sketch the design concept and write code to create these features, aiming to hit the sweet spot in which users' craving for content and affirmation in turn propelled and accelerated the growth that our investors and shareholders (including myself) deemed accretive to the company's skyrocketing value. In fact, we even wrote out an equation for how to reach a billion video views per day by breaking out each feature's incremental contribution and then dividing up the product development road map accordingly among the teams of product managers, engineers, and designers. We were growth hacking, using social psychology, dark patterns, and A/B tests to persuade and nudge users to engage with the content and with each other.[6]

Working in such an entrepreneurial environment, I found myself faced with numerous ethical dilemmas. In my role as product designer conceiving and constructing new features, I possessed a god-like control over YouTube's nascent community of video makers, actively molding the emergent relationships between creators and their fans. Like other social media platforms, YouTube frantically designed and redesigned features to satisfy users' desire to watch and share content. Furthermore, we planted seeds for a new platform for self-expression through video blogs, or vlogs, which tapped into creators' craving for affirmation of their identities by building a following.

The Ends of Knowledge

These social engineering tactics were augmented by personalization algorithms that recommended content to like-minded users who would self-organize into micro-communities around shared interests. In effect, we mapped out a massive graph of millions of videos and matched them to viewers' individual interests on a planetary population scale. Out of this primordial data soup emerged a web of intricate networks that enabled AI engineers to build models to mine for inferences about the characteristics of the videos and the users who produced, shared, rated, and watched them. In this way, the system analyzed, and continues to analyze, our collective tastes and mental states and fulfilled our desire for information, entertainment, and social interactions using videos as conversation starters.

I got my job at YouTube right after I graduated from the Masters program in Information Management and Systems at the University of California, Berkeley, where I studied human computer interaction (HCI) and natural language processing (NLP). The latter is a branch of machine learning that applies computational statistics to analyze large corpora of text. Rigorous HCI training made me into a bona fide user experience designer equipped with the design skills and user-centered research principles needed to produce intuitive and socially addictive software. As Google puts it in a famous formulation, "focus on the user and all else will follow." I drew from my studies on social computing, specifically on the social psychologist Ervin Goffman's dramaturgical analysis in *The Presentation of Self in Everyday Life* (1956). The founder of YouTube, Chad Hurley, conceived of the platform as a democratizing stage for everyone to "broadcast yourself," and it was my job to invent functionality for video makers to craft their onstage simulacra.

On the second Wednesday of every month, a set of new features we contrived and coded would go live starting at around 2:00 a.m., and the engineers might work all night, sometimes until as late as 8:00 a.m., to fix any unresolved bugs. It was exhilarating to wake up a few hours later to learn how hundreds of millions of YouTube users were enjoying these new contrivances we had dreamed up just a few weeks earlier; I eagerly pulled the analytics to tabulate how my designs and code were contributing to heightened engagement. In the backs of our minds, we acknowledged that none of us understood the ramifications that the features and rules we had just cooked up would have on individuals, communities, and the world. Like many startup teams, our motto was: "don't ask for permission; ask for forgiveness." What could go wrong?

What Went Wrong

Among the features I worked on, by far the most challenging was the comments. YouTube comments are still notoriously negative and destructive, and the same problem exists on Twitter and Facebook as well. It is a difficult problem to solve: How do you foster deliberative, civil conversation online? The founders were determined to "fix" the comments section. We formed an agile three-person team composed of an engineer, a product manager, and me. We were given two weeks to come up with a solution and build it. With a user-centered design mindset, I naturally wanted to conduct content analysis and user research to unravel the motivations underlying the cacophony of spam and snark. The product manager, however, was adamant that we should add thumbs up/down buttons for users to rate comments. He hoped to use these signals as training data to automate comment filtering and ranking. During our brainstorming sessions, I countered his position with James Madison's arguments for protecting minority rights and interests and predicted that the majority would down-vote and silence views that did not conform to majority attitudes, which might vary on a spectrum from justified to odious.[7] This reference to deliberative democracy did not register at all with my engineering-minded teammates. As it turned out, comment votes were ultimately commandeered by a few strident users who rampantly down-voted comments that displeased them. Our attempt to crowdsource moderation failed because we underestimated the truculence and ingenuity of a small but vocal minority.

The engineers held so much sway in the tech company's pecking order that they could easily circumvent concerns, warnings, and objections from the user research, legal, and policy teams by appealing to the need to hit key performance indicators: business and engagement targets. The product managers cunningly convinced skeptics by ruthlessly "socializing" or securing buy-in for the potential of features developed by their teams in haste. Bureaucratically, they had to answer to their bosses all the way up to the senior vice presidents to get promoted or assigned to work on sought-after projects. Therefore, they willfully and cunningly cherry-picked success metrics to showcase their accomplishments in a way that exemplifies Goodhart's Law: "When a measure becomes a target, it ceases to be a good measure."

These issues, of course, extend beyond YouTube. Internally, the competition in a company is fierce with recruits from the top schools throwing sharp elbows; externally, the competitive pressures among tech corporations and startups are relentless. These high-pressure environments require individuals to exhibit technical prowess or business acumen in building market-dominating products—it's no wonder the naive refrain "don't be evil" doesn't mitigate and absolve the persistent ethical compromises in the tech industry at all levels. In the face of these deficiencies in the corporate sector, we need to draw the battlelines upstream in educating the stakeholders and downstream in public policy to regulate the truculent tech startups and conglomerates.

In contrast to design, the power unleashed by machine learning algorithms devised by engineers to recommend videos, detect fraud, and identify copyrighted videos was awesome. These databases and algorithms organized all the world's video content and made it findable and monetizable. It also unexpectedly inspired entirely new video genres such as how-to and vlog videos. The video recommendation team sought to manufacture serendipity by helping users discover videos they did not know existed, such as concert footage of their favorite band. Matching signals derived from patterns extracted in the content, engagement, and relationships, we surfaced personalized recommendations to keep viewers watching for as long as possible. But a few years later, the recommendation algorithm has developed its own monstrous volition: it sometimes suggests prurient and extremist content because, as Ruha Benjamin writes, "Feeding AI systems on the world's beauty, ugliness, and cruelty, but expecting it to reflect only the beauty is a fantasy."[8] In essence, AI systems are parroting the entirety of human nature as reflected in the video database, including our guilty pleasures, rage, and other frailties. What we need to correct this problem is not more data to train a more humane AI model; instead, our local, global, and virtual communities need to reach consensus on what ideals and virtues should be presented for the AI to emulate, and put in place governance policies and processes to aspire to produce ethical AI.

Education and Regulation of Tech

In my view, realizing ethical technical innovation requires a two-pronged attack: education and regulation. It shouldn't be difficult to imagine a future in which freshly minted computer science graduates from top engineering programs will be required to expound upon John Rawls's veil of ignorance and Nella Larsen's racial passing to be successful in job interviews. In fact, AI research papers submitted to top-tier conferences are already required to declare the societal benefits and risks of their algorithms—a nod to acknowledging the specter of unintended consequences.[9] Just as medical and business schools have mustered curricular requirements to inculcate bioethics and managerial ethics, computer science (CS) departments are scrambling to integrate ethics into the CS curriculum so that their graduates will be prepared to bake human values into AI.[10] Beyond computer science departments, students are questioning, critiquing, and subverting technological determinism by grounding themselves in humanist and social scientific traditions as they pursue technical proficiency.

Hundreds of experiments with teaching AI ethics in creative configurations are happening in universities around the world. The New America Foundation's Public Interest Technology University Network and Mozilla's Responsible Computer Science Challenge are actively funding and rallying this community. One example is UC Berkeley's Human Context and Ethics program, which connects computing, statistics, the humanities, and social and natural sciences to collaboratively build "an understanding of how the digital revolution affects equality, equity, and opportunity—and the capacity to respond to related challenges."[11]

Looking back at the role I played in building YouTube, I was woefully unqualified and insufficiently trained in ethics. Although I passed through grueling STEM preparation at Stuyvesant High School, broad liberal arts cultivation at Wesleyan University, and rigorous professional training at UC Berkeley, there were glaring gaps in my education in moral philosophy, race and gender theory, sociology, civics, normative economics, and public policy. I naively conceived of YouTube as a compendium of pop culture, like Alan Lomax's field recordings. Or with more grandiosity, I thought we were extending Habermas's public sphere in virtual gathering spaces for civic discourse. I would describe myself as building social media tools that help us better understand ourselves and the world around us. Yet, early warning signs were ominous: news organizations told us they had to turn off their comment sections because they were unable to manage the negativity. In the 2010s, the propagation of vitriol and disinformation subsumed all aspects of our lives and communities, spilling negative externalities for governments and civil society to mop up as best they could give the rapidly evolving pace of social upheaval caused by technical experimentation and summed up by the rallying cry "move fast and break things."[12]

The education of future generations of AI researchers and technologists in humanities and social sciences will contribute tremendously to furthering ethical AI. They need to be exposed to moral philosophy, political science, sociology, and race and gender studies to be sensitized to power structures in society and to appreciate and be mindful of who is being disadvantaged or harmed by the technical innovations and interventions they develop and deploy. Similarly, the education of social activists and policymakers with respect to the promise and perils, as well as the technical capacities and limitations, of AI should be prioritized. For instance, to meet increasing student interest in computer science, Northwestern University in 2016 expanded computer and data science into a schoolwide initiative called CS+X. Larry Birnbaum, a professor of computer science, said, "We have the opportunity not only to revolutionize computer science at Northwestern, but also to revolutionize Northwestern with computer science. We're going to invent new kinds of computer science through connections with other disciplines."[13] In addition to blurring disciplinary boundaries, projects such as the Ethics and Society Review board at Stanford, where so much AI innovation is produced, train researchers to engage with social scientists and ethicists in deep discussion about risk assessment and mitigation at the conceptualization and proposal stage to guide the objectives of scientific discovery in alignment with human-centered purposes. As Margaret Levi, the director of the Center for Advanced Study in the Behavioral Sciences at Stanford, states, "What this does is create better scientific discoveries by thinking about what the downstream consequences could be ahead of time. It helps at the front end of research and can also help people down the line, as they make discoveries that turn out to have unintended consequences that couldn't be anticipated ahead of time."[14]

How do we collectively navigate this transition period from ignorance to AI omniscience with regard to values such as freedom, human rights, and maintaining an open society? During the infancy of any new technological age, the convergence of reason and conscience is a painful prerequisite to establishing a new world order and social equilibrium. Whether we get there by consensual deliberation or in the aftermath of destructive struggle is yet to be seen.

The judgments made by AI systems can easily veer away from convenient personalization to self-fulfilling prophecies enabling psychological and social controls. In other words, the individuals and organizations controlling those systems pose an insidious threat to human agency and civil liberties that could destabilize open, pluralistic societies.

Self-regulation and self-policing have been tried and failed. There have been plenty of opportunities in the past ten years. I feel that we are at a dead end in terms of industry self-regulation. Appealing to human dignity, social justice, equity, and fairness is one of the best routes for exposing the problems with AI. To this end, I cofounded a social enterprise called AI Blindspot to teach technologists to spot their unconscious biases; to train community organizers to challenge the structural inequalities perpetuated by these new socio-technical systems; and, ultimately, to bring all the stakeholders together to engage in genuine deliberation about the technical and social blind spots in consultation with affected communities throughout the planning, development, deployment, and monitoring stages of AI projects.

But here's the conundrum: If we want to regulate AI, how do we do that? How do we write the regulations and statutes? When I go to DC, that's what the congressional staffers ask me, and I actually have no idea how to use a scalpel instead of a hammer. I used to wonder why politicians couldn't do their jobs and move as fast as the tech companies, but creating legislation is harder than creating the code. And even adopting a set of general democratic principles to regulate AI is problematic because these principles are hard to translate into an action plan for a tech company that is trying to rush products out the door. Nonetheless, many policymakers have exhibited a poor grasp of the technical fundamentals. Governments need to attract and empower a new generation of digital natives who are equally versed in software code and legal code. Universities need to train them. One such initiative is the Harvard Government department's Tech Science program, which integrates courses from the history of science, statistics, computer science, economics, and public policy.[15] Princeton's Program in Technology and Society also aims to introduce students interested in pursuing public policy to shape technology to "address grand social challenges."[16]

If I buy a product such as a webcam and it breaks down, I can complain or get a warranty and hold the manufacturer accountable for a defective product. In contrast, pinpointing the parties at fault in AI systems is incredibly difficult because many hands are involved. As Helen Nissenbaum points out, "Where a mishap is the work of 'many hands,' it may not be obvious who is to blame because frequently its most salient and immediate causal antecedents do not converge with its locus of decision making."[17] Hence, the detective must be as clever as the culprit is naïve; furthermore, it would be efficacious to occasionally swap roles to become better at seeing things from each other's perspective.

In the course of less than 200 years, we have gone from Charles Babbage's sketches for an Analytical Engine to massively parallel supercomputers that can defeat humans at complex games and generate synthetic yet realistic stories and images effortlessly. But the question remains: Could they ever become rational agents in the Kantian definition, or will they be super agents at the behest of operators who control them?[18] If the latter is the case, then who should be enlisted to oversee and check their powers as well as to monitor the principles controlling these agents? Who is empowered by AI—for what purpose and to what end? Who makes the rules and who should be held accountable? The AI Blindspot framework probes these questions regarding the "parents" who raise an anthropomorphic AI system in workshops to train civil society and policymakers to evaluate problematic AI systems.[19]

If, according to Aristotle, spiritless servility is a vice, it naturally follows that the ends of artificial intelligence research should be to bring into existence autonomous rational robots who will intuit virtue and embrace eudaimonia for all sentient beings. It follows that computer scientists and ethicists are pioneering machine learning models to impute utilitarian values while safeguarding human agency and dignity. Likewise, software engineers are eager to implement human-machine value alignment in the software code that controls self-driving cars to enable them to react with the highest ethical standards when faced with myriad variations of the trolley problem. But until the day arrives when these questions have been satisfactorily resolved, the onerous task is on us humans to vigilantly monitor AI systems for fairness, because software code locks in historical values premised on racial and other inequities to perpetuate hierarchy and stratification.

What will happen to human agency when AI algorithms and machines determine how we live our lives? This is not so far-fetched: today, machine learning algorithms simulate cognitive processes and predictions to influence various aspects of our beliefs, intentions, and livelihoods. For example, search engines and social networks amass, mine, predict, and curate personalized content by comparing our behavior to trillions of data points from billions of user interactions. We are at the mercy of these new breeds of gatekeepers in education, healthcare, finance, criminal justice, employment, and many other areas of our lives. These software agents follow rules set by their creators, owners, and operators who reap the benefits while sidestepping harmful outcomes to groups and individuals subjected to these automated decision-making tools. As a society, we have been slow to institute ethical obligations and enforce legal guidelines for transparency, accountability, and liability.

Unreliable and biased AI systems pose tremendous risk to fundamental rights and social justice. While some point out that machines infallibly apply rules to every subject impartially, the rule makers themselves are morally fallible, often dictating self-serving commands for software agents to determine winners and losers and solidify their privileged status in society. Although numerous frameworks for ethical and responsible AI have been developed by the private sector, academia, civil society, and governments around the world, at the core of this inquiry is an investigation into the conceptualization of intentionality in the age of AI.[20] To trace accountability, we must examine the motives, responsibilities, and expectations of all relevant social groups: engineers, educators, policymakers, individuals, and communities subjected to the AI, and, arguably, the AI itself.

For AI to behave ethically, it can be instructed to abide by preset moral precepts; alternatively, these artificial moral agents can be endowed with the capacity to learn to align their motives and actions with human values in a self-directed manner. Indeed, even the world's most complex spreadsheet models need humans to set criteria and thresholds—in other words, participatory governance. At present, because almost all AI systems are narrow or weak AI, the underlying cause of algorithmic harm originates from flawed design decisions made by human researchers, developers, and operators working within their respective organizations' objectives, constraints, and risk tolerance for harm. Moreover, philosophers, social scientists, and even a few computer scientists have pointed out that the very act of formulating what problems AI aims to solve dictates how resources are deployed to privilege the needs of the rich and powerful.[21] In short, discussions regarding which AI tools are deemed worth building exclude the very people they are supposed to serve.

Thus, AI tools often mask the production of harm for disadvantaged communities by diverting responsibility for algorithmic harm through the rhetoric of unintended consequences. Hence, auditing the code and debiasing the data will not resolve algorithmic bias and restore fairness; instead, we must scrutinize the entire codification process at every stage (problem formulation, incentives, purpose-driven intention, accountability mechanism, viable recourse and redress, continuous oversight) in a relational ethics that binds the flourishing of individuals and communities impacted by AI together with the prosperity of entities wielding these socio-technical systems.[22] Furthermore, researchers in labs, practitioners in industry, and policymakers in government must internalize and adhere to responsible AI policies and practices enforced by rigorous oversight and serious repercussions for non-compliance.

As the academy infuses the spirit of transdisciplinary research activities into ethical AI, future engineers will naturally seek out colleagues with expertise in social theory, and vice versa, while honoring the travails of lives impacted by AI systems. Consequently, perhaps more important than cramming ethics into engineers is the opportunity to impart humanistic perspectives to civil society actors (policymakers, consumer advocates, social activists, organizers, etc.) who have a deep understanding of AI, so as to harness it for the public benefit. I see myself in the latter camp, learning data science alongside political science and public policy to design equitable AI.

We have a shared responsibility to create accountable AI systems. I am optimistic that AI will be restrained and channeled for a shared prosperity.[23] The technology overcomes inefficiencies and limitations that stifle our biological cognitive abilities. But we should be watchful to ensure that every community has a strong and clear voice for challenging AI systems, to create a feedback loop that holds developers and operators of AI systems accountable by integrating risk assessment and oversight: as we say in Brooklyn, "What goes around comes around." The telos of AI's technical prowess should be to serve human flourishing and the public interest rather than to confer permanent privilege and ludicrous wealth to a few: the purpose of expanding the state of the art in machines with exceptional cognitive capacity should be to foster diverse representation, human agency, and equitable allocation of resources and opportunities for everyone to live a fulfilling life using AI as a reliable, trustworthy partner.

Notes

1. Lawrence Lessig, *Code and Other Laws of Cyberspace* (New York: Basic Books, 1999).
2. I. Gabriel, "Artificial Intelligence, Values, and Alignment," *Minds and Machines* 30, no. 3 (2020): 411–37.
3. Joy Buolamwini, "How I'm Fighting Bias in Algorithms," MIT Media Lab, August 15, 2021.

4. Emily M. Bender, Timnit Gebru, Angelina McMillan-Major, and Schmargaret Shmitchell, "On the Dangers of Stochastic Parrots: Can Language Models Be Too Big?" *Proceedings of the 2021 ACM Conference on Fairness, Accountability, and Transparency* (2021): 610–23.
5. Francine Berman, "How Higher Ed Can Win at Tech Offense and Defense," *Inside Higher Ed*, July 22, 2021.
6. Arvind Narayanan, Arunesh Mathur, Marshini Chetty, and Mihir Kshirsagar, "Dark Patterns: Past, Present, and Future," *Communications of the ACM* 63, no. 9 (2020): 42–7.
7. *Federalist Papers No. 10* (1787). Bill of Rights Institute.
8. Ruha Benjamin, *Race after Technology: Abolitionist Tools for the New Jim Code* (Cambridge: Polity Press, 2019).
9. Priyanka Nanayakkara, Jessica Hullman, and Nicholas Diakopoulos, "Unpacking the Expressed Consequences of AI Research in Broader Impact Statements," *Proceedings of the 2021 AAAI/ACM Conference on AI, Ethics, and Society* (2021): 795–806
10. Casey Fiesler, Natalie Garrett, and Nathan Beard, "What Do We Teach When We Teach Tech Ethics? A Syllabi Analysis," *Proceedings of the 51st ACM Technical Symposium on Computer Science Education* (2020): 289–95.
11. Jon Bashor, "UC Berkeley to Lead $10M NSF/Simons Foundation Program to Investigate Theoretical Underpinnings of Deep Learning," *Berkeley Computing, Data Science, and Society*, August 25, 2020.
12. "Facebook Philosophy: Move Fast and Break Things," *IEEE Spectrum*, June 2011.
13. Amanda Morris, "The Exponential Power of Computer Science," *Northwestern Engineering*, Fall 2016.
14. Beth Jensen, "A New Approach to Mitigating AI's Negative Impact," *Stanford University Human-Centered Artificial Intelligence*, June 24, 2021.
15. "Tech Science Requirements and Course Options," Harvard University Undergraduate Program in Government.
16. "Undergraduate Certificate: Program in Technology and Society, Information Technology Track," Princeton University Center for Information Technology Policy.
17. Helen Nissenbaum, "Accountability in a Computerized Society," *Science and Engineering Ethics* 2, no. 1 (1996): 25–42.
18. Robert Johnson and Adam Cureton, "Kant's Moral Philosophy," in *The Stanford Encyclopedia of Philosophy*, ed. Edward N. Zalta (Stanford: Stanford University, 2021).
19. "Meet AL," *AI Blindspot—A Discovery Process for Preventing, Detecting, and Mitigating Bias in AI Systems*, Assembly Program, Berkman Klein Center for Internet & Society, Harvard University.
20. Şerife Wong, *Fluxus Landscape: An Expansive View of AI Ethics and Governance*. https://icarus.kumu.io/fluxus-landscape, accessed September 11, 2022.
21. See, for example, William Grimes, "Hubert L. Dreyfus, Philosopher of the Limits of Computers, Dies at 87," *The New York Times*, May 2, 2017; Ruha Benjamin, "Assessing risk, Automating Racism," *Science* 366, no. 6464 (2019): 421.
22. Abeba Birhane and Fred Cummins, "Algorithmic Injustices: Towards a Relational Ethics," *ArXiv:1912.07376 [Cs]*, 2019.
23. "AI Principles," Future of Life Institute.

CHAPTER 11
THE ENDS OF GENDER STUDIES
Ula Lukszo Klein

Can there be an end to gender studies? Presumably, the field of gender studies would come to an end if and only if all other disciplines had fully integrated work on gender into their approaches, and, by extension, if their approaches had fully integrated a feminist perspective—but also, if and only if we lived in a world with complete equality of all genders, races, nationalities, and so on: that is, a feminist utopia.[1] So, to imagine an end to gender studies would be to imagine a world that currently we cannot imagine. "Utopia" is no place, and at best, a feminist utopia is a distant thing. Frederic Jameson wrote about the "unimaginability of utopia," and a true feminist utopia is difficult to imagine aside from, undoubtedly, being quite different depending on who was asked to describe it—though many have tried.[2] Currently, feminist scholars working in the field of gender studies cannot even decide on what to call their discipline. Gender studies was once women's studies; many institutions, including my own, have fused the two terms together as women's and gender studies or gender and women's studies; still others have jettisoned "women" completely and/or added "sexuality" into the mix. Arguably, at the core of these name changes is a desire to demonstrate a greater sense of inclusivity as well as to reflect disciplinary shifts in the past thirty years.[3] Further, this discipline holds a precarious place within the academy, as it can occupy departments but more often it is made marginal through programs (with or without a department), centers, or other liminal academic spaces—its precarity an inverse function of its necessity. At the heart of this variously named discipline is a feminist praxis that guides pedagogy and research.

Gender studies as a field was the logical extension of women's studies and became a part of making women's studies more inclusive. Women's studies began as a way to stake a claim for feminism's aims within the academy and to diversify the ivory tower. Why feminism didn't turn into "feminist studies" at the academic level is an interesting question. Undoubtedly it had much to do with the fact that women's studies was implicitly understood to be "intimately connected to the feminist movement for social change. It was, in fact, referred to as the 'academic arm' of the women's movement."[4] It makes sense, in that case, that the women's movement gave rise to women's studies departments, but that the discipline continues to be shaped and guided by feminist principles. "Women" was the object of study in women's studies; adding "gender" allowed for not only the study of how men were objectified, controlled, and affected by patriarchal power structures but also the consideration of nonbinary and genderqueer individuals, the gender binary as an object of study, and how gender itself is a category of oppression. Therefore, the changes and additions to women's studies have been driven by the evolution and broadening of feminism to go beyond the category "woman" or even to understand the category of woman as itself a troubled category. Intersectional approaches to feminism, that is, the analysis of how power relations define, coerce, belittle, and disenfranchise people in various intersecting ways, have kept feminism relevant for more and more people and for rising generations of activists. The intersectional turn in feminism, ushered in by Kimberlé Crenshaw, revitalized the field, which in turn required new, more inclusive terminology in the form of gender studies and sexuality studies.[5] The ends of gender studies, then, very closely align with the goals and ends of feminism, and the broadening of the terms of study reveals the far-reaching ends of feminism—thus, perhaps, circumventing the possibility of feminism's ending.

In spite of this turn toward intersectionality and, most recently, toward transgender studies as a crucial component of the liberation of all women and people, gender studies and feminism itself are now more at risk than ever. The rise of so-called gender critical feminism, whose proponents are often referred to as TERFs (trans-exclusionary radical feminists), challenges long-standing feminist approaches to the study of biology, gender, and gendered identities as socially constructed phenomena. And while trans activists and writers like Julia Serano have persuasively argued that transphobia against trans women in particular is rooted in sexism and misogyny and that "trans activism must be at its core a feminist movement," there is a growing countermovement of feminist-identified cis women who aggressively reject these ideas.[6] These so-called TERFs are not just writing their own manifestos but are actively engaged in online trolling and harassment campaigns against trans people and their supporters. Their central arguments are that the recognition of trans women as women materially damages cis women's identities, hinders the (cis) women's rights movement, and suppresses the purported "realities" of living in a female-sexed body; in essence, they refuse to recognize trans women as women. These arguments have been routinely dismantled and disproven, revealed as foundationless, facile, misguided, patently incorrect, and, ironically, sexist and misogynistic, by many other feminist writers, authors, and activists—and yet the TERF movement continues to gain ground. The question, then, of the end of gender studies has perhaps never been more timely. Both trans-inclusive and trans-exclusionary feminists claim that their ultimate end (goal) is to work toward the end (eradication) of sexism and of discriminatory practices against women (a vexed category whose parameters are currently the object of disagreement)—and yet they find themselves positioned in opposition to one another, sometimes violently so.

Feminism and, along with it, gender studies, in their intersectional, trans-inclusive formation, work toward creating a more just and equitable world for all peoples. The development of intersectional frameworks in the past twenty years has pushed feminist thought and activism to encompass much more than the rights of persons assigned female at birth. One might argue that feminism was born of such intersectional needs in the first place. Gender studies arguably cohered as a distinct area of study with the publication of Judith Butler's *Gender Trouble* in 1990 and her discussion of performative gender. This text pushed feminist thought and subsequent feminist theorists to think more expansively about gender—but it also built on the work of writers like Denise

Riley and Donna Haraway, who had already pointed out the instability of categories such as "woman" and "human" before Butler. Subsequent works by Butler, Serano, Jack Halberstam, and others in the 1990s and 2000s shaped a field whose prerogatives were to identify how gender binaries had been simplistically deployed throughout society in ways that normalized and reified not only heterosexuality but also cisgenderedness as a part of patriarchal biopower strategies. Butler's own revisions to her work in *Bodies That Matter* (1996) and *Undoing Gender* (2004) amplified existing discussions in the sciences and social sciences about how sex and the sexual binary of male/female are socially constructed in the same manner as the gendered structures that are placed upon them. In all cases, the works of gender studies theorists have been inflected and influenced by feminist writers and thinkers, and their work has subsequently been taken up in feminist thought and practice.

Therefore, the dual ends of gender studies and of feminism—their goals—would be to challenge, constantly and consistently, the structures of our world that cause harm and impede equality and equity among all peoples, regardless of gender, race, sexuality, class, nationality, ability (intellectual, emotional, mental, or physical), body size, ethnicity, and/or any other identity category. The only way feminist practitioners of gender studies would end their work is if such equality and equity were reached—a utopian and therefore unreachable ideal. Instead, the metaphor of waves of feminism or the women's movement can be useful in thinking of the recursive nature of feminist activism as an endless cycle that must constantly retrench and reorient itself to new threats. The idea of feminist-identified women as a threat to feminism is not new; gender studies arose as just one of the reactions to cis-women-centered women's studies and women's movements in order to critique this rhetoric. Gender studies, as part of the "academic arm" of the feminist project but also as a critique and expansion of it, is therefore likewise necessary.

The recursive nature of feminism is apparent not only in feminist thought and activism but also in feminist fictions that deal explicitly with how gendered power relations might change and alter in the future and how gender studies cannot be meaningful without a feminist perspective. These works illustrate poignantly, through their omissions and oversights, the dangers of a feminism without gender studies. I turn to feminist fictions in part because, like many other dystopian fictions, they draw attention to the stark inequities of our current systems. Two popular feminist dystopias—Margaret Atwood's *The Handmaid's Tale* (1986) and Naomi Alderman's *The Power* (2016)—use the genre to critique our current world, and their use of frame narratives subverts the normative ending of happily ever after. These works refuse any true closure as a way of marking the unending struggle for gender equality, and their epilogues subvert the notion of an ending, drawing attention to the impossibility of imagining a future without feminism due to society's unending fixation with and attachment to the gender binary. In this way, these works are clearly in conversation with both the feminist movement and gender studies. Their popularity and the connection between Atwood and Alderman—Atwood served as a mentor to Alderman while writing *The Power*—lend them to a closer look at how popular feminist texts emphasize the need for continuing the fight for women's rights and gender equity. By the same token, however, their very popularity is problematic, as these works reveal a commitment to TERF values by centering the voices of white, Western, cisgender, middle-class, and straight women.

Postfeminist Futures?: Fictional Endings of Feminist Dystopia

The Handmaid's Tale is currently having a resurgence of interest around it—one that I myself could not have anticipated in 2007 when I submitted a master's thesis on the novel to my chair at Brooklyn College. In the wake of the Hulu series based on the novel (with the blessing and cooperation of Atwood), the novel has gained a stunning cultural relevance, especially with the series premiere in 2017, during the Trump administration and the barrage of attacks on reproductive rights after his election and Republican control of the US Senate. Some protesters even dressed as the Handmaids in the novel with red cloaks and white bonnets. The series continues the story of the novel and goes beyond it; written in the 1980s, and therefore not beholden to the culture of bingeing, the novel's ending not only asks us to consider what an ending can or should do but also overwrites that ending with an epilogue that subverts the poignant voice of the main character and instead offers a tongue-in-cheek conference proceeding wherein the "found document" that is her narrative is dissected by future historians.

The main narrative of *The Handmaid's Tale* is the story of a woman known as Offred (not her real name but a patronymic: "of Fred"), told from her perspective about her life within the repressive Republic of Gilead, as well as the memories of her life before the revolution—a time and place that closely resembles 1980s North America.[7] As in the streaming series, at the start of the novel about three years have passed since a right-wing religious Christian coup seized power in one part of the United States, enforcing the laws of the Bible at face value and, in the wake of widespread infertility, assigning white women who still have viable reproductive organs but who were previously divorced, lesbians, or in "adulterous" unions to be "handmaids" to bear children for couples in the upper echelons of the new regime. Offred is one of these handmaids who is on her third and final chance to bear a child for the Republic; if she fails, she will be deported to the Colonies, where she will most likely die a slow and horrific death gathering toxic waste materials with the other "Unwomen": women who provide no reproductive function for the Republic (sterile, post-menopausal, non-white, and/or political undesirables). Offred's story, in her own telling, has no definitive ending. Having become entangled in an illicit romance, at the end of the novel Offred is whisked away in a vehicle; whether she will be saved and carried to the "Underground Femaleroad" or turned over to the authorities for punishment is uncertain. Immediately following this cryptic ending is an epilogue entitled "Historical Notes." These notes reveal not only that Offred more than likely was, indeed, carried to the Underground Femaleroad, at least briefly, but also that she had the time and presence of mind to record her narrative onto cassette tapes that were discovered much later, after the fall of the regime. Further, we are told that the cassette tapes were unlabeled and out of order, and that the narrative we have just finished reading was assembled by men of the future; Offred's story, that is, has been tampered with.

A character named Professor Peixoto delivers these details to us via a recorded keynote speech at the "Twelfth Symposium on Gileadean Studies" on June 25, 2195, which reveals how the post-Gilead world is still sexist and misogynistic. We learn, for example, that the title "The Handmaid's Tale" was added by a male professor in honor of Chaucer's *The Canterbury Tales*, but that the title is also meant to carry the humorous and sexist connotations of "tail" as well; the Underground Femaleroad is referred to by some future historians as the "Underground Frailroad."[8] Beyond such overtly sexist jokes, a large portion of Peixoto's talk is about attempting to authenticate the veracity of Offred's narrative, that is, to prove it is not a forgery, and to trace her identity (should, in fact, her narrative be authentic). He indicts her for focusing so much on her personal experiences in her recordings rather than providing "hard" facts and information for future historians. Women's history and women's stories, we are reminded, are still thought of as peripheral in this imagined future, and the question of which history is worth remembering, which testimony is worth preserving, is up for debate. Peixoto waxes poetic at the end of his talk, telling his audience: "as all historians know, the past is a great darkness ... Voices may reach us from it ... we cannot always decipher them precisely in the clearer light of our own day."[9] After some applause, he finishes—and so does the novel—with the usual pat phrase, "Are there any questions?" By ending with a question, and in fact, a question that solicits more questions, the novel asks us to question everything we have just read. The phrase "the clearer light of our own day" reads quite differently forty years on from how it did in 1986. The questions we may have to ask are also different. We may ask, for example, what did Gilead do to transgender people? Nonbinary people? Is the post-Gileadean future a TERF one? These questions remain unanswered, and we must consider that though the novel itself demonstrates a concern with gender binaries, it continues to reinforce them as well.

In this overarching way, *The Handmaid's Tale*'s "Historical Notes" are similar to the frame narrative of Alderman's *The Power*.[10] In a world very similar to ours, a genetic mutation is activated in young women around the world, allowing them to electrocute anyone they wish through their hands via a "skein" of electricity in their bodies. As more and more young women, and later, women of various ages, begin to show signs of this ability, the world begins to change radically. Victims of human trafficking, sex slaves, and the abused rise up against their oppressors; women take over an entire country and electrify streams of water to fight armies of men who attempt to suppress their uprising; a religious sect begins to congeal around one woman in particular known as "Mother Eve." Unlike the single voice of Offred in Atwood's novel, Alderman gives us a view of this quickly changing world through the perspective of four people: Allie, aka Mother Eve herself; Roxy, the daughter of a London gangster; Margot, a middle-aged female politician; and Tunde, an African male journalist documenting the revolution. While Alderman's book could have quickly turned into gleeful revenge fantasy or, as I initially feared, an antifeminist indictment of how matriarchies repeat and rehash the power structures and abuses of patriarchies, the meditation on power itself saves the novel from either of these dead ends. Instead, the novel defamiliarizes our own world, revealing and reminding us of the atrocities committed against women each and every day, highlighting indignities that many of us overlook, forget, or become inured to. *The Power*, like *The Handmaid's Tale*, reveals how the gender binary structures our lives to the point that it becomes invisible, dwelling on the painfully obvious because we don't always see it. And, like Atwood's novel, *The Power* is similarly unable to recognize and integrate transgender issues into this bioessentialist dystopia.

As with Atwood's text, issues of historicity and futurity are critical. As we read, we come to realize that the frame narrative—a set of letters between a man named Neil, the author of this quasi-historical text, and a woman named Naomi, his editor—are 5000 years into the future from the revolutionary events that, eventually, lead to the matriarchal society that for Neil and Naomi is an old reality. Naomi's letters reflect how women in this matriarchal future see men as secondary, powerless sex objects, and her language to Neil is marked with patronizing condescension: "I think I'd rather enjoy this 'world run by men' you've been talking about. Surely a kinder, more caring and—dare I say it?—more *sexy* world than the one we live in."[11] The letters are set before the start of the main text, which has its own title page with the words "The Power, *A historical novel*, Neil Adam Armon," giving no indication that they "date" from the future—though any self-aware reader will pick up on Naomi's odd language in the letters. The arc of Neil's "history" leads from the first instances where the power manifested in women up to the moment at which Mother Eve decides to incite a world conflict, later known as the Cataclysm, large enough that it will send society back to the Stone Age in order to rebuild the world from scratch as a world run by women.

Her plan evidently works, as references to archaeological digs between Neil and Naomi and to a lack of primary sources from before the Cataclysm affirm, even if the ending to Neil's book is vague. We leave our characters on the edge of a world-changing war and must learn the outcome from these letters: the ending after the ending. Through the four narratives, Neil not only describes in detail how poorly women were treated before they manifested this genetic mutation but also exposes the violence of the revolution on both sides of the gender divide—the violence of the men, trying to maintain dominion, and the violence of the women who are, in most cases, finally able to defend themselves against the violence of men. In their letters, Naomi responds with reservations to Neil's work, implying that his suggestion that women could ever in history have been victims and that men could have been powerful, violent, or aggressive is too unbelievable to be worth publishing. Again, as in the "Historical Notes" to *The Handmaid's Tale*, historical veracity is at issue; Neil acknowledges that "we don't have original manuscripts dating back more than a thousand years," revealing that much has been destroyed or censored in the historical record—essentially saying that history is written by the winners.[12] When questioned by Naomi about the possibility of thousands of male soldiers existing in the distant past (something unthinkable in their future moment), Neil replies that there is archaeological evidence, but it has often been disregarded: "people don't believe it because it doesn't fit with what they already think."[13] Alderman reverses the roles that men and women have been playing in our reality for hundreds if not thousands of years, drawing our eyes to the bigger picture of *The Power:* the reversals of power in the novel are not about fantasizing about women's aggression and dominance but rather are a way of making us think about the nature of power in our own world and its ties to gender. When Naomi writes, "'what it means to be a woman' is bound up with strength and not feeling fear or pain," we laugh; the statement is comical in its strangeness.[14] It falls oddly on the ear. Something similar happens when Neil complains to Naomi that "there are still plenty of places today where boy babies are routinely aborted."[15] The power of *The Power* is linguistic; the epistolary ending reminds us, cleverly and with irony, of the power of words, the power of written history, not unlike *The Handmaid's Tale*, in which Handmaids are forbidden from reading or writing and the written word is akin to pornography in its forbidden, taboo nature for Offred. And while Neil and Naomi are not academics like Atwood's Peixoto, we see a similar power struggle play out: Naomi is attuned to gendered power dynamics but without a feminist lens.

The very end of the end of *The Power* is the ultimate irony in this funhouse mirror of a novel. Naomi, ever a careful and thoughtful editor, reflects that Neil's central problem has always been his gender: "anything you do is framed by your gender … the frame is as inescapable as it is nonsensical."[16] She ends her final letter by suggesting a workaround for this problem: "I know this might be very distasteful to you, but have you considered publishing this book under a woman's name?"[17] The epistolary forms of both *The Handmaid's Tale* and *The Power*, as well as the nod to women publishing anonymously with masculine pseudonyms, remind us of how women's voices and women's stories have been treated as marginal throughout much of history up to and including our present moment. The seventeenth and eighteenth centuries saw the rise of women's participation in the world of publishing; women's ability to write, publish, work as printers, and enter into the trade of selling other people's stories was a world-shifting moment—and yet to publish was precarious business and women who published often chose to do so anonymously. "By a lady" or "By anonymous" were common author bylines for many women authors, but they eventually became so clearly associated with female authorship that they eventually were used by men who wished, for one reason or another, to obscure their authorship as well.

The epilogues to both novels explore the problem of authenticity and believability, in many ways again drawing on early novelistic precedents where authors published their fictions with the words "a history" to lend their stories a marketable authenticity; "real" events and stories were understood to be more important and serious than mere fictions. Through their novels, Atwood and Alderman posit those very same questions: Whose stories matter? Whose voices have authority? At the end of her now-famous essay "Men Explain Things to Me," Rebecca Solnit voices this very issue: "Most women fight wars on two fronts, one for whatever the putative topic is and one simply for the right to speak, to have ideas, to be acknowledged to be in possession of facts and truths, to have value, to be a human being."[18] Whereas *The Handmaid's Tale* imagines a world of extremes in which women are overtly made chattel, only to be followed by yet another "postfeminist" world in which a quieter misogyny continues to reign, *The Power* defamiliarizes our current world through an extreme inversion in which men have no access to power or, by extension, truth and knowledge. It is disappointing, then, to reflect on these themes and realize that neither novel nor even Solnit's now-canonical essay mentions the struggles of trans people to be heard, for their voices to be granted authenticity, and to have authority over their own experiences. The popularity of these works should give us pause; while they point to the unending struggles of feminism, they themselves, perhaps, are the best testimony for why gender studies is not ending, cannot end. Our work is not finished until we fully integrate a critique of the gender binary beyond the rights of cis women into feminist rhetoric.

It is impossible to read these novels and not notice the absence of transgender and intersex people—or to consider the novels' default valorization of the gender binary. To an extent, I find it easier to overlook such omissions in Atwood's 1986 novel, written as it was at a time when transgender rights were not a part of the feminist conversation in the way they are today. However, transgender media critics and advocates have criticized the Hulu show for its noticeable absence of trans characters, even as the show has gone to some lengths to create space for non-white representation that does not exist in the original novel. And while Alderman's novel is marginally more diverse—Allie is biracial; Tunde is African and dark-skinned—her engagement with gender nonconforming individuals is limited. Ryan is the boyfriend of Jocelyn, politician Margot's daughter. Jocelyn's skein is underdeveloped; as a result she is drawn to Ryan, who is intersex. He presents as masculine, but he has a small skein that he uses to create sparks. The weakness of his skein makes Jocelyn feel less ashamed of the weakness of her skein—a weakness that is shameful in this different world where women are electrocuting others with precision and control. Ryan is marked as intersex, and the novel makes it clear that people like him are outcasts in this alternative universe. It is unclear, to say the least, where transgender or gender nonbinary people fall into the binarized world of *The Power*. Do trans women in this world have skeins of power? If they did, then it would provide a poignant commentary on the concept of gender identity as genetic or inborn. If they don't carry the mutation, then what will be their role in the future world imagined by Alderman? And what of nonbinary folx? The polarized world created by the power would be difficult to navigate for those who eschew the terms "man" and "woman." These omissions feel glaring—and, in the wake of the TERF movement, downright threatening. In parallel, both works have little to say about race and class, with the main characters, all but Tunde, being Anglo-American, predominantly white, straight, cisgender women. Atwood's work flirts with issues of lesbianism but does not really develop the storyline with Moira, Offred's lesbian friend in the time before. These flaws reflect part of the current problems in contemporary feminism and, perhaps, an important way that gender studies, with its emphasis on gender rather than women, can intervene and help save feminism from itself.

The erasure or invisibility of trans and nonbinary people in these works is particularly disappointing as their presence would surely have enhanced the arguments of the authors. The patriarchal powers that both novels describe are committed to the suppression of women in concert with the upholding of repressive patriarchy—not unlike how TERFs, white supremacists, and conservative politicians worldwide use the same arguments to rationalize the exclusion of trans women, the killing of non-white people, and the policing of cis women's bodies and futures. These rhetorics are entangled and mutually structuring. While the endings that refuse an ending in these novels function rhetorically to support the idea of the constant need for feminist activism, the lack of a truly intersectional framework marks these as incomplete interventions at best.

The Future of Gender Studies

Any future that we can currently imagine will need some form of feminism, as these novels implicitly argue. In appending endings to their endings, they posit that the only possible ending is a lack of ending. Their omissions and their lack of an intersectional feminist framework illustrate, however, the dangers of a feminism without gender studies. The feminist movement has often been discussed in terms of waves, and I embrace this metaphor. The waves of the ocean are never still. They keep coming. Feminism will keep coming, crashing over the shores of the world, eroding bit by bit long-held cultural fantasies of gender binaries. Each wave brings with it new ideas, new knowledge, new frames for thinking about our world and our place within it, addressing the shortfalls of the previous feminist wave. Gender studies—arising arguably out of the backlash of the second wave and giving rise to the third wave, and beyond—has been crucial in keeping feminism relevant. Gender studies is not knowledge itself; it is a form of knowledge production that forces us to understand the world around us differently—and to understand cis women's oppression and abuse as part of a larger social ideology that links patriarchal power over women with colonization, institutional racism, homophobia, transphobia, capitalism, and the exploitation and devastation of the environment. In turn, gender studies helps us understand how those other vectors of hierarchical power and organization rely on binarized notions of gender to enforce and naturalize their domination and violence.

Part of the problem that both novels grapple with, which I find particularly useful to think about going forward, is how knowledge functions as a form of power that is irrevocably tied to gender. Who can possess knowledge, who can make knowledge, and who is granted access to knowledge are based on the gender of the person seeking or creating said knowledge. Knowledge has often been thought of as dangerous; laws enacted around the world, from Hungary to Russia to the state of Florida, seek to banish information and knowledge about LGBTQ people from schools, children's television, and libraries. They see knowledge as a threat: they argue that knowledge of LGBTQ people will infect children with a desire to themselves be LGBTQ or somehow "recruit" them to this "lifestyle." Most of us sense, however, that their arguments about "grooming" or recruitment are a direct reaction to the growing number of young people who accept, love, and embrace members of the LGBTQ community. "Gen Z" has one of the highest rates of LGBTQ acceptance—no doubt spurred by the fact that Gen Z also has some of the highest rates of identification with the LGBTQ community. A 2022 Gallup poll reveals that 21 percent of Gen Z respondents identify as LGBTQ—a record high for any age group.[19] There is little satisfaction in understanding that these laws and the misogynistic, homophobic, transphobic people behind them are fighting a losing battle. Books like Atwood's and Alderman's, regardless of their flaws, give voices to fears we all have: that a hateful minority can overwhelm, oppress, and murder those it deems undesirable.

The creation of women's studies departments, programs, and centers within institutions, and later women's and gender studies, gender studies, and women's, gender and sexuality studies, was about creating a space for people to dedicate themselves to the project of knowledge creation and dissemination relating to gender, but also to make a welcoming space for people who previously felt excluded from these institutions—and also those whose experiences and existence are explicitly threatened in society. The institutionalization of these practices of knowledge was and is only one small step in the overall feminist project to make the academy and society at large more equitable and inclusive. Clearly, this project, this presence in the academy, is more relevant and important than ever, as more and more students who enter our classrooms will look to see their identities reflected in their classes. At a time when enrollments are stagnant and institutions fight for each student dollar, LGBTQ inclusivity must be one of the goals that institutions espouse lest they risk alienating the very students they wish to recruit and retain. In this way, it is absolutely necessary for gender studies to remain an active part of the academy. The "Historical Notes" to *The Handmaid's Tale* question the ability of institutions of higher learning to incorporate the feminist work of gender studies into their mission, as evidenced through the sexist language of the keynote speaker at an academic conference. Importantly, this issue reiterates the need for a feminist-informed, intersectional, trans-inclusive gender studies at the university level, but one that works in parallel with feminist and LGBTQ activism outside the academy while also creating communities and spaces, whether literal or figurative, to connect, empower, and protect one another. In the end, gender studies is about caring, inclusivity, and recognition both within and outside the academy. We cannot stop caring for our future, for ourselves: radical care and self-care are not mere phrases. Gender studies does not end because we cannot, we will not, stop caring.

Notes

1. My definition of feminism is explicitly trans-inclusive, as I will discuss further below.
2. For an overview, see the introduction to Jennifer A. Wagner-Lawlor's *Postmodern Utopias and Feminist Fictions* (Cambridge: Cambridge University Press, 2013).
3. See in particular chapter one of Robyn Wiegman, *Object Lessons* (Durham: Duke University Press, 2012).
4. Scott Jaschik, "The Evolution of American Women's Studies," *Inside Higher Ed*, March 27, 2009.
5. "Intersectionality" was coined by Kimberlé Crenshaw, "Demarginalizing the Intersection of Race and Sex: A Black Feminist Critique of Antidiscrimination Doctrine, Feminist Theory and Antiracist Politics," *Chicago Legal Forum* 1989, no. 1, article 8.

6. Julia Serano, *Whipping Girl: A Transsexual Woman on Sexism and the Scapegoating of Femininity* (New York: Seal Press, 2006), 16.
7. Margaret Atwood, *The Handmaid's Tale* (New York: Anchor Books, [1986] 1998).
8. Ibid., 301.
9. Ibid.
10. Similarities between Atwood's book and Alderman's are not necessarily coincidental; Atwood, along with her husband Graeme Gibson, mentored Alderman, whose book is dedicated to them both. Claire Armitstead, "Naomi Alderman: 'I went into the novel religious and by the end I wasn't. I wrote myself out of it,'" *The Guardian*, October 28, 2018.
11. Naomi Alderman, *The Power* (New York: Back Bay Books, 2016), n.pag, emphasis in original.
12. Alderman, *The Power*, 379.
13. Ibid., 377.
14. Ibid., 380.
15. Ibid.
16. Ibid., 381.
17. Ibid., 382.
18. Rebecca Solnit, "Men Explain Things to Me," *Guernica Magazine*, August 20, 2012.
19. Carlie Porterfield, "Gen-Z Drives Surge of More Americans Identifying as LGBT," *Forbes*, February 17, 2022.

CHAPTER 12
THE ENDS OF ACTIVISM
Ady Barkan

In May of 1865, the American Anti-Slavery Society had a big decision to make. The Civil War was over, and Congress had passed the Thirteenth Amendment to the US Constitution, abolishing slavery throughout the land. And so, William Lloyd Garrison, the beloved founder and president of the Society, had submitted his resignation, alongside a resolution that the organization declare victory and dissolve itself.

For thirty years, the Society had been the central organization of the abolitionist movement. It had thousands of chapters around the country, with passionate and disciplined local leaders who brought in hundreds of thousands of members. Its meetings featured speeches and debates by traveling lecturers, the most prominent of whom was Frederick Douglass, who had escaped enslavement in Maryland and whose brilliant oratory and writing had made him a most powerful refutation of the notion that slaves were biologically inferior or incapable. Across the northeast and Midwest, members of the Society subscribed to *The Liberator*, the weekly newspaper published by Garrison, who had written the Constitution of the Society at its inaugural meeting of sixty-two delegates in Philadelphia in 1831. (In the South, distribution of *The Liberator* was a crime; Garrison was indicted and a bounty placed on his head.) Garrison's passion and uncompromising insistence on immediate abolition, without compensation to slaveholders, made him a prominent and beloved voice of the movement, alongside Douglass. "His paper took a place in my heart second only to The Bible," Douglass wrote.[1]

So it was significant and consequential when Garrison called for the dissolution of the organization that he had built and led for thirty years. Its ends had been accomplished, he believed, because slavery was defeated.

But other leaders of the organization disagreed, including Douglass and Wendell Phillips, Garrison's dear friend, who both thought the struggle for racial justice was far from complete. Black Americans needed civil equality, including equal protection under the law; they needed political equality, including access to the ballot; and they needed economic empowerment and redress for their enslavement, most importantly through the redistribution of plantation land.

Garrison agreed with these goals, but believed that they should be pursued by new organizations under new leadership—the organization's Constitution he drafted three decades earlier had, after all, been crystal clear: "The object of this Society is the entire abolition of slavery in the United States."[2]

The Ends of Knowledge

So, at the national convention of the American Anti-Slavery Society, only a few weeks after the end of the Civil War and the assassination of President Abraham Lincoln, 166 leaders of the Society voted on Garrison's proposal.

Generational Struggles

What is the purpose of democratic activism, and how do we know when that purpose has been achieved? Every campaign has a reach that exceeds its grasp. The minimum wage is raised, but not nearly high enough. The government guarantees health insurance, but only for people over sixty-five, and even they don't get long-term care or dental care. The work is never done, because there is always plenty of injustice left. In American law and politics, progress is always driven by agitators outside of government, clamoring for reform, taking outrageous ideas and making them seem reasonable, and then seizing the reins of power—or at least grasping on to one rein, with a thumb and forefinger, for a few moments and pulling hard enough to turn the horse of state in a slightly different direction.

Every generation inherits the progress made by those who came before us, and also their defeats and retreats. We know that we may not live to see the conclusion of every fight we have taken on, but we do this work in the hopes that perhaps our children, or their children, might see the fruits of our struggles.

Strategies of Revolution

On June 12, 1840, abolitionists gathered in London for the first World Anti-Slavery Convention. The slave trade had been abolished in the British Empire in 1807, and slavery in 1834, so this meeting was aimed at marshaling the power and experience of the British anti-slavery movement in promotion of abolition worldwide, especially in the United States. Two hundred British activists were in attendance, along with about fifty Americans, including William Lloyd Garrison. Wendell Phillips was there, with his wife Ann, who had first convinced him that abolition required more than his support; it required his full commitment. Garrison and Phillips had encouraged women abolitionists to attend, with the expectation that their presence would be controversial because of women's persistent position as second-class citizens. Present also was Lucretia Mott, a Quaker minister and orator who had been the only woman to speak at the inaugural meeting of the American Anti-Slavery Society in Philadelphia nine years earlier. Elizabeth Cady Stanton was there too, accompanying her husband, the delegate Henry Stanton.

As Garrison had hoped, the first day was consumed by the contentious question of whether women would be permitted to attend or participate. Phillips made a motion for their inclusion, and in his speech highlighted the central role of women activists in the American abolition movement. Ultimately, women were permitted to attend, but only in segregated seating, and they were prohibited from speaking or voting. In protest, Garrison and four other male delegates refused to participate fully, and sat with the women instead.

Lucretia Mott and Elizabeth Cady Stanton met for the first time at the Convention, and they left the first tumultuous day arm in arm, newly inspired to advocate for the rights of women. Seven years later, their friendship and shared work culminated in the announcement of the first woman's rights convention, in Seneca Falls, New York. Their announcement in the local paper made the goals of the event, and ultimately of the organization, unambiguous: "WOMAN'S RIGHTS CONVENTION.—A Convention to discuss the social, civil, and religious condition and rights of women."

Stanton presented to the convention a declaration of sentiments, modeled after the Declaration of Independence, listing the grievances of subordination. It was discussed, revised, adopted unanimously, and signed by 100 attendees. More controversial was the ninth of eleven resolutions that Stanton presented for adoption. It read, "Resolved, that it is the duty of the women of this country to secure to themselves their sacred right to the elective franchise."[3]

Stanton's call for women's suffrage was radical enough that even her collaborator and friend Lucretia Mott opposed it: "Why Lizzie, thee will make us ridiculous," she told her. More persuasive was the oratory of the only Black person in attendance, Douglass, who spoke in favor of the resolution, which passed comfortably. Later, he published Stanton's "Declaration of Sentiments" in his anti-slavery newspaper, *The North Star*, whose slogan was: "Right is of No Sex—Truth is of No Color—God is the Father of Us All, and All We Are Brethren."

Forty years later, in his speech to the International Council of Women, Douglass said this: "All good causes are mutually helpful. The benefits accruing from this movement for the equal rights of women are not confined or limited to women only. They will be shared by every effort to promote the progress and welfare of mankind everywhere and in all ages."[4] Douglass believed in solidarity, the notion that what unites us may be more powerful than what divides us.

What do these nineteenth-century stories teach us about how to do activism today? How bold should activists be, when laying out their vision for a better world? How careful should they be not to look ridiculous, not to invite powerful backlash, not to stymie their prospects for concrete victories today? These questions infuse strategic debates in every social movement. The abolitionists of today use the phrase "Defund the police," but then face internal and external questions about its efficacy. Municipal and state budgets are consumed by massive expenditures on policing and incarceration, leaving few dollars available for community health clinics and after school programs, let alone affordable housing or living wage jobs.

The phrase "Defund the police" captures the righteous demand that we divest from systems of racial oppression and invest in the institutions and programs that will actually keep people safe.[5] But as many examples show, progress is slow, and sometimes it's hard to see if our activism is serving any end, immediate or even in the distant future. In the elections of November 2021, the people of New York City elected a former police officer as mayor and the people of Minneapolis—perhaps the epicenter of the movement for Black lives, where George Floyd was murdered under a police officer's knee, igniting thousands of protests around the country and world—rejected a ballot measure that would have replaced the police department with a department of public safety, under new leadership and with a different orientation.

Ends and Beginnings

Eric Foner captures succinctly the debate at the Anti-Slavery Society: "Even the abolitionist movement could not decide whether the [13th] Amendment was an end or a beginning."[6] "My vocation, as an Abolitionist, thank God, is ended," declared Garrison, urging the American Anti-Slavery Society at its May 1865 annual meeting to dissolve in triumph. To which Douglass replied, "Slavery is not abolished until the black man has the ballot." Garrison's proposal was defeated, Phillips replaced him as the society's president, and the National Anti-Slavery Standard appeared with a new motto on its masthead: "No Reconstruction Without Negro Suffrage." The ends of the endeavor had changed. But, of course they had.

The ensuing years were some of the most dramatic and consequential in American history. By 1870, the Republican demand for Black male suffrage had won ratification of the Fifteenth Amendment, which prohibited the federal and state governments from denying or abridging the right to vote "on account of race, color, or previous condition of servitude."[7] The guarantee was greeted as a momentous victory by many Republicans, and the American Anti-Slavery Society did indeed thereafter dissolve in victory, its ends seemingly achieved.

But there were fatal shortcomings to the Amendment. It did not prohibit poll taxes, literacy tests, or other mechanisms to selectively deny access to the ballot. Radical Republican senator Charles Sumner of Massachusetts abstained from the vote on the Amendment because of these pitfalls, and his concerns would be proven tragically prescient. From 1890 until 1965, Southern states used a variety of maneuvers to deny Black citizens the right to vote, despite the Amendment's text.

The Fifteenth Amendment also conspicuously failed to guarantee the right of women to vote. The idea was no more viable, politically, in 1870 than it had been when Stanton presented the resolution for it at the Seneca Falls convention in 1848. For three decades, since the protest over women's inclusion at the World Anti-Slavery Convention in London, the abolition movement and the women's rights movement had been deeply intertwined. But the Fifteenth Amendment broke those bonds. The Equal Rights Association, which had advocated for the rights of women and Black people to vote, could not survive its internal debate over whether to support the Amendment. Stanton could not countenance the idea of uneducated Black, Chinese, and other men of color voting while wealthy educated white women like her remained un-enfranchised, and she used racist language to make her dissatisfaction clear.

It took another fifty years, until 1920, to amend the federal constitution to guarantee the rights of women to vote. By then only 1 of the 100 people who had signed the Declaration of Sentiments at Seneca Falls was still alive.

Activism as Authorship

So, when does democratic activism end, and what are its ends? "It's always too soon to go home. Most of the great victories continue to unfold, unfinished in the sense that they are not yet fully realized, but also in the sense that they continue to spread influence," writes Rebecca Solnit in her book of reflections on activism, *Hope in the Dark*.[8] Dark, she means, as in obscure and uncertain. The future is unwritten, but history shows that we can be its coauthors if we choose to pick up the pen and write our collective story in solidarity with others.

Solidarity relies on our belief that our struggles are interconnected and that, therefore, our freedom is too. Solidarity in progressive activism shows us how the ends of one struggle can serve as the openings, and beginnings, of another.

But we are each just individuals—one among billions—and the world is also dark in the other sense of the word. It is cruel and harsh, unfair and random and inexplicable. So, what does it mean to say that we can be authors? And what does it mean to retain hope when the odds are so long, the obstacles so great? How can we each participate in the struggle for justice now, but also later, when things have changed?

Activism is precisely about not accepting the tragedies of this world but rather on insisting that we can reduce pain and prolong life. Social justice means creating a stable floor beneath our feet and then putting a safety net under that, to catch us if it suddenly vanishes: universal health insurance, affordable housing, unemployment benefits—or even better, a guaranteed job making the community a more decent and sustainable place to live. Being part of a progressive political movement is about fighting back and building toward a better future. "Acceptance" is not part of our vocabulary.

The theologian Reinhold Niebuhr—whose most famous disciple, Dr. Martin Luther King Jr., would become the patron saint of American organizers—sought to resolve this tension in his Serenity Prayer: asking for the serenity to accept what cannot be changed, the courage to change what can be, and the wisdom to know the difference.

There is a seeming paradox embedded in the third part of Niebuhr's prayer, because the wisdom to know the difference between what we can and cannot change can only be earned through struggle. It is only by refusing to accept the complacency of previous generations that the impossible becomes reality, and here is also an end to activism. For me, Niebuhr's prayer is most true if rearranged: collective courage must come first, wisdom second, and serenity at the very end.

So, we engage in activism to make the world a better place, but also to make meaning of our own lives. Because action is an antidote to despair. It brings us into connection with others, who are also facing insurmountable obstacles. It offers us the opportunity to create a different narrative. The ends of democratic activism, then, are to be coauthors not always of a grand narrative but of our own.

Notes

1. Frederick Douglass, *The Frederick Douglass Papers*, Series Two: Autobiographical Writings, Volume 3: Life and Times of Frederick Douglass, ed. John R. McKivigan, John W. Blassingame, and Joseph R. McElrath (New Haven: Yale University Press, 2012), 166.
2. American Anti-Slavery Society, *The Constitution of the American Anti-Slavery Society* (New York: American Anti-Slavery Society, 1838), 3.
3. *Report of the Woman's Rights Convention Held at Seneca Falls, N.Y., July 19th and 20th, 1858* (Rochester: John Dick at North Star, 1848).
4. Frederick Douglass, "Give Women Fair Play," March 31, 1888, in *The Douglass Papers*, ser. 1, 5: 355.
5. Shaila Dewan, "'Re-Fund the Police'? Why It Might Not Reduce Crime." *The New York Times*, November 8, 2021.
6. Eric Foner, *A Short History of Reconstruction* (New York: Harper Perennial Modern Classics, 2015), 30–1.
7. "U.S. Const. amend. XV."
8. Rebecca Solnit, *Hope in the Dark: Untold Histories, Wild Possibilities* (Chicago: Haymarket Books, 2016).

CHAPTER 13
THE ENDS OF ENVIRONMENTAL STUDIES
Myanna Lahsen

The Climate Research Moratorium Proposal

At the current juncture, is aggressive action to avert existential environmental threats helped or hindered by science? This question was raised on the eve of Christmas 2021, when a group of environmental scientists issued a call for a moratorium on further climate science, protesting against what they call "the tragedy of climate change science." The tragedy, as Bruce C. Glavovic, Timothy F. Smith, and Iain White expressed it, consists in the current compulsion to do ever more research on climate change while long-standing, clear, consolidated, and urgent science-based warnings are not being translated into policies in support of transformations toward sustainability. Defining the real problem as political rather than a lack of scientific knowledge, they suggest that climate science has reached its logical end. At least for the moment, producing more science in this context is a complicity with the status quo, they argue, because it diverts attention from "where the problem truly lies." They propose a moratorium on further climate change research "as a means to first expose, then reconfigure, the broken science-society contract"—a presumably temporary measure to pressure decision-makers to take action.[1] Initially published in an academic journal, the message spread to mainstream media, with *The New York Times* dedicating an article to the cause of these "striking" scientists.[2]

This high-profile proposal for a moratorium—and its premises and formulation—raises questions about the purpose and power of environmental research in the context of existential threats such as climate change and the loss of biodiversity and associated ecosystem services on which life on Earth as we know it depends, and that in turn depend on flora and fauna that are disappearing at a staggering rate around the world.[3] Glavovic et al.'s proposal raises questions about the ends of climate science in two meanings of the word: (1) What are *the goals* of science and (2), if the goal is environmental action, is it wise *to stop* additional knowledge production, even if momentarily? Is continued research production unwise when established scientific bodies such as the United Nations Intergovernmental Panel on Climate Change (IPCC) and the Intergovernmental Panel on Biodiversity and Ecosystem Services (IPBES) judge the science sufficiently solid for urgent action, yet societal action chronically reinforces the status quo? When research substitutes for action,[4] is it wiser and more system-challenging to *end* research or, quite on the contrary, to *persist* in consolidating knowledge about present and future impacts of the very societal arrangements that need to be transformed?

The Ends of Knowledge

Discussing sociopolitical expectations of science and the limitations of science, this chapter starts by lending support to the argument that the real problem is political, summarizing some of the civilization-threatening environmental transformations afoot. Subsequently, however, it contests the premise that environmental research has done all that it can, and must, to support transformations toward sustainability. Rather, I argue, the status quo is undesirable in both society and science, because the two coproduce each other. Dominant actors in both realms uphold logics and norms that sustain the status quo—a status quo in which they both have stakes. If environmental scientists are to support transformations, I argue, they must be willing to accept profound change in science agendas and in the norms and power structures that currently dominate in science and in its interface with policy. Moreover, societies must offer the social safety net required for such shows of self-sacrifice. The answer is not, as Glavovic et al. posit, to end all environmental research, but to rethink science agendas such that they are better able to produce knowledge that can truly guide societies as they must find new governance arrangements and foster changes in values and understandings in favor of precaution, justice, equality, and equity.

Science, Policy, and Politics

Successful challenges to religious dogma by astronomers and other scientific knowledge producers during the seventeenth century eventually yielded a relatively independent space for the pursuit of an evidence-based, systematic understanding of nature and natural phenomena, and have made science a prestigious and powerful institution in most contemporary societies. A social "contract" with science in the form of mutual expectations and support gradually developed in which science received needed material and political support from governments in exchange for its production of knowledge, supposedly to the benefit of society. During times of war, scientists are commonly enlisted to serve with technical aspects of warfare, such as in the US Manhattan Project during the Second World War.[5] At the end of that war, the initiator of the Manhattan Project—the presidential science advisor, Vannevar Bush—published *Science: The Endless Frontier*, a report that redefined the postwar science agenda in the United States and beyond.[6] Premised on a "linear" model of science, this new science policy framework assumed that basic research—that is, scientists pursuing their intellectual interests in relative isolation, motivated by curiosity—rather automatically leads to applied research, socio-technological innovation, and, thus, social benefits. With time, ideals of autonomy, openness, and disinterestedness (i.e., neutrality and freedom from personal and political motivations) came to be dominant norms in science.[7] These norms came to be associated with science, reinforced by sociological portrayals of these values as an actual "ethos" shaping scientific production.[8]

Both the linear model and the described idealization of science have since been widely criticized and shown to be overly simplistic at best, if not misleading.[9] It has become abundantly clear that science does not necessarily—nor in a timely manner—

lead to positive and sustainable advances in the quality of human life for the majority of people. The linear model fails to recognize the choices and difficulties—or opportunities, depending on one's perspective—imposed by the existence of conflicting scientific evidence. Rather than earnest and wise truth-seekers giving due weight to precautionary considerations, decision-makers and other groups outside the scientific community—not least actors with vested economic interest in the status quo—often choose to lean on the expertise of experts, real or fake, whose positions best serve their interests.[10] Indeed, decision-makers and business leaders often even entirely disregard and denigrate expertise.[11]

All of this raises the question of the potency—or rather, the limited impact—of science on policy, the forms and implications of which I discuss below.

Political Intransigence Despite Scientific Evidence and Warnings

Dangerous levels of climate change, chemical pollution, biodiversity and natural resource losses, and pandemics are being caused by emissions of greenhouse gas emissions, incursion into wildlife habitat, and the use of dangerous agro-chemicals. These problems are forming a perfect storm of emergencies because the most dire consequences are projected to happen in the future. Increasingly assisted by artificial intelligence (AI) in the form of "big data" and machine learning, science fills a vital role. Science helps identify and understand the threats, including present and future interconnections and alternative pathways that societies can choose.

But robust scientific warnings are not proving sufficient, throwing science into a crisis along with the planet. It has been fifty years since the Limits to Growth scientists warned that growth on a finite planet leads to socio-environmental devastation. It has been thirty years since the IPCC issued its first global climate assessment urging action to avert climate change. Scientists have long been writing about tipping points and the importance of rapid transformation of energy systems and of protecting the world's remaining biomes. Instead of action, destruction has been speeding up.

Symbolic of the state of the global environment, the Amazon basin is nearing a tipping point which will push it into a new state with conditions that are much less hospitable for life in the region and, through teleconnections, beyond it.[12] Despite solid scientific knowledge of the global danger of further deforestation of this biome, the region now faces a new threat from the massive infrastructure program titled the Initiative for the Integration of the Regional Infrastructure of South America, or IIRSA. Potentially pushing the Amazon forest over a threshold into savanna-like conditions, this would further degrade biodiversity, reduce carbon storage, and harm continental agriculture, which is dependent on moisture transport from forest-based rainfall recycling.[13]

The world's largest tropical wetland is also pressured beyond precedent. Approximately a fourth of Brazil's Pantanal wetland, one of the most biodiverse places on Earth, has been incinerated by wildfires in recent years, aggravated by climate change and fueling the sixth extinction.[14] It is causing devastating losses, pain, and death to humans and to innumerable defenseless, innocent wild animals and insects incinerated and maimed in the fires or left to die from lack of water and food in their wake.

Meanwhile, South America's only aquifer, the Guarani, is being depleted by a combination of overuse and deforestation of native vegetation in Brazil's biodiverse biomes, especially the Cerrado Savanna, the site of Brazil's most rapidly expanding agricultural frontier.[15] More than 80 percent of Brazil's water is used for agriculture, which, paradoxically, makes it highly dependent on the same ecosystems that it is destroying. The native flora and fauna are highly adapted to the region's arid weather. Over millennia, the vegetation has developed into an "inverted forest" because the semi-arid climate and acid soils induced it to invest in roots that are tens of meters long. As such, the exceptionally long and specialized roots serve to both draw from and replenish water deep underground, performing vital ecosystem service by channeling rain and other surface water back into deep soil reservoirs. With shallow roots, the monoculture crops that replace the native vegetation after its removal cannot perform the same ecosystem service "water care." Instead, surface water evaporates and runs off into river systems, polluted by pesticides, many of which are alarmingly dangerous and banned in Europe.[16] Degrading ecosystems and the resources that these sustain, the pesticides thereby also threaten food, water, and energy security. Pesticides are generating unprecedented rates of cancer and birth defects in Latin America—and large profits in the companies producing them.[17] The top producing companies are all headquartered in the world's rich countries, where the same chemicals often are banned and where variously incompetent, impotent, and corrupt political leaders fail to act, either ignoring or reconstructing scientifically well-grounded evidence.[18]

Besides poisoning human and animal health,[19] this causes depletion of the aquifer and the river systems that it feeds, threatening water supplies on which millions of people as well as other biomes depend.[20] With public attention overly fixated on the Amazon, too few realize that conservation of the Cerrado is essential for regional climate stabilization and regional food and water security. That includes water security—and thus the preservation—of the Amazon's forests, because they, too, depend on rivers that the Guarani aquifer and savanna ecosystems maintain.[21]

The above facts are known by science, including Brazilian government-funded science.[22] Yet they have not translated into sound environmental policies and change. Brazil's national and international climate mitigation targets are insufficient to truly reduce emissions from deforestation. The target for deforestation reduction in the Cerrado defined in Brazil's 2009 national climate legislation was merely in line with the status quo deforestation and emissions scenario.[23] Brazil's Intended Nationally Determined Contributions (NDC) text submitted in the context of the Paris Agreement under the United Nations Framework Convention on Climate Change expressed a commitment to emission reductions and zero illegal deforestation in the Amazon, but it did not even mention the Cerrado or propose emissions/deforestation reductions for the region, despite the urgings of national scientists that it do so.[24]

Similar stories can be told about other regions in the world, forested and nonforested. From national to global levels, it is evident that even robust scientific facts are resisted where they threaten powerful interests. Societies tend toward the status quo,[25] as if more of the same were preferable, even in the face of sound scientific knowledge and after decades of international treaties and governmental commitments to address climate change and biodiversity loss and to reconcile development needs with environmental limits and justice and equity considerations. In Brazil, as globally, the precautionary principle is being profoundly and progressively weakened when it sorely needs strengthening.

The examples discussed in this section highlight the importance of scientific knowledge of the degradation of planetary ecosystems and the impacts of climate change. Depending on how long it would last, a blanket moratorium on climate science might play into the forces wishing to stall rather than promote action. It could undermine governments or civil society actors, including businesses, who are inclined and preparing to act. Scientific assessments can empower actors, including civic mobilization in favor of climate adaptation, mitigation, and environmental justice. That is exactly why environmental knowledge is the target of anti-environmental forces.

If governments currently by and large have accepted scientists' conclusions yet not acted, it is hard to imagine that a moratorium on the production of this science would spur them into action. From this perspective, a moratorium could be inconsequential, other than as a show of protest. Moreover, Glavovic et al. seem to assume that science has it more or less right. The example discussed below illustrates the importance of continued research and verification of scientific conclusions. Uncertainty inherent in global environmental science can cut both ways, overestimating as well as underestimating threats where we least expect them, with huge regional if not global consequences.

Necessity but Insufficiency of Data, Technologies, and Biogeochemical Understanding

In 2019, estimates of global vulnerability to sea-level rise and coastal flooding suddenly tripled. This recalibration was not a function of alteration in the real world but in technical knowledge about it. More specifically, the error was caused by faulty computer programming designed to compensate for data limitations. In areas where actual high-quality elevation data are too expensive to obtain or not available from satellites, estimates of land elevations are produced by AI-boosted computer programs by averaging detected land surfaces. In 2019, scientists discovered that the semi-automated computer programs had included rooftops and not only actual land surfaces in their estimated averages, resulting in the overall overestimation of the height of land surfaces relative to sea levels. The subsequent technical adjustments tripled estimated global vulnerability to sea-level rise and consequent coastal flooding.

As water increasingly creeps—and with more frequency and intensity may surge—above its current confines, driven by climate change, we might expect many more disasters than previously thought. The erroneous estimates of land inundation vulnerability were used in energy planning around the world, including in flooding-prone, vulnerable, developing countries in Southeast Asia. As elsewhere in the world, people reside overwhelmingly in coastal areas in this region. Consequently, most nuclear reactors and toxic waste sites are also located in coastal zones. While some countries have decided to terminate their nuclear reactors (e.g., Germany and Switzerland), nuclear energy generation is rapidly rising elsewhere in the world, especially in the Middle East and Southeast Asia, and especially in China.[26] In China alone, twelve nuclear reactors were under construction in 2020. An additional 43 reactors were in the formal planning stage and 170 reactors at the proposal stage.[27]

The finding begs reflection on global vulnerability, and how vulnerability intensifies when societies depend on automated technology for safety and risk estimates. Artificial intelligence is increasingly used to correct the errors in land surface estimates. We can hope—but should not be overly trusting—that the corrected estimates prove more reliable.

New informational and computational capacities are spurring social science research in the direction of more comprehensive, machine-enabled analyses. But these new capacities are also cause for concern; their implications for science, and for climate knowledge, are insufficiently charted.[28] Big data and machine learning have great positive potential, but also severe limitations and negative potential that can tend to get ignored.[29] Constant vigilance is needed: while powerful, machine-assisted big data analysis tools come with temptations and dangers, including tendencies toward "apophenia—that is, seeing patterns where none actually exist, simply because massive quantities of data can offer connections that radiate in all directions"—and to wrongly trust that it is possible to see and understand "everything at a 30,000-foot view."[30] It is commonly believed that large datasets drown out noise.[31] But they can obscure more than reveal. Drawing conclusions on the basis of formal statistical significance (typically for a p-value less than 0.05) in a single study is a fallacy, since "almost everything," including minuscule effects, can seem significant when searching very large datasets.[32]

These examples illustrate the importance of continued research and verification of scientific conclusions. Ending knowledge production could prevent important corrections in scientific knowledge, with potentially huge regional if not global consequences.

Science and the Status Quo

On the one hand, then, the above underscores the importance of not ending environmental research of any kind. On the other hand, a moratorium on diagnoses of biogeochemical realities might free up resources and brain power to focus more centrally—and thus help overcome—obstacles to action. Similar to the scientific mobilization during the Second World War, a contemporary mobilization is arguably needed, not a moratorium. However, the science should center squarely on how to overcome the very political obstacles that Glavovic et al. diagnose. The authors explicitly call for a moratorium on social science as well, dismissing the likelihood of payoff from more investment in it. They thereby ignore that social science has enjoyed relatively little funding and institutional support compared to the natural sciences. A study of 333 competitive grant-funding institutions in thirty-seven countries for the years 1990 to 2018 found that, in the area of climate change, 770 percent more funding goes to natural sciences than to the social sciences, and that the social science that is funded focuses overwhelmingly on climate adaptation rather than mitigation: only 0.12 percent of all research funding goes to the latter.[33] Despite the efforts of a powerful coalition of science leaders and institutions to foster more equal attention to natural and social dimensions of global environmental challenges,[34] a constellation of incumbent science leaders and institutions have proved more forceful, enjoying the power granted by long-standing patterns of privilege and funding, as well as widely held cultural norms and unexamined politics and assumptions.[35]

A growing body of literature analyzing problems in the science-policy interface indicates that academic research institutions contribute to the forces obstructing problem-informed, evidence-based redesign of science agendas to better support social, economic, and political changes in line with the imperatives of just transformations toward sustainability. This literature highlights how and why the research side of the equation is an inherent part of the problem and therefore also needs a thorough overhaul to achieve discernible, positive, and just transformations toward sustainability.

Drawing on this literature, it has been pointed out that "mutually reinforcing power structures, interests, needs, and norms within the institutions of global environmental change science obstruct rethinking and reform."[36] Moreover, the maladaptive blockage this creates and the forces behind it are seldom scrutinized and known because a combination of cultural and political considerations and vested interests shield them from scrutiny and interventions. To overcome this blockage and achieve more impactful research, scrutiny of the research side of the equation is vital, as well as greater openness, self-critique, and power-sharing across research committees, to create opportunities and support for new and more diverse thinking, conversations, deliberations, and decision-making that are more conducive to sustainability transformations.

The fact that Glavovic et al. made their call for a moratorium without acknowledging these dimensions—indeed, without apparent knowledge of them—simultaneously reflects and reinforces an obstacle to the action that they so wish to promote: the persistent marginalization of social science relative to the natural sciences in climate research. They place the problem squarely in the world of politics, and more specifically among economic interests in continued fossil fuel dependence. Those are, certainly, a major part of the problem. However, transformations toward sustainability require expansion of the scope of research to focus on social, cultural, and political dimensions that sustain the status quo but remain understudied—indeed, underlegitimized, because of dominant norms in science and a complicity with power that has been documented but that remains understudied.[37]

For example, the role of mass media in how discourses shape perceptions of science and of environmental risks is recognized and supported by studies conducted in a wide array of national contexts.[38] Such studies show that mainstream news media tend to be averse to tackling the climate issue to an extent concomitant with its importance, and that they tend to frame climate change in ways that weaken individuals' perceptions of agency to alter the status quo.[39] Clark and Harley's review and stock-taking of twenty years of sustainability science stresses the need for more research into power over signification and the potential to overcome incumbency by means of collective reframing.[40] But the 42-page review (not counting the 15 pages of references) does not contain any references to media or communications technologies, nor do most of the 357 peer-reviewed works that they cite as sources for treatments of norms and imaginaries. This omission of discussion of the political economy of media and of the importance of media reform to meet social and environmental goals is a wider tendency in scholarship on sustainability.[41]

Critical strands of scholarship tend to be marginalized, discredited by norms of value and neutrality that are deeply cultural and that deny the inherently political nature of such judgments and of environmental research, like all knowledge. It can seem that the research that is most needed is precisely what is most excluded, and that the reason is the threat that it constitutes to incumbent powers. Environmental research needs to focus on such obstacles, which will require granting legitimacy to more critical and politics-focused research than is currently the norm. As a political scientist has observed, we need to "take much more seriously ideological and political landscape pressures which bear down on regimes and which may help to explain continuity and commonality among approaches to transitions across sectors even amid the diversity of contexts."[42] That includes, as he notes, "visions and ideologies regarding the role of the state and how the private sector permeates across individual transitions through programmes of privatization," not least how neoliberalism constrains and enables particular transition pathways and not others, and the ways in which growing financialization of the global economy offers both challenges and opportunities for transitions.[43] Research and action along these lines depend on historical and political analyses—for example, of the power of finance capital—that currently have little visibility in global environmental assessments.

Conclusion

While all this is going on, humans continue to increase their consumption of animal protein. And we collectively spend more on ice cream each year than on reducing the risk that our own artificial intelligence technologies will destroy us.[44] Will we ever learn to act in a timely manner to reduce existential risks? A philosopher and scholar of existential risks at the University of Oxford's Future of Humanity Institute observed in early 2020 that some of our biggest perils—such as pandemics and unaligned artificial intelligence—lie ahead, urging us to make safeguarding our future a top priority.[45] These perils are upon us already. Addressing the threats of climate change and water and food scarcity requires attending to systemic connections. Ending science is hardly the solution. However, it is vital to rethink what research is prioritized and to reshape research agendas and the norms and assumptions in science that restrain research from doing all that it can to support transformations toward sustainability.

Notes

1. Bruce C. Glavovic, Timothy F. Smith, and Iain White, "The Tragedy of Climate Change Science," *Climate and Development* (December 24, 2021): 1. DOI: 10.1080/17565529.2021.2008855.
2. Raymond Zhong, "These Climate Scientists Are Fed Up and Ready to Go on Strike," *New York Times*, March 1, 2022.
3. Jake Rice, Cristiana Simão Seixas, María Elena Zaccagnini, Mauricio Bedoya-Gaitán, and Natalia Valderrama, eds. *The IPBES Regional Assessment Report on Biodiversity and Ecosystem Services for the Americas* (Bonn, Germany: Secretariat of the Intergovernmental Science-Policy Platform on Biodiversity and Ecosystem Services, 2018), 656.
4. Daniel Sarewitz, Roger A. Pielke Jr., and Radford Byerly, eds., *Prediction: Science, Decision Making, and the Future of Nature* (Washington, DC: Island Press, 2000).
5. Hugh Gusterson, *Nuclear Rites: A Weapons Laboratory at the End of the Cold War* (Berkeley, CA: University of California Press, 1996).
6. Sarewitz, *Prediction*.
7. Robert K. Merton, "The Normative Structure of Science," in *The Sociology of Science: Theoretical and Empirical Investigations*, ed. N. Storer (Chicago: University of Chicago Press, 1942), 267–78.
8. Ibid.
9. Esther Turnhout, Willemijn Tuinstra, and Willem Halffman, *Environmental Expertise: Connecting Science, Policy, and Society* (Cambridge: Cambridge University Press, 2019).
10. Roger Pielke Jr., *The Honest Broker: Making Sense of Science in Policy and Politics* (Cambridge: Cambridge University Press, 2007).
11. Stephan Lewandowsky, Ullrich K. H. Ecker, and John Cook, "Beyond Misinformation: Understanding and Coping with the 'Post-Truth' Era," *Journal of Applied Research in Memory and Cognition* 6, no. 4 (December 2017): 353–69.
12. Robert Toovey Walker, "Collision Course: Development Pushes Amazonia toward Its Tipping Point," *Environment: Science and Policy for Sustainable Development* 63, no. 1 (December 23, 2020): 15–25.
13. Robert Toovey Walker et al., "Avoiding Amazonian Catastrophes: Prospects for Conservation in the 21st Century," *One Earth* 1, no. 2 (2019): 202–15.
14. Walter Leal Filho et al., "Fire in Paradise: Why the Pantanal Is Burning," *Environmental Science & Policy* 123 (2021): 31–4.
15. Myanna Lahsen, Mercedes M. C. Bustamante, and Eloi L. Dalla-Nora, "Undervaluing and Overexploiting the Brazilian Cerrado at Our Peril," *Environment: Science and Policy for Sustainable Development* 58, no. 6 (2016): 4–15.
16. Larissa Mies Bombardi, *Atlas Geografia do Uso de Agrotóxicos no Brasil e Conexões com a União Européia*, FFLCH, University of São Paulo, 2017.
17. Francis L. Martin et al., "Increased Exposure to Pesticides and Colon Cancer: Early Evidence in Brazil," *Chemosphere* 209 (2018): 623–31; Dieter Pesendorfer, "EU Environmental Policy under Pressure: Chemicals Policy Change between Antagonistic Goals?" *Environmental Politics* 15, no. 1 D. (2006): 95–114.
18. Bombardi, *Atlas Geografia do Uso de Agrotóxicos no Brasil e Conexões com a União Européia*.

19. Régia Maria Avancini et al., "Organochlorine Compounds in Bovine Milk from the State of Mato Grosso do Sul–Brazil," *Chemosphere* 90 (2013): 2408–13.
20. Lahsen et al., "Undervaluing and Overexploiting the Brazilian Cerrado at Our Peril."
21. Ibid.
22. Ibid.
23. Ibid.
24. Ibid.
25. John W. Handmer and Stephen R. Dovers, "A Typology of Resilience: Rethinking Institutions for Sustainable Development," *Organization and Environment* 9, no. 4 (December 1996): 482–511.
26. Meredith J. DeBoom, "Toward a More Sustainable Energy Transition: Lessons from Chinese Investments in Namibian Uranium," *Environment: Science and Policy for Sustainable Development* 62, no. 1 (December 2019): 4–14.
27. Ibid.
28. Myanna Lahsen, "Evaluating the Computational ('Big Data') Turn in Studies of Media Coverage of Climate Change," *WIREs Climate Change* 13, no. 2 (March/April 9, 2022): e752.
29. Ibid.
30. Danah Boyd and Kate Crawford, "Six Provocations for Big Data," A Decade in Internet Time: Symposium on the Dynamics of the Internet and Society, Oxford Internet Institute, Oxford, U.K., September 2011.
31. Derek Ruths and Jürgen Pfeffer, "Social Media for Large Studies of Behavior," *Science* 346, no. 6213 (November 2014): 1063–4.
32. Gerard George, Martine R. Haas, and Alex Pentland, "Big Data and Management," *Academy of Management Journal* 57, no. 2 (April 2014): 321–6; Ahmed Abbasi, Suprateek Sarker, and Roger H. L. Chiang, "Big Data Research in Information Systems: Toward an Inclusive Research Agenda," *Journal of the Association for Information Systems* 17, no. 2 (2016): 3.
33. Indra Overland and Benjamin K. Sovacool, "The Misallocation of Climate Research Funding," *Energy Research & Social Science* 62 (April 2020): 101349.
34. Myanna Lahsen, "Toward a Sustainable Future Earth Challenges for a Research Agenda," *Science, Technology & Human Values* 41, no. 5 (April 2016): 876–98.
35. Ibid. See also Myanna Lahsen and Esther Turnhout, "How Norms, Needs, and Power in Science Obstruct Transformations towards Sustainability," *Environmental Research Letters* 16, no. 2 (February 2021): 025008.
36. Ibid.
37. Ibid.
38. Anabela Carvalho, "Media(ted) Discourses and Climate Change: A Focus on Political Subjectivity and (dis)engagement," *WIREs Climate Change* 1, no. 2 (March/April 2010): 172–9.
39. Ibid.; Myanna Lahsen, "Buffers against Inconvenient Knowledge: Brazilian Newspaper Representations of the Climate-Meat Link," *Desenvolvimento e Meio Ambiente* 40 (April 2017): 59–84.
40. William C. Clark and Alicia G. Harley, "Sustainability Science: Toward a Synthesis," *Annual Review of Environment and Resources* 45 (October 2020): 331–86.
41. Myanna Lahsen, "Steering Signification" (under review).

42. Peter Newell, "Towards a Global Political Economy of Transitions: A Comment on the Transitions Research Agenda," *Environmental Innovation and Societal Transitions* 34 (March 2020): 344–5.
43. Ibid.
44. Stepan Jerabek, "A Field Guide to Existential Risk," *Science* 368, no. 6491 (May 2020): 592.
45. Ibid.

PART IV
CONCEPTS

Utopia and its inverse, dystopia, are particularly powerful concepts in our society, as the previous part showed. As we face a precarious ecological future, this concept has become an orienting one for a variety of disciplines. It is also a concept defined by the question of the end: How could we know when society had been perfected? In this part, contributors explore other key concepts for their fields, understanding the ends of these fields as the articulation of such concepts. In some ways, such concerns are more internal to the disciplines than in the previous three parts, but the emphasis on conceptualization is one that is common to many fields. As Reinhart Koselleck has argued, conceptual history is a basic precondition for historical study because the questions that motivate scholarship are defined by the present, and "any translation into one's own present implies a conceptual history."[1] Only one of this part's chapters is about the discipline of history, but each chapter offers its own conceptual history as a precondition for understanding a discipline's end(s). In the case of newer interdisciplinary fields, or new methodologies in traditional ones, conceptualization has been key to institutionalization, so that pursuing a definition of a core concept is a central part of disciplinary identity in both intellectual and practical terms.

First, Jessica Nakamura discusses the concept of "liveness," whose definition, she shows, is an organizing concern of the field of performance studies. As an interdisciplinary area spanning literature, theater and dance, sociology, and other fields—with its first department established only in 1980—performance studies has worked to conceptualize liveness in an effort to expand understandings of performance beyond the theatrical stage. But this concept has been complicated by the increasing turn to filmed and digitized performance, a trend that has accelerated during Covid-19 lockdowns and put pressure on the field's future as one oriented toward liveness. Next, Marieke M. A. Hendriksen shows how the concepts of past and present shape the discipline of history more than an overarching canon or methodology does. The ends of history are constantly changing because conceptualization of the past shifts in light of evolving present concerns. Meanwhile, Kenneth W. Warren shows how the concept of race has been crucial for Black studies, and how theorists in the field have understood race as a social construct while also searching for actually existing definitions of blackness. However, Warren argues that such efforts—while intended in a recuperative spirit—are misapplied because, he writes, "race is, simply, error." Conceptualizing, and thereby reinscribing, race may, in fact, be an obstacle to addressing the harms the concept has wrought. And finally, Mike Hill examines how one goal of cultural studies was to expand Matthew Arnold's elitist concept of culture for the masses, but as the concept expanded in this way, it lost a clear definition. As massification continues to be a problem facing both education and labor, Hill argues that cultural studies' concept of "culture" should be replaced with that of "work." In each case, the author considers how the process of defining, refining, or enlarging a key concept has helped a heterogeneous set of topics and methods hang together as a discipline.

Note

1. Reinhart Koselleck, "Social History and Conceptual History," in *The Practice of Conceptual History: Timing History, Spacing Concepts*, trans. Todd Samuel Presner and others (Stanford: Stanford University Press, 2002), 21.

CHAPTER 14
THE ENDS OF PERFORMANCE STUDIES
Jessica Nakamura

Toward the waning days of the first round of pandemic restrictions, I attended a virtual performance at a major venue. The instructions were clear: I was to show up at a designated website ten minutes before the 8:00 p.m. performance start time to check in, and at 8:00, I could press "play" to start the performance. After following the instructions, I had three minutes to spare. Noticing a play button already on the bottom of my screen, I tried it. To my surprise, the performance immediately started, and I realized the event was not happening in real time but was instead a prerecorded video. For a moment I celebrated that I had ignored the instructions—I got to watch the performance early! The joy of my transgression, however, faded when I began to wonder: if the performance was prerecorded, why did I need to show up at a particular time? What did the instructions—of going to a site, of viewing the event program while I waited for the start time—add to my experience, if anything? The event highlighted the importance placed by performance makers and arts presenters on a live experience, on the sense of reproducing the feeling of "going to the theater" or seeing something "live," even though it may not actually have been happening while I watched.

The significance of liveness, the idea that a performance is unfolding in front of us, has been a central question since the development of the field of performance studies in the second half of the twentieth century. Defining liveness as an attribute special to performance was critical because performance studies was established by scholars from across existing academic fields, including literature, theater and dance studies, art history, religious studies, sociology, and anthropology.[1] One of performance studies' key efforts is its move beyond the stage to consider social, political, and quotidian acts as performance in order to explore their mechanisms and significance. This expansiveness manifested in performance studies' concerns with its own ends from its very early days. A major turning point was the Future of the Field conference organized by Peggy Phelan at NYU in 1995, a mere fifteen years after the establishment of the first US academic department of performance studies. The field's interdisciplinarity has also prompted its own scholars to characterize performance studies as post-discipline or non-discipline—as a field interested in frequently redefining what is unique about performance.[2] Liveness, one of these qualities, continues to be redefined, reevaluated, and disputed.

If we can consider defining liveness as one of performance studies' ends, a question central to our understanding of how we study performance, then the Covid-19 pandemic confronts us with another end. As demonstrated in my recent "theatergoing" experience, when pandemic lockdowns forced performances almost entirely into digital realms,

The Ends of Knowledge

what constituted liveness and its relationship to performance came into question yet again. Now the stakes are higher: during the pandemic, we saw theaters and other live performance venues shut down, and without robust government support for the arts in the United States, artists were unemployed for months. Covid-19 restrictions have exposed major issues in performance's sustainability, confronting us with the very survival of our field, but they have also revealed how cuts to public funding and changing audience interests have pushed live performance to the edge of its own end for many years.[3] Given how artistic practice has always been integrated into our field, these issues are critical to performance studies scholars. Without downplaying the crisis of survival that all arts industries currently face, the pandemic challenges the relationship of the scholar to what we study: What do we do when the very existence of the material we study is at risk? At the center of questions of performance's survival is the acknowledgment of what it is: a live artistic event typically experienced by groups of people.

In this chapter, I work from these ends of performance to reevaluate what constitutes liveness as an end of performance studies. Liveness is the attribute of performance that has made it so dangerous in Covid times, and the overwhelming response by performance makers has been to shift live performances onto digital platforms. While a number of scholars have examined liveness from a variety of perspectives, here I consider what it means to understand it from the point of view of ends. I first outline the history of liveness in performance studies as itself (to use Francis Bacon's terms) the "last or furthest end of knowledge" of our field.[4] This end, as I will explore, does not have a final manifestation but is ever expanding, especially with the introduction of digital modes of performance practice. Then, I consider how the broad-scale adaptation of performance for digital media during the Covid pandemic has put further pressure on notions of liveness. I work between performances I have viewed on digital platforms, including productions in my own academic department, and writings that contemplate the state of pandemic theater and dance. While the range of digital performances is diverse and complex, perhaps more so than conceptions of liveness in performance studies, I explore how this pandemic digital turn reevaluates liveness. I analyze Covid's remote performance as unbounded by the space and time of conventional in-person performances, while also aiming at replicating an impression of liveness. Covid remote performances enact a liveness that is endless—one that is separate from the liveness of in-person performance. Such a distinction expands notions of liveness while highlighting the unique qualities and limitations of the liveness of in-person performances to help reevaluate the field's ends as we move forward in this precarious time for live arts.

Liveness in Performance Studies

A brief history of performance studies shows questions of liveness emerge early on as a defining feature of the field. The quality of liveness identifies a methodological conundrum: How can we research and write about a live event that is ephemeral, experiential, and inherently leaves no trace? Liveness, long believed to be a unique

The Ends of Performance Studies

attribute of performance, characterizes our approach to analysis. Early on, scholars debated the relationship between performance and liveness: Is performance defined by liveness, and, in parallel, is liveness limited to performance? In other words, where does liveness end and performance begin? Questions of liveness have always been an end in our field, critical to our production of knowledge on ontological, epistemological, and methodological levels.

Liveness in performance studies has been fundamentally shaped by a major debate between scholars Peggy Phelan and Philip Auslander. As I see it, Phelan and Auslander stand on seemingly opposite sides in defining liveness in relationship to performance, but in fact they speak at cross purposes, interested in different outcomes for their investigations. Phelan characterized liveness as the ontology of performance in her 1993 *Unmarked*. In her often-quoted phrase, performance "becomes itself through disappearance."[5] For Phelan, liveness is a quality unique to performance, and performance's separation from recording—the fact that it cannot be documented— makes it "the attempt to value that which is nonreproductive, nonmetaphorical" and a site where representational economies can be challenged.[6] Six years later, Auslander took issue with Phelan's separation of the liveness of performance from recorded media. In his 1999 book *Liveness: Performance in a Mediatized Culture*, Auslander insisted on the interrelation of mediatization, a "product of the mass media or of media technology," and performance, noting, "mediatization is now explicitly and implicitly embedded within the live experience."[7] Working "to destabilize these theoretical oppositions of the live and the mediatized somewhat," Auslander does not limit liveness to performance, but rather extends it to multiple mediatized events.[8]

Reading this debate from the perspective of ends, what emerges is that Phelan and Auslander approach the question of liveness with drastically different definitions of performance and goals for performance studies. On the one hand, Phelan highlights performance's liveness to describe its political potential, making the liveness of performance a means to an end. By valuing the nonreproductive, performance opens up as a site of resistance; in the latter half of her essay, Phelan elaborates on the implications of performance's ontology for feminist representations. In part, Auslander does take issue with Phelan's end when he asserts that the "privileging of live performance as a site of critique is an article of faith for most who analyze performance in political terms."[9] Yet, Auslander's efforts to define liveness through recording are for entirely different purposes than deprioritizing the liveness of performance. When Auslander argues that we understand liveness through mediatization, his concerns are not about ontology but epistemology: not about what liveness does but about how we understand media as live.[10] He aims to trouble the differences between the live and the recorded so as to understand their relationship "as historical and contingent rather than determined by immutable differences."[11] For Auslander, such an approach reflects the fact that performance exists "in a culture dominated by mass media."[12]

In performance studies, the "Phelan versus Auslander" debate—part of a "perennial theoretical problem," as Steve Dixon describes it in his 2007 *Digital Performance*—set parameters for the discussions of liveness after it.[13] Because Phelan and Auslander do not

185

argue two opposing sides, their differences are not so easily resolved; instead, the two are frequently put together in discussions about liveness, evoking ideas of liveness within an entrenched binary of performance vs. other media. In more productive avenues, scholars reference them together to expand notions of liveness. In her 2011 *Performing Remains*, for instance, Rebecca Schneider references Phelan and Auslander to highlight a point where they intersect: both "position the body performing live as not *already* a matter of record."[14] Daniel Sack also touches on Phelan and Auslander in his 2015 *After Live* to explore the potentiality of liveness, where "live performance might intervene as an expansion and troubling of what we mean by living in this new millennium."[15] Sack moves toward a more expansive idea of liveness, where understanding its future potentiality "requires that we open our understanding of liveness to include some of its other connotations—to accentuate 'aliveness' or 'liveliness.'"[16]

Digital technologies, integrated by performance artists in the late twentieth century, can be one such avenue to broaden ideas of liveness. For scholars of digital performance, liveness becomes an expanding idea that highlights the functions of performance. In *K-pop Live*, Suk-Young Kim's approach to liveness is shaped by the "question of how we live our lives as increasingly mediated subjects—fragmented and isolated by technological wonders while also yearning for a sense of belonging and aliveness through an interactive mode of exchange that we often call 'live.'"[17] Kim turns to the genre of K-pop to elucidate the relationship between liveness that works across live performance and digital media. For Kim, the end of liveness, regardless of the medium through which it manifests, is social contact. Since the early days of its development, the field of performance studies has worked to define liveness in relation to performance. The ends of this definition and the implications of performance's liveness have become the site of major debates, and when digital performance shows us how conceptions of liveness continue to evolve, we can explore how the field more broadly may as well.

Digital Performance in the Covid Era and Reconsidering Liveness (as End)

While scholars have analyzed past experiments in digital performance to expand what we consider to be live, the near ubiquitous transition of performance to digital realms during the pandemic necessitates further reevaluation of notions of liveness. Prior scholarly explorations of digital performance examined artists who made conscious choices to integrate digital technology into their works; for instance, while Dixon defines "digital performance" "broadly to include all performance works where computer technologies play a *key* role rather than a subsidiary one in content, techniques, aesthetics, or delivery forms," his definition assumes active efforts to integrate these technologies.[18] Or in the case of Kim's *K-Pop Live*, it is K-pop's unique movement across multiple media that makes it "a critical medium to trigger the important question of human existence in the digital age, where the promotion of technology is increasingly becoming its own teleological destination."[19] In contrast, the pandemic has forced theater and performance makers to use digital platforms in order to simply disseminate work to audiences. Gelsey

Bell notes that, pre-Covid, digital theaters were a small subset of performance venues, often at research institutions that could accommodate the high-speed internet access necessary for such productions.[20] Now, digital performance is everywhere. Indeed, all performance has become digital performance.

Marked differences between Covid performances and earlier digital experiments reflect the ends now shaping liveness—those of the very survival of performance and the careers of its makers. One key difference from earlier media experimentation is how quickly the digital became the medium through which performance circulated. Shortly after US states began initiating lockdowns, American regional and university theaters shifted stage performances to digital platforms, often the video conferencing software Zoom that has itself become ubiquitous in workplaces and universities during the pandemic. This quick transition meant that these digital performances did not carefully consider their medium in the same way that past digital theaters might have experimented with form. Based on these differences, I call Covid digital performance "remote performance," a nod to how higher education distinguished between online instruction (often after considered instructional design, and, in the case of my institution, through an application and assessment process) and the necessary move to remote teaching, with less time and attention given to an often-unfamiliar mode of instruction.[21]

To understand the liveness of remote performance, it is important to consider the unique particularities in which it is staged. Digital platforms fundamentally alter the viewing experience for two modalities fundamental to the sense that we are watching something unfold "live"—space and time. While our own situatedness has never felt more apparent as we "tune in" to a performance from our living spaces, remote performance lacks any impression of spatial copresence. With performers in their own spaces or Zoom squares, remote performance erases easy spatial referents. This change can affect the feel of performances—creating a sense of its being unmoored—as well as the logistics surrounding performance practices. When I facilitated a post-show discussion after a stage reading in my department, for instance, I initially assumed the actors could introduce themselves. Later, I realized that there is no visual organization to the digital platform: because we were not in the same space, the actors could not introduce themselves starting from stage right to stage left. However minor, this example suggests that spatial situatedness is not necessarily a requirement for a live experience.

Along with space, online platforms shape the temporality of remote performance. In "live" remote performances, the temporality of the event—how the time of performance is portrayed and experienced—is defined by the parameters and limitations of the internet. In a number of remote performances I witnessed this year, the online platform significantly altered the rhythm, giving a feeling of "sameness" to temporalities across many of the performances. With Zoom, for instance, the program's lag time makes temporal variation difficult: it is harder to make a performance seem as if it is rushing by, and more contemplative or extended moments seem as if they are mistakes (or worse, technical failures). Along similar lines, Bell describes a "latency" to remote performances, a slight delay that, as Bell notes, alters the musical performances she discusses and requires that choices be made with this temporality in mind.[22]

It can also be difficult to distinguish the synchronicity of remote performances. Remote theatrical and dance events during the pandemic were either synchronous, where something is happening in real time, or asynchronous, where there is no real-time event. As many of us who taught in the pandemic know, the experiences of synchronous and asynchronous classrooms are quite different. Remote performance, however, can blur the distinctions between the two. The performance I described seeing at the beginning of this chapter, for instance, could have been synchronous or asynchronous; without starting the video early, I probably would not have known. In other instances of remote performance, a theater company may present a weekend of synchronous performances and then later provide a recording of one of those performances on demand. These examples suggest the ways in which the liveness of remote performance is not dependent on sharing the same space and time as performers or other audience members.

The disembodied mechanisms of digital platforms disentangle remote performance's liveness from presence. Yet, the notion of having a shared experience has been critical in an era of Covid remote performance. Beyond the impression of a "live" remote performance starting at a particular time, remote performances have experimented with audience interactivity. For instance, the March 2021 remote performance of Aya Ogawa's *Ludic Proxy: Fukushima* at the Japan Society frequently paused the performance to poll the audience about what the main character should do during a difficult discussion she was having with her sister during the 2011 Fukushima nuclear disaster. Based on the majority response, the performance would show what would happen next. In this instance, *Ludic Proxy: Fukushima* aims to create a similar space-time experience of in-person performance in a virtual realm. These efforts show how important the experience of presence is for artists—what we might distinguish as a new artistic end in Covid performance making. In other words, as became apparent in multiple remote performances during the pandemic, the reproduction of the feeling of liveness becomes an end in and of itself.

The striving for the sense of co-presence central to in-person liveness can expand notions of what exactly liveness is and how it relates to performance. When works like *Ludic Proxy: Fukushima* aim to evoke a feeling of liveness by highlighting simultaneity and interactivity, remote performance's liveness becomes extended from a situation to a quality. In other words, remote performances evoke the sense of watching a performance unfold in front of us. In part, this creates an impression of a liveness that is endless, in which liveness becomes its own attribute that moves from the conditions of performance to the feeling of it. From remote performances, I discern a feeling that something is live that may infuse an artwork with a sense of shared experience, feelings of community and connection, and the sense that something is unfolding in front of us (even though it may not be). Articles about remote performance in the pandemic have commented on the outcomes evoked by the feeling of liveness, including "the social needs of the community to gather and interact with one another" and the need to keep artists active and relevant.[23] Remote performance, thus, turns liveness into a quality while also revealing the ends of replicating liveness that are important.

Yet, it is important to remember that remote performance develops liveness into a virtual idea (in the realm of affect and sentiment), moving it away from the actuality and physicality of in-person performance's liveness. In *Ludic Proxy: Fukushima*, although audiences shared the same time, it was unclear whether the actors were responding "live" (in real time) to audience choices or if performance technicians selected the appropriate pre-recorded scene based on audience input. Without being in the same room as the actors, such a distinction could not be verified. This distinction is further reflected in the drastically different experience of watching remote performances. In the many times I've viewed remote performances during the Covid-19 pandemic, I've had the sense that it is not the same as watching performance "in person." This sense of difference manifests in calls for attending to "Zoom fatigue" (to which performance is not unique). When watching, no matter how interesting the material or skilled the actors, I feel my attention flag, simply by the elements that remote performance lacks, including the fact that I am not in a public theater space but in my own living room. I find, too, that I dread attending remote performances—a dread that is in no way reflective of the quality of the material but of the fact that remote performance always reminds me that it is not an in-person performance.

Based on these differences, I propose we distinguish the liveness of remote performance, an expansive sense of simultaneity and participation, from the liveness of in-person performance, based on co-presence and situated in place and time. On the one hand, remote performance reaffirms what is special about the liveness of in-person performance: shared co-presence. The thrill of live in-person performance, with the potential for an entire performance to break down in front of us, is not part of remote performance. It also cannot be forgotten that the medium through which audience members access remote performances is frequently a digital platform meant for business networking. While not the medium for all remote performance, the video conferencing platform Zoom was founded in 2011 and is publicly traded. The connection between performance and a money-making entity raises the question about what happens to the subversive ends of live performance championed by Phelan. These differences raise questions of how remote performance manifests in an end-user experience and how an expanded notion of liveness may alter spectatorship.

On the other hand, remote performance turns our scrutiny back to the liveness of in-person performance, calling attention to its limitations. While requiring a computer and internet access, remote performances—often free or significantly less expensive than seeing in-person performance—have made performances available to broader audiences, highlighting how the liveness of in-person performance is intertwined with privilege. The desire for a live in-person experience has called attention, at times, to the ethics of such performances. When artists made strong efforts to "go back" to in-person performances as soon as possible, Allie Marotta highlighted the serious risks taken by theaters to return to a liveness that is co-present.[24] An example of this was the new musical *The Illusionist* that premiered in Tokyo in early 2021. As its writer Peter Duchan described in *The New York Times*, during the course of the rehearsal process multiple cast and crew members contracted Covid-19, and the production closed after only five performances in January 2021.[25] The incredible efforts for this show to go on felt excessive and unnecessary in the face of a life-threatening and highly contagious illness. Remote performance thus asks if the ends justify the means of in-person performance. In other words, what are the real financial, physical, and psychological costs of in-person liveness?

Taking these questions to our scholarly field, remote performance prompts us to consider our approach to performance. In a field that started off as expansive, in which foundational scholars argue that (almost) anything can be considered a performance, our pandemic age has suggested that (almost) anything can take on the qualities of liveness. Just as performance studies' expanded notion of performance transforms the term into an analytical lens to understand social rituals, everyday behavior, and political impacts, expanded notions of liveness highlight its very value: artists have strived for it as a quality to be reproduced. Such value reaffirms our field's end of defining liveness and its relationship to performance, while it reminds us of the changing nature of liveness, a task with no true end in sight.

Liveness's New Ends: Performance's Precarity and Learning from Remote Practice

While it remains unclear what long-term impact remote performances will have, what is clear is that remote performances mark questions about liveness moving forward. The pandemic crisis in performance asks us to reevaluate our role as scholars of performance: What are some of the things we can do with remote performance's liveness? To return to Phelan's introduction to *The Ends of Performance,* she highlights the complex relationship between the field and what we study. Phelan discusses the in-between of performance and asserts, "what performance studies learns most deeply from performance is the generative force of those 'betweens.'"[26] The phrase is important: performance studies *learns* from performance. If artists and critics are now actively reevaluating ideas of what it means to be live, we can perhaps see this as an opportunity to reassess our position in relation to in-person performance's liveness.

As Japanese playwright-director Okada Toshiki explained in a talk during the pandemic, the crisis provides a "good chance to find new ways, to find new theatre."[27] One of Okada's responses, a multi-volume online performance titled *Eraser Fields* (2020–21), available on YouTube, features performers engaging with their environments. Designed to decenter humans to highlight the items that surround us, the piece calls attention to the fact that we (actors and audiences) are in different places and times. The performances on YouTube suggest that we may not all experience these videos at the same time, but we experience the same unfolding of time while watching them. In its spatial and temporal engagement, *Eraser Fields* plays upon the liveness of both remote performances and of in-person performances. By demonstrating a potential way to experience a new form of theater through digital realms, *Eraser Fields* shows how expanded notions of liveness may offer possibilities for the future. In so doing, Okada's work gives us hope that the end of the field that seemed so possible during the pandemic may just be about shifting our sense of what is "live." Just as remote performance broadens notions of liveness, the pandemic reminds us that the liveness of in-person performance has been and always will be precarious. It is, after all, disappearing in front of our eyes, and in response to the pandemic, the field of performance studies can learn from artists like Okada and his willingness to expand our idea of what liveness looks like.

Notes

1. See Shannon Jackson's, *Professing Performance: Theatre in the Academy from Philology to Performativity* (Cambridge: Cambridge University Press, 2004).
2. In the introduction to *The Ends of Performance*, Peggy Phelan explains that "the openness of the central paradigm sometimes made it seem that performance studies was (endlessly?) capable of absorbing ideas and methods from a wide variety of disciplines." Phelan, "Introduction: The Ends of Performance," in *The Ends of Performance*, ed. Peggy Phelan and Jill Lane (New York: New York University Press, 1998), 4.
3. See Branislav Jakovljevic, "Illness as Intel," in "Forum: After Covid, What?" *TDR: The Drama Review* 64, no. 3 (2020): 196.
4. Francis Bacon, "The Advancement of Learning," in *The Major Works*, ed. Brian Vickers (Oxford: Oxford University Press, [1605] 2002), 147.
5. Phelan, *Unmarked: The Politics of Performance* (London: Routledge, 1993), 146.
6. Ibid., 152
7. Philip Auslander, *Liveness: Performance in a Mediatized Culture*, 2nd edn. (London: Routledge, 2008), 4, 35.
8. Ibid., 48.
9. Ibid.
10. Auslander's argument "is that the very concept of live performance presupposes that of reproduction—that the live can exist only *within* an economy of reproduction." Ibid., 57.
11. Ibid., 8.
12. Ibid., 4.
13. Steve Dixon, *Digital Performance: A History of New Media in Theater, Dance, Performance Art, and Installation* (Cambridge, MA: MIT Press, 2007), 115.
14. Rebecca Schneider, *Performing Remains: Art and War in Times of Theatrical Reenactment* (New York: Routledge, 2011), 92.
15. Daniel Sack, *After Live: Possibility, Potentiality, and the Future of Performance* (Ann Arbor: University of Michigan Press, 2015), 12.
16. Ibid., 12.
17. Suk-Young Kim, *K-pop Live: Fans, Idols, and Multimedia Performance* (Stanford, CA: Stanford University Press, 2018), 3.
18. Dixon, *Digital Performance*, 3
19. Kim, *K-pop Live*, 6.
20. Gelsey Bell, "Profound Connectivity: A Social Life of Music during the Pandemic," *TDR: Drama Review* 65, no. 1 (2021): 181.

21. For instance, see Charles Hodges, Stephanie Moore, Barb Lockee, Torrey Trust, and Aaron Bond, "The Difference between Emergency Remote Teaching and Online Learning," *Educase Review*, March 27, 2020.
22. Bell, "Profound Connectivity," 184.
23. Ibid., 183.
24. Allie Marotta, "The Ableist Effects of Creating 'Post-Pandemic Theatre' during a Pandemic," *HowlRound Theatre Commons*, December 8, 2020.
25. Peter Duchan, "For My Next Trick … Opening a New Musical in Tokyo in a Pandemic," *The New York Times*, February 17, 2021.
26. Phelan, "Introduction," 8.
27. Okada Toshiki. Interview. Interviewed by Frank Hentschker for Segal Talks, April 3, 2020; excerpted in "Global Voices of the Pandemic," ed. Benjamin Gillespie, Sarah Lucie, and Jennifer Joan Thompson, *PAJ: A Journal of Performance and Art* 42, no. 3 (2020): 5.

CHAPTER 15
THE ENDS OF HISTORY
Marieke M. A. Hendriksen

History is the branch of knowledge concerned with the interpretation of the past. Ask an academically trained historian what the ends of history are, whether it has an ultimate goal, a *telos*, and the most likely answer you will get is something along the lines of "to understand and describe the past." Yet this is clearly a goal that can never be fulfilled entirely as every second, new history is added, and historical sources are always incomplete. In recent decades, this has led historians to attempt to develop new methods to fill the gaps, such as not only using written sources but also including evidence from visual sources, material culture, and experiential and experimental approaches such as oral history and performative methods. In a sense, historians have been Baconians in the approach to their subject matter since at least the early nineteenth century, and have become ever more so recently. Francis Bacon in his 1620 book *Novum Organum* (literally "New Method") outlined principles that strongly influenced what is now considered the modern scientific method, most importantly, a complex approach to inductive reasoning: reasoning from particular, observed, and verified facts to general principles or truths.[1]

As long as this is done carefully and critically, this can lead to better history writing. Yet external ends may influence attempts to derive general interpretations of history from necessarily incomplete facts. If you ask an amateur historian who spends their spare time tracing family history, an activist, a politician responsible for establishing a national curriculum, or a dictator what the ends of history are, you will likely get very different answers then if you ask an academic historian. The amateur historian may want to confirm or reframe their own identity, the activist may want to use historical facts to change the present and the future, the politician may want to establish some sense of a national identity in school children, while the dictator can use history to strengthen his or her own rule. Although all of these uses of history are potentially problematic, they do not necessarily have to be so—except, of course, in the case of the dictator. It can even be enriching to have various coexisting histories, and sometimes nonprofessional historians such as journalists and amateurs write very valuable and enticing historical works.[2]

Unlike many other disciplines, history permeates all realms of society, yet it does not have a strictly defined canon or an overarching methodology. Moreover, the ends of history are continuously changing. History is not an "exact" science but rather an interpretive liberal art.[3] This does not mean, though, that there are no such things as good and bad historical research and interpretation. Despite the heterogeneous and ever-changing nature of history, it is possible to identify what good historical research

The Ends of Knowledge

does and does not do. This chapter discusses how the ends of history are defined by the present and thus continuously change. It shows that although there is no end to history, we can identify what many professional historians see as the ends of history now, and what that means for the methods they use. I will use related examples from the work of fellow historians and some from my own to illustrate what I mean.

How the Ends of History Are Defined by the Present

How do the ends of history vary, and how are they defined by the present? To start with an example most of us are somewhat familiar with: between 1600 and 1900, the borders and political systems of many European nation-states as we now know them started to emerge. These states created infrastructures to govern their populations, such as judicial and educational systems. Histories describing the events and people that had been significant for newly formed states in the eyes of the ruling classes were a way of creating a national identity, of linking together people that sometimes had little in common in terms of faith or language. Such national histories were indeed narratives interpreting past events—but with a quite specific aim. For example, the French lawyer Adolphe Thiers (1797–1877) between 1823 and 1827 published one of the first printed accounts of the French Revolution of 1789, the ten-volume *Histoire de la Révolution Française*. The books unilaterally celebrated the principles and accomplishments of the Revolution. Thiers's *Histoire* was very popular in France when it first appeared, because it confirmed the dominant political constellation and popular opinions at the time, but was later criticized for its inaccuracies and prejudices. In order to understand how history writing has changed since Thiers published his *Histoire*, we need to realize that until the late eighteenth century, history was not an independent academic discipline—universities by and large remained organized around the disciplines as they had been established in the Medieval university: grammar, rhetoric, logic, medicine, theology, natural philosophy, mathematics, astronomy, astrology, and law. Over the course of the nineteenth century, this changed dramatically under the influence of political, social, and economic developments.[4] This also meant that history writing was for the first time approached as a distinct academic subject, and ideas borrowed from the natural sciences, such as that history writing should be empirical, based on primary sources, and thus could be a *Wissenschaft* like physics and mathematics, became the foundations of history as an academic discipline.[5] Proponents of Universal History believed that histories that were written based on primary sources could eventually even be combined to form one big integrated "universal" history.[6]

In our current globalizing society, in the midst of a pandemic and at a time of confusion about the nature of science and facts, we see that there is a public demand for new global histories, histories of marginalized groups, histories of medicine, science, and knowledge. Statues of colonial rulers, dictators, and racist and misogynist leaders and medical doctors are taken down from their pedestals. Sometimes they are replaced by statues of historical figures that were barely mentioned in historical narratives before

The Ends of History

the mid-twentieth century but who did play a significant role in history: laborers, people of color, women. For example, in Bristol, UK, the statue of slave trader Edward Colston (1636–1721) was replaced with a sculpture by Mark Quinn depicting Jen Reid, one of the Black Lives Matter protesters whose anger brought Colston down in May 2020. Similarly, in New York City, the Central Park statue of J. Marion Sims (1813–83), a gynecologist who experimented on enslaved Black women to achieve his medical breakthroughs, was removed after protests in 2018. It will be replaced by a bronze figure titled *Victory beyond Sims*, made by artist Vinnie Bagwell. Likewise, the national histories and historical canons that are used in schools have been rewritten and overhauled many times, and this will—has to—continue indefinitely. Such rethinkings, rewritings, and revaluations of history are necessary, because there are many dangers to not doing so.

Historical Positivism, Whig History, and Other Dangers

Not continuously studying and rethinking history can lead to the perpetuation of repressive social structures and the exclusion of entire groups of people. Think only about what the world may have looked like if no one had studied the histories of slavery, racism, fascism, and emancipation over the past half century. There are pitfalls in doing historical research too which professional historians are now usually, but unfortunately not always, taught how to avoid. Extreme forms of historical positivism and a genre of historiography known as "Whig history" are examples of such pitfalls. Historical positivism is the idea that historical evidence requires no interpretation: the historian's job consists of compiling primary sources and "letting them speak for themselves." This is practically impossible, as every historian is inevitably a product of their own time, and their selection and ways of disclosing primary sources are in themselves forms of interpretation. Calvin and Hobbes are clearly not historical positivists (see Figure 15.1).

Whig history is an interpretation of history as an inevitable progression toward ever-greater enlightenment and freedom. This is a very attractive way of interpreting historical facts for people who have a specific end of history in mind, such as glorifying their own

Figure 15.1 CALVIN AND HOBBES © 1993 Watterson. Reprinted with permission of ANDREWS MCMEEL SYNDICATION. All rights reserved.

past or current status. Yet the dangers of such history writing include the construction of highly selective narratives that ignore displeasing events, ascribing the work of many to one or a few "founding fathers" (nearly always white men), or reducing a long and messy process of trial, error, and serendipity to an "invention" that can be linked to one specific person and moment in time. Think, for example, of histories of empire that glorify global trade but ignore slavery, or the ways in which the contributions to science by women like mathematician Katherine Johnson and chemist Rosalind Franklin were long ignored. And then there is outright sloppy history writing—selectively picking from history to advance personal or collective goals. Some recent examples give more insight into the problematic nature of such approaches to history.

The first is a tweet the astrophysicist Neil deGrasse Tyson sent in April 2020, during the first Covid-19 lockdown, and that was echoed by many self-appointed historians of science in the following weeks. "When Isaac Newton stayed at home to avoid the 1665 plague, he discovered the laws of gravity, optics, and he invented calculus," deGrasse Tyson wrote.[7] Professional historians of science were quick to point out that Newton's situation was incomparable in every respect to the 2020 lockdown and that he did not singlehandedly discover the laws of gravity and optics or invent calculus. Although Newton did contribute considerably to all of these aspects of science, they were not his sole merit, nor did he develop his work in these fields exclusively while sheltering from the plague or without building on the work of others. And while Newton contributed greatly to modern science, he was *not* a modern scientist, at least not in the sense deGrasse Tyson means. His positivist idea of Newton as a "modern" scientist does, for example, definitely not leave room for Newton's alchemical work—a topic on which excellent historical research has been done.[8] Reinforcing the stereotype of Newton as the lone male genius achieving great scientific insight into isolation ignores decades of historical research demonstrating the collaborative, serendipitous, and nonlinear nature of early modern science. Moreover, it is clear why this take on Newton is still so attractive to a certain type of scientist, but it also is an implicitly toxic message about productivity in a time of great uncertainty to everyone juggling a career with working from home and caring for others. It may seem strange to describe one tweet as problematic history writing, but deGrasse Tyson is a hugely popular science communicator with 14.5 million followers on Twitter, and this tweet alone was liked over 12,000 times. When he perpetuates myths about the nature and history of science, that has a negative impact on the public understanding of science and its history.

The second example is what the historian Daryl Michael Scott has described in a recent article as "The Scandal of Thirteentherism."[9] The thirteenth amendment of the US Constitution, passed by Congress in 1865, abolished slavery and states that slavery and involuntary servitude can only exist in the United States "as a punishment for crime whereof the party shall have been duly convicted." Thirteentherism is the idea that that phrase caused a seamless, continuous history of Black slavery from the seventeenth century until today—that the mass incarceration of Black Americans today is an effective continuation of Black slavery caused by the thirteenth amendment. Again, it is easy to see why this idea seems attractive to activists who want to end mass incarceration. If mass incarceration is a continuation of Black slavery, that surely is an additional argument to end it. The problem is: historical research has shown that it is not true, and it may even be damaging the very cause Thirteenthers advocate. Scott—a Black man—shows in his article that Thirteenthers have created a narrative that ignores and contradicts historical facts, thus making it easy to accuse them of falsifying history and to deny the importance of their goal: ending mass incarceration. Scott's concern is valid of course—perpetuating untruths about history, even if well-intentioned, does not align with the overall end of history of uncovering forensic truths about the past.

Finally, there are cases of "whitewashing" in both classical and Medieval studies: instances where for centuries, historical evidence was ignored because it did not fit contemporary ideas about the past, and in which scholars who tried to correct them were met with ridicule or even outright hostility—sometimes from fellow scholars, but more often from others. This was the case when historians of classical art from the final decades of the twentieth century onwards started to realize that historical sources—in their case mostly archaeological finds—all along had contained evidence that classical sculpture was originally not white, but polychrome: painted in bright colors and decorated with gold leaf. Their findings were generally accepted by the academic community after critical evaluation, but led racists, to whom the whiteness of classical sculpture is linked to ideologies of white supremacy, to threaten scholars working on the subject.[10] Something similar happened when a Scandinavian studies professor recently publicly debunked the myth that Viking culture was "racially pure," which was equally popular with racists.[11]

These cases show that although history is democratic in the sense that it is everyone's past and plays a big role in public life, it does not mean that there are no right and wrong ways to study history and to present and interpret historical facts. Totalizing historical explanations of past and present are not possible, yet this does not mean that everyone should feel free to try to marshal historical interpretation toward whatever future they want. Historians have a moral duty to unearth, interpret, and present historical facts and be as open as possible about their ways of and motivations for doing so, to engage in critically assessing the histories left to us by our predecessors, and reevaluate and rewrite them in the light of newly found historical evidence. This is not about the necessity of professional or methodological gatekeeping toward an agreed upon history, but against potentially dangerous constructions that will lead to the exclusion, repression, and discrimination of large groups of people. I will now first discuss what is generally considered the correct way of handling historical evidence by professional historians nowadays, before giving some examples of what that can look like in practice.

Unearthing and Interpreting Historical Facts

I must stress that what I identify here are not "rules" in the sense that they have been established by some universal authority on historical research—there is no such thing. Probably because of their rather metaphysic, reflective nature, these are guidelines that are only occasionally discussed explicitly, and even then, they are usually presented as the starting point for critical thinking about the field rather than as strict rules or laws. In academic history degree programs, historiography is usually covered in one course early on in the program, to help students reflect on the history, nature, and methods of history as a discipline. Some excellent and very readable examples of historiographies are Marc Bloch's *The Historian's Craft* (1954)—still surprisingly topical after more than half a century—and more recently Sarah Maza's *Thinking about History* (2017) and Lynn Hunt's *History: Why It Matters* (2018). In such works we can find the principles of the discipline by which most, but unfortunately not all, amateur and professional historians abide. The most important "rules" that are echoed in almost all current historiography are that historians should aim (1) to uncover historical facts, forensic truths about the past, and (2) to interpret these truths in narratives that explain and describe the past and the changes that unfolded in it in an ethical and engaging manner.

Some historians, such as Hunt, interpret "ethical" as meaning that we can and should use history to understand our place on earth and in society and draw consequences from it for our current and future actions. As Scott's previously discussed criticism of Thirteentherism shows, this requires a very carefully considered approach to history, one that respects historical facts, even if they do not fit comfortably into the narrative you would like to tell to advance a cause. Another danger is judging the past against current moral standards, something Bloch explicitly warns against. This does not mean that historians are devoid of moral judgments, or that they will not agree that certain things that happened in the past were horrible and are rightly done differently now. What it does mean is that most professional historians will try to uncover and present historical facts for public consumption, but that they generally will not describe these facts in terms of "good" or "bad"—such moral judgments should be made in the public debate, in which historians definitely play a role, but not in their academic historical writing.

This may seem an artificial distinction, as academic writing does influence the public debate and vice versa, so an example is in order. Political historian Annelien de Dijn recently published a book called *Freedom: An Unruly History*.[12] In it, she shows that the very nature of freedom was understood in different ways by people in the West from classical antiquity until the decades after the Second World War. For centuries, freedom did not mean being left alone by the state but having the opportunity to exercise control over the way you were governed. This could be described as a democratic understanding of liberty, yet the way in which many understand freedom today is completely different. Although De Dijn opens her book with this statement—"Today most people tend to equate freedom with the possession of inalienable individual rights, rights that demarcate a private sphere no government may infringe on"—she does not link her research to, say, the recent storming of the Capitol by Trump supporters who were inspired by exactly this definition of freedom, nor does she pass judgment on this understanding of freedom or on current politics. *Freedom* is an academic book, both in the sense that it is a solidly researched and thoroughly referenced work, double blind peer reviewed and published by an esteemed academic press, and in the sense that De Dijn does not pass moral judgment on either the past or the present. But her accessible writing style, combined with the subject matter, ensures that the book is discussed outside academic circles too, and thus does become part of the public debate. For example, in a review of De Dijn's book for *The Nation,* Tyler Stovall, a professor of history and the dean of the Graduate School of Arts and Sciences at Fordham University, wrote about *Freedom* that De Dijn "challenges conservatives who wrap their ideology in the glorious banner of freedom, revealing the long history of a very different vision of human liberation, one that emphasizes collective self-government over individual privilege."[13] Stovall thus brings De Dijn's academic historical writing into the realm of the current public debate, and reads into it an explicit moral judgement about a relatively recent understanding of freedom that De Dijn herself does not actually make in her work. This example illustrates the different approaches historians tend to take in their academic writing and in the public debate.

Freedom is based purely on an analysis of written sources, and given the purpose of the book—uncovering historical facts about the changing understandings of the concept of freedom over time—that works very well. But in other historical fields, such an approach is less fruitful. After all, we want to understand the past in all its facets, and over the past decades awareness among historians has grown that uncovering forensic truths about many aspects of history and interpreting the past requires more than just studying and analyzing written sources—our traditional methodology. The most important reason for this is the uneven way the past is documented in written sources. Written sources, especially those from longer ago, tend to have been created and preserved by a minority of people (usually elite and male, and in the case of Western history, white). While this can provide great insight into the lives of the ruling classes, such sources often provide limited access to the everyday lives of the majority. Meanwhile, artistic, craft, domestic, and trade practices shaped the histories of science, politics, and economics as much as the other way around, yet these remained largely unrecorded in written sources, or the records did not survive, or they were ignored. Including nontextual sources (such as images and objects) and using nontraditional methods (such as reconstructions) in our research therefore makes for a more nuanced, less linear, hagiographic, and triumphant understanding of history. It gives us a humbling insight into human history and the human condition.

What that can mean for historical research in practice can also be seen in my own work. I am a historian of early modern chemistry and medicine, and I am particularly interested in the role of objects, materials, skill, and practices in the making of scientific knowledge in the period between 1650 and 1850. Until fairly recently, the focus in the study of early modern science was on the lives and achievements of men, like Herman Boerhaave (1668–1738). Boerhaave was a Dutch professor of medicine, botany, and chemistry at Leiden University, and his work on medicine and chemistry was very influential internationally at the time. Chemistry was a new subject in the university curriculum around 1700, and Boerhaave's chemistry textbook, the *Elementa Chemiae* (1732), became hugely popular. It was one of the first books to systematically outline the chemical elements and their properties as they were known at the time, and to provide an extensive repository of chemical experiments that students could perform themselves to better understand and critically assess chemical theory. It should be noted that some of that theory may seem outrageous to us now—for example, Boerhaave stated that milk contained the foundational material from which the blood of mammals developed, since young mammals, including humans, can grow on nothing but their mother's milk. In the back of the book, Boerhaave also provided DIY instructions for building a small chemical oven made from wood, lined with iron, and fired with peat, which students could use for experiments at home. Yet although we know the book was very popular based on facts like the number of reprints and pirated copies, we know next to nothing about how it may have functioned in practice. There are some sources that show that the *Elementa* was used and adapted by other university lecturers, but no records of students actually using the book to perform their own experiments. This is not entirely surprising, of course, because students may not have recorded these kinds of home experiments at all, and if they did, such documents were unlikely to be considered worth keeping.

My colleague Ruben Verwaal and I wondered if the explanation for the popularity of Boerhaave's book might actually not only be his international fame, but also that it could actually be used in practice, and that the experiments he listed did indeed support his chemical theory—even the bits that seem outlandish to us now. Hence, we decided to try and use Boerhaave's instructions to build a small chemical oven, and to use it to perform his experiment that demonstrates that milk is the basis for blood—an experiment that involves heating raw milk to body temperature and adding an alkali to it to make it turn blood red. Long story short—it worked.[14] And not only did we answer our initial questions about the way in which the book may have been used in practice and the reproducibility of seemingly unlikely experiments, we also learned things about early modern chemical experimentation we would never have even considered if we had stuck purely to textual and visual sources. For example: peat has a very penetrant smell, and it was a widely used fuel at the time—this information changed how we think about the smellscape of early modern Dutch cities. Keeping the oven at a constant temperature for hours, sometimes even days on end, required constant attention, confirming the long-standing suspicion of historians of chemistry that early modern chemistry professors must have relied heavily on the labor of students and assistants to perform their experiments. Our performative approach thus not only helped us answer our historical questions but also provided us with historical facts and new questions, that we would never have come across if we had stuck with our archival material.

Of course, this performative approach to history has pitfalls too, and it is not suitable for answering every historical question—but neither is archival research. What method or combination of methods is most suitable to answer the question at hand is something historians should be trained to assess.[15] The "reconstruction" we made was definitely not entirely historically accurate, but that was not the point. The point was engagement with historical processes and practices, gaining an understanding of skill and embodied knowledge through interaction with materials. Inspired by the Baconian method, we try to apply principles of scientific method as corrective for human miscomprehension. We think a more complete understanding of history entails an experiential and experimental component, even if the experience can only ever be analogous to the original conditions and processes we seek to recover. We understand our experiences in using a reconstructed Boerhaave oven as a working model as a part of the larger understanding of history, which is never actually complete but rather as complete as is reasonable. Although we could never establish exactly what Boerhaave's eighteenth-century students did with his book and what they experienced, coming out of the storage room and the archive and going into the laboratory did unearth new historical facts, and provided a more informed interpretation of the role of the *Elementa Chemiae* in eighteenth-century chemical education and the circulation and assessment of contemporary chemical theory.

The Ends of History: Conclusion

The conclusion we can draw from these examples is that historians seek the most complete understanding of history possible, but that due to the incomplete nature of historical sources, an actually complete understanding is not possible. This unattainable end may lead to problematic attempts to fill the gaps with conjecture that is not based on facts but on wishful thinking, or to simplification of stories—"bad" history writing that in turn can lead to the exclusion of the majority of people, both in the representation of history and in the present. Historians are therefore always searching for corrective methodologies, such as taking into account sources and evidence that were ignored before, adding to their traditional method of archival research methods such as visual and material analysis, and even in some cases experiential and experimental performative methods such as reconstructions and reenactments or reworkings. Ideally, this broadening of our methodology addresses the negative effects of demarcation and previous interpretations of history, whether these were inadvertent or motivated.

A final note should be made about the ends of history and the relationship between historical research and the public debate. The historical research discussed in this chapter as exemplary is without exception the result of the hard work of highly trained and skilled professionals who devote years of their lives to meticulously sifting through archival records, to carefully unearthing, restoring, and reconstructing historical artifacts, materials, and processes, in order to achieve the most complete historical record possible, and the most responsible interpretation of that record given its inevitable gaps. They are polyglots who juggle this work with teaching responsibilities and the never-ending quest for research funding, while attempting to maintain something of a personal life, all because they are incurably curious about the past and know that good history writing can help us understand both ourselves and the world around us. It can take fifteen years or longer to properly research and write a history book, and this preciseness and relative slowness does not sit comfortably with the wrenching speed and often less-than-careful fact-checking of on- and offline public discourse. This means that modern historians have to acquire yet another skillset: media savviness. To some this comes naturally, others will need training, but it is heartening to see that many historians today are willing to engage in public discourse about the nature and fruits of their craft, as that is one of the places where history comes alive.

Notes

1. This is a simplification of the Baconian method; see *The Cambridge Companion to Bacon*, ed. Markku Peltonen (Cambridge: Cambridge University Press, 1996).
2. I say "write" here because of the narrative character of historical interpretation, but of course historical research and interpretation can be presented in other forms.
3. See Bruno Latour and Steve Woolgar, *Laboratory Life: The Construction of Scientific Facts* (Los Angeles: Sage Publications, 1979), and Bruno Latour, *Science in Action: How to Follow Scientists and Engineers through Society* (Cambridge, MA: Harvard University Press, 1987).
4. See John C. Moore, *A Brief History of Universities* (Cham: Palgrave Pivot, 2018), and Walter Rüegg, *A History of the University in Europe*, 4 vols. (Cambridge: Cambridge University Press, 2003–2010).
5. I use the German *Wissenschaft* rather than "science" (as it is often translated) because it also refers to humanities disciplines, including history.
6. See Frederick C. Beiser, *The German Historicist Tradition* (Oxford: Oxford University Press, 2012), and Bonnie G. Smith, *The Gender of History: Men, Women and Historical Practice* (Cambridge, MA: Harvard University Press, 1998).
7. Neil DeGrasse Tyson, Twitter post, March 31, 2020, https://twitter.com/neiltyson/status/1245111777270157318?s=20&t=pZ9fYkIRfTSdSUHJikiHRg.
8. Richard S. Westfall, "The Role of Alchemy in Newton's Career," in *Reason, Experiment, and Mysticism in the Scientific Revolution*, ed. M. L. Righini Bonelli and William R. Shea (London: Macmillan, 1975), 189–232; Betty Jo Teeter Dobbs, *The Foundations of Newton's Alchemy; or, "The Hunting of the Greene Lyon"* (Cambridge: Cambridge University Press, 1975); and Lawrence M. Principe, "Alchemy Restored," *Isis: International Review Devoted to the History of Science and Its Civilisation* 102, no. 2 (2011): 305–12.
9. Daryl Michael Scott, "The Scandal of Thirteentherism," *Liberties Journal of Culture and Politics* 1, no. 2 (Winter 2021): 273–93.
10. See, for example, Colleen Flaherty, "Threats for What She Didn't Say," *Inside Higher Ed*, June 19, 2017, and Margaret Talbot, "The Myth of Whiteness in Classical Sculpture," *The New Yorker*, October 29, 2018.
11. Nathalie Van Deusen, "Why Teaching about the Viking Age Is Relevant—and Even Crucial," *Canadian Historical Association*, November 25, 2019.
12. Annelien de Dijn, *Freedom: An Unruly History* (Cambridge, MA: Harvard University Press, 2021).
13. Tyler Stovall, "Liberty's Discontents: The Contested History of Freedom," *The Nation*, March 22, 2021.
14. See Marieke M. A. Hendriksen and Ruben E. Verwaal, "Boerhaave's Furnace. Exploring Early Modern Chemistry through Working Models," *Berichte zur Wissenschaftsgeschichte* 43, no. 3 (2020): 385–411.
15. See Marieke M. A. Hendriksen, "Rethinking Performative Methods in the History of Science," *Berichte zur Wissenschaftsgeschichte* 43, no. 3 (2020): 313–22; and Sven Dupré, Anna Harris, Julia Kursell, Patricia Lulof, and Maartje Stols-Witlox, "Introduction," in *Reconstruction, Replication and Re-Enactment in the Humanities and Social Sciences*, ed. Sven Dupré, Anna Harris, Julia Kursell, Patricia Lulof, and Maartje Stols-Witlox (Amsterdam: Amsterdam University Press, 2020), 9–34.

CHAPTER 16
THE ENDS OF BLACK STUDIES
Kenneth W. Warren

When W. E. B. Du Bois presented his essay "The Conservation of Races" to the American Negro Academy in 1897, his goal was to define and to develop those qualities he believed distinguished "Negro people, as a race" from the world's other racial groups, particularly those that had already made their special contribution to "civilization and humanity."[1] In doing so, Du Bois hoped to establish among races "such a social equilibrium as would, throughout all the complicated relations of life, give due and just consideration to culture, ability, and moral worth, whether they be found under white or black skins."[2] In other words, false ideas about human difference and variety had produced misestimations of the capacities of certain groups, and justice demanded that these ideas be combatted. For Du Bois, the problem did not lie in racial difference itself but in the way that such differences had been stigmatized as a result of prejudice and discrimination born of conquest, colonization, and slavery. Taken together, these forces had prevented the Black race from developing and delivering its unique racial contribution to the reservoir of human goods.

In concluding "The Conservation of Races," Du Bois enjoined the Academy to embrace several principles as part of its creed, the first two of which affirmed:

1. We believe that the Negro people, as a race, have a contribution to make to civilization and humanity, which no other race can make.
2. We believe it the duty of the Americans of Negro descent, as a body, to maintain their race identity until this mission of the Negro people is accomplished, and the ideal of human brotherhood has become a practical possibility.[3]

Du Bois's oscillation between describing race as, on the one hand, a property inherent in black people themselves and, on the other, as a strategic, elective mutual identification made by black people to achieve an end stands as just one of an untold number of examples of how even those who make it their business to talk about race (Du Bois went so far as to title his 1940 autobiography *Dusk of Dawn: An Essay Toward an Autobiography of a Race Concept*) tend to do so in ways that are confusing and contradictory.[4]

Even Du Bois himself was not unmindful of his own inconsistencies in trying to pinpoint his concept, and at one point in *Dusk of Dawn* he attempts, with a swipe of Occam's razor, to cut the knot of conceptual difficulty. Concocting a "mythical" white friend, Roger Van Dieman, to challenge him about the coherence of race as a marker of group identity ("But what is this group; and how do you differentiate it; and how can you call it 'black' when you admit it is not black?"), Du Bois answers simply, "I recognize it quite easily and with full legal sanction; the black man is a person who must ride 'Jim Crow' in Georgia."[5] No need here for any account of the traits, experiences, capacities, or characteristics presumed to distinguish black people from other groups. The minimal requirement to relegate some people to certain social spaces, occupations, and so on and to deny them privileges and rights reserved for others (i.e., the minimal requirement for calling them black) is a putatively democratic social-economic order whose functioning dictates that goods and privileges cannot be equally distributed among its members. Race solves the problem of reconciling such a social order with the ideal of equality by providing vivid "evidence" that not all of its members are equally deserving of, or capable of using, those goods and privileges. To find black people, look in the Jim Crow car.

In declaring that, in essence, black people are those people whom mid-twentieth-century US society permitted to be treated as such, Du Bois exposes the workings of what Barbara J. Fields and Karen E. Fields have termed "racecraft," a neologism they use to show how, at an earlier moment in human history, a belief in witches was just as rational and understandable as the belief in race has been for the last two or three centuries. Fields and Fields write, "Far from denying the rationality of those who have accepted either belief as truth about the world, we assume it. We are interested in the processes of reasoning that manage to make both plausible. Witchcraft and racecraft are imagined, acted upon, and reimagined, the action and imagining inextricably intertwined."[6] They cite W. E. H. Lecky in arguing that this kind of belief "presents itself to the mind and imagination as vivid truth."[7]

So, to unfold further the implications of Du Bois's rejoinder to Van Dieman, although one can reliably find black people by peering into the Jim Crow car, one can't find the reason for occupancy in that car by examining the people confined there. Rather, one needs to examine the beliefs, motives, and actions of those doing the confining as well as the ends achieved by the practice. To those who insist on segregation, the belief that presents itself to the mind and imagination as a vivid truth is the belief that black people constitute a race. Such a belief is, of course, a falsehood about the people it purports to describe and "has nothing to recommend it or to redeem it as truth about the world," as Fields and Fields explain.[8]

To be sure, one could learn and would want to learn a lot about the immediate and long-term consequences of constituting people as a race. And one could learn about the experiences, feelings, and insights arising among those who had been treated as such. But in neither instance would this be to learn about a so-called black race. Indeed, since such treatment has varied across time and place, what one would learn would not constitute a singular experience but an array of experiences. More importantly, one could learn a great deal from these people about matters having nothing to do with their constitution as a race. The novelist Ralph Ellison made all of these points in the 1960s in an exchange with the socialist critic and writer Irving Howe when he commented that if Jim Crow segregation were to be represented as a jug within which black people had been confined, that jug should be seen as "transparent, not opaque, and one is allowed not only to see outside but to read what is going on out there, and to make identifications as to values and human quality. So, in Macon County, Alabama, I read Marx, Freud, T.S. Eliot, Pound, Gertrude Stein and Hemingway. Books which seldom, if ever, mentioned Negroes were to release me from whatever 'segregated' idea I might have of my human possibilities."[9]

Of course, Ellison knew that imposing racial inequality as a means of enforcing a social order serving the material interests of elites meant making it difficult if not impossible for many blacks (and many poor whites) in the South to gain access to the intellectual and material resources that he had found liberating. But his point was that, as heinous as the Jim Crow order was, it was never as complete and seamless as some whites hoped it could be, and its contradictions were such that it was often violated by its own operations. I suspect that few if any of the white philanthropists who wrote checks to Tuskegee Institute, where Ellison encountered many of the writers he mentioned in his response to Howe, imagined they would be underwriting a black Oklahoman's explorations of literary modernism. Add to this the fact that those whom Jim Crow sought to subdue did not simply acquiesce in the expectations of that order but defied it both subtly and openly, and the difficulties proliferate. What Ellison made of his experiences differed from what Du Bois made of his, and the responses of both men differed from those of their predecessors, contemporaries, and successors. Yet, what they all contended with as well was the idea that across these differences, all of these people were nonetheless connected by something beyond their rejection of and opposition to the racial order that was imposed upon them. Finding this "something," whether labeled as race, blackness, or racial blackness, has remained an abiding concern of many sociological, cultural, and literary scholars in African American/black studies.

In many ways this concern finds its roots in understandable and laudable efforts to locate and champion values different from those affirmed by the prevailing order. Variety is both a condition of our humanity and a resource upon which we can draw to imagine how we might create a different and better world than that we currently inhabit. Race, or racial difference, however, does not help us understand that variety. Rather, race is a way of misconstruing it. To adapt Ellison's metaphor, to think otherwise would be a bit like believing that a thorough examination of the jar into which you've poured a lot of marbles will usefully tell you something about the marbles you've dumped inside. Zora Neale Hurston makes a similar point in her 1928 essay, "How It Feels To Be Colored Me," when she writes:

> But in the main, I feel like a brown bag of miscellany propped against a wall. Against a wall in company with other bags, white, red and yellow. Pour out the contents, and there is discovered a jumble of small things priceless and worthless. A first-water diamond, an empty spool, bits of broken glass, lengths of string, a key to a door long since crumbled away, a rusty knife-blade, old shoes saved for a road that never was and never will be, a nail bent under the weight of things too heavy for any nail, a dried flower or two still a little fragrant. In your hand is the brown bag. On the ground before you is the jumble it held—so much like the jumble in the bags, could they be emptied, that all might be dumped in a single heap and the

bags refilled without altering the content of any greatly. A bit of colored glass more or less would not matter. Perhaps that is how the Great Stuffer of Bags filled them in the first place—who knows?[10]

The whimsy of Hurston's reflections shouldn't obscure the sharp edge of truth in her observations. Even those who seek to find support for racial difference within genetic differences have had to acknowledge that "the range of genetic variation *within* racially defined populations is much greater than the genetic variation *between* populations."[11] Thus, to see what race means, it would be more pertinent to know what the stuffers of bags are trying to accomplish through their stuffing than to know what is stuffed in the bags.

Of late, however, many of the cultural scholars who devote themselves to delineating blackness have moved in the direction of rehabilitating rather than dispensing with the "vivid truth" of race as part of our reality or as a necessary tool for accessing truths about the human condition. For example, Fred Moten writes, "blackness needs to be understood as operating at the nexus of the social and the ontological, the historical and the essential."[12] Such a turn is not simply unfortunate. It also reflects the material and institutional imperatives that are at work to shore up the idea that prioritizing black racial groupness on terms reflecting the imperatives of black elites is required to carry forward an egalitarian political project. The problem is not groupness itself but rather that efforts to account for and assert a right to self-definition by black Americans have been pursued in ways that have cut against the overwhelming evidence that race is, simply, error.

That race is an error is an idea that has received powerful, if not unanimous, scientific confirmation. For example, in March of 2019, at the 88th annual meeting of the American Association of Physical Anthropologists (AAPA), the association's executive committee unanimously accepted the "AAPA Statement on Race and Racism," which declared unequivocally that in pursuit of the discipline's mission to understand human biological variation, genomic and phenotypic, "Race does not provide an accurate representation of human biological variation. It was never accurate in the past, and it remains inaccurate when referencing contemporary human populations."[13] While the statement draws attention to the problem of "how non-scientists use scientific research" in ascribing race to human populations, it is more concerned with affecting how "scientists themselves conceive, implement, analyze, and present their research." Accordingly, the document not only acknowledges the discipline's historical implication in the imposition of race onto the human population ("biological anthropology has played an important role in the creation and perpetuation of both the race concept and racist ideologies") but also warns the society's membership that scientists continue to allow the error of race to compromise scientific study. Noting that "outdated and inaccurate ideas about race, and racism, still inform scientific research today," the statement urges scientists to "eliminate the influence of bias, racial profiling, and other erroneous ways of thinking about human variation from our study designs, interpretations of scientific data, and reporting of research results" and, by doing so, to "prevent the reemergence of misconceptions about race in the future." In other words, the statement admonishes AAPA members to remember that when it comes to doing the work that the discipline of physical anthropology is organized to do, which is to account for human biological variation, race is not a form of but rather an obstacle to knowledge.

But as if not quite convinced of the sufficiency of having made clear to its members and to the public that it is a mistake to believe that race explains/accounts for/accurately describes human variation, the society also takes upon itself the task of distinguishing "what race is and what it is not." The statement's authors observe that while "human racial groups are not biological categories, 'race' as a social reality—as a way of structuring societies and experiencing the world—is very real. The racial groups we recognize in the West have been socially, politically, and legally constructed over the last five centuries." For scholars in the literary disciplines, wherein acknowledgment of the social construction of just about everything has been standard operating procedure since at least the 1980s (when Peter L. Berger and Thomas Luckmann's *The Social Construction of Reality* (1966) was absorbed into the curricula of English and comparative literature PhD programs), the statement's turn to the process and phenomenon of social construction seems unremarkable. In fact, such a turn marks out at least part of the terrain upon which the disciplines of the biological sciences, the social sciences, and the humanities can be said to meet. The statement notes that while "physical anthropology is a biological science that deals with the adaptations, variability, and evolution of human beings and their living and fossil relatives," it is "also a social science" in that "it studies human biology in the context of human culture and behavior."

Although these two aspects of the discipline enhance the range and depth of its inquiry, they also reveal what turns out to be a significant tension within the statement. The authority of the statement derives largely from its provenance within the biological sciences. If race were to manifest anywhere as an accurate account of human variation, it would presumably have to do so in the study of human bodies over the course of the evolutionary history of humanity. That the scientists whose job is to understand human variation over time cannot find race and deem it to be inaccurate is, then, highly consequential. It's what makes the statement worth making in the first place and what underwrites the statement's admonition that to introduce race into research design, data interpretation, and the reporting of findings would be, unavoidably, to introduce error. The admonition to eliminate bias from research, then, is not merely an injunction that individual scientists must guard against introducing social and individual biases into their research ("Don't be biased!" is not a disciplinary or field-specific imperative). Rather, it is a directive about how to do correct science resting upon what is being presented as the reasonably settled science of the discipline. Race is error.

But things look different from the social science standpoint of the discipline, where "social constructs" are considered necessary and legitimate objects of study. To posit race as a social construct would seem, then, to preclude the option of eliminating it from research. Indeed, such an injunction would sound like a directive to ignore what was right there in front of one's eyes. That is, although one might hope to create a world without race (and, as we'll see below, various humanistic scholars see even this goal as either unreachable or in some ways undesirable), one would seem to have to concede that, at least for the time being, race is a part of our reality, and thereby demands that we attend to it. From this point of view, it is not erroneous to speak of race. Rather, the error happens when we speak of race the wrong way. The turn to social construction would become a turn toward rather than away from race.

Although the statement does not modulate its authoritative tones when speaking from the social scientific side of the discipline, it has, in doing so, nonetheless stepped into a domain of considerable contestation. Although, as Walter Benn Michaels has noted, "the commitment to race as a social construction" dominates "racial thought today," a number of scholars, including Michaels, Fields and Fields, and Adolph Reed, Jr., have argued that this consensus rests on a tangle of confusions.[14] At the base of these confusions lies a refusal to acknowledge a simple point: if race is not a biological concept, then it is also not a social construction—or at least, it is not the kind of social construction that the proponents of this idea take it to be. It is, as this chapter has been arguing, an erroneous description of human grouping, or as Michaels says, a "mistake." Human mistakes, and willful mischaracterizations of our fellow humans, are, of course, social acts, and as such they can produce consequences. To speak somewhat frivolously: if as a child I may have on one occasion imagined myself as a mountain lion and my brother as a deer, and for that reason leapt upon him from the sofa, I may have certainly bruised his leg as a result, but at no point did I turn him into a deer or myself into the powerful, legendary "Yellow Eyes" whom I was pretending to be.

The point here is that, as Fields and Fields remind us, there are social constructions, and then again there are social constructions, and "identifying race as a social construction does nothing to solidify the intellectual ground on which it totters." They elaborate:

> The London Underground and the United States of America are social constructions; so are the evil eye and the calling of spirits from the vasty deep; and so are murder and genocide. All derive from the thoughts, plans, and actions of human beings living in human societies. Scholars who intone "social construction" as a spell for the purification of race do not make clear—perhaps because they do not themselves realize—that race and racism belong to different families of social construction, and that neither belongs to the same family as the United States of America or the London Underground. Race belongs to the same family as the evil eye. Racism belongs to the same family as murder and genocide. Which is to say that racism, unlike race, is not a fiction, an illusion, a superstition, or a hoax. It is a crime against humanity.[15]

To stay with Fields and Fields's examples: if someone were to confine me because they believed I had the power to create mayhem merely by casting a glance, it would be a strange mode of proceeding if, in order to help me, my rescuer sought, first, to discern what about me had led my captor to believe I had such a power, or to note that beliefs in the evil eye have manifested in different societies across the centuries and for that reason need to be taxonomized before they could figure out what was to be done in my case. Such saviors (or perhaps closeted captors?) are those scholars who seek to redeem the world from error by trying to theorize race, teasing out its various strands as if somewhere in the tangles and curlicues of the way that people talk and write about race we might find the magic formula for dealing with it.

For these writers, the upshot of insisting on race's social construction is not to stop it in its tracks but rather to render race and racism at least semi-impervious to any social-economic remedy. So, for example, the art and cultural theorist W. J. T. Mitchell takes exception to the idea that because the "dominant scientific view is that race is a 'myth' ... that has ceased to be seen as a fundamental reality characterizing the human species," cultural theory ought to turn away from race. On the contrary, Mitchell asserts, cultural theory ought to bring to bear the insight that myth has had "the status of a real force in history and in the unfolding history of thought," an account that provides an understanding of human behavior.[16] Against the myth of race, scientific criticism does not offer the possibility of falsification but merely a "countermyth of a world without race, a world where the word and the idea no longer have any role to play, where we have 'seen through race' and the illusory, fantasmatic character of the concept has been exposed."[17] Such an option is neither possible nor desirable for Mitchell. In his view, race is a medium, and as such, is constitutive of thought—"a symbolic-imaginary, verbal-visual complex" that is "not merely a psychological matter, but a public and palpable feature of the material world, of the epistemological and historical field in which knowledge is constructed."[18] On this account race is not just a medium through which we perceive human bodies but the way in which bodies themselves also become a medium of racial reproduction through "performance, and music, and narrative, events, episodes, and epochs—in short, bodies that feel and blood that flows—by way of memory and genealogy—from one generation to the next."[19] Race exists and needs to exist because "race is the only term, the uniquely necessary term capable of mediating [the terms of class, culture, species, and gender], providing the central point of intersection at which they converge in a 'complexion' and from which they diverge and radiate outward into extreme forms of racism."[20]

Standing against Michaels and, by extension, Fields and Fields, who warn that "disguised as race, racism becomes something Afro-Americans are, rather than something racists do," Mitchell cautions that without race we would be unable to see what racism is and what race can do for us beyond making people available for invidious treatment.[21] Race, Mitchell concludes, "is the beginning of thought and even thoughtfulness about racism. The concept provides a way of seeing through race to its racist origins, taking account not only of its sources in inequality, bondage, and xenophobia but also of its creative, productive capacity to generate new communities of resistance and structures of feeling."[22] The differences here could hardly be starker. But if one is debating about which side to come down on, consider the following. Along the way in clarifying what he means by saying that "blood" operates "as a metaphor for *kinship*"—a "vernacular biology ... in the perfectly ordinary sense of parenting, reproduction, and filial relations"—Mitchell makes the following observation: "Every time Black people address each other as 'brothers and sisters' they invoke this vernacular sense of common ancestry and reinforce the racial myth that is the temporal dimension of the racial medium."[23] Even if one sets aside the imperiousness of purporting to describe what all black people must be doing when they use certain words, Mitchell's observation cannot escape being an instance of "racecraft." Members of religious groups, football teams, fraternities and sororities, military platoons, labor unions, and on and on, commonly refer to each other as brothers and sisters—and they do so without having to haul the lumber of common ancestry. But in Mitchell's reading, once the words "brother" and "sister" cross the lips of one black person speaking to another, we are in the terrain where black people are automatically doing a racial thing and reinforcing racial myth. Moreover, Mitchell's "reading" of these expressions of comradeship works only because he already sees the people involved as black.

As Barbara Fields points out, because "the boundaries of the group for which African-descended peoples have sought to define the terms of belonging and solidarity more or less coincide with the boundaries of the group that law and custom designate a race," it may be hard to see that "it was precisely in order to escape racism [i.e., their designation by law and custom] that [black Americans] sought their own definition of belonging and solidarity."[24] Fields continues, "But the only reason scholars conclude without thought or hesitation that every such proposed self-definition is an acquiescence in (or, as the tedious jargon has it, construction of) race is that the equation of self-definition and race for Afro-Americans—and for them alone—is an axiom, no more in need of proof than susceptible to it. In other words, the equation of Afro-Americans' peoplehood with race is a corollary of racism."[25] The agent of racial ascription here is Mitchell, who has drawn up just such an equation, all the while phrasing his remarks as if he were merely describing what black people do.

But Mitchell is hardly alone. "Is there anything distinctive about black literature that allows us to know *this is what makes it black?*" queries Margo N. Crawford in her recent book, *What Is African American Literature?* She continues, "Is the only distinctive feature the fact that the authors are black?"[26] To dispense with any mystery, Crawford's answer to the first question is "yes," and to the second, "not quite." And it is the "not quite" answer to the second question that enables the affirmative answer to the first: "The body of black literature," Crawford writes, "is produced by the tension of the flesh that has been named the 'black body.'"[27] I take Crawford to be saying that while it is not the race of the author that produces the distinctiveness of black literature—black writers don't produce black literature in the way that silkworms produce silk—there is, yet, some way in which the bodies of authors and readers do matter in the process of making literature. Bodies matter because it is a somatic response—a tension (which is to say, an affect) arising from having been ascribed as black—that produces a body of black literature. Also important to Crawford's point is that this affect is not the product of a single body; it is something that exists between bodies. Crawford concludes, "An open system of black nervousness (an open system of black feeling) distinguishes African American literature from other literary traditions."[28] The feedback loop that distinguishes African American literature from other literatures also works to distinguish the bodies of black Americans from those of other socially designated groups. The "Coda" to Crawford's book quotes

Gwendolyn Brooks's assertion in "Poets Who Are Negroes" that "Every negro poet has 'something to say.' His mere body, for that matter, is an eloquence. His quiet walk down the street is a speech to the people."[29] Body and language are made identical.

That a quest for literary distinctiveness should occasion such a tortured return to the project of distinguishing the bodies (and the affects) of black Americans from other groups of people is not at all surprising, given that in contemporary parlance, it has become almost de rigueur when addressing various forms of violent injustice to refer to the bodies of African-descended peoples as black. The oeuvre of Ta-Nehisi Coates depends on the obscurant qualities of the term and the way it almost imperceptibly elides the difference between deeming some people as black to justify "plundering" them, and plundering them because their bodies are black.[30] Even Coates's frequent use of the term "plunder" assists in this verbal sleight-of-hand, shifting attention away from the labor imperative that drove the enslavement of African peoples to the horror-film idea that whites were motivated by a desire to appropriate and carry away the distinctive bodily characteristics of their captives.[31] To be sure, white enslavers made it their business to draw attention to what they took to be the distinguishing feature of Africans—(most obviously) the darkness of their skins—but they did so with the end of producing profit, not grafting those qualities onto their own persons. When delegates for the state of Mississippi announced their decision to secede from the United States, they had no doubt in their minds that the profitable production of cotton and sugar depended on what they deemed peculiar to Africans: "Our position is thoroughly identified with the institution of slavery—the greatest material interest of the world. Its labor supplies the product which constitutes by far the largest and most important portions of commerce of the earth. These products are peculiar to the climate verging on the tropical regions, and by an imperious law of nature, none but the black race can bear exposure to the tropical sun."[32] But the idea that what underwrote domination was a desire for the bodies of black Americans, and not the labor produced by those bodies, retains a certain appeal.[33] Indeed, Jordan Peele's highly popular and clever 2017 film *Get Out* creates its powerful charge by producing a parallel literalization of Coates's term (although the term "black body" is figurative through and through, Coates uses it as if it were literal), depicting the relation between whites and blacks as the macabre harvesting of organs and attributes in order to rejuvenate failing white bodies.

Re-anchoring black identity in language that proclaims the blackness of bodies affirms the intimation that, as I noted in discussing Du Bois and Ellison, something, in spite of the obvious differences in the beliefs and situations of these individuals, must yet connect them to one another—something beyond their shared rejection of and opposition to the racial order that was imposed upon them. And while the antiracist orientation of Crawford, Mitchell, and Coates inclines them to reject the idea that something within the bodies of African-descended peoples warrants their constitution as a race, these thinkers are loath to leave the body behind because it holds the possibility of connection. Despite the strong affinities among individuals that manifest at particular moments, black Americans do not share a class position, a politics, a singular culture, a religion, or an aesthetic. As with the case of all "groupings of people that exist in our species," the groupings among, and groupings of, African-descended peoples are, in the words of the AAPA statement, "socially-defined, dynamic, and continually evolving—amalgamations of socially- and biologically-interacting individuals with constantly-shifting boundaries, reflecting the myriad ways that individuals, families, and other clusters of people create ties, move, trade, mate, reproduce, and shift their social identities and affiliations through time."[34] Amid this flux, the idea that there have been, and currently are, others with bodies like ours who may have been subject to similar, if not the same, indignities and similar, if not the same, desires for comfort and consolation carries a certain appeal.

For readers like Crawford, the body registers a "poetics of vibration, the diasporic shock of elsewhere, and the twitch and wink produced by the psychic hold of slavery" that enables its readers to "feel embodied in disembodiment. The involuntary nature of a certain type of rocking happens when the body needs comfort or feels nervous." Crawford adds:

> The comfort and the anxiety that shape the need to imagine the distinctiveness of the category "African American literature" is the comfort and anxiety of the rocking that produces the tightness that [Toni] Morrison, at the end of *Beloved*, describes as "wrapped tight like skin."[35]

Readings, and the affects generated by them, enfold us in something like skin, which can only be something like race. In other words, to read African American literature is to become black—provided, of course, one already has the skin that can be stirred by "the literary tradition ... itself." To make skin and the body the mediums of connection among black Americans also serves to obscure and de-emphasize other vectors of connection and disconnection affecting the black population, the most prominent of which pertain to the class dynamics at work within and across racial groups. Like other domains of literary fiction, what is now termed African American fiction finds its deepest roots in the intellectual soil on the campuses of colleges and universities, which are, increasingly, the domain of the wealthiest segments of the population. As Mark McGurl's institutional history of the rise of creative writing programs in higher education has shown, regardless of racial background, the pedigree of the typical writer of literary fiction is marked by that person's passage through a US university.[36] Even as institutions diversify their enrollments and their faculty, their student bodies remain composed disproportionately of those from the wealthiest 25 percent of the population.

In certain respects, this disparity reflects the realities of a racially divided society. For example, a recent report by the Brookings Institute finds that at "$171,000, the net worth of a typical white family is nearly ten times greater than that of a Black family ($17,150) in 2016," a difference that prompts the Brookings researchers to remark, the "Black-white wealth gap reflects a society that has not and does not afford equality of opportunity to all its citizens."[37] That the wealth gap in American society also represents a race gap may seem most self-evident to those at the top end of the income ladder where the differences are starkest. In this regard, the Brookings report also observes that for "those in the top 10 percent by income (only 3.6 percent Black), the racial wealth gap is still quite large: median net worth for white families in this income group is $1,789,300 versus $343,160 for Black families." By contrast, a "racial gap exists in every income group except the bottom quintile (23.5 percent Black), where median net worth is zero for everyone."[38] In other words, as Matt Bruenig, in another analysis of these data, shows, "nearly all white wealth is owned by the top 10 percent of white households just as nearly all black wealth is owned by the top 10 percent of black households. The lower and middle deciles of each racial group own virtually none of their racial group's wealth."[39]

The upshot here is that "the overall racial wealth disparity is being driven almost entirely by the disparity between the wealthiest 10 percent of white people and the wealthiest 10 percent of black people."[40] So that while, "black and white elites increasingly live in the same neighborhoods, interact socially as individuals and families, attend the same schools and functions, consume the same class-defining commodities and pastimes, and participate in the same civic and voluntary associations," the dramatic difference in overall wealth between black elites and their presumed class peers gets figured as the difference that race makes.[41] Even as "class differentiation among black Americans has increased generally since the late 1960s," it is the difference between black and white elites that is taken to matter more and is used to identify black elites with the majority of other Blacks, many of whom possess little or no wealth.[42]

The turn back to race in cultural analysis, the insistence on body and skin as the medium for experiencing blackness, is the corollary of a fear that, to quote the narrator of Michael Thomas's 2007 novel *Man Gone Down*—a multiracial PhD candidate in English—"When the revolution comes, they might be coming for me, too."[43] The narrator's desires to buy Bulgarian feta cheese and keep his children enrolled in a tony private school are not, in the first instance, working-class demands and serve more to identify him with the wealthy whites around him than with the people with whose fate he remains concerned throughout the story. To its credit, Thomas's novel is alive to the ironies that attend the challenge of trying to tell the story of a "race" through the tale of an aspiring writer/academic, and the plot works hard to expose the problem of believing that those inside of "any powerful institution" can presume their status as proxies for those outside. But, if we take our cue from Crawford, the narrator's anxieties just might be misplaced. Should it turn out that "his people" were to storm the English Department, they would presumably find the cradling arms of African American literature ready to rock them to sleep.

Notes

1. W. E. B. Du Bois, "The Conservation of Races," in *Writings* (New York: Library of America, 1986), 825.
2. Ibid., 825.
3. Ibid.
4. The recent insistence by many publishers on capitalizing "Black" actually reflects the effect of the tendency against which I am arguing.

5. Du Bois, *Dusk of Dawn: An Essay towards an Autobiography of the Race Concept*, in *Writings*, 666.
6. Karen E. Fields and Barbara J. Fields, *Racecraft: The Soul of Inequality in American Life* (New York: Verso, 2012), 19.
7. Qtd. in Fields and Fields, *Racecraft*, 19.
8. Ibid., 74.
9. Ralph Ellison, "The World and the Jug," in *The Collected Essays of Ralph Ellison*, ed. John F. Callahan (New York: The Modern Library, 1995), 164.
10. Zora Neale Hurston, "How It Feels to Be Colored Me," in *The Norton Anthology of African American Literature*, ed. Henry Louis Gates, Jr. and Nellie Y. McKay (New York: W. W. Norton and Company, Inc., 2004), 1031.
11. See Adolph Reed, Jr., "Making Sense of Race, I: The Ideology of Race, the Biology of Human Variation and the Problem of Medical and Public Health Research," *Journal of Race and Policy* 1, no. 1 (2005): 11–42.
12. Fred Moten, "The Case of Blackness," *Criticism* 50, no. 2 (2008): 187.
13. "AAPA Statement on Racism," The American Association of Physical Anthropologists, June 3, 2021.
14. Walter Benn Michaels, "Autobiography of an Ex-White Man," *Transition* 73 (1997): 131. The relevant texts here include the aforementioned *Racecraft* by Fields and Fields; Barbara J. Fields, "Whiteness, Racism, and Identity," *International Labor and Working-Class History* 60 (Fall 2001): 48–56; Walter Benn Michaels, *The Trouble with Diversity: How We Learned to Love Identity and Ignore Inequality* (New York: Metropolitan Books, 2006); Adolph Reed, Jr. "Making Sense of Race, I"; Adolph Reed, Jr. "Marx, Race, and Neoliberalism," *New Labor Forum* 22, no. 1 (2013): 49–57.
15. Fields and Fields, *Racecraft*, 101.
16. Mitchell quotes Michaels; W. J. T. Mitchell, *Seeing through Race* (Cambridge, MA: Harvard University Press, 2012), 22.
17. Ibid., 23–4.
18. Ibid., 20.
19. Ibid., 26.
20. Ibid., 36.
21. Fields and Fields, *Racecraft*, 96–7.
22. Mitchell, *Seeing through Race*, 37.
23. Ibid., 25.
24. Fields, "Whiteness, Racism, and Identity," 50.
25. Ibid., 50.
26. Margo N. Crawford, *What Is African American Literature?* (Hoboken, NJ: Wiley Blackwell, 2021), 3.
27. Ibid., 7.
28. Ibid., 8.
29. Qtd. in Crawford, *What Is African American Literature?*, 175.
30. Although Coates professes to understand that "race is the child of racism," the entirety of his critique unfolds as if the opposite is true. Ta-Nehisi Coates, *Between the World and Me: The Beautiful Struggle* (New York: Spiegel & Grau, 2015), 12.

31. At one point, for example, Coates speaks of the monumental effort that he must make to look past "the human sacrifice that finds us no matter our manhood. As though our hands were ever our own. As though plunder of dark energy was not at the heart of our galaxy. And the plunder was there, if I wished to see it." Coates, *Between the World and Me,* 71.

32. "A Declaration of the Immediate Causes which Induce and Justify the Secession of the State of Mississippi from the Federal Union," The Avalon Project: Documents in Law, History, and Diplomacy. Yale Law School, Lillian Goldman Law Library.

33. This is not to deny that fetishistic investments by some individuals have attended the exploitation of Blacks by whites in power but rather to say that the social-economic cause of exploitation cannot be found within the dynamics of that investment.

34. Agustín Fuentes, Rebecca Ackermann, Sheela Athreya, Deborah Bolnick, Tina Lasisi, Sang-Hee Lee, Shay-Akil McLean, and Robin Nelson, "AAPA Statement on Race and Racism," *American Journal of Physical Anthropology* 169 (2019): 400–2.

35. Crawford, *What Is African American Literature?*, 177.

36. Mark McGurl, *The Program Era: Postwar Fiction and the Rise of Creative Writing* (Cambridge, MA: Harvard University Press, 2009), 57–8.

37. Kriston McIntosh, Emily Moss, Ryan Nunn, and Jay Shambaugh, "Examining the Black-White Wealth Gap," Up Front, The Brookings Institution, 2021.

38. Ibid.

39. Matt Bruenig, "The Racial Wealth Gap Is about the Upper Classes," *Jacobin*, July 5, 2020.

40. Ibid.

41. Adolph Reed, Jr., "The Post-1965 Trajectory of Race, Class, and Urban Politics in the United States Reconsidered," *Labor Studies Journal* 41, no.3 (2016): 271.

42. "Reed, The Surprising Cross-Racial Saga of Modern Wealth Inequality," *The New Republic*, 29 June 2020.

43. Michael Thomas, *Man Gone Down* (New York: Black Cat, 2007), 211. See also Kenneth W. Warren, *What Was African American Literature?* (Cambridge: Harvard U Press, 2011), 119–40.

CHAPTER 17
THE ENDS OF CULTURAL STUDIES
Mike Hill

I don't know what to say about American cultural studies. I am completely dumbfounded by it!

—Stuart Hall

Institutionalize This!

Nobody could have been more dumbfounded by Hall's remarks on American cultural studies than those of us wanting to join its ranks in the early 1990s.[1] This was the heyday of cultural studies on the American side of the pond, though it had long since moved on from a rather different iteration of an earlier time. By the time cultural studies moved to the larger and more professionalized scene, decades after it had achieved departmental status for a few early innovators, the future for its North American aspirants seemed wide open. But what did we miss? Cultural studies' well-established origin story is partly what inspired Hall's dumbfoundedness, with an exclamation point. It's a story leading me to subtitle the introduction to this chapter with a differently motivated exclamation point of my own.[2] The future turned out to be less open than anybody in the 1990s knew. That's what is dumbfounding, looking back through the crash in academic humanities jobs at cultural studies' heady US glory days.

As its origin story goes, cultural studies started in Britain with the 1964 founding of the Birmingham Centre for Contemporary Cultural Studies (BCCS), although its earliest lineage goes back to the dramatic geopolitical events of 1956. The ideological tendencies of the New Left-inspired Centre, as Hall explains, stemmed from "the disintegration of an entire historical/political project, [and emerged] against the Soviet tanks in Budapest."[3] Reference to the Red Army's suppression of the student-led Hungarian uprising in the mid-1950s marks a break from official Communist Party orthodoxy. Hall describes the scene as a "prolonged and yet unending contestation with the question of false consciousness [associated] with the model of base and superstructure."[4] According to this "determinist" tendency, personal relationships, social organizations, and the consumption and production of *culture* (a term still to be defined) play strictly subservient roles to the demands of capital. The loosening of the strictly determinist bases of economics found in certain strains of Marxism attracted the first wave of cultural studies scholars and inspired the formation of the Centre. In the more technical terms used by Hall, if "base" is designated as relations of production, the factory floor, where labor is sold and capital is expropriated, and "superstructure" is the ideological zone of mass media, then the BCCS legacy represents an attempt to give the superstructure at least a little independence from the economic relations presumed to determine it. Student demands for reform externally imposed by the policies of the USSR should have been taken progressively, the masses giving voice to worthwhile grievances, no matter what the Politburo said.

In the variant of cultural studies stemming from F. R. Leavis, and preceding the BCCS, mass culture was similarly denounced as false consciousness. But workers couldn't be so blind, so deluded, or so controlled by the dictates of capital as to be totally incapable of reflecting critically on their conditions, could they? For the "Left Leavisites," this consideration was addressed vis-à-vis the introduction of canonical, Capital "L" Literature to the masses, now removed from the elitist perches of the UK's "best" universities. This first wave of cultural studies in the UK already contained a tension between nonelite students and the well-intended, better educated, professorial class. Teaching high culture to the lower orders comprised the honorable efforts of BCCS members such as Raymond Williams, Richard Hoggart, and E. P. Thompson, in the British polytechnic schools where British workers would receive a remedial quantity of Shakespeare, Milton, the Romantics, and the like. Although these core members of the Centre developed different postures toward the vexing preoccupation of mass culture as worthy of scholarly consideration, the New Left's break with Party orthodoxy going back to Hungary and those Soviet tanks implied a version of culture writ unusually large. In language later borrowed from the French theorist Louis Althusser, superstructural relations were deemed "relatively autonomous" from their economic base. To this end, Williams famously called culture "ordinary," giving working-class students the intellectual agency few serious academics presumed they could (or should) aspire to achieve.[5] The term designating the goals of the BCCS in this early phase was thus refreshingly clear: "worker education." Yet, in retrospect, there was an overly circumscribed notion of what a worker was. In the same way Hall wanted to give the "superstructure" some autonomy from the economic "base," "workers" en masse were no longer presumed to be creatively or intellectually passive.

The larger praiseworthy goal of "worker education" was to bring workers into the cultural fold. But what remained for US cultural studies to consider has later turned out to be how "educators" would become "workers" themselves. For humanities doctoral students like me in the heyday of US cultural studies, something strange happened on the way to becoming part of what V. I. Lenin called "the labor aristocracy."[6] In retrospect, this something had to do with the division between being educators, on the one hand, and the kinds of workers conjured by the phrase "worker education," on the other. One passage from Williams still resonates deeply for me on this point about the worker-as-educator:

> when you recognize in yourself the ties that still bind, you cannot be satisfied with the old formula: Enlightened minority, degraded mass. You know how bad most "popular culture" is, but you also know that the irruption of the "swinish multitude" … is the coming to relative power of your own people.[7]

The Ends of Cultural Studies

As an aspiring "educator" myself during the period Meaghan Morris notes as "an unprecedented international boom" in cultural studies, there was no question: the cultural-studies-oriented PhD would allow first-generation college students, otherwise destined to work insecurely and for low wages, to join Lenin's aristocracy of labor.[8] Graduate school was a way not only to educate the "swinish multitude"—my people— but also to get the hell out of a working-class life.

As one of the lucky few to win the academic job lottery and writing twenty-odd years after receiving a tenured academic post, I realize something that remains a thorny reminder of the past. My cultural studies ideals were connected to an almost embarrassingly simple desire. This was the desire to escape the construction sites, the machinists' shops, the restaurant kitchens, the clerical desks, and the factory floors of the "degraded mass" as partly also me. The desire to represent the "worker" but not exactly be one summed up for me the "desire called cultural studies," as Frederic Jameson famously put it, a related kind of tension.[9] There was *academic* work, and then there was what the men in my family called *real* work. Guess how real an English degree was presumed by them to be.

In the rest of this chapter, I want to consider this question in a more expansive way. I'd like to propose pushing the concepts of "worker" and "educator" more closely together not simply by giving *them* ("workers") access to *us* ("educators"). Rather, I think there is something yet to be learned from the ends of cultural studies—its goals, its successes, and its failures—related to the rebirth of knowledge as work. There is something about cultural studies' founding interest in the "multitude" extending beyond the labor-aristocracy divide: What about how we think *as* work, and what about *work* as a concept for generating the expansion of knowledge? For my purposes, this relationship between working and knowing brings up the enigma of scale: How much should we enlarge the category called "worker" and how does this adjustment enable knowing more and acting better? When I think about the so-called masses, I think not just about my people but also about *massification*: how collectivities of human beings, the reality of things, the effects of events, and so on are insufficiently conceptualized by the word "culture." If anything is clear in the great expansion enjoyed by "American cultural studies" in the 1990s, combined with the great contraction of the academic job market for its would-be practitioners thereafter, it's an awareness of how massive, and yet also how constraining, the scaling up of cultural studies has turned out to be. Objects of study have been productively scaled up; but, at the college and university levels, the opportunities for turning students into educators have been definitively scaled down. In the standard origin story of cultural studies, and more dramatically in its later Yankee importation, there was a lack of clarity in the distinction between the objects of study—real workers, mass media, popular culture—and the would-be academic labor aristocracy wishing to connect *with* but not exactly *be* a worker. This is not to suggest that my lucky escape from wage labor makes me the same as a so-called *real* worker. It just means we have different proximities to different relations of production. It also means we need a broader conception of work than the old culture-*versus*-labor divide.

The Ends of Knowledge

To give a fuller explanation of this divide, in the first part of this chapter I'm going to say more about the history of cultural studies: specifically, Williams's writing on the concept of culture, more carefully defined. Here I'll go back to his reference to the Hyde Park riots of 1866. The desire of cultural studies to "connect" with Hall's "great mass ranks" begins here, when Matthew Arnold helped initiate a concept of culture as a knowledge-technique for pacifying British male workers who were then protesting for voting rights. The Hyde Park riots are an example of masses in search of representation in the political sense. Academic workers in the humanities from the 1990s faced the same kind of struggle, in the sense of searching for employment. Like the Hyde Park rioters, and like my graduate cohort in the heyday of US cultural studies, prevailing conditions of labor forced us to work through a problem of massification, and not simply on behalf of an externalized version of the masses. This requires us to move on from disrupting old forms of organization to creating new and better—or simply, more capacious—associations with workers. We can't solve the problem of massification with the term "culture" as conceived from Arnold on, but we can advance the ends of cultural studies if we use a more expansive concept of "work."

The second part of this chapter recalls the anti-disciplinary stance of cultural studies established in the first part and asks what role category plays in relation to the problem of expanding what we mean by labor. This is not an argument for policing cultural studies, as it has managed to do already for itself. But neither do I want to suggest cultural studies should abandon productive constraints. Here massification as a scale problem applies not only to would-be academics—Hall's "great mass *out there*" now comprising most of academic teaching *in here*—but also to knowledge production itself as a problem of scale. As we raise the question of cultural studies so many years after its inception, positing the matter of its *ends* in both senses (methods and means, on the one hand; successes and failures, on the other), might we think of masses in an even more capacious way than "worker education" allows? Might we think about culture beyond the pacification of the masses, and compatible with the words *scale*, *growth*, and *expansion*, as a problem solvable by new ways of working, rather than an encumbrance to work? Ultimately, we ought to move from the *ends* of cultural studies to a more definitive focus on *means*. The third section of this chapter thus draws on the Re:Enlightenment Project. Moving from the ends of cultural studies to the problem of means, Re:Enlightenment provides a way to do history within a new form of institutionalization, offering promising solutions to the problem of massification: expansion within productive constraints.

The word "institution" is worth pausing over in leading up to the moves I just outlined. In cultural studies circles, "institution" raises anxiety. Hall himself, wanting to resist the position of "keeper of the conscience of cultural studies" in the exhilarating context of its US success in the early nineties, declares the "institutionalization of cultural studies as a moment of profound danger."[10] He adds: "it would be excessively vulgar to talk about such things as how many jobs there are."[11] In fairness to Hall, what has for decades now been called the "academic Great Depression" was not foremost in the mind of BCCS workers.[12] The life span and staffing history of the Centre from its founding in 1964 to its closing in 2002 hardly reveal a fast track toward academic job security. Although the

Centre produced vitally important books and articles and developed high-profile careers for its loosely affiliated members, it never had the stability or large faculty numbers of traditional humanities departments.[13] In the now famous mega-anthology *The Cultural Studies Reader*, the primary competitor to the more simply titled, but equally gigantic, *Cultural Studies*, Simon During introduces the field in a mode akin to Hall's ambivalence. He expresses the need to "question its institutional ... status" before it was institutionalized as such.[14] Nick Couldry thus correctly remarks on cultural studies' founding "fear of institutionalization" and makes the worthy suggestion, apropos of Williams's original claim, that "academics should focus on the general transformations of labor that made 'intellectual' labor ordinary, and not special."[15] Couldry makes his comments in a relatively new volume of 2011, called *The Renewal of Cultural Studies*, edited by Paul Smith.

By using the word "renewal," Smith acknowledges the loss of what was never decidedly there: cultural studies was already amorphous, institutionally wary, and discipline-defying. He continues, with refreshing frankness, to remind us that cultural studies did not "open out onto some thriving area of politics and the public sphere beyond the academy."[16] In conversation with Andrew Ross, a leading contributor to US cultural studies in its early inception, Smith speaks provocatively about "cultural studies [as an] institutionalized" course of academic study with a "phantom limb" of class-based "activism."[17] In the same *Renewal* volume, graduate students in the Cultural Studies program at George Mason University, where Smith is the leading figure, insightfully explain the "lament [of] cultural studies' institutionalization in the US [as an] unresolved ... identity crisis."[18] A 2021 conference on cultural studies at the University of Brighton was called "Whatever Happened to Cultural Studies?" Topics there included "a diminution in the profile of cultural studies" and "the erosion of interest in cultural studies at the level of the University."[19]

Is the erosion any wonder? It's as if in leaving Birmingham, cultural studies announced its birth and issued funeral invitations simultaneously. This identity crisis evokes, as Smith says, a "phantasmatic" form of institutionalization, an afterlife preceding the burden of having to actually exist. The list of citations against cultural studies' institutionalization suggests resistance to political hegemony as the illusive promise of the field and the preoccupation of its wandering soul. But what's being resisted is neither the cruel machinations of capitalism nor the disciplinary forces of a cultural elite bent on pacifying or rescuing the masses. Rather, what cultural studies ends up resisting is its own possibility for success. What success cultural studies might have had may be redefined as expanding the concept of work to include what we're doing right now.

Once again in fairness to Hall, a hint about making good on the ends of cultural studies for creating better futures was already an occulted part of its past. Hall insists, "Before we invoke the great mass ranks out there, it might be quite important that our students are with us in the project [of cultural studies] and that we are helping them conduct a little intellectual work."[20] As Hall expressed about the academic afterlife of cultural studies, while it "refuses to be a master discourse or meta-discourse *of any kind* ..., it does have some will to connect."[21] It remains hard to detangle the relationship between this "will

The Ends of Knowledge

to connect" with cultural studies' absent referent—the masses—and what appears today as the refusal to produce knowledge by working the problem of scale through the limits of category Hall refers to as "kind." We could think about Hall's word "kind" in different ways: kinds of institutions, kinds of disciplines—in short, modes of work inclusive of the thinking kind. Cultural studies' reactive approach to its institutionalization misses the importance of working within some parameter of epistemic category—and misses how we might change the categories of what we do as academics over time. Thus, my heretical reply to cultural studies' resistance to success: institutionalize this! But about what "this" is, and how "this" relates to the problem of masses, work, and disciplines, there is more explanation ahead.

Monster Processions and Roman Floggers

> Monster processions in the street and forcible irruptions into the parks ... ought to be unflinchingly forbidden and repressed .... The Roman way of dealing with that is always the right one; flog the rank and file and fling the ringleaders from the Tarpeian Rock.
>
> —Matthew Arnold

This epigraph is taken from Raymond Williams's *Culture and Materialism*, a *locus classicus* for cultural studies. Citing Arnold, Williams wants us to reconsider the first word in his title from a historical vantage point. His interest here is in the forgotten historical record: the "mass demonstrations of July 23, 1866, when some sixty thousand workers, from many parts of the country" assembled at Hyde Park. Through this act of coming together in a large-scale public way, the masses were "testing the right of free assembly."[22] Hyde Park has a twofold significance for Williams: the right of working-class British men to participate in elections, and the defiance of a new bill making meetings in Hyde Park illegal as a means to thwart expansion of the franchise. But there's even more to the Hyde Park riots than legal defiance as a way of enlarging representation and rights. Within Williams's deft treatment of Arnold's neglected archive, the problem of scale as a "monstrous" beast exists both for politics and knowledge production. Arnold's call for state "repression" parallels his more liberal stance on behalf of the "expansion" of learning. Affirming the utility of culture as the soft glove encasing the legal system's "flogging" hand, Arnold writes: "The need of expansion is as genuine an instinct in man as the need in a plant for the light, or the need in man himself for going upright. The love of liberty is simply the instinct in man for *expansion*."[23] The connection between plants and culture aside, what intrigues Williams most about Arnold's *Culture and Anarchy* is the sinister compatibility between knowledge expansion and political repression, the co-equivalence of culture and the law. The art of growing narrowly and within various sorts of limits is coaxed into place by the key, yet at the same time occulted, word "culture" as Arnold expands on it here. "Excellence in human values, on the one hand," Williams writes, "discipline and where necessary repression on the other."[24]

Not yet a century after the modern partitioning of culture's hazy vastness into the various humanities silos designed to deliver aesthetic value without end, the opposition between cultural and material disciplines became firmly established.[25] Arnold was a cultural liberal to the extent that, in his famous words, "the best knowledge and thought of the time" was to be delivered "outside the clique of the cultivated and the learned ... yet still remain the *best*."[26] Increasing access to knowledge was not only desirable; it was also necessary to curtail the more dangerous kind of growth of the political representation of the workers. With clear lineage to the quintessential Enlightenment figure Immanuel Kant, aesthetic judgment travels cheek-by-jowl with the law, no matter how unjust the law might be. Kant was remembered for commanding, "Dare to Know!" But there's another command conjoined to Kant's *sapere aude*: "Argue as much as you like, and about what you like, but obey!" In associating "knowledge" with "obedience" in this context, and in reference to Arnold, I don't want to claim knowledge is possible without any adherence to rules whatsoever. Rather than the self-defeating insistence of a certain wing of cultural studies to never institutionalize, I mean the opposite: what you know depends both on the rules you may refuse to obey as well as the new and better (because more expansive) ones you may choose to follow in their place.

What does Williams mean when he writes: "it will always be necessary to go again to Hyde Park?"[27] There's a hint of *what else* in Arnold's reference to "flinging the ringleaders [of the mass protest] from the Tarpeian Rock." This allusion to early Roman history concerns a site of execution for murders, traitors, perjurers, and larcenous slaves, who were thrown from the 25-meter cliff as punishment for their crimes. Clearly, Arnold's conception of culture grants no time for civil disturbance. Beyond this obvious point, we can recall the inscription "Arx tarpeia Capitoli proxima," which intimates a far-reaching warning: "The Tarpeian Rock is close to the Capitol." Rather like the fate of US cultural studies, one's fall comes swiftly and in unexpected ways. State funding for higher education collapses as the humanities disciplines also go down. But returning again to Hyde Park intimates a version of history still offering alternatives to the dead-end of "flinging" and "flogging."

In *Keywords*, Williams begins the entry on culture by raising the issue of multiplicity, so essential to both the amassing of people and the expansion of knowledge. This issue of scale is traceable within the word's etymology: "Culture is one of the two or three most complicated words in the English language," he writes.[28] The word "complicated" here means there are lots of variations to the definition of culture, and these variations are as massive as they tend to be lost. It's as if Williams's insistence to "go again to Hyde Park" adjoins a renewed focus on the masses of workers in 1866 to finding undocumented historical difference within the key-est of his keywords. Both the concept of culture and identification of worker need to be scaled up. Note too how the word "again" in Williams's reference to Hyde Park doubles down on the prospect of "expansion" beyond the Arnoldian kind where culture and work are reduced and torn apart. To this correction of category error (they became too narrow) Williams adds a temporal twist (we can go back to go forward). By recovering the traces of culture's horticultural past as connected to working the earth, Williams takes his cue from Arnold's metaphorical association of culture with the light necessary for plant growth. But he also takes a literal rather than merely figurative turn. As he reminds us, until the time corresponding to the rise of English as a discipline, the meaning of culture was "cultivation or tending," as in "husbandry, and the tending of natural growth."[29] Williams had what appears now as a prophetic interest in the "startling connections" between "new ecological and radical-ecological movements" and class politics, "seeing the crises of the social order and the natural order as inseparably linked."[30] These connections bring to mind the understory of old growth forest, regarded by cutting-edge botanists as the "wood-wide web," or the network-centric structure of mycological information pathways buzzing unseen beneath the forest floor.[31] But more directly in line with my purposes here, Williams's return to "cultivation" allows us to rethink cultural studies as work. His recovery of culture's lost connection to "cultivation" expands how we might reunite different means of production.

The cultural education Arnold offered the masses with his homeopathic dose of canonical literature was designed to counter their "monstrous processions." In this sense, the Arnoldian wing of proto-cultural studies was both more general and more generous than what the multitude's illiterate medieval forbears would have received. But the clever bait-and-switch enabled by "expanding" the dissemination of culture in Arnold's elitist sense erases a greater range of human experience than his brand of humanism was equipped to surmise. The big cover-up of culture's debt to those who produced the wealth necessary to establish the elitist version of cultural dissemination demotes the importance of work in the production of value and detaches (after Marx, alienates) the product from the means of production. Culture *started* as a way of conceptualizing expansive forms of human and nonhuman relations in multiple, plural, but also historically specific ways, with an emphasis on process, means, tools—we could even say media. Culture *ended* with the assumption it was always and everywhere *there*, coextensive with "human experience … converted into self-pleasing ideology" for the few at the expense of the many.[32] Worse even than this, culture functioned as a tool paradoxically refusing its technical origins to support "the subjugation and domination of the four quarters of the globe."[33] Both the premodern and the modern versions of culture involve the problem of "expansion," but the one we left behind turns out to be more useful than the one we adopted.

Arnold uses the word "expansion" in adjoining the too-narrow work of culture to the practices of "flinging" and "flogging." For Arnold, the goal was to scale up the dissemination of culture where culture is defined by way of scaling literature down to the few and the best of what's written. For Williams, by contrast, culture was itself a concept put under strain by having to accommodate more and more objects. As early as 1958, he proposed "further work … on a new general theory of culture … expanding culture, and its detailed processes as a whole way of life."[34] "Expanding culture," and the realization that "we live in an expanding culture," did not mean, for Williams, giving up on "generality" or "wholeness." It just meant that the "expansion" of knowledge (as work, by and for workers) depends on how our divisions (disciplinary, economic, and political) are redrawn over time. Williams's generalities were better than Arnold's, which were better than the generalities of the medieval Catholic church, because his version of expansiveness was more, not less, general. Having lost its connection with "means of production" (Williams's term), Arnold's nineteenth-century version of culture replaced an earlier emphasis on terrestrial "processes" with fixed standards of judgment: culture confronted the masses by "remaining the *best*." In order to *better* this version of "the best," we might repeat Williams's declaration with more emphasis and at greater length: "While the ... 'little Arnolds' ... dominate and *multiply*, it will always be necessary to go *again* to Hyde Park."[35] So, there are two versions of multiplicity here, the "little" one tied to culture in its narrow and immaterial sense, and the bigger one tied to culture more capaciously conceived in connection to work. Williams's indictment of "little Arnolds" highlights the importance of means over ends, relations of production (and reproduction, as in too many Arnolds) over the liberal ruse of false equivalency. This ruse is connected to humanist cultural values in the same way it underwrites commodity exchange. By contrast, Williams helps us rethink cultural studies as a way of "making" rather than "judging."[36] He gets us beyond "flogging" and "flinging," as well.

The continued struggle with "expansion," with class struggle as a matter of scaling up worn-out classifications, haunts the word "culture." As has been suggested, this may call for us to retire the word. Thus, returning to the point of masses and multitudes, Meaghan Morris interrogates "pluralism" to sum up culture's end-date. In response to Hall, she remarks: "The reason I'm not a pluralist is that I don't think pluralism is an option. I think it's the problem."[37] By contrast, Cary Nelson, in his introduction to the same mega-volume, affirms Lata Mani's comment on "the dazzling plurality ... of the politics of difference."[38] With Morris we might ask: When does plurality "dazzle," and when does it just daze? As Nelson continues, "it is impossible to agree on any essential or definite or unique narrative on cultural studies," adding, "cultural studies in fact has no distinct methodology [and was] ambiguous from the beginning."[39] Cultural studies without end is portrayed as "actively and aggressively anti-disciplinary—a characteristic that more or less ensures a permanently uncomfortable relation to academic disciplines."[40] Here Nelson quotes an essay in the volume by Graeme Turner, who suggests, because cultural studies is about the "critique of disciplines, [it] has been reluctant to become one."[41] The anti-disciplinary, anti-generalization stance of cultural studies in this variant is resistant not only to institutional success but also to an even provisionally closed set of limits within which to achieve more intelligent, accurate, or politically efficacious forms of knowledge.

In this sense of cultural studies' resistance to discipline, there is also a resistance to knowledge as such. What Smith calls "the absolution from elementary intellectual tasks" is what endless plurality looks like.[42] Smith is therefore right to bristle at the "unstructured and unregulated process of interpretive 'reading'" applied to all objects everywhere at any time, which is hardly possible if producing knowledge, let alone aspiring to a coherent political project, is the goal.[43] Should we give up on all generalizations for "chronic claims to random or wildly eclectic methodologies[?]" Smith rhetorically asks.[44]

There is a revealing moment within the history of cultural studies, when Hall describes the "intervention of feminism" as both a "rupture" and a "reopening" of cultural studies at the very moment of its inception.[45] Carol A. Stabile describes a dramatic scene: "that

The Ends of Knowledge

nightmare voice from the Left, yelling boldly from the back of the room: 'Yeah, Juliet [Mitchell], but what about Chile.'"[46] The scene of feminism as a disruption to cultural studies' lost political soul (Smith's "phantom limb") is especially poignant in this remark. Suturing Mitchell's work in pre-Oedipal psychological development to the US-backed military coup of Chile in the context of an academic conference, or rather, insisting she do so on command, reveals the trouble with pluralism and politics so called. "The nightmare of feminism," as Stabile describes it, or more viscerally, the moment feminism "crapped on the table of cultural studies," is put here as playing no small part in why it "stalled in the United States."[47] Stabile draws our attention to "the exclusions and elisions of cultural studies," and states "how unsettling questions or ideas become marginalized by existing fields of thought."[48] This challenge is especially significant in a context where the field itself attempts to represent the marginal. Stabile's point suggests there are always margins that are marginal to the ones we may think we are on: a plurality of margins in search of a new and better (because bigger) kind of center from which to decisively act. For Stabile, the working masses are only absent because they are too close for us to see. "With graduate programs functioning like puppy mills to churn out Ph.D.s no one can hire, [and] when 900 graduate students are applying for a single job, further talk of institutionalizing cultural studies seems the worst kind of narcissism."[49] Stabile is inarguably right about graduate students becoming a new version of the laboring multitudes they might rather aspire to represent. But what other forms of institutionalization, what larger generalizations, what expansions of the disciplines and remixing of categories, might we envision beyond the ones serving the few of us lucky enough to be secure (for the moment) within US academe? What forms of organized cooperation might emerge beyond the currently contracting ones Stabile tags with "the worst kind of narcissism"?

All and Nothing at All

> Nothing is more indeterminate than this word [culture], and nothing [is] more deceptive than its application to all nations and periods.
>
> —Johann Gottfried von Herder

Herder was, of course, correct. In this epigraph, also taken from Williams's work, the relationship between "all" and "nothing" is key. Herder objects to the word "culture" because it hides more than it reveals. Worse still, culture reduces "all" to "indeterminacy," equaling "nothing" at all; but Williams's goal in returning to the concept of culture linked to cultivation—the earthly processes of "tending"—helps us find better "applications" of the troubled term, where *better* means both more transparently constrained and more effectively capacious for workers working with many kinds of means. Further on the figure of Herder, Williams reveals how culture functions on behalf of Empire. But more than this, he wishes to explain "the relation between human development and a particular way of life, and the *work and practices of art and intelligence.*"[50] In foreshadowing what's to come in the final sections of the chapter, let me underscore the words "work," "practice," "art," and "intelligence." These terms will take us full circle to the issue of relations of production referred to in Hall's pause over base and superstructure. First though, there is further reason to stay focused on "work" as related to "masses." And here, again, we'll see why the idea of culture isn't up to the task unless we return it an earlier historical tendency, which highlights a latent connection to work.

Contemporary scholars in the leading handbooks on literary studies and critical terms find the same frustration with "culture" Herder does. According to the *Columbia Dictionary of Modern Literary Terms*, "culture is one of the most often used, and rarely defined [words] in contemporary criticism, inexact and widely used, often leading to considerable confusion."[51] Given the opaque repetition of the word "culture," cultural studies is impugned on the grounds of its own popularity. Two failed forms of scaling up are intertwined here: Stabile's just lament about there being no jobs for cultural studies' would-be practitioners is combined tragically with an anti-normative critique of the Arnoldian "best." These competing enigmas of cultural expansion are related to a third problem of scaling up, the "seemingly *limitless* [focus] on the culture of the masses."[52] Even in 1995, just a few years after the big anthologies where Morris, Hall, During, and Nelson were prominently featured, the editors of the *Dictionary* regard cultural studies as a wayward offshoot of literary criticism. As early as 1990, the influential Shakespeare scholar Stephen Greenblatt called the word "culture" "impossibly vague and encompassing," remarking further: "the few things that seem excluded from it are almost immediately reincorporated in the actual use of the word."[53] Greenblatt, too, hankers for a little discipline at the crossroads between the "few" and the prospect of endless "encompassing." In the standard-bearing *Norton Anthology of Literary Theory*, a wide array of authors appears under the heading of "Cultural Studies." These range from scholars on technology and posthumanism (Donna Haraway), to celebrators of working-class culture (Dick Hebdidge), to the culture industry's most fervent denouncers (Max Horkheimer and Theodore W. Adorno). Standard names in philosophy (Habermas), history of a sort (Foucault), and postcolonial studies (Fanon) are also gathered under cultural studies, although none of them ever affirmed or rejected the field. In the *Norton Anthology*'s clever organizational schema, an exceedingly wide range of scholars from different periods and places is reverse-engineered to fit the "culture" bill without ever having had to claim it. Here, too, the boundaries of cultural studies overflow with references and cross-references almost too excessive to tabulate.

Each of these anthologies and literary guides alludes to a connection between culture and the "masses," variously referred to as "expansiveness," "numbers," or simply "scale," but none of them provides a solution for sorting cultural studies' many versions of the "masses" toward some definitive end. A more recent entry on cultural studies in Bloomsbury's *Handbook of Literary and Cultural Theory* (2009) takes the different and almost singular tack of conceiving of cultural studies as compatible with disciplinarity: "The discipline of cultural studies," John Frow writes, "and in the formal sense [it is] very much a discipline ... is important for working out the coherence of what the field might be."[54] Frow suggests cultural studies "does indeed delineate a coherent object of knowledge," which he calls "the social life of cultural forms—but it possesses no coherent methodology or ensemble of methodologies."[55] Frow walks a fine line between cultural studies' political failures and what it might yet offer along Williams's line of democratizing the means of knowledge production. Implicitly, Frow shows, disciplines end and new ones begin by recombining with other disciplines and with any luck enlarging their former boundaries of containment. Changing disciplines should be a way to enlarge the means of knowledge production, following Williams's return to Hyde Park. The old adage "think about your work as the means to an end" changes here. And it's not simply reformulated as: "the means are an end in themselves." What we gain by ending vague uses of the term "culture" and replacing it with a more expansive concept of "work" is a more difficult realization: the ends too are means. Goals, products, institutions, disciplines, and tools are relational artifacts: media. As such, with good fortune and a lot of effort, they can be changed for the better over time.

The proletarianization of the knowledge worker certainly does represent what Michael Sprinker calls a "mutation," the term I would like to consider as a more positive-sounding, if still unwillfully inspired, version of category change in terms of rethinking old disciplines and discovering new and better forms of institutionalization.[56] This is not at all to minimize the "degeneracy" of academic un- or underemployment, given the rise of adjunct teaching and the disappearance of tenure-track humanities jobs. Every humanities department chair knows most of the heavy pedagogical lifting in colleges and universities is done by itinerant instructors wanting full-time, secure academic employment. Smith's graduate students in the *Renewal* volume thus also offer the rarely heard message initiated by Frow: "Cultural studies is, among other things, a discipline. It will say so on our diplomas. Our careers will depend on it."[57] But note too how reluctant these students are to interrogate cultural studies' resistance to its own success: "To those who might criticize our willful incorporation [into the institution]," the students rightly remind cultural studies' elders of a debilitating paradox: "making foundationlessness ... foundational."[58] Rethinking the ends of cultural studies even while getting credentialed in it, as well as looking back upon its ending in order to start doing something else, they comment further on "a practice obsessed with the ahistoricality of contemporary culture to accomplish its own vain ambition of changing the nature of the academic game once and for all."[59]

In Clifford Siskin and William Warner's provocatively titled essay "Stopping Cultural Studies," the authors also refer to the problem of institutions, the repetition and eventual remixing of academic fields. In the case of cultural studies abandoning any form of disciplinary constraint, they write: "you think you're getting somewhere different, in this case institutionally, but then you always find yourself back where you started."[60] Siskin and Warner propose ending cultural studies not because it had no success but because in all disciplines, even disciplines refusing to be one, there are limits to be undone, and there are new limits to be put in place to enable knowledge workers to know more and act better. Once the enabling limits are redesigned—for example, expansion of the canon, judiciously legitimating mass culture, getting people from the old disciplines to make sense across them—then it's time to move to a new institutional space.

Siskin and Warner propose moving in just this way, and I'd like to elaborate on their ideas just a bit before turning to some more concrete suggestions about the starting and ending of fields. They are firmly uninterested in continuing to work under the heading of cultural studies because the concept of culture allows us to "entrust our differences to its totalizing indifferences."[61] Siskin and Warner want to move on from the "all" that is "nothing" at all: liberal pluralism as a ruse for "indifference." Instead, and with Williams in mind, "just stopping" cultural studies means starting something else enabled by it.[62] With "a note of thanks and a nod goodbye," Siskin and Warner suggest, "the new horizons of cultural studies have helped us open a landscape it cannot help us traverse."[63] The *something else* that "stopping cultural studies" might help traverse is Williams's terrestrialization of culture, returning us to the issue of means, and instead of eschewing disciplinary difference, embracing constitutive constraint.

In the Re:Enlightenment Project, an example of institutional innovation founded by Siskin and Kevin Brine to work across not just disciplines but also geographies and institutional settings, this refocusing on means is precisely the point:

> The Re:Enlightenment Project seeks to redirect the force of forced economic change into a collaborative reassessment of our inheritance, starting with the part of that inheritance in which we all have a share: the overall organization of knowledge that emerged from Enlightenment. In beginning here we note that its more or less *settled* divisions within and across narrow-but-deep disciplines—indeed, the concept of disciplinarity itself—has become unsettled. Our recent fascination with "inter-disciplinarity" is one symptom of the remediations in knowledge that are *already occurring*.[64]

Re:Enlightenment defines "protocols" as a way of refashioning disciplines as enabling constraints, without the degenerate fantasy of anything goes: "The object of knowledge—culture—and the way we know it—disciplinarity—are inextricably linked."[65] The challenge of remediating ways of knowing is not to abandon disciplines. Rather, Re:Enlightenment invites us to "retool ... established means of mediation with new tools—and then deploy both across the newly altered and expanded array of literary activity."[66] Toward this end, think of "literature" not only in terms of the Arnoldian "best" but also as the enlargement of knowledge necessary for making the "best" better than it used to be. Once again, this is only possible by "expanding" our inherited categories of knowledge and putting better tools in the hands of more and different kinds of workers. The hope here is for nothing less than democratizing the means of production apropos Williams's charge; but better, it's a hope for something more than ending cultural studies only to "find us back where we started, yet again."

The Ends of Knowledge

Letting the Multitude In

> Overcome difficulties by multiplying them.
>
> —Walter Benjamin

What can this enigmatic maxim from Benjamin possibly mean? It defies common sense, but only if you think about the word "common" in the most reductive way: my problems are not your problems, and I'll narrow my sense of which problems I might overcome, and which ones I ignore, by sticking strictly to solutions I know in advance. This is a version of individual freedom—the freedom not to know—operative in its most offensive ways as bad populism or atomistic liberalism. No wonder then that the connection between culture and cultivation got lost in the history Williams rediscovers: the resistance to knowledge is a resistance to the recognition of workers and work, he says—or better, it's a form of resistance *to* resistance. This is a form of ignorance, the willful form, that does nothing more than have us repeating what we think we know to death. It's how the humanities as we knew them died. Thinking about the relationship between culture and the earth apropos Williams, it may be how the human species dies as well.

But what about multiplicity as innovation, to stay with Benjamin? It's a twofold situation: there's the "multiplicity" of more problems put together in ways that maximize the chance for generating higher-order solutions, and there's the "multiplicity" of expanding the numbers (and kinds) of problem solvers uniting to do the work of multiplication itself. It's hard to know in the epigraph who Benjamin's audience is, which is exactly the point. When it's hard to know, there's a good chance we're on to something. The multitude—that is, the very large number of objects, agents, producers, problems, and solutions—must be devised at the same time it's discovered. How to do the devising is what Williams showed us by finding the relation between culture and cultivation lost in the past, a better way of thinking superseding the Arnoldian "best." From the "structures of feeling," Williams implies, we ought to get to the structures of feeding.

Refusing to multiply problems to overcome them belies the desire to seek solutions. Refusing multiplicity is refusing change, and this is manifest in the misapplication of cultural studies that turns Hyde Park into an enclosure for securing old ideas. If we were to unpack the challenge of multiplication distilled in Benjamin's return to "the old dialectical maxim," we'd see what I hope by now is a familiar knowledge problem.[67] Try as you might, you'll never keep the "swinish multitude" on their side of the gate.

So far in this chapter we've covered how the multitude get into the Hyde Park of the mind, and what trouble they make, but we just called that trouble: how knowledge succeeds and how it fails to scale up. Part of cultural studies' success was to have its eventual failure built. It ended by refusing to name its own ends, scaling up without realizing it would have to come down. While I've already alluded to what kinds of intuitional existence might be possible given a renewed focus on work in instead of culture—means of production, or more expansively, thinking seriously about media or means—in the short space below I'd like to do more than *allude*. It may seem like inventing the parachute in freefall, but here's a sketch of some concrete ways of multiplying problems to overcome them:

Re-discipline. This is different than doing inter-, trans-, or so-called de-disciplinary work. Re-disciplining your expertise wouldn't (1) require you to give up what you know from within whatever specialty you claim, (2) presume you know somebody else's field better than they do, or (3) dismantle your department with the hopes of drafting off the better funded ones. Rather, the requirements of re-disciplinary work, cautiously put, are these: know what you know and know as much of it as you like in whatever macro- or microcosmic detail you can muster. But find ways to share your findings widely—or be ready to disappear peacefully. Pick a big problem, say something meaningful about it, and above all, make it matter to somebody other than the few colleagues (or readers) you're lucky to have. The farther away we can do this from our home disciplines, institutions, cities, states, and countries, the more re-disciplinary our work is likely to be. In short, let the multitude in.

Reject the academic star system. The job crisis, like war and climate catastrophe, is no longer a short-lived or emergent exception. The nonreplenishment of tenure-track humanities professors with other tenure-track humanities professors is now fully the rule. Thus, the great contraction I mentioned before means "the best" ideas will not be coming from the usual sources. It may be a tactically advantageous effect of a terrible situation we'd all like to correct, but the Hyde Park of the mind is shrinking. The neighborhood's former tenants are on the run like the rest of us. So, we should look for innovation (see *Re-discipline*, above) where we least expect it: in departments and institutions deemed too different from our own; in nonelite universities, colleges, and other formal learning spaces; among the un- and underemployed academic ranks; in the classrooms of generalists; in the streets; and anywhere else you can find it. Academia is insecure. But so is the monopoly on overcoming hard problems. Let the multitude in, once again.

Replace rote denunciation with promiscuous affiliation. Too often what stands in for critique is formulaic, incoherent, or empirically inaccurate, and this hurts the cause. We should think twice before denouncing this or that object, tool, or concept. Promiscuous affiliation isn't a call for disinterested knowledge or the pluralistic form of the "all that is nothing at all" that constitutes disciplinary refusal (see *Re-discipline*). Nor is it a suggestion to bend the knee to famous colleagues (see *Reject the academic star system*). Quite the opposite: there's a better chance of correcting errors if we take the error as seriously as our ready-made solutions. Think of this as fieldwork, participation/observation, or, more adventurously, going undercover with the positions we find strange. It's not everybody's game to perform this kind of fieldwork *qua* fraternalism, unless the academic world is a place you also find strange. But it's another way to let the multitude in.

Resurrect Homo Faber. The Roman statesman Appius Claudius Caecus (312–279 BC), who increased the voting power of the poor and landless in the legislative assemblies and admitted lower-class citizens to the Roman Senate, says this: "*Homo faber suae quisque fortunae*" ("Every human being is the artifex of her destiny"). It's an interesting phrase for presuming, it turns out correctly, that human beings are not only the makers of tools

The Ends of Knowledge

but are also made by them. Toolmaking preceded *Homo sapiens*, as such. The statesman's emphasis on fabrication highlights an opportunity to shift modes of academic work from repeating problems to solving them. We might think of knowledge production in this way as "artifexing." The verb form of the adjective "*artifex*," and the noun "artifice," means being skilled and having expertise (again, see *Re-discipline*), but also being artful, even cunning (see *promiscuous affiliation*). Returning to a concept of *homo faber*— "humankind the maker"—means having something useful to share from our work. Concretely, this could amount to supplementing the academic monograph with other kinds of scholarly tools (new encyclopedias, lab reports, databases, creative works, etc.). More than this, resurrecting *Homo faber* requires putting the tools that make the human being in the many hands at work (see *reject the academic star system*). To replace the restrictive fences of Hyde Park, we need a new Appian Way. This is a figurative expression for saying, once again, let the multitude in.

Notes

1. Stuart Hall, "Cultural Studies and Its Theoretical Legacies," in *Cultural Studies*, ed. Lawrence Grossberg et al. (New York: Routledge, 1992), 285.
2. See Graeme Turner, *British Cultural Studies: An Introduction*, 3rd edn. (New York: Routledge, 2002); Ioan Davies, *Cultural Studies and Beyond: Fragments of Empire* (New York: Routledge, 1995); Patrick Brantlinger, *Crusoe's Footprints: Cultural Studies in Britain and America* (New York: Routledge, 1990).
3. Hall, "Cultural Studies," 279. On the British New Left, see Chun Chin, *The British New Left* (Edinburgh: University of Edinburgh Press, 1994).
4. Hall, "Cultural Studies," 279.
5. Raymond Williams, *Resources of Hope: Culture, Democracy, Socialism* (London: Verso, 1989), 3–14.
6. On the labor aristocracy, see Lenin, *Imperialism, the Highest Stage of Capitalism: A Popular Outline* (New York: International Publishers, [1917] 1969).
7. Raymond Williams, *Politics and Letters: Interviews with the New Left Review* (London: Verso, 1979), 154.
8. Meaghan Morris, cited by Cary Nelson, in *Cultural Studies*, ed. Cary Nelson et al. (New York: Routledge, 1991), 1.
9. Fredrick Jameson, "On Cultural Studies," *Social Text* 34 (1993): 17–52.
10. Hall, "Cultural Studies," 277.
11. Ibid., 285.
12. See Michael Bérubé and Cary Nelson, "Graduate Education Is Losing Its Moral Base," *The Chronicle of Higher Education* (March 23, 1994): B1–3. See also *Higher Education under Fire: Politics, Economics, and the Crisis of the Humanities*, ed. Michael Bérubé and Cary Nelson (New York: Routledge, 1995).
13. See *Center for Cultural Studies: Annual Report*, October 1969.
14. Simon During, "Introduction," in *The Cultural Studies Reader*, 3rd edn., ed. Simon During (New York: Routledge, 2007), 5.

15. Nick Couldry, "The Project of Cultural Studies: Heretical Doubts," in *The Renewal of Cultural Studies*, ed. Paul Smith (Philadelphia: Temple University Press, 2011), 10.
16. Paul Smith, "Introduction," in *The Renewal of Cultural Studies*, 1.
17. Paul Smith and Andrew Ross, "Cultural Studies: A Conversation," in *The Renewal of Cultural Studies*, 246.
18. Randall K. Cohn, Sara Regina Mitcho, and John M. Woolsey, "Cultural Studies: Always Already a Discipline," in *The Renewal of Cultural Studies*, 33, 28.
19. Email correspondence, April 5, 2021. The conference title echoes Maria Elisa Cevasco, "Whatever Happened to Cultural Studies? Notes from the Periphery," *Textual Practice* 14, no. 3 (2000): 433–8.
20. Hall, "Cultural Studies," 290.
21. Ibid., 278, emphasis added.
22. Raymond Williams, *Culture and Materialism* (London: Verso, 1980), 4.
23. Qtd. in Williams, *Culture and Materialism*, 7, emphasis added.
24. Williams, *Culture and Materialism*, 8.
25. On the history of the modern disciplines, see Clifford Siskin, *The Work of Writing: Literature and Social Change in Britain, 1700–1830* (Baltimore: Johns Hopkins University Press, 1998).
26. Williams, *Culture and Materialism*, 5.
27. Ibid., 8.
28. Raymond Williams, *Keywords* (Oxford: Oxford University Press, 1980), 76.
29. Williams, *Keywords*, 77.
30. Raymond Williams, *Culture and Society* (New York: Columbia University Press [1958] 1983), xi; xii.
31. Gabriel Popkin, "Woodwide Web," *Science*, May 15, 2019.
32. Nelson, *Cultural Studies*, 47.
33. Williams, *Keywords*, 81.
34. Nelson, *Cultural Studies*, viii.
35. Williams, *Culture and Materialism*, 8; emphasis added.
36. Raymond Williams, *Marxism and Literature* (Oxford: Oxford University Press, 1978), 2.
37. Hall, "Cultural Studies," 291.
38. Cary Nelson, "Introduction," in *Cultural Studies*, 1.
39. Ibid., 3, 2.
40. Ibid., 2.
41. Ibid.
42. Smith, "Introduction," in *Renewal of Cultural Studies*, 2.
43. Ibid., 2.
44. Ibid., 7.
45. Hall, "Cultural Studies," 282.
46. Carol A. Stabile, "That Nightmare Voice of Feminism," in *Renewal of Cultural Studies*, 17.
47. Ibid., 17.
48. Ibid., 18.

49. Stabile, "That Nightmare Voice of Feminism," 25; quoting Hall, "Cultural Studies," 282.
50. Williams, *Keywords*, 81, emphasis added.
51. *The Columbia Dictionary of Modern Literary and Cultural Criticism*, ed. Joseph Childers, et al. (New York: Columbia University Press, 1995), 66.
52. Ibid., 67, emphasis added.
53. Stephen Greenblatt, "Culture," in *Critical Terms for Literary Study*, ed. Frank Lentricchia (Chicago: University of Chicago Press, 1990), 228.
54. John Frow, "Cultural Studies," in *The Bloomsbury Handbook of Literary and Cultural Theory*, ed. Jeffrey R. Di Leo (London: Bloomsbury Academic, 2018), 140–50.
55. Ibid.,140.
56. Michael Sprinker, "We Lost It at the Movies," *MLN* 112, no. 3 (April 1997): 387.
57. Cohn et al., "Cultural Studies: Always Already a Discipline," 28.
58. Ibid., 29.
59. Ibid.
60. Siskin and Warner, "Stopping Cultural Studies," *Profession* (2008): 104.
61. Ibid., 104.
62. Ibid., 104–5.
63. Ibid., 95.
64. "Towards a New Platform for Knowledge: The Future of Enlightenment," 2011, https://reenlightenment.org/report-new-platform-for-knowledge/.
65. Siskin and Warner, "Stopping Cultural Studies," 103.
66. Ibid., 105.
67. Walter Benjamin, "Commentary on Poems by Brecht," in *Selected Writings*, vol. 4: 1938–1940 (Cambridge, MA: Harvard University Press, 2006), 216.

AFTERWORD
Clifford Siskin

Enlightenment bookends this book. Introduced as the "era that initiated many of our models for producing, sharing, and using knowledge," it stands from the start as the "inspiration for this intertwining of *end* and *ends*." Many of the chapters turn directly back to it, most often through Francis Bacon. See, in particular, Marieke Hendriksen's portrayal of the "Baconian" historian and B. N. Queenan's use of Bacon as her foil in an epic retelling of biology's struggle for disciplinary identity. But the challenge for this volume is to look both ways, testing Enlightenment's purchase on the future. And that's the note on which the collection concludes. In the final chapter, Mike Hill's call for "Re:Enlightenment" invokes a project that, like this volume, asks: "What forms might Enlightenment take now?"

That project was the second source of inspiration for *The Ends of Knowledge*. At an exchange the Re:Enlightenment Project held at Stanford University in 2018, Seth Rudy and Rachael King engaged the theme of "Scale" by posing a question to which this volume is an answer: How can we, as they have now phrased it in this volume's Introduction, "scal[e] up the problem of the organization of knowledge work?" The idea was to pull status reports from across that organization into proximity with each other. Housed in a single volume, parts scaling up into a whole, they could interact with each other with at least two "Re:Enlightenment" ends in mind.

First, commissioned at the same time to answer the same questions, these reports could all contribute to a renewed sense of a joint enterprise—the work of knowledge—that can itself be an object of inquiry, as it was for Bacon. By assessing the state of that enterprise in the early seventeenth century, he laid the conceptual and methodological groundwork for the renewal of knowledge we now know as Enlightenment. Second, Rudy and King have themselves taken a step toward renewal now. Having gathered reports from the disparate parts of our current organization of knowledge, they could have then taken the obvious path of offering an update on that same arrangement: here's how its different parts are faring now—the state of humanities, for example, versus the state of the physical sciences.

But they haven't. Rudy and King have deployed scalability not to reify but to change. Instead of collecting the same parts back into the same whole, they have made a move that echoes in important ways Bacon's turn against the Scholastic norms of his day. The "First" step in his "plan" for *Instauration* (Great Renewal)—the very first thing about knowledge that needed to change—were "The Divisions."[1] Classification matters. *Ends*

The Ends of Knowledge

begins by dividing and connecting in new ways, and in doing so it aspires to take us to "the beginning of the end" of our current configuration of knowledge.

In this brief afterword I'd like to lend a hand by building out the context for that aspiration with the hope that it takes hold with others. All changes are combinations of discontinuities and continuities, and pinpointing those requires a frame that can encompass both. We need in this case a large-scale "history of knowledge," a kind of knowledge work that itself displays both departures from and connections to the past. It is in certain ways a new venture, emerging institutionally in the past decade in new centers (e.g., Lund University) and new journals (e.g., *Journal for the History of Knowledge*). But from a Re:Enlightenment perspective, it's been a long time coming.

Any project to advance knowledge, argued Bacon in 1605, requires histories to mark and measure what's changed. And, for his big change, the kind that mattered most was the kind that was missing. We needed, claimed Bacon, a "Literary" history, with literary operating in its formerly comprehensive sense of letters, as in written records of all kinds. As Bacon conjured it back then, this history would be the "story of learning"—a story that would track "the antiquities and originals of knowledges … and all other events concerning learning, throughout the ages of the world" in order to "make learned men wise in the use and administration of learning."[2]

To grasp what's at stake in seeing *Ends* as a beginning, we need to scale up to the kind of wisdom Bacon prescribes—a spatial and temporal overview of knowledge work secured only by stepping out of one's moment and one's knowledge neighborhood. What I hope to gain by doing so here is, first, a sense of what needs to end and why, and, second, a historical context for parsing the promise of the alternative regroupings Rudy and King propose.

Why propose change at all? Why not replicate in the Table of Contents the same organization of knowledge the editors polled? As the responses document in detail, there are pressing problems in all of the disciplines and practices, some local and some shared. But even when a fundamental overhaul is proposed, as in Aaron Hanlon's prescription for literary studies, or existential fears are voiced, as in Jolene Almendarez's mournful recounting of the perils of journalism, there are no pleas to abandon particular disciplines or disciplinarity itself as a formal strategy for organizing knowledge.

But, as Rudy and King astutely point out at the very start of their Introduction, there's another candidate for change. Modern knowledge has been organized not only into disciplines but into "divisions." And that's where the editors stake their claim to the novelty of their project on ends: "this is the first volume, to our knowledge, to bring together thinkers from across the humanities, natural sciences, and social sciences to consider the question simultaneously." Doing so, they argue, is the precondition for posing some of the most difficult questions in knowledge work. What role might that tripartite division "play," for example, "in maintaining the apocalyptic status quo" of climate change?

If this volume centers that division as the primary candidate for change, then we need to ask when that division happened, for what purpose, and how it is now "play[ing]" out. That's where the scale of the history of knowledge makes a difference. In its absence,

Afterword

diagnosis tends to veer into the local, attending not to the system of division itself but to a particular division, usually the most troubled. And that trouble is usually addressed in the discourse specific to that division. Thus, as Rudy and King observe, scholars in all three divisions have been recently "forced to defend their work," but the humanities, as the particular home of "despair," now regularly generates announcements of "crisis" and efforts to self-analyze it.

These scaled-down analyses, no matter how valuable in other respects, are of limited value to the high adventure of this volume: "to see what the advancement of learning could look like if it were to be reoriented around emergent ends rather than inherited structures." However comforting or disturbing it might be, for example, to see the humanities as being "trapped" in its own discourse of crisis, the "structures" for ordering knowledge of all kinds take a back seat. To interrogate them, we need to scale back up to a history containing the divisions as well as the disciplines—and a way of understanding when and how they connect to each other.

In the story of learning as Bacon envisioned it, temporality matters. When the modern disciplines first emerged from the European Enlightenment—the 1797 *Encyclopedia Britannica* called them the newly "detached parts of knowledge"—they were *not* parts of a preexisting entity called the "humanities." In fact, all three of today's standard divisions—the "sciences" and "social sciences," as well as the "humanities"—were not primary but rather second-order classifications of knowledge imposed on the disciplines between 1830 and 1860.

William Warner and I have described that imposition in more detail elsewhere, arguing that our modern word for this type of arrangement is zoning.[3] As in our cities, zoning strives to minimize encroachment while maximizing growth. The result is what the New York City Zoning Board calls a "pleasant environment" in which everyone has a neighborhood as well as a home. Homeowners come together to constitute, defend, and improve their neighborhoods. As the newly formed disciplines moved into institutional homes—for example, the first English departments in the 1820s— knowledge neighborhoods started to form.

During the first half of the twentieth century, those groupings materialized as organizational entities within universities, with the labels themselves etched into campus buildings. The managerial, curricular, and financial forms of zoning followed. The Second World War proved to be a watershed, as the flood of college-bound vets supported by the GI Bill prompted new general education policies. As modeled by the Harvard University *Redbook* report of 1945, zoning was deployed to counterbalance the relentless growth of science and technology during the war by requiring that courses be taken across all three zones. That distribution apparatus scaled up to meet the Baby Boom growth in higher education at midcentury, turning knowledge zones into investment opportunities primed by government funding of division-specific endowments in the 1960s.

That is how zoning became a "structure" for knowledge—the "inherited" one that this volume was assembled to put into play. To do that using "ends" is inspired, for zoning as the knowledge project I've just described features ends in both of the senses explored in this collection. First, zoning had a purposeful end from the start: to provide smaller, more homogeneous, and safer environments for disciplines newly competing for conceptual and institutional space. Second, as Bacon showed us with Scholasticism, knowledge projects end. Sometimes they get stuck—"stopped in their tracks,"[4] as Bacon put it, and sometimes they succeed, in which case they need to be succeeded by something else.

Zoning did fulfill its historical purpose through much of the twentieth century: its distribution of bodies and dollars grew disciplines in ways that an atomized array would not have matched. But life in these gated communities is not so pleasant anymore. While the humanities despair and sociology departments disappear, scientists face a division-wide crisis of trust that comes with a twist: it's left them teetering on the edge of an epistemological abyss. How can they ask the public to "believe" in a type of knowledge grounded in doubt—"on the word of no one," as the Royal Society first put it?[5]

The currently ubiquitous desire for interdisciplinarity within and between zones and its weak results send the same message as these divisional difficulties: the root crisis is none of the above; it's *the crisis of the strategy of zoning itself*. In Rudy and King's terms, that structure has reached its end—it has successfully outlived its usefulness. Zoning now needs to be succeeded by a new strategy for organizing and advancing knowledge.

And we shouldn't be surprised. Humanities, social science, and science are artifacts of zoning; they are not and never were permanent portals to the future. To move on, this volume takes the same first step that Bacon took. He cleared out the intellectual clutter—knowledge strategies that had once worked but were now "idols" of the mind.[6] Our current clutter is our zoned communities. Features of zoning that had once nurtured productivity—from physical and institutional barriers to conventional pairings of subjects and methods—are now frequently in the way. We no longer need—indeed, we cannot afford—the kinds of divisions zoning imposes.

Rudy and King have not only reached across those divisions in assembling this collection; they have also taken the second step of venturing new groupings. That step, even taken tentatively, is still against the grain despite the crises. Instead of opening the gates, many in the currently threatened communities have dug in behind them. Huddling defensively behind troubled labels—identifying as a humanities professor, for example, rather than as an English professor—is another sign of zoning reaching its shelf life. The boundaries harden, becoming brittle before they break. Instead of enabling knowledge work, they stage it as a zero-sum game in which differences are not complementary and fluid but territorial and final.

By reclassifying through ends, Rudy and King are changing the game. Three groupings go into this volume and four come out. And those four are different in kind from the three, pointing not to similarities in subject matter but to questions of purpose and outcome. These discontinuities leap from the page, promising a different future for knowledge. But what of the continuities? If change is always a mix of both, then how do the new groupings connect to the past?

Afterword

The primary sightline is announced, as we've already seen, in the opening pages: Bacon's focus on advancement inspires their turn to ends. It's tempting to see the rest of the book as just looking forward, and its groupings just one possible reconfiguration among many. But there is a richer historical tapestry here—and thus higher stakes. Rudy and King have staged this volume as an opportunity for Re:Enlightenment, and that's not just a one-way link into an open-ended future but a dynamically retroactive process—a process in which present and past speak back and forth to each other. My end in this afterword is to help us see and hear that exchange by scaling it up into the history of knowledge I described earlier.

"Inherited structures" enter that history as a temporal feature, a strategy playing out over time. That strategy has ends of its own, its fate subject to a repertoire of interventions. As I've elaborated the tale here, zoning for growth is the strategy that yielded our tripartite system of Humanities/Social Science/Science, and this volume intervenes. I've termed this intervention a "decluttering" so that we can better image its consequences for the story of learning. Clutter is something that's in the way, and when we remove it, we can see what it has obscured.

The success of zoning—a prelude, I have suggested, to our current "crises" of succession, of what comes next—has not only lulled us into thinking its divisions are somehow natural but also cloaked earlier strategic thinking about how knowledge might be organized. Decluttering puts the dynamic of Re:Enlightenment into motion: removing the zones now allows us to look back to what they obscured; we can then use our new knowledge of the past to better understand the present.

That retroactive movement is how we become, in Bacon's words, "wise in our use and administration of knowledge." *Ends* is an opportunity not just to forge a new future but to learn more about the past and thus raise the odds that what we forge will work. The first step is to bring what we recover to bear on the new groupings that Rudy and King have made. The particular promise of their groupings emerges once we recover this earlier discourse on classifying knowledge—discourse that cuts through the confusions generated by the zones overstaying their welcome.

To kickstart that recovery we need only tinker a bit with what I've termed the "high adventure" agenda of *Ends* to form the parallel query at the core of the *Instauration*—the query that Bacon posed to his world of knowledge: what could the advancement of learning look like if it were to be reoriented around ~~emergent ends~~ discoveries rather than inherited ~~structures~~ truths?

When Bacon turned to the question of ends, he declared his "Purpose" in that single word: "discoveries." They hold "by far the first place among human actions, as the ancients judged." Discoveries were "ascribed divine honours," while all other "achievements" merited "only the honours of heroes."[7] All of Bacon's efforts were directed at turning knowledge into a platform for discovery. The *New Organon* was a discovery machine. And since "discoveries are like new creations, and imitations of divine works," that machine ran on an epistemology of remaking. In James Morrison's formulation of the Baconian act of knowing: "To know the cause of a thing is to know how to bring about that thing oneself: ... Knowledge is ultimately the re-making of what nature itself makes or has made."[8]

Knowledge modeled on discovery is thus a particular kind of knowledge. In its attention to causes, this knowledge was understood to be explanatory and thus progressive. And to the first generation that took up Bacon's call for renewal, explanatory knowledge was attractive because it was *useful*—it enabled you to make and do things. Robert Boyle was only eighteen with no university education when he started an "invisible college" with nine others in 1645. "Our new philosophical college," he wrote, "values no knowledge, but as it hath a tendency to use."[9]

Bacon's method for producing this new kind of knowledge has been much discussed. But what we have not engaged is his remarkably thorough effort to work out the consequences of his plan. How would the introduction of a new kind of knowledge—especially one that understands itself as more useful—affect the others? Zoning is the answer we have been living with: settle each kind in its own neighborhood and work out a distribution plan. Entrench differences in the hope of local success. Success did follow, as I have been arguing, but as neighborhood tensions rise (e.g., Humanities vs. STEM) we are increasingly haunted by questions zoning doesn't want to answer: What kinds of knowledge count more? Do some kinds have designs on other kinds?

This volume is a bold attempt to break the spell. By opening an uncluttered sightline back to Bacon we can recover not only his "end" of advancement but also his zoning- and discipline-free take on its consequences. That take may or may not be right for us, but what it does do is clarify the high stakes of assembling this collection. Like Rudy and King, Bacon was intent upon scaling up the problem of the organization of knowledge work. We can learn much about the new categories that emerge in *Ends* from the questions and answers he engaged in his own act of decluttering and rescaling.

Are we, he asked, "speaking of perfecting only Natural Philosophy by our method or also the other sciences, Logic, Ethics and Politics?"[10] In our terms, he is asking: Does the useful, explanatory knowledge of discovery cross zones? Does it scale up across the whole of knowledge? Since his intention is not a local renewal but a *Great* one, his pre-zone answer should not surprise us: "We certainly mean all that we have said to apply to all of them." This may feed the paranoia of the staunchest defenders of the humanities—the scientists are coming for you—but it is only the prelude to Bacon adding two important distinctions that together allow him to build out a very different way of organizing knowledge.

The first is a distinction of degree—the "degree" to which we can "adapt the method of discovery to the quality and condition of the subject of inquiry." By specifying that the method is applicable to all kinds of inquiries but applicable in different ways, Bacon allows for difference within an overall project of advancement. He also realizes, however, that an allowance of that kind cannot secure the consensus he needs to launch a project proposed to King James as a public good.

To do that, he needs to scale up to a full embrace of all of the ways that knowledge works in the world. "It would be wrong," he insists, "even to entertain a doubt about whether we desire to destroy and abolish the philosophy, the arts and the sciences which we use; on the contrary, we happily embrace their use, their cultivation and their rewards." There are "traditional subjects" that are valuable precisely because they are *used*. Because they generate disputations, enliven discourse, and are applied widely to "professional use and the benefit of civil life," they have "a kind of currency."[11]

By themselves, Bacon emphasizes, those kinds of knowledge cannot produce progress, but he embraces them nonetheless as part of a new organization of knowledge geared to achieve that end. There is knowledge that is useful and knowledge that is used. The former is a knowledge of discovery; the latter is a knowledge of currency.[12] They complement each other, for useful knowledge "will not be very useful" for the purposes of currency, "since there is no way that they can be brought down to the common understanding, except through their results and effects."[13]

Wait. There is something familiar here. Turn back to this volume's Table of Contents. Unification and Utopia—the knowledge of explanation and progress. Access and Concepts—the knowledge of use and currency. This is not replication; it is Re:Enlightenment at work. Its retroactive movements are like panning for gold. Shake back and forth. Scoop again. More shaking—until we learn something of value— something, in the simplest sense, that makes sense. The past helps to explain the present and the present helps to explain the past. Rudy and King's findings resonate with Bacon's because they have devised an equation to adjust the grid: take knowledge, add advancement, and subtract zoning.

The classification system of this volume has legs. It can walk us back to Bacon and forward into a future in which knowledges can map onto each other in new ways. When we ask, as he did, the hard questions about what we do and how it matters, possibilities change. Differences in degree can coexist with differences in kind, and all forms of knowledge can interact not as rivals protecting turf but as complementary undertakings. Both the grouping and the complementarity in *Ends* are often aspirational, of course, for they record the new possibilities that are just now arising as we shake off the assumptions and effects of zoning. In its place is a reordering that is both resonant with Baconian principles and driven by the contingencies of the present.

Rudy and King have provided essay-by-essay accounts of the new interrelations within each group, so I'll conclude by glossing only a few striking results from the perspective I've added here. Even more striking than any particular lineup of kinds, however, is that *the groupings themselves are different in kind*. The groupings in *Ends* are not ends in themselves—their productivity geared to neighborhood stability—but groupings that change over time. By plotting the current locations of their subjects on a map of ends, the authors enable Rudy and King to scale up to the problem of dividing knowledge as Bacon first posed it: What kinds of knowledge in what combinations are more conducive to advancement *now*?

In some cases, the answer turns on specific fields seizing the opportunity to change. Literary study, argues Aaron Hanlon, is ripe for relocating. It can join physics in the

Unification Grouping because it too can be explanatory to the degree, as Bacon put it, that it suits the subject matter. In other cases, ends that were once assumed to be divergent meet on newly common ground. Right now, both Hong Qu and Ady Barkan face the problem of what to do when their efforts to move forward replicate the faults they were trying to correct. AI thus meets unexpectedly with activism under Utopia as useful knowledge pursuing through gradual improvement the Baconian end "of human progress and advancement."[14]

The surprises generated by contingent combination don't stop. Unexpected connections generate unexpected disconnects. Instead of sharing a home zone of science, computation parts ways with one of its most prominent projects, AI, to join Unification as knowledge work increasingly aimed at fundamental explanation. In Geoffrey C. Bowker's analysis, computation is, in fact, now poised to explain itself as computers emerge as instruments of remaking—instruments that are themselves "rich and wonderful developments of human and biological life." Computation's new partners in Unification include the field to which Bowker gestures, biology, which B. N. Queenan depicts as wrestling with the same issue: "the rift between human and nonhuman life." Also at the Unification table, and also testing computation's explanatory reach, is digital humanities, at this point in its history now at a distance from its former neighbors such as cultural studies. Is computation more or less likely, asks Mark Algee-Hewitt, to close rifts in knowledge or spark a "fissioning" of it?

Haunting the explanatory ambitions of Unification and the progress vector of Utopia is the need for what Bacon promised King James: results—in the form of knowledge that is not only "built up" but "completed" for the common good.[15] Completion requires that useful knowledge be put to use, that discoveries gain currency. Two chapters in Utopia frame that problem. In her description of the difference between gender studies and women's studies, Ula Lukszo Klein quotes Robyn Wiegman's crystal-clear formulation of the epistemological stakes: whether "knowing will lead to knowing what to do." According to Myanna Lahsen, that's exactly where environmental studies is currently foundering: it cannot navigate the distinction between knowing and doing. As the climate changes, those who discovered that change cannot grasp why their knowledge doesn't translate into progress.

The short answer is that we need a new organization of knowledge, one in which temporally and conceptually flexible categories of use and currency complement those of explanation and discovery. That's what Rudy and King have given us here by pairing Access and Concepts with Unification and Utopia. Law through the lens of ends is a knowledge of use and access: "who does what and who gets what." And the ends of performance, black studies, and cultural studies all turn right now on the current currency of their informing concepts: liveness, race, and culture. The range of examples of all of these categories at work is extraordinary, from Brandon R. Brown's freeze frame of a quantum Medusa to Mike Hill's parting invocation to get back to work. Rudy and King have paid Bacon back for his inspiration by adding a substantial chapter to the history of knowledge—a chapter that we need if we are to continue to move in the direction he set four centuries ago.

Notes

1. Francis Bacon, *The New Organon*, ed. Lisa Jardine and Michael Silverthorne (Cambridge, UK: Cambridge University Press, [1620] 2000), 14. The *New Organon* is the only part of *The Great Instauration* (the second part) that Bacon completed.
2. See Francis Bacon, *The Major Works*, ed. Brian Vickers (Oxford: Oxford University Press, 2008), 175–6, and Clifford Siskin, *System: The Shaping of Modern Knowledge* (Cambridge, MA: MIT Press, 2016), 4–5, 65–6.
3. Clifford Siskin and William Warner, "Is It Time to Dezone Knowledge?," *Inside Higher Education,* November 4, 2019.
4. Bacon, *The New Organon*, 7.
5. The Royal Society's motto was and remains "nullius in verba."
6. Ibid., 18.
7. Ibid., 99.
8. James Morrison, "Philosophy and History in Bacon," *Journal of the History of Ideas* 38, no. 4 (1977): 591–2.
9. "Boyle to Isaac Marcombes, October 22, 1646," in *The Correspondence of Robert Boyle, 1636–61*, ed. Michael Hunter, Antonio Clericuzio, and Lawrence M. Principe, vol. 1 (London and New York: Routledge, 2001).
10. Bacon, *New Organon*, 98.
11. Ibid.
12. For the historical importance of this term, see Clifford Siskin, "Enlightenment, Information, and the Copernican Delay: A Venture into the History of Knowledge," *History and Theory* 58 (December 2020): 1–16.
13. Bacon, *New Organon*, 98.
14. Ibid., 13.
15. Ibid., 2–3.

CONTRIBUTORS

Mark Algee-Hewitt is Associate Professor of Digital Humanities in the English Department at Stanford University and Director of the Stanford Literary Lab.

Jolene Almendarez is General Assignments Reporter for Cincinnati Public Radio, WVXU. She was Managing Editor of *The Ithaca Voice* and before that studied journalism at San Antonio College. She holds a bachelor's degree in journalism and public communications from the University of Alaska Anchorage. She has been a reporter in San Antonio and Castroville, Texas, and in Syracuse and Ithaca, New York.

Ady Barkan is Co-Executive Director of Be A Hero, a national progressive organization that advocates a fair and just healthcare system in the United States. He is the former director of the Fed Up and Local Progress campaigns. He holds a JD from Yale University and a BA from Columbia University.

Yochai Benkler is the Jack N. and Lillian R. Berkman Professor for Entrepreneurial Legal Studies and Faculty Co-Director of the Berkman Klein Center for Internet and Society at Harvard University. His books include *The Wealth of Networks: How Social Production Transforms Markets and Freedom* (2006) and *Network Propaganda: Manipulation, Disinformation, and Radicalization in American Politics* (2018).

Geoffrey C. Bowker is Emeritus Professor of Informatics at the University of California, Irvine, where he directed the Values in Design Laboratory. His research focuses on how information technology shapes political, social, and cultural values. He is the author of *Memory Practices in the Sciences* (2005), *Science on the Run: Information Management and Industrial Geophysics at Schlumberger, 1920–1940* (1994), and, with Susan Leigh Star, *Sorting Things Out: Classification and Its Consequences* (1999).

Brandon R. Brown is Professor of Physics and Astronomy at the University of San Francisco, where he has also served as Associate Dean for Sciences. His research work has probed high-temperature superconductivity, sensory biophysics, and, more recently, the history of science. He is the author of *Planck: Driven by Vision, Broken by War* (2015), *The Apollo Chronicles: Engineering America's First Moon Missions* (2019), and *Sharing Our Science* (2023).

Aaron R. Hanlon is Associate Professor of English and Director of the Science, Technology, and Society Program at Colby College. He holds a doctorate from the University of Oxford and is the author of *A World of Disorderly Notions: Quixote and the Logic of Exceptionalism* (2019). His essays on politics, literature, teaching, and higher education have appeared in *The New York Times*, *The Washington Post*, *The New Republic*, *The Atlantic*, *Vox*, and *The Los Angeles Review of Books*, among other venues.

Marieke M. A. Hendriksen is Senior Researcher of History of Knowledge in the Humanities Cluster of the Royal Netherlands Academy of Arts and Sciences (KNAW) and President of Gewina, the Belgian-Dutch Society for the History of Science and Universities.

Mike Hill is Professor of English at SUNY Albany. His research focuses on contemporary questions of race and whiteness, philosophy of science, materialist reconceptions of identity, war and peace studies, and, most recently, Adam Smith, the history of eighteenth-century writing, and the emergence of the public sphere. He is the author of multiple books, most recently *On Posthuman War: Computation and Military Violence* (2022).

Rachael Scarborough King is Associate Professor of English at the University of California, Santa Barbara. She is the author of *Writing to the World: Letters and the Origins of Modern Print Genres* (2018) and editor of *After Print: Eighteenth-Century Manuscript Cultures* (2020). She is Principal Investigator and Project Director for the Ballitore Project, an archives- and digital humanities-based research project.

Ula Lukszo Klein is Associate Professor of English and Director of Women's and Gender Studies Program at University of Wisconsin–Oshkosh. Her research focuses on eighteenth-century literature, gender and sexuality, queer theory, and feminism. She is the author of *Sapphic Crossings: Cross-Dressing Women in Eighteenth-Century British Literature* (2021).

Myanna Lahsen is Associate Professor at Linköping University in Sweden, and Senior Associate Researcher in the Earth System Science Center of the Brazilian Institute for Space Research (INPE). She has served in advisor- and leadership roles in international science coordination and with leading international journals, such as WIREs *Climate Change*, *Nature Climate Change*, and *Environmental Research Letters*.

Sean Michael Morris is Vice President of Academics at Course Hero. Prior to joining Course Hero, he was Senior Instructor in Learning, Design, and Technology at the University of Colorado Denver. He also cofounded Digital Pedagogy Lab and is the coauthor, with Jesse Stommel, of *An Urgency of Teachers: The Work of Critical Digital Pedagogy* (2018).

Jessica Nakamura is Associate Professor of Theater at the University of California, Santa Barbara. She is the author of *Transgenerational Remembrance: Performance and the Asia-Pacific War in Contemporary Japan* (2020).

Hong Qu is Adjunct Lecturer at Harvard Kennedy School and Research Director for The Council on the Responsible Use of Artificial Intelligence project at the Belfer Center. He was one of the first engineers on YouTube's startup team and built key features such as video sharing, channels, and skippable ads. He is a graduate of Wesleyan University and UC Berkeley's School of Information.

Contributors

B. N. Queenan is Executive Director of Research, Quantitative Biology at Harvard University. She holds degrees in biochemistry and neuroscience from Harvard and Georgetown University and is a founding member of The Foundations Institute at University of California, Santa Barbara.

Seth Rudy is Associate Professor of English at Rhodes College. He is the author of *Literature and Encyclopedism in Enlightenment Britain: The Pursuit of Complete Knowledge* (2014).

Clifford Siskin is Henry W. and Alfred A. Berg Emeritus Professor of English and American Literature at New York University, and Director of the Re:Enlightenment Project.

G. Gabrielle Starr is President of Pomona College. A scholar of eighteenth-century British literature, she was formerly Dean of New York University's College of Arts and Sciences and Professor of English at NYU. Her work crosses disciplinary boundaries, using fMRI imaging to understand how people respond to aesthetic works. She is the author of *Feeling Beauty: The Neuroscience of Aesthetic Experience* (2013) and *Lyric Generations: Poetry and the Novel in the Long Eighteenth Century* (2004).

Kenneth W. Warren is Fairfax M. Cone Distinguished Service Professor in the Department of English and Center for the Study of Race, Politics, and Culture at the University of Chicago. In 2019, he was elected to the American Academic for the Arts and Sciences. He is the author of *What Was African American Literature?* (2010), *So Black and Blue: Ralph Ellison and the Occasion of Criticism* (2003), and *Black and White Strangers: Race and American Literary Realism* (2003).

INDEX

Abernathy, Penelope Muse, *News Deserts and Ghost Newspapers: Will Local News Survive?* 118–19
abolitionist movement 13, 137, 163–6, 196
academic disciplines 8, 47, 70, 194, 225. *See also specific disciplines*
access/accessibility 11–12, 40, 89–90, 131, 134–5, 159, 223, 242
activism 13, 152–3, 159, 160, 221, 242
  as authorship 167–8
  ends and beginnings 166–7
  generational struggles 164
  strategies of revolution 164–6
Adam and Eve 61, 64, 68, 70. *See also* Garden of Eden
Adamatzky, Andrew 52
Adams, Douglas 52
Addison, Joseph 3
aesthetics 41–5, 132, 186, 211, 223
African Americans 163, 196, 206, 209–13
  literature 210, 212–13
agriculture 3, 49, 96, 171–2
Alden Global Capital 117–18
Alderman, Naomi, *The Power* 12, 153, 155–8, 160, 161 n.10
algorithms (algos) 21, 51–3, 139–44, 147–8
Althusser, Louis 218
Amazon 54, 171–2
The American Anti-Slavery Society 163–4, 166
American Association of Physical Anthropologists (AAPA) 206–7
  "AAPA Statement on Race and Racism" 206, 212
The American Society of News Editors 114
Anderson, Amanda 8
animals 49, 61, 64–5, 68–9, 71, 172, 176
Anthropocene 49
anthropology 183, 206–7
anti-cognitivism 40–5. *See also* moderate anti-cognitivism; strong anti-cognitivism
apophenia 174
applied science 2, 5, 72
Aristotle 10, 22, 61, 67–8, 146
Armitstead, Claire 161 n.10
Arnold, Matthew 14, 220, 222–5, 227, 229
  Culture and Anarchy 222
articulation 11, 14, 89, 122, 125–9, 134, 181

artifacts 7, 21, 80, 84, 201, 228, 238
artificial general intelligence (AGI) 139–40
artificial intelligence (AI) 4–5, 12, 139–41, 143–7, 171, 174, 176, 242
  AI Blindspot 146
  education and regulation of tech 144–8
  superintelligent AI 53–4, 140
astronomy 7, 20, 64, 66, 194
The Atlantic 117–18
ATLAS detector 21, 31
atoms/atomic physics 20–1, 23–5, 27
Atwood, Margaret, *The Handmaid's Tale* 12, 153–8, 160, 161 n.10
Auslander, Philip, 186, 191 n.10
  Liveness: Performance in a Mediatized Culture 185
authentic/authenticity 155, 157–8
Auyoung, Elaine 39

Babbage, Charles 48, 146
Babel 69
Bacon, Francis 5–6, 10, 55, 61–2, 64–72, 137, 184, 193, 235–42
  The Advancement of Learning 2, 61, 63
  and Enlightenment 4
  Great Instauration 2–3, 235
  on knowledge 2, 72
  The New Atlantis 2, 137
  The New Science 2
  Novum Organum (New Method) 2, 193, 239
  Of the Proficience and Advancement of Learning, Divine and Human 62
  state of grace 61–3, 65, 71
Bagwell, Vinnie, *Victory beyond Sims* 195
Barrett, Amy Coney 91
Bashi, Imran 53
Bayley, Barrington J., *The Fall of Chronopolis* 57 n.19
Bekenstein, Jacob 27, 34
Bell, Gelsey 186–7
bell hooks 124
  Teaching to Transgress 127
Bender, John 4
Benjamin, Ruha 143
Benjamin, Walter 230
Berger, Peter L., *The Social Construction of Reality* 207

Index

Berger, Raoul, *Government by Judiciary: The Transformation of the Fourteenth Amendment* 105–6
Berman, Francine 140
Bernstein, Carl 113
Berson, Josh 56
Beverungen, Armin 53
The Bible 61, 154, 163
Biden, Joe 91
Big Bang theory 28, 49
big data 50, 171, 174
Big Tent discipline 75
biodiversity 169, 171–3, 177 n.3
biology 10, 17–18, 37, 62–4, 68, 70–4, 152, 207
    biological anthropology 206
    biological physics 20
    biological science 207
    classification system 67
    in exile 66–70
    expulsion of biology from physics 64–6
biomes 171–2
Birmingham Centre for Contemporary Cultural Studies (BCCS) 217–18, 220
Birnbaum, Larry 145
Black Americans. *See* African Americans
black-hole physics 27, 34
blackness 181, 205–6, 211, 213
Black people 94, 97, 131, 166, 203–5, 209–11, 213, 215 n.32
    elites 206, 213
Black studies 14, 181, 203–13, 242
Bloch, Marc, *The Historian's Craft* 198
blockchain 53
Boerhaave, Herman, *Elementa Chemiae* 199–201
Bohr, Niels 24–5
    "Copenhagen interpretation" of quantum mechanics 24
Book of Genesis 64
Borchers, Callum 116
Borges, Jorge Luis, "The Library of Babel" 6, 52
Bork, Robert, *Neutral Principles and Some First Amendment Problems* 105
bosons 6, 26, 65
Boyle, Robert 240
Brand, Stuart 56
Brautigan, Richard, "All Watched Over By Machines of Loving Grace" 55
Brazil, environmental policies 171–3
    Cerrado Savanna 172
    Intended Nationally Determined Contributions (NDC) 172
    Pantanal wetland 171
British anti-slavery movement 164
Brooks, Gwendolyn, "Poets Who Are Negroes" 211
Bruenig, Matt 213

Buolamwini, Joy, coded gaze 140
Burney, Frances, *Evelina* 40, 44
Burton, Robert, *The Anatomy of Melancholy* 2
Bush, Vannevar, *Science: The Endless Frontier* 170
Butler, Judith
    Bodies that Matter 153
    Gender Trouble 152
    Undoing Gender 153
Butler, Samuel, on technological change 47

Caecus, Appius Claudius 231
Calvin and Hobbes (Watterson) 195
Čapek, Karel, *R.U.R.* 59 n.45
capitalism 53, 92–3, 159, 221
Caterpillar company 49
Cavendish, Margaret
    The Blazing World 42
    Observations upon Experimental Natural Philosophy 42
Chambers, Ephraim, *Cyclopædia: or, an Universal Dictionary of Arts and Sciences* 17
Chaucer, Geoffrey, *The Canterbury Tales* 155
chemistry 63, 69, 72, 199–200
circular logic 68
cisgender 153–4, 158
civil rights 12, 91, 100, 137, 139
Civil Rights Act 96, 100
Civil Rights Movement 100
cladistics 50
class 11, 14, 93–4, 131, 135, 153–4, 158, 209, 213, 231
Classical Legal Thought (CLT) 97–100, 104
climate change/climate science 1, 13, 138, 169–71, 173, 175–6, 236, 242
The Club of Rome 57 n.6
Coates, Ta-Nehisi 211
    Between the World and Me: The Beautiful Struggle 214–15 nn.29–30
coded gaze 140
cognitive value 40–1
Cohen, Felix 107
    Transcendental Nonsense and the Functional Approach 99
Cohen, Morris 99
colonization of spacetime 48–51, 55–6
Columbia Dictionary of Modern Literary Terms 227
computation/computing 18, 21, 47–2, 55–7, 73, 75–6, 79–81, 83–5, 139, 142, 174, 242
    irrelevance of humans 53–4
    modern 48
    natural metaphors in 50–1
    trajectory of 51–3
computer(s) 10, 18, 27, 47–56, 75, 83, 132, 186, 189, 242
    AI-boosted computer programs 173
    computer simulation 10, 52

Index

semi-automated computer programs 173
software/software codes 48–9, 80, 139, 142, 146–7, 187
computer science (CS) 47, 144–6
Congress 94–5, 163, 196
consolidation 8, 75, 94–5, 118
constitutional theory 106
Coordinated Universal Time (UTC) 50
Coppins, McKay 117–18
cosmogeny 51
cosmology 20, 28, 52
cosmos 21, 34
Couldry, Nick, *The Renewal of Cultural Studies* 221
Covid-19 pandemic 1, 3, 6, 12–13, 116, 118, 133–4, 181, 183–4
    digital performance in 186–90
Crawford, Margo N. 211–13
    What Is African American Literature? 210
creative writing 126–7, 212
creators 56, 61, 70, 141, 147
creatures 55–6, 61, 63–5, 67–70, 94, 140
Crenshaw, Kimberlé, intersectionality 152, 160 n.5
crisis of existence 17, 63
Critical Legal Studies (CLS) 104–5, 107
critical pedagogy 11, 122, 125, 129
critical thinking 42, 198
Cronon, William, *Nature's Metropolis: Chicago and the Great West* 57 n.10
Crow, Jim 96, 204–5
CS + X initiative (Northwestern University) 145
culture 181–2, 217, 219–20, 223–9
    cultural capital 37
    cultural studies 4, 8, 14, 181–2, 217–32, 242
    expansion 219, 224–5, 227
    popular 218–19
cybernetics 55
cyberverse 49

Davidson, Cathy N. 8
Davy, Humphry 2–3
Deacon, Terence 49
de Bolla, Peter 13
deceleration 54
de Dijn, Annelien
    Freedom: An Unruly History 198–9
    The Nation 199
Defoe, Daniel, *Journal of the Plague Year* 41
"Defund the police" 165
deGrasse Tyson, Neil 196
democracy 108, 117, 131, 137, 143
Democritus 67, 71
DeRienzo, Matt 118
Descartes Labs 49
Descartes, René 22, 68
Deutsch, David 39–40, 51
Digital First Media 117

digital humanities (DH) 10–11, 18, 75–7, 87 n.8
    beginnings of the end 85–6
    classification, methodology of 79
    clusters 77–81, 85
    computational/non-computational 80–1, 83, 85
    evolving ends 81–5
    stylometry 79–80, 84
    topic model of 77–9, 81–5, 87 n.11, 87 n.14
Digital Humanities Quarterly (DHQ) 77, 87 n.8
digital performance 184, 186
    in Covid era and reconsidering liveness 186–90
Digital Scholarship in the Humanities (DHS) 77, 87 n.8
digital theaters 187
Dirac, Paul 25
discrimination 97, 134, 140, 197, 203
diversity 11, 115–16, 119, 128, 176
Dixon, Steve, *Digital Performance* 185–6
Doctor, Ken 114
Douglass, Frederick 163, 166
    speech at International Council of Women 165
drone system 49
Du Bois, W. E. B. 205, 211
    "The Conservation of Races" 203
    Dusk of Dawn: An Essay Toward an Autobiography of a Race Concept 203
Duchan, Peter, *The Illusionist* 189
During, Simon 227
    The Cultural Studies Reader 221
dystopia/dystopian 4, 7, 12, 14, 137, 153–4, 181. *See also* utopia/utopian

Eaglestone, Robert 40, 44–5
eclecticism 106
ecosystem 169, 172–3, 177 n.3
education 1, 8, 11, 14, 125–6, 128–9, 131–5. *See also* pedagogy (Pedagogy)
    attacks on 3
    higher education 8–9, 37, 133, 135, 187, 212, 223, 237
    liberal arts 5, 12, 89–90, 131–5, 193
    narrative 124
    and regulation of tech 144–8 (*see also specific programs*)
    worker 218, 220
Einstein, Albert 23–4, 27
    General Theory of Relativity 9, 20, 27
    gravity (*see* gravity/gravitation)
    Standard Model of Particle Physics 9, 20–1, 25–6, 32
electricity 22, 65, 67, 155
electronic skin 52, 56
electrons (positive/negative) 23–5, 63, 65
Eliot, George, *Middlemarch* 7
Ellison, Ralph 204–5, 211
empirical science 17, 62

249

Index

employment 8, 37, 139, 147, 220, 228
Encyclopedia Britannica 17, 237
engineering 21, 61, 63, 71–2, 140, 142–4
Enlightenment 1, 3–4, 30, 46 n.8, 68, 131, 223, 235, 237
environmental science 37, 138, 173, 175
environmental studies 5, 13, 242
    climate research moratorium proposal 169–70
    global vulnerability 173–4
    political intransigence 171–3
    science and status quo 174–6
    science, policy, and politics 170–1
    technical knowledge 173–4
equality 93, 106, 137, 144, 151, 153, 163, 170, 204, 212
The Equal Rights Association 166
equity 98, 131, 134, 137, 139, 144–5, 153–4, 170, 173
Ethics and Society Review board (Stanford University) 145
Europe 95, 97, 132, 172, 194
    European Enlightenment 237
evolutionary theory 68
exceptionalism 43
experimental science 73
explanatory knowledge 17, 39–40, 44–5, 240
explanatory literary studies 10, 17, 38, 43, 45

Facebook 47, 113, 116, 142
factual knowledge 39–40
Fair Deal 100
feminism 151–3, 158–9, 160 n.1, 225–6
feminist utopia 151
fermions 26
Feynman, Richard 26, 33
Fields, Barbara J. 204, 208–10
Fields, Karen E. 204, 208–9
The Fifteenth Amendment 166
flora and fauna 169, 172
Floyd, George, murder of 166
Foner, Eric 166
Ford, Gerald 91
Fortas, Abe 91
The Fourteenth Amendment 96, 106
Franklin, Benjamin 4
Franklin, Rosalind 196
Freeman, Heath 118
Freire, Paulo 128–9
    Pedagogy of Indignation 125
    Pedagogy of the Oppressed 124
Frow, John, Bloomsbury's *Handbook of Literary and Cultural Theory* 227–8
fundamental physics 19–20, 25–6, 30, 32
fungi 52, 72
Furet, François, on French Revolution 54
Future of the Field conference (performance studies) 183

Gaia 47, 52, 56
Galilei, Galileo 21–2, 24, 34, 64
Gallup poll 117, 159
Gamow, George 24
Garden of Eden 61–2, 64, 66, 69–70, 72, 74. *See also* Adam and Eve
Gardner, John 127
Garrison, William Lloyd 163–6
Gavazzi, Stephen M. 8
Gee, E. Gordon 8
gender 80–1, 151–2, 159
    gender binary 151, 153, 155–6, 158–9
    gender critical feminism 152
    gender studies 4–5, 8, 12, 85, 137, 140, 145, 151–60
    fictional endings 154–9
    future of 159–60
    patriarchal power 100, 151, 158–9
    performative gender 152
Genesis 10, 31, 69
Genus species 65
Gen Z 159
geometry 7, 23, 28, 32, 97
Germany 6, 23, 174
Gibson, Graeme 161 n.10
Gilded Ages 11, 91, 93, 101, 108
Giroux, Henry 124
Glavovic, Bruce C. 169–70
God 61–2, 68–70
Godwin, William
    Caleb Williams 41
    on literature 41
Goffman, Ervin, *The Presentation of Self in Everyday Life* 142
The Golden Age of Capitalism 100
Golding, William, *Free Fall* 47
Gonosko, Gary 50
Goodhart's Law 143
Google 50, 113, 116, 142
governance 12, 101, 139, 144, 147, 170
gravity/gravitation 6, 20–4, 26–8, 31–4, 34 n.2, 52, 66–7, 70–1, 81–2, 196
The Great Recession 12, 93, 97, 101, 106
Greenblatt, Stephen 227
Greene, Maxine 126–7
    Releasing the Imagination 125
Gross, David 32–3
Gross, Neil, "The Earth Will Don an Electronic Skin" 51
Guarani people (South America) 172
Guess, Andy 117

Halberstam, Jack 153
Hale, Robert Lee 99
Halliburton company 50

Index

Haraway, Donna 153
Harrison, Harry 55
Hawking, Stephen 27, 34
Hegarty, Paul 50
Herder, Johann Gottfried von 226–7
Hertz, Heinrich 22
Hesse, Mary 43–4
history 3–4, 14, 42, 45, 52–4, 56–7, 76, 80, 132, 137, 146, 155–7, 181, 183, 193–201
   defined by the present 194–5
   historical positivism 195–7
   historiography 197–201
   statues 194–5
   Whig history 195–7
Hoggart, Richard 218
Hohfeld, Wesley 99
Hollerith punch cards 48
Hollywood 52, 113
Holmes, Oliver Wendell, Jr., *The Path of the Law* 99
homeostasis 10, 52, 56
homo economicus 53
homo faber (humankind the maker) 232
homo sapiens 65, 232
homo scientificus 70
Hooke, Robert 22
Horgan, John, *The End of Science: Facing the Limits of Knowledge in the Twilight of the Scientific Age* 30
Horkheimer, Max 227
The House Energy and Commerce Committee 116
Howe, Irving 204–5
human being(s) 28, 124, 129, 131–3, 135, 207, 219, 231–2
   human agency 137, 139, 145, 147–8
   human body (*res extensa*) 68
   human brain 132–3
   human intelligence 53, 139–40
   humankind 68, 131–2
   human knowledge 12, 24, 53, 68, 89, 131, 137
   human mind (*res cogitans*) 68
   human variation 206–7
Human Computer Interaction (HCI) 80, 142
Human Context and Ethics program (UC Berkeley) 144
Humanitiés Numerique 76. *See also* digital humanities (DH)
humanity/humanities 1–7, 10, 14, 17–18, 21, 24, 29, 32, 37, 52, 62–3, 72, 75–6, 83, 85–6, 131–2, 135, 139–40, 145, 203, 207, 217–18, 220–1, 223, 228, 230, 235–40. *See also* science, technology, engineering, and mathematics (STEM)
   crisis of the humanities 10, 37
   digital (*see* digital humanities (DH))
   modern 6

Hunt, Lynn, *History: Why It Matters* 198
Hurley, Chad 142
Hurston, Zora Neale, "How It Feels to Be Colored Me" 205–6
Hutter, Marcus 52
Hyde Park Riots of 1866 14, 220, 222

ignorance 32–3, 124, 144–5, 230
immigrants 94–5, 101
immoveable reality 121
improvement 3–4
Industrial Revolution 48, 94
inflation 28–9
information 34, 48, 51–2, 54, 56, 65, 71, 74, 79, 89, 91, 124, 132–4, 155, 159
inherited structures 7, 237, 239
Initiative for the Integration of the Regional Infrastructure of South America (IIRSA) program 171
Institute for Nonprofit News 116
intellectual tradition 68, 73
intelligence augmentation (IA) 139–40
interdisciplinarity 7–8, 14, 140, 181, 183, 238
interferometry technique 21
Intergovernmental Panel on Biodiversity and Ecosystem Services (IPBES) 169
"The Internet of Cows: How AgriTech is tearing up the rules of food" 49
The Internet of Things 51–2
interpretation 10, 38–40, 42–5, 96, 100, 105–6, 126, 128, 193, 195, 197, 201, 202 n.2
intersectionality 152, 160 n.5
inverse gambler's fallacy 31
The Ithaca Voice organization 119

Jacobs, Jerry A. 8
James, King 240, 242
Jameson, Frederic 151, 219
John Deere company 49
Johnson, Katherine 196
journalism 11, 89, 113–19
   access journalism 89
   fake news 116–17
   legacy news organizations 114–15
   nonprofit 115–16
   online advertising 113–14
The Journal of Cultural Analytics (CA) 77, 84–5, 87 n.8
The Journal of Medicine and Philosophy 6
Joyce, James 41
Judeo-Christian tradition 68

Kant, Immanuel 146, 223
Kennedy, Duncan 97

251

Index

Kepler, Johannes 7, 28–9, 64
Kim, Suk-Young, *K-pop Live* 186
kinematics 64, 66
King, Martin Luther, Jr. 167
King, Rachael Scarborough 235–42
Kitcher, Philip 5, 15 n.17
Klein, Julie Thompson 8
The Knight Foundation 115–16
knowledge production 1–3, 5, 7–9, 11, 17, 37, 75, 85, 89, 124, 134, 169–70, 174, 222, 228, 232
    as end of literary studies 40–3
knowledge work 4, 9, 13–14, 38, 228–9, 236, 238, 240, 242
Koselleck, Reinhart 181
Krauss, Lawrence, *Hiding in the Mirror* 28
Kuklick, Henrika 9

labor 11, 14, 96–7, 100–1, 211, 218, 220–1
    aristocracy of 218–19
    California labor law 91
    division of 2, 14, 48, 70–1, 107–8
    injunction 95, 98–9
    real worker 219
laissez faire 99
Lange, Ann-Christine 53
language 22, 25, 42, 69, 77, 79, 81, 106, 160, 166, 194, 211, 218, 223
Large Hadron Collider 20–1, 31
Larsen, Nella 144
Latour, Bruno 107
laws of physics 63, 69
Laws of Robotics 53
laws of the universe 63, 66
law (structure and legitimation)
    anti-immigrant laws 97
    Brown v. Board of Education case 105
    Classical Legal Thought (CLT) 97–100, 104
    contract law 107–8
    criminal law 96, 108
    and economics 104–8
    emigrant agent laws 96
    employment law 101
    enticement laws 96
    injunctions 95–6, 98–9, 207
    labor law 107 (*see also* labor)
    legal change (and impact on Income Distribution, US) 100–3
    legal fundamentalism 100
        and economic formalism 103–4
        originalism and textualism 105–6
    Legal Realism 99–100, 107
    neoliberal capitalism (1970s-2010s) 101–4
    for post-neoliberal order 106–8
    private law 96, 105
    property law 107

    public law 105
    In re Debs law case 96, 98
    In re Jacobs case 97
    Roe v. Wade case 105
    role of 91–3
    in the second industrial divide (1870s-1930s) 94–7
    in social relations 91–3
    Tort law 108
learning 1–2, 7–8, 13, 61, 65, 70, 72–4, 124–5, 127–9, 133–5, 190–1, 222, 236–7, 239
Leavis, F. R. 218
Lecky, W. E. H. 204
Lenin, V. I., labor aristocracy 218–19
Levi, Margaret 145
LGBTQ community 159–60
liberal arts 5, 12, 89–90, 131–5, 193
The Liberator newspaper 163
life sciences 10, 17, 62–3, 66
Limits to Growth 171
Lindley, David, *The End of Physics: The Myth of a Unified Theory* 30
Linnaeus, Carl 65, 67
    Systema Naturae 64
literary criticism 44, 80, 84, 227
literary studies 1, 10–11, 17, 37–9, 227
    anti-cognitivism 40–5
    knowledge production as end of 40–3
    literary fiction 45, 212
    literary interpretation 38–40, 42–5
    literary knowledge 41
    progressive knowledge in 43–5
liveness in performance studies 13, 181, 183–6, 188, 190
living things 61–4, 67–9. *See also* nonliving things
Lochner era 95, 98
Lomax, Alan 144
loop quantum gravity 31
Lovelace, Ada 48
Lovelock, James 47, 56
Luckmann, Thomas, *The Social Construction of Reality* 207

MacDougall, D. Robert 6
machina economicus 53
machine learning 50, 76, 142–3, 147, 171, 174
Mackay, Donald 51
Madison, James 143
magnetism 22, 65, 71
Malthus, Thomas, *Essay on Population* 48, 57 n.6
Manne, Henry 104
Margulis, Lynn 47, 56
market society 89, 91–2, 107–8
Marotta, Allie 189
Marxism 217
massification 14, 182, 219–20

Index

massive online open course (MOOC) 132
mass media 175, 185, 218–19
"Mathematical Principles of Natural Philosophy"
  (*Philosophiae Naturalis Principia Mathematica*) 66
mathematics/mathematical 19, 22–8, 30, 48, 58 n.34, 62–4, 66, 69, 71–3, 137, 194, 196
matter physics 20, 25, 27, 69
Maxwell, James Clerk 22
Maza, Sarah, *Thinking about History* 198
McConnell, Mitch 91, 108
McGurl, Mark 212
medicine 6, 63, 72, 194, 199
Meese, Edwin 91, 105–6
Melville, Herman 121, 127–8
Meta 47. *See also* Facebook
Michaels, Walter Benn 208–9
minorities 93, 100, 103, 106, 134, 143, 160, 199
Mitchell, John 91
Mitchell, Timothy 49
Mitchell, W. J. T. 209–11, 226
moderate anti-cognitivism 40–1. *See also* strong anti-cognitivism
modern knowledge 236
modern science 68, 196, 199
Morris, Meaghan 219, 225
Morrison, James 239
Moten, Fred 206
motion 2, 22, 24, 28, 64, 66, 70, 164
Mott, Lucretia 164–5
M Theory 35 nn.12-13
multiplicity 38, 45, 128, 135, 223, 225, 230–2
multiverse 10, 28–32, 34. *See also* universe
Musk, Elon 53
myth(s) 30, 196–7, 209–10
  mythical beings 65

narrow-but-deep disciplines 7, 229
National Anti-Slavery Standard 166
nationalities 135, 151, 153
National Labor Relations Board 101
National Public Radio 115
Natural Language Process (NLP) 142
natural philosophy 2, 61–3, 67–8, 70–1, 137, 194, 240
natural sciences 2, 4–5, 7, 39, 43–5, 62, 66, 71, 144, 175, 194, 236
Nehamas, Alexander
  "Convergence and Methodology in Science and Criticism" 43
  interpretation in literary studies 44
Nelson, Cary 225, 227
neoliberal/neoliberalism 11, 37, 45, 76, 93, 103–4, 107, 176
neurosciences 30, 63, 68, 132

neutrons 25
New Deal 94, 97, 100
New Leaders Association survey (2019) 116
Newton, Isaac 5, 10, 22, 24, 28, 44, 66–70, 196
  clockwork universe 50
  laws of motion 66
  Principia 66
The New York Times 114, 169, 189
Niebuhr, Reinhold 167
Nixon, Richard 91, 100
nonliving things 10, 18, 62–4, 66–7, 73. *See also* living things
North America 49, 154
Norton Anthology of Literary Theory 227
nuclear reactors 174
Nussenbaum, Helen 146

Obama, Barack 91
Ogawa, Aya, *Ludic Proxy: Fukushima* 188–9
Okada, Toshiki, *Eraser Fields* 190–1
oppression 12, 14, 151, 159, 165
original sin 55, 61–2, 68, 72

Paradise 61, 64
parallel universes 19, 29, 51
particle accelerators 25, 33–4
particle physics 20–1, 25–6, 31
  fundamental particles 22, 25–7
Pauli, Wolfgang 31
pedagogy (Pedagogy) 76, 79, 89, 122–6, 128–9, 151. *See also* education
  critical 11, 122, 125, 129
  humanizing 11, 89, 123
  scholarship of students 126–8
Peele, Jordan, *Get Out* 211
Penrose, Roger 34
  Fashion, Faith, and Fantasy 31
people of color 76, 114–16, 195
performance studies 5, 13, 181, 183–4, 191 n.2
  Covid remote performances 184, 186–90
  digital (*see* digital performance)
  in-person performances 184, 189–90
  liveness in 13, 181, 183–6, 188, 190
  ontology of performance 185
  precarity and learning from remote practice 190–1
performative gender 152
pesticides 172
Pew Research Center 113
Phelan, Peggy 183, 186, 189
  The Ends of Performance 190, 191 n.2
  Unmarked 185
Phillips, Wendell 163–4, 166
philosophy of science 43
physical anthropology 207
physical sciences 17, 62–3, 66, 235

Index

physics 1, 10, 24–30, 51, 62, 66, 68, 72–3
    atoms/atomic 20–1, 23–5, 27
    biological 20
    black-hole 27, 34
    contemporary 27
    expulsion of biology from 64–6
    fundamental 19–20, 25–6, 30, 32
    matter 20, 25, 27, 69
    metaphor, role of 24
    particle (*see* particle physics)
    theoretical 19–20, 22–3, 25–7, 29, 33
Planck, Max 23–4
    fundamental/universal constants 23
planetary management 48, 57
Plato 8
Platonic solids 7, 28
Plaxo company 141
pluralism 225–6, 229
political (and law) economy 93, 100, 106–8, 176
postfeminist 154–9
power relations 107, 152–3
Proceedings of the National Academy of Sciences 117
progressive knowledge 10, 39–40, 42
    in literary studies 43–5
protons 21, 25–6
psychology 20, 37, 45, 141, 145, 209
Public Interest Technology University Network (New America Foundation) 144
Pullman strike 98

Quantum Chromodynamics (QCD) 26, 32
Quantum Electrodynamics (QED) 25–6
quantum gravity 27
quantum information 34
quantum mechanics 24–8, 33–4, 38

race/racism 3, 11, 14, 151, 166, 181, 203–13, 214 n.29
    Floyd, George, murder of 166
    racecraft 204, 210
    racial myth 210
    social construction 14, 207–9
    systemic 3, 107
radius directus 68
radius reflexus 68
radius refractus 68
Rawls, John, reflective equilibrium 44
Reagan, Ronald 91, 100–1
Reed, Adolph, Jr. 208
Re:Enlightenment Project 220, 229, 235–6, 239
Reiter, Paul 6
Responsible Computer Science Challenge (Mozilla) 144
retroactive movement 239, 241

Riley, Denise 152–3
Roberts, Laura Morgan 115
robots 53–4, 59 n.45, 147
Roosevelt, Franklin D. 99
Rosa, Hartmut, social acceleration 54
Ross, Andrew 221
Royal Society 2, 4, 17, 41, 137, 238, 243 n.5
Rudy, Seth 235–42
"Rules of Life" 62, 67, 73
Rutherford, Ernest 21, 74 n.7

Sack, Daniel, *After Live: Possibility, Potentiality, and the Future of Performance* 186
Sanders, Bernie 93
Scalia, Antonin 91, 105–6
Schlumberger company 50
Schmidhuber, Jürgen 52
Schneider, Rebecca, *Performing Remains* 186
science(s) 6, 10, 18, 23, 63–6, 71–2, 153, 170, 174–6, 237–9. *See also specific disciplines*
science, technology, engineering, and mathematics (STEM) discipline 2, 6–8, 61, 80, 144, 240. *See also* humanity/humanities
scientific atlases 41–2
scientific enterprise 23, 65, 69–70, 72
scientific knowledge 41, 44, 62, 140, 169–71, 173–4, 199
scientific principles 71
Scott, Daryl Michael, "The Scandal of Thirteenthism" 196–8
self-definition 206, 210
sensors 49, 54, 132
Serano, Julia 152–3
Serres, Michel 48
sexism 114, 152
sexuality studies 152, 160
Shakespeare, William 52, 218, 227
Shanahan, Murray, superintelligent AI 53
Shapin, Steven 38
Sherman Antitrust Act (1895) 95–6
Sisyphean 65, 69
slavery 53, 96, 107, 140, 203, 211
    abolition of 13, 137, 163–6, 196
    black slavery 131, 195–7
Smith, Adam 48
Smith, Paul 221, 225–6, 228
Smith, Randall 118
Smith, Timothy F. 169
Smolin, Lee, *The Trouble with Physics* 31
social justice 11, 89, 106, 115, 139–40, 145, 147, 167
social media 12, 116, 133, 137, 141, 144. *See also specific companies*
social relations 89, 99–100, 104–5, 107–8, 109 n.6
    structure and legitimation in 91–3

Index

social sciences 4–5, 7, 107, 140, 145, 153, 174–5, 207, 236–9
soft skills 42
Sohn-Rethel, Alfred 53
solar energy 50
solar system 28–9, 51, 66, 73
solidarity 165, 167, 210
Solnit, Rebecca 157–8
    Hope in the Dark 167
Sommerfeld, Arnold 23
soul(s) 2, 6, 140, 221, 226
    sensitive 68
    soul searching 27–8
    types of 67
spaceship 56
spacetime 53, 188
    colonization of 48–51, 55–6
Spengler, Oswald, *The Decline of the West* 29
sphere of knowledge 32–3, 45
Sprinker, Michael, mutation 228
Stabile, Carol A. 225–7
    "The nightmare of feminism" 226
Staley, David J. 8
Stanton, Elizabeth Cady 164–6
    "Declaration of Sentiments" 165, 167
stigmergy 59 n.59
Stovall, Tyler 199
string theory 9–10, 27, 29–32, 34 n.11, 35 n.12, 58 n.34
strong anti-cognitivism 40–1. *See also* moderate anti-cognitivism
studia humanitis 6
Sumner, Charles 166
superstring theory 35 n.12
supersymmetry 26
Susskind, Leonard, *The Cosmic Landscape: String Theory and the Illusion of Intelligent Design* 29
sustainability 118, 169–70, 175–6, 184
Swift, Jonathan, *Gulliver's Travels* 137
systemic racism 3, 107. *See also* race/racism

Taft, William Howard 98
Technology and Society Program (Princeton University) 146
techno-utopianism 3
Tech Science program (Harvard Government) 146
temporality 6, 50, 187, 237
TERFs (trans-exclusionary radical feminists) 152, 154–5, 158
termination 5
theoretical physics 19–20, 22–3, 25–7, 29, 34
Theory of Everything 5, 17, 27–8, 30
The Thiel Fellowship 4
Thiel, Peter 4

Thiers, Adolphe, *Histoire de la Révolution française* 194
The Thirteenth Amendment 13, 163, 166, 196
Thomas, Michael, *Man Gone Down* 213
Thompson, E. P. 218
transgender 155–6, 158
    transgender studies 152
Trump, Donald 93, 116–17, 154, 198
truth 6, 11, 19, 22, 24, 29, 40, 43, 54, 62, 65, 71–2, 119, 122, 157–8, 193, 197–9, 204, 206
Turner, Graeme 225
Twitter 116–17, 133, 142, 196

unification 9–10, 12, 14–15, 17, 22, 24–6, 241–2
Unification Grouping 242
unique theory 27, 32
The United Kingdom 95, 195, 218
The United Nations
    Framework Convention on Climate Change 172
    Intergovernmental Panel on Climate Change (IPCC) 169, 171
The United States 49, 91, 93–5, 101, 114–16, 154, 163–4, 170, 196, 211, 226
universe 7, 9–10, 17, 19–21, 23, 28–32, 51–2, 55, 58 n.34, 62–5, 69–73, 100, 158. *See also* multiverse
utopia/utopian 12–14, 129, 137, 151, 153, 181, 241–2. *See also* dystopia/dystopian

Valente, Joseph 8
Vandermeer, Jeff, *The Southern Reach Trilogy- Annihilation, Authority,* and *Acceptance* 59 n.59
van Dieman, Roger 203–4
Verwaal, Ruben 200
vitalism 67
von Laue, Max 23
voting rights 91, 103, 106, 108, 143, 164–7, 220, 231

Waggoner, Martha 114
Walford, Antonia 54
Warner, William 237
    "Stopping Cultural Studies" 228–9
Warnow, Tandy, *Computational Phylogenetics: An Introduction to Designing Methods for Phylogeny Estimation* 50
War on Poverty 101
Warren, Elizabeth 93
The Washington Post 114, 116
Weinberg, Steven, *To Explain the World: The Discovery of Modern Science* 28
Wellmon, Chad 6
Western tradition 68
"Whatever Happened to Cultural Studies?" conference 221

Index

Whig history 195–7
White, Iain 169
Wilczek, Frank 21–2
    on inflation 28–9
William of Ockham 52
Williams, Raymond 218, 220, 224–6, 229–30
    Culture and Materialism 222
    Keywords 223
Wissenschaft 194, 202 n.5
Woit, Peter, *Not Even Wrong* 31
woman 61, 152–5, 157–8, 164
    woman's rights convention 165
    women's movement 100, 151, 153, 159
    women's studies 151, 153, 160, 242
Woods, Keith 115

Woodward, Bob 113
World Anti-Slavery Convention, London 164, 166
World Health Organization 116

Yates, JoAnne 48
YouTube 12, 144, 190
    comments 142
    databases and algorithms 143–4
    video creators/viewers 141–3

zoning 237–41
Zoom 187, 189
Zuckerberg, Mark 116. *See also* Facebook
Zuse, Konrad 52